EU Consumer Law

Published by:
Richmond Law & Tax Ltd
12-14 Hill Rise
Richmond TW10 6UA
United Kingdom
Tel. +44 (0) 20 8614 7650
Fax +44 (0) 20 8614 7651
info@richmondlawtax.com
www.richmondlawtax.com

ISBN 1 904501 21 4

British Library Cataloguing in Publication Data
A catalogue record for this publication is available from the British Library

Cover design by Bill Anderson Associates
Printed and bound by Antony Rowe Ltd

EU Consumer Law

Dr Paolisa Nebbia
Lecturer in Law, University of Southampton

Tony Askham
Partner, Bond Pearce

RICHMOND

Table of Contents

TABLE OF CASES xv

TABLE OF LEGISLATION xix

1. INTRODUCTION 1

2. THE DEVELOPMENT OF EU CONSUMER PROTECTION 5

A. No reference to consumer protection in the Treaty of Rome 5
1. The Paris summit of 1972 6
2. The recognition of consumer rights at EC level 6
3. The contribution of the *Cassis de Dijon* case 7
4. The Single European Act 1986 7
B. The consolidation of EC consumer protection policy: the Treaty on European Union 8
C. The Treaty of Amsterdam and consumer protection 10
D. Internal market policy and consumer policy 11
1. Internal market policy as the way to introduce consumer protection measures 11
2. Gaps in the internal market policy from the point of view of consumer protection 12
3. Legal problems linked to cross-border consumer complaints 16
E. The EC consumer protection programmes 21
1. The preliminary programme: 1975 21
2. The second programme: 1981 25
3. A new impetus for consumer protection policy 26
F. Community consumer policy in the internal market 28
1. The first three-year action plan: 1990–1992 28
2. Post internal market consumer policy: the second three-year action plan: 1993–1995 30
3. The third three-year action plan: 1996–1998 31
4. The fourth three-year action plan: 1999–2001 34
G. Consumer policy strategy 2002–2006 35
H. The notion of the consumer in EC legislation 36
I. Some selected ECJ decisions on consumers 38
J. Means of consumer participation in the EC decision making process 41
1. The consumer movement in the European Union 41
2. EC structures for consumer representation 42
3. Procedures for consumer participation and representation 46
K. Legislative achievements under EC consumer policy: an overview 47
1. Legislative initiatives within the competence of the

Health and Consumer Protection Directorate-General 47
2. A selection of initiatives outside the scope of the Health and Consumer Protection Directorate-General but still relevant in terms of consumer protection 52
3. The Commission's 2001 Green Paper on Consumer Protection 54
L. Non-legislative achievements under EC consumer policy 54
1. Stimulation of cooperation between national authorities 54
2. Consumer information projects 55
3. Consumer education programmes 56
4. Consumer access-to-justice projects 57
5. Stimulation of research and training 57
6. Stimulation of consumer–supplier dialogue 57
7. Framework proposal for financing EU activities in favour of consumers 58
M. EC consumer policy in an international context 58
1. EC consumer policy and the European Free Trade Association 58
2. The links between EC consumer policy and EC external trade policy 59
N. Concluding remarks: future challenges for EC consumer policy 59

3. PRODUCT LIABILITY AND GENERAL PRODUCT SAFETY 61

1. Introduction 61
2. Council Directive (EEC) 85/374 on the approximation of the laws, regulations and administrative provisions of Member States concerning liability for defective products 62
3. Parliament and Council Directive (EC) 2001/95 on general product safety 66

4. SAFETY OF AGRICULTURAL PRODUCTS AND FOODSTUFFS 73

A. Introduction 73
B. General principles and requirements of safety 75
1. Introduction 75
2. Regulation 178/2002 laying down the general principles and requirements of food law, establishing the Food Safety Authority and laying down procedures in matters of food safety 75
C. Material in contact with foodstuffs 82
1. Introduction 82
2. Council Directive (EEC) 89/109 on the approximation of the laws of the Member States relating to materials and articles intended to come into contact with foodstuffs 82

3. Council Directive (EEC) 84/500 on the approximation of the laws of the Member States relating to the ceramic articles intended to come into contact with foodstuffs 85
4. Commission Directive (EC) 2002/72 relating to plastics materials and articles intended to come into contact with foodstuffs 87
5. Commission Directive (EEC) 93/10 relating to materials and articles made of regenerated cellulose film intended to come into contact with foodstuffs 89
D. Food additives 91
1. Introduction 91
2. Council Directive (EEC) 89/107 on the approximation of the laws of the Member States concerning food additives authorised for use in foodstuffs intended for human consumption 92
3. Council Directive (EC) 94/35 on sweeteners for use in foodstuffs 96
4.European Parliament and Council Directive (EC) 95/2 on food additives other than colours and sweeteners 98
5. European Parliament and Council Directive (EC) 94/36 on colours for use in foodstuff 100
6. Council Directive (EEC) 88/388 on the approximation of the laws of the Member States relating to flavourings for the use in foodstuff and to source material for their production 102
E. Specific products 104
1. Introduction 104
2. Council Directive (EEC) 89/108 on the approximation of the laws of the Member States relating to quick-frozen foodstuffs for human consumption 104
3. Council Directive (EC) 2001/112 relating to fruit juices and certain similar products intended for human consumption 107
4. Council Directive (EC) 2001/113 relating to fruit jams, jellies and marmalades and sweetened chestnut puree intended for human consumption 109
5. Council Directive (EC) 2001/111 relating to certain sugars intended for human consumption 110
6. Council Directive (EC) 2001/110 relating to honey 111
7. Council Directive (EC) 2001/114 relating to certain partly or wholly dehydrated preserved milk for human consumption 112
8. Parliament and Council Directive (EC) 2000/36 on cocoa and chocolate products intended for human consumption 113
9. Parliament and Council Directive 99/4 (EC) on coffee and

chicory extracts 115
10. Hormones in meat: Council Directive (EC) 96/22 concerning the prohibition on the use in livestock farming of certain substances having a hormonal or thyrostatic action and of beta-agonists 117
F. Novel foods and genetically modified organisms (GMOs) 118
1. Introduction 118
2. Parliament and Council Regulation 258/97 concerning novel foods and novel food ingredients 119
3. Parliament and Council Directive 2001/18(EC) on the deliberate release into the environment of genetically modified organisms 121
G. Dietetic foods and food supplements 122
1. Introduction 122
2. Council Directive (EEC) 89/398[1] on the approximation of the laws of the Member States relating to foodstuffs intended for particular nutritional uses 122
3. Parliament and Council Directive (EC) 2002/46 on the approximation of the laws of Member States relating to food supplements 124
H. Organic food 127
1. Introduction 127
2. Council Regulation 2092/91 on organic production of agricultural products and indications referring thereto on agricultural products and foodstuffs 127
I. Traditional products 128
1. Introduction 128
2. Council Regulation 2081/92 on the protection of geographical indications and designations of origin for agricultural products and foodstuffs 129
3. Council Regulation 2082/92 on certificates of specific character for agricultural products and foodstuffs 130

5. WATER 133

1. Introduction 133
2. Council Directive (EEC) 80/778 relating to the quality of water intended for human consumption 134
3. Council Directive (EEC) 76/160 concerning the quality of bathing water 138
4. Council Directive (EEC) 80/777 on the approximation of laws relating to the exploitation and marketing of natural mineral waters 140

6. COSMETICS 143

1. Introduction 143
2. Council Directive (EEC) 76/768 on the approximation of the laws of the Member States relating to cosmetic products 144
3. Analysis of cosmetic products 152

7. DANGEROUS SUBSTANCES AND PREPARATIONS 155

1. Introduction 155
2. Council Directive (EEC) 67/548 of 27 June 1967 on the approximation of laws, regulations and administrative provisions relating to the classification, packaging and labelling of dangerous substances 156
3. Commission Decision (EEC) 85/71 concerning the list of chemical substances notified pursuant to Council Directive (EEC) 67/548 on the approximation of laws, regulations and administrative provisions relating to the classification, packaging and labelling of dangerous substances 165
4. Parliament and Council Directive 1999/45 concerning the approximation of the laws, regulations and administrative provisions of the Member States relating to the classification, packaging and labelling of dangerous preparations 165
5. Commission Directive (EEC) 91/155 defining and laying down the detailed arrangements for the system of specific information relating to dangerous preparations in implementation of Article 10 of Directive (EEC) 88/379 171
6. Council Directive (EEC) 76/769 on the approximation of the laws, regulations and administrative provisions of the Member States relating to restrictions on the marketing and use of certain dangerous substances and preparations 172

8. TOYS 181

1. Introduction 181
2. Council Directive (EEC) 88/378 on the approximation of the laws of the Member States concerning the safety of toys 181

9. TOBACCO PRODUCTS 187

1. Introduction 187
2. Parliament and Council Directive (EEC) 2001/37 on the approximation of the laws, regulations and administrative provisions of the Member States concerning the manufacture, presentation and sale of tobacco products 188
3. Parliament and Council Directive 2003/33 (EC) on the

approximation of the laws, regulations and administrative provisions of the Member States relating to the advertising and sponsorship of tobacco products 190
4. Council Directive (EEC) 89/552 of 3 October 1989 on the coordination of certain provisions laid down by law, regulation or administrative action in Member States concerning the pursuit of television broadcasting activities 191

10. COMMUNITY WARNING AND INFORMATION SYSTEMS 193

1. Introduction 193
2. RAPEX 194
3. Information and reaction to public health problems: Council Decision (EC) 1786/2002 197

11. INFORMATION 199

A. Introduction 199
B. Presentation and labelling of foodstuffs 199
1. Introduction 199
2. Parliament and Council Directive (EC) 2000/13 on the approximation of the laws of the Member States relating to the labelling, presentation and advertising of foodstuffs for sale to the ultimate consumer 200
3. Parliament and Council Directive (EC) 98/6 on consumer protection in the indication of the prices of products offered to consumers 204
4. Council Directive (EEC) 90/496 of 24 September 1990 on nutrition labelling for foodstuffs 205
5. Council Directive (EEC) 87/357 on the approximation of the laws of the Member States concerning products which, appearing to be other than they are, endanger the health or safety of consumers 207
6. Specific products 208
C. Presentation and labelling of non food-products 211
1. Introduction 211
2. Price indication 212
3. Components of footwear: Council and Parliament Directive (EC) 94/11 on the approximation of laws, regulations and administrative provisions of Member States relating to the labelling of material used in main components of footwear for sale to consumers 212
4. Textile names: Parliament and Council Directive 96/74 on textile names 213
5. Parliament and Council Directive (EC) 1999/94 relating

to the availability of consumer information on fuel economy and CO2 emissions in respect of the marketing of new passenger cars 214
6. Legal Council Directive 92/75 on the indication by labelling and standard product information of the consumption of energy and other resources by household appliances 215
7. Parliament and Council Regulation (EC) 1980/2000 on a revised Community eco-label award scheme 216
8. Legal Labelling of medicinal products: Parliament and Council Directive 2001/83 on the Community code relating to medicinal products for human use 217
D. Language 220
1. Introduction 220
2. Community legislation 220
3. The case law 221
4. Communication from the Commission to the Council and the Parliament concerning language use in the information of consumers in the Community 221

12. ADVERTISING AND UNFAIR COMMERCIAL PRACTICES 223

1. Introduction 223
2. Council Directive (EEC) 84/450 concerning misleading and comparative advertising 224
3. Comparative advertising 225
4. Television advertising: Council Directive (EEC) 89/552 of 3 October 1989 on the coordination of certain provisions laid down by law, regulation or administrative action in Member States concerning the pursuit of television broadcasting activities 227
5. Advertising of medicinal products: Council and Parliament Directive 2001/83 relating to medicinal products for human use 230
6. Proposal for a Parliament and Council Directive concerning business to consumer commercial practices in the internal market and amending Directives (EEC) 84/450, (EC) 97/7 and (EC) 98/27, COM(2003)356 final 234

13. CONSUMER CONTRACTS 237

A. Introduction 237
B. Market transparency 238
1. Introduction 238
2. Council Directive (EEC) 85/577 of 20 December 1985 to

protect the consumer in respect of contracts negotiated away from business premises 239
3. Council Directive 87/102 on the approximation of the laws, regulations and administrative provisions of the Member States concerning consumer credit 241
4. Council and Parliament Directive (EC) 97/7 on the protection of consumers in respect of distance contracts 246
5. Parliament and Council Directive 2002/65 concerning the distance marketing of consumer financial services 251
C. Substantive control 255
1. Introduction 255
2. Council Directive (EEC) 93/13 on unfair terms in consumer contracts 255
3. Council and Parliament Directive 1999/44 on certain aspects of the sale of consumer goods and associated guarantees 262
D. Cross-border protection of consumers' interests 265
1 Introduction 265
2. Council and Parliament Directive 98/27 on injunctions for the protection of consumers' interests 266

14. ELECTRONIC COMMERCE 269

1. Introduction 269
2. Parliament and Council Directive 2000/31 on certain legal aspects of information society services, in particular electronic commerce, in the internal market 270
3. Communication from the Commission to the Council, the Parliament and the ECB – application to financial services of Article 3(4) to (6) of the Electronic Commerce Directive, COM(2003)259 273

15. HOLIDAYS AND TRAVEL 275

1. Introduction 275
2. Council Directive (EEC) 90/314 of 13 June 1990 on package travel, package holidays and package tours 275
3. Council and Parliament Directive (EC) 94/47 on the protection of purchasers in respect of certain aspects of contracts relating to the purchase of the right to use immovable properties on a timeshare basis 279
4. Council Regulation (EEC) 295/91 of 4 February 1991 establishing common rules for a denied-boarding compensation scheme in scheduled air transport 282
5. Council Regulation 2027/97 on air carrier liability in

the event of accidents 283

16. FINANCIAL SERVICES 285

A. Introduction 285
B. Credit transfers and payment systems 285
1 Introduction 285
2. Council and Parliament Directive (EC) 97/5 on cross-border credit transfers 285
3. Commission Recommendation (EEC) 88/590 of 17 November 1988 concerning payment systems and in particular the relationship between the cardholder and the card issuer 287
4. Recommendation 97/489 concerning transactions by electronic payment instruments and in particular the relationship between issuer and holder 289
C. The insurance industry 292
1. Introduction 292
2. Council Directive (EEC) 92/49 of 18 June 1992 on the coordination of the laws, regulations and administrative provisions relating to direct insurance other than life assurance and amending Council Directive (EEC) 73/239 and Council Directive 88/357 292
3. Parliament and Council Directive (EC) 2002/83 concerning life assurance 293
4. Parliament and Council Directive 2000/26 on the approximation of the laws of the Member States relating to insurance against civil liability in respect of the use of motor vehicles and amending Council Directives (EEC) 73/239 and (EEC) 88/357 295

INDEX 299

Table of Cases

A and Others v The National Blood Authority [2001] 3 All ER 289 64

Badische Erfrischungs-Getrdnke GmbH & Co KG v Land Baden-Wiirttemberg (Case C-17/96) [1998] 1 CMLR 341 141
Bayerische Hypotheken und Wechselbank AG v Edgar Dietzinger (Case C-45/96)[1998] ECR I-1199 39
Berliner Kindl Brauerei AG v Andreas Siepert (Case C-208/98) [2000] ECR-I 1741 242
Bertrand v Paul Ott (Case C-150/77) [1978] ECR 1431 39
Buet v Ministère Public (Case C-328/87) [1989] ECR 1235 14
Bureau Européen des Unions de Consommateurs v Commission (Case C-170/89) [1991] 1 ECR I-5709, [1992] 1 CMLR 820 41, 59

Cape SNC v Idealservice (Case C-541/99) [2001] ECR I-9049 256
Club Tour, Viagens e Turismo SA v Alberto Carlos Lobo Gonçalves Garrido, and Club Med Viagens Ld (Case C-400/00) [2002] ECR I-4051 39, 275
Cofidis SA v Jean-Louis Fredout (Case C-473/00) [2002] ECR I-10875 40, 260
Commission v Belgium (Case 102/79) [1980] ECR 1473 140
Commission v France (Case C-246/91) [1993] ECR I-2289 150, 151
Commission v France (Case C-52/00) [2002] ECR I-3827 14, 64, 65, 84, 85
Commission v Germany (Case C-205/84) [1986] ECR 3755 36
Commission v Germany (Case C-237/90) [1992] ECR I-5973 136
Commission v Greece (Case 429/85) [1988] ECR 843 158
Commission v Greece (Case C-29/90) [1992] ECR I-1917, [1994] 3 CMLR 675 151
Commission v Greece (Case C-154/00) [2002] ECR I-3879 14, 31, 64, 65
Commission v Italy (Case C-372/99) [2002] ECR I-819 261
Commission v Italy (Case C-14/00) [2003] ECR I-513 115
Commission v Italy (Case C-365/00) 7 March 2002 151
Commission v Netherlands (Case C-144/99) [2001] ECR I-3541 261
Commission v Spain (Case C-92/96) (1998) 138
Commission v Spain (Case C-12/00) [2003] ECR I-459 115
Commission v United Kingdom (Case C-337/89) [1992] ECR I-6103 135
Commission v United Kingdom (Case C-56/90) [1993] ECR I-4109, [1994] 1 CMLR 769 139
Commission v United Kingdom (Case C-300/95) (1997) 64
Consorzio del Prosciutto di Parma e Salumificio Santa Rita v Asda Stores Ltd (Case C-108/01) [2003] 2 CMLR 21 130
Criminal proceedings against André Ambry (Case C-410/96) [1998] ECR I-7875 279
Criminal proceedings against Di Pinto (Case C-361/89) [1991] ECR I-1189 39, 239
Criminal proceedings against Geffroy (Case C-366/98) [2001] ECR I-222 221
Criminal proceedings against Sterbenz (Case C-421/00) [2003] ECR I-1065 200

Denkavit Futtermittel GmbH v Land Baden-Wurttemberg [1991] ECR I-3069 199
Denmark, Germany and France v Commission (Cases C-289/96, C-293/96 and C-299/96) [1997] ECR I-1541 130
Dillenkofer v Germany (Cases C-178, 179, 188, 189, 190/94) [1996] ECR I-4845 278

El Corte Inglés SA v Cristina Blázquez Rivero (Case C-192/94) [1996] ECR I-1281 245
Estée Lauder Cosmetics GmbH & Co. OHG v Lancaster Group GmbH (Case C-220/98) [2000] ECR I-117 148

Faccini Dori v Recreb (Case C-91/92) [1994] ECR I-3325 241
Ford-Werke AG and Ford of Europe Inc v Commission (Joined Cases 25, 26/84) [1985] ECR 2725, [1985] 3 CMLR 528 46, 66
Francesco Benincasa v Dentalikit Srl (Case C-269/95) [1997] ECR I-3767 39
Fratelli Graffione v Ditta Fransa (Case C-313/94) [1996] ECR I-6039 40

Germany v Parliament and Council (Case C-376/98) [2000] ECR I-8419 190
Goerres (Case C-385/96) [1998] ECR I-4431 221
Groupement des Producteurs, Importateurs et Agents Généraux d'Eaux Minérales Etrangeres, VZW (Piageme) v Peeters NV (Case C-85/94) [1991] ECR I-2971 141
Gut Springenheide GmbH v Oberkreisdirekto des Kreises Steinfurt-Amt fur Lebensmilleluberwachung (Case C-210/96) [1998] ECR I-4657 40, 59

Heininger (Case C-481/99) [2001] ECR I-9945 39
Hünermund and others v Landesapothekerkammer Baden-Württemburg (Case C-292/92) 223

Idealservice Srl and Idealservice MNRE Sas v OMAI Srl (Case C-542/99) [2001] ECR I-9049 40
Italy v Caldana (Case C-187/84) [1985] ECR 3013, [1989] 1 CMLR 137 156

KO v De Agostini and TV Shop (Case C-34–36/95) [1997] ECR I-3843 227
KO v Gourmet International Products AB (GIP) (Case C-405/98) [2001] All ER (EC) 308 223

Leclerc- Siplec (Case C-412/93) [1995] ECR I-179 223

Nissan case (Case C-373/90 Complaint against X) [1991] ECR I-131 224

Oceano Grupo Editorial SA v Rocio Murciano Quintero (Cases C-240–244/98) [2000] ECR I-4941 40, 260

Piageme v Peeters (Case C-369/89) [1995] ECR I-2955 221

R v Minister of Agriculture, ex parte Fédération Européene de la Sante Animale (FEDESA) (Case C-331/88) [1990] ECR I-4023, [1991] 1 CMLR 507 39
Rewe-Zentral v Bundesmonopolverwaltung für Branntwein (Cassis de Dijon case) (Case 120/78) [1979] ECR 649 7
RTI (Reti Televise Italiane SpA) and Others v Ministero delle Poste e Telecommunicazioni (Joined Cases C-320, 328, 329, 337, 338, 339/94) [1996] ECR I-6471, [1997] 1 CMLR 346, ECJ 230

Sanchez v Medicina Asturiana SA (Case C-183/00) [2002] ECR I-3901 65

Satellitenfernsehen GmbH, Kabel 1, K 1 Fernsehen GmbH (Case C-6/98) [1999] ECR I-7599 228
Simone Leitner v TUI (Case C-168/00) [2002] 2 CMLR 6 39, 278

Toshiba Europe GmbH v Katun Germany GmbH (Case C-112/99) 225
Travel Vac SL v Manuel José Antelm Sanchis (Case C-423/97) [1999] ECR I-2195 240

Veedfald v Aarhus Amtskommune (Case C-203/99) [2001] ECR I-3569 64
Verband Sozialer Wettbewerb eV v Clinique Laboratoires SNC and Estée Lauder Cosmetics GmbH (Case C-315/92) [1994] ECR I-317 15, 40, 148
Verein für Konsumenteninformation v Österreichische Kreditversicherungs AG (Case C-364/96) [1998] ECR I-2949 279
Verein Gegen Unwesen in Handel und Gewerbe Köln eV v Mars GmbH (Case C-470/93) [1995] ECR I-1923 40

Table of Legislation

Animals and Animal Products (Examination for Residues and Maximum Residue Limits) Regulations 1997 (SI 1997/1729) 117
Agreement on Agriculture 122
Agreement on Sanitary and Phytosanitary Measures (SPS Agreement) 122
Agreement on Technical Barriers to Trade (TBT Agreement) 122
Asbestos Products (Safety) Regulations 1985 (SI 1985/2402) 179

Broadcasting Act 1990 230

Ceramic Ware (Safety) Regulations 1988 86
Chemicals (Hazard Information and Packaging for Supply) Regulations 2002 (SI 2002/1689) 171, 172
Classification, Packaging and Labelling of Dangerous Substances Regulations 1984 (SI 1984/1244) 164
Coffee Extracts and Chicory Extracts (Wales) Regulations 2001 (SI 2001/1440) 117
Consumer Credit Act 1974 245
Consumer Protection Act 1987 65, 86
s 4(1)(e) 64
s 4(10)(e) 63
Consumer Protection (Cancellation of Contracts Concluded away from Business Premises) Regulations 1987 (SI 1987/2117) 241
Consumer Protection (Distance Selling) Regulations 2000 (SI 2000/2334) 251
Consumer Protection Stop Now Orders (EC Directive) Regulations 2001 (SI 2001/1422) 268
Control of Misleading Advertisement Regulations 1988 (SI 1988/915) 226
Cosmetic Products Regulations 1978 (SI 1978/1354) 151
Cosmetic Products (Safety) (Amendment) Regulations 1985 (SI 1985/2045) 151
Cosmetic Products (Safety) (Amendment) Regulations 1987 (SI 1987/1920) 151
Cross-Border Credit Transfers Regulations 1999 (SI 1999/231) 287

Dangerous Substances and Preparations (Safety) (Consolidation) Regulations 1994 (SI 1994/2844) 179
Dangerous Substances and Preparations (Safety) (Consolidation) (Amendment) Regulations 1996 (SI 1996/2635) 179
Decision (EEC) 69/414 setting up a Standing Committee for Foodstuffs ([1969] OJ L291/9) 84, 97
Decision (EEC) 74/234 relating to the institution of a Scientific Committee for Food ([1974] OJ L136/1) 84
Decision (EEC) 84/133 introducing a Community system for the rapid exchange of information on dangers arising from the use of consumer products ([1984] OJ L70/16) 54, 194, 208
Decision (EEC) 85/71 concerning the list of chemical substances notified pursuant to Council Directive (EEC) 67/548 ([1985] OJ L30/33) 165
Decision (EEC) 86/138 concerning a demonstration project with a view to introducing a Community system of information on accidents involving consumer products ([1986] OJ L109/23) 55, 56

Decision (EEC) 88/383 providing for the improvement of information on safety, hygiene and health at work ([1988] OJ L183/34) 71
Decision (EC) 94/3092 concerning development of the Community information system on accidents at home and leisure ([1994] OJ L331/1) 193
Decision (EC) 95/260 setting up a Consumer Committee ([1995] OJ L162/37) 2, 43
Decision (EC) 96/335 establishing an inventory and a common nomenclature of ingredients employed in cosmetic products ([1996] OJ L132/1) 146
Decision (EC) 97/579 setting up Scientific Committees in the field of consumer health and food safety ([1997] OJ L237/18) 84
Decision (EC) 99/283 of 25 January 1999 establishing a legal framework for the financing of the EC's activities in favour of consumers ([1999] OJ L34/1) 34
Decision (EC) 99/372 adopting a programme of Community action on injury prevention in the framework for action in the field of public health ([1999] OJ L46/1) 193, 198
Decision (EC) 2000/323 setting up a Consumer Committee ([2000] OJ L111/30) 2, 43
Decision (EC) 2002/247 suspending the placing on the market and import of jelly confectionery containing the food additive E 425 konjac ([2002] OJ L84/69) 96
Decision (EC) 2002/1786 on information and reaction to public health problems ([2002] OJ L271/1) 194, 197
Art 3 197
Directive (EEC) 65/65 on the approximation of provisions laid down by law, regulation or administrative action relating to proprietary medicinal products ([1965] OJ L22/369)
Art 1 140
Directive (EEC) 67/548 on the approximation of laws, regulations and administrative provisions relating to the classification, packaging and labelling of dangerous substances ([1967] OJ L196/1) 52, 155, 156, 165, 166, 167, 170, 173
Art 1 157
Art 2 157
Art 5 158
Art 6 158
Art 7 162
Art 8 160
Art 9 160
Art 10 160
Art 11 160
Art 13 161, 165
Art 13(1) 160
Art 15 161
Art 16 161
Art 18 162
Art 20 163
Art 21 163
Art 23 163
Annexes 164
Annex I 158, 159, 162, 165
Annex II 162, 169
Annex III 162

Annex IV 162
Annex V 158, 167
Annex V, Pt B 167
Annex V, Pt C 168
Annex VI 158, 167, 169
Annex VII 158
Annex VIII 158
Annex IX 161, 169
Annex J 161
Directive (EEC) 70/189 amending for the second time Council Directive 67/548/EEC on the approximation of the laws, regulations and administrative provisions relating to the classification, packaging and labelling of dangerous substances ([1970] OJ L59/33) 164
Directive (EEC) 71/144 amending for the third time Council Directive 67/548/EEC on the approximation of the laws, regulations and administrative provisions relating to the classification, packaging and labelling of dangerous substances ([1971] OJ L74/15) 164
Directive (EEC) 71/307 on textile names ([1971] OJ L185/16) 47
Directive (EEC) 72/166 on the approximation of the laws of the Member States relating to insurance against civil liability in respect of the use of motor vehicles, and to the enforcement of the obligation to insurance against such liability ([1972] OJ L103/1) 295
Directive (EEC) 73/146 amending for the fourth time Council Directive 67/548/EEC on the approximation of the laws, regulations and administrative provisions relating to the classification, packaging and labelling of dangerous substances ([1973] OJ L167/1) 164
Directive (EEC) 73/239 on the coordination of laws, regulations and administrative provisions relating to the taking-up and pursuit of the business of direct insurance other than life assurance ([1973] OJ L228/3) 36, 292
Art 1 292
Directive (EEC) 73/241 approximating the laws of the Member States relating to cocoa and chocolate ([1973] OJ L228/23) 115
Directive (EEC) 75/324 on the approximation of the laws of the Member States relating to aerosol dispensers ([1975] OJ L147/40) 155
Directive (EEC) 75/409 amending for the fifth time Council Directive 67/548/EEC on the approximation of the laws, regulations and administrative provisions relating to the classification, packaging and labelling of dangerous substances ([1975] OJ L183/22) 164
Directive (EEC) 75/440 laying down standards for surface water intended for the abstraction of drinking water ([1975] OJ L194/26) 136
Directive (EEC) 76/160 concerning the quality of bathing water ([1976] OJ L31/1) 133, 138, 140
Art 3 138
Art 4 138
Art 5 139
Art 6 139
Art 7 138
Art 8 139
Arts 9–11 139

Art 13 140
Annex 138
Directive (EEC) 76/766 on the approximation of the laws of the Member States relating to alcohol tables ([1976] OJ L262/149) 211
Directive (EEC) 76/768 on the approximation of the laws of the Member States relating to cosmetic products ([1976] OJ L262/169) 47, 143, 144, 151, 153
Art 1 144
Art 2 145
Art 4 145, 146
Art 5 145
Art 5(1) 148
Art 5(2) 148
Art 5a 146
Art 6 147
Art 6(1)(b) 148
Art 6(1)(c) 148
Art 6(1)(d) 148
Art 7 148
Art 7(2) 147, 148
Art 7(3) 150
Art 7a 149
Art 8 150
Art 9 150
Art 10 149
Art 12 151
Annexes 148, 150
Annex II 145
Annex III 145, 147
Annex IV 145, 147
Annex VI 145, 147
Annex VII 145, 147
Annex VIII 147
Directive (EEC) 76/769 on the approximation of the laws, regulations and administrative provisions of the Member States relating to restrictions on the marketing and use of certain dangerous substances and preparation ([1976] OJ L262/201) 155, 172, 212
Art 1(2) 173
Art 1(3) 173
Art 2(1)(a) 173
Annexes 179
Annex I 174, 179
Annex II 176
Directive (EEC) 76/893 on materials and articles intended to come into contact with foodstuffs ([1976] OJ L340/19) 82
Directive (EEC) 76/907 adapting to technical progress Council Directive 67/548/EEC on the approximation of the laws, regulations and administrative provisions relating to the classification, packaging and labelling of dangerous substances ([1976] OJ L360/1) 164

Directive (EEC) 77/94 on the approximation of the laws of the Member States relating to foodstuffs for particular nutritional uses ([1977] OJ L26/55) 123
Directive (EEC) 78/63 on the classification, packaging and labelling of pesticides 155
Directive (EEC) 79/112 on labelling, presentation and advertising of foodstuffs ([1979] OJ L33/1) 95, 106, 114, 115, 141, 221
Art 14 221
Directive (EEC) 79/267 on the coordination of laws, regulations and administrative provisions relating to the taking-up and pursuit of the business of direct life assurance ([1979] OJ L63/1) 36
Directive (EEC) 79/370 adapting to technical progress for the second time Council Directive 67/548/EEC on the approximation of the laws, regulations and administrative provisions relating to the classification, packaging and labelling of dangerous substances ([1979] OJ L88/1) 164
Directive (EEC) 79/581 on indication of prices of foodstuff ([1979] OJ L158/19) 37, 204
Directive (EEC) 79/661 adapting to technical progress Annex II to Council Directive 76/768/EEC on the approximation of the laws of the Member States relating to cosmetic products ([1979] OJ L192/35) 152
Directive (EEC) 79/831 amending for the sixth time Council Directive 67/548/EEC on the approximation of the laws, regulations and administrative provisions relating to the classification, packaging and labelling of dangerous substances ([1979] OJ L259/10) 164
Directive (EEC) 80/590 determining the symbol that may accompany materials and articles intended to come into contact with foodstuffs ([1980] OJ L151/42) 89
Directive (EEC) 80/777 on the approximation of laws relating to the exploitation and marketing of natural mineral waters ([1980] OJ L229/1) 134, 140
Art 1 141
Art 1(5) 141
Art 2 141
Art 3 141
Art 4 141
Art 5 141
Art 6 141
Arts 7–9 141
Art 14 140, 142
Annex I 141
Annex II 141
Directive (EEC) 80/778 relating to the quality of water intended for human consumption ([1980] OJ L229/11) 133, 134
Art 3 135
Art 4 134
Art 4(2) 135
Art 6 135
Art 7 135
Art 8 135
Art 9 135
Art 10 136
Art 11 135
Art 12 136
Arts 13–15 136

Art 15(2) 136
Art 16 135
Art 17 136
Art 17a 137
Art 20 137
Annex I 135, 136
Annex II 136
Annex III 136
Directive (EEC) 80/1335 on the approximation of the laws of the Member States relating to methods of analysis necessary for checking the composition of cosmetic products ([1980] OJ L383/27) 153
Directive (EEC) 81/957 adapting to technical progress for the third time Council Directive 67/548/EEC on the approximation of the laws, regulations and administrative provisions relating to the classification, packaging and labelling of dangerous substances ([1981] OJ L351/5) 164
Directive (EEC) 82/232 adapting to technical progress for the fourth time Council Directive 67/548/EEC on the approximation of the laws, regulations and administrative provisions relating to the classification, packaging and labelling of dangerous substances ([1982] OJ L106/18) 164
Directive (EEC) 82/368 adapting to technical progress for the second time Annex II to Council Directive 76/768/EEC on the approximation of the laws of the Member States relating to cosmetic products ([1982] OJ L167/1) 152
Directive (EEC) 82/434 on the approximation of the laws of the Member States relating to methods of analysis necessary for checking the composition of cosmetic products ([1982] OJ L185/1) 153
Directive (EEC) 82/828 amending for the third time Council Directive 76/769/EEC on the approximation of the laws, regulations and administrative provisions of the Member States relating to restrictions on the marketing and use of certain dangerous substances and preparations ([1982] OJ L350/34) 175
Directive (EEC) 83/189 laying down a procedure for the provision of information in the field of technical standards and regulations and providing for regulatory transparency in the internal market for information-society services ([1983] OJ L109/8) 182
Directive (EEC) 83/229 on the approximation of the laws of the Member States relating to materials and articles made of regenerated cellulose film intended to come into contact with foodstuffs ([1983] OJ L123/31) 83, 90
Directive (EEC) 83/264 amending for the fourth time Council Directive 76/769/EEC on the approximation of the laws, regulations and administrative provisions of the Member States relating to restrictions on the marketing and use of certain dangerous substances and preparations ([1983] OJ L147/9) 175, 176
Directive (EEC) 85/514 on the approximation of the laws of Member States relating to methods of analysis necessary for checking the composition of cosmetic products ([1983] OJ L291/9) 153
Directive (EEC) 83/574 adapting to technical progress for the third time Annex II to Council Directive 76/768/EEC on the approximation of the laws of the Member States relating to cosmetic products ([1983] OJ L332/38) 152
Directive (EEC) 84/5 on the approximation of the laws of the Member States relating to insurance against civil liability in respect of the use of motor vehicles ([1984] OJ L8/17) 297

Directive (EEC) 84/449 adapting to technical progress for the sixth time Council Directive 67/548/EEC on the approximation of the laws, regulations and administrative provisions relating to the classification, packaging and labelling of dangerous substances ([1984] OJ L251/1) 164
Directive (EEC) 84/450 concerning misleading and comparative advertising ([1984] OJ L250/17) 37, 47, 127, 224, 234, 235, 266, 267
Art 2 224
Art 2(1) 224
Art 3 224
Art 3a 225
Art 4 225
Art 6 226
Art 7 14, 226
Directive (EEC) 84/500 on ceramic articles intended to come into contact with foodstuffs ([1984] OJ L277/12) 85
Art 1 87
Art 2 86, 88, 110
Art 3(1) 88
Art 3(3) 88
Art 3(5) 89
Art 4 89
Art 7 88
Art 8 88
Annexes 87, 88
Annex I 86, 88
Annex II 86, 89
Annex III 89
Directive (EEC) 85/374 on product liability ([1985] OJ L210/29) 8, 13, 16, 32, 52, 61, 65
Art 1 62
Art 2 62
Art 3 63
Art 4 62
Art 5 63
Art 6 63
Art 7 63
Art 7(e) 63
Art 9 64
Art 13 65
Art 15 64
Art 16 64
Art 226 63
Directive (EEC) 85/490 on the approximation of the laws of the Member States relating to methods of analysis necessary for checking the composition of cosmetic products ([1985] OJ L295/30) 154
Directive (EEC) 85/577 to protect the consumer in respect of contracts negotiated away from business premises (Doorstep Selling Directive) ([1985] OJ L372/31) 14, 20, 39, 48, 239, 266
Art 1(1) 239

Art 1(2) 239, 241
Art 1(3) 239, 241
Art 1(4) 239, 241
Art 3 240
Art 3(2)(c) 240
Art 4 240, 259
Art 5 241
Art 6 241
Art 7 241
Art 8 241
Directive (EEC) 86/431 adapting to technical progress for the seventh time Council Directive 67/548/EEC on the approximation of the laws, regulations and administrative provisions relating to the classification, packaging and labelling of dangerous substances ([1986] OJ L247/1) 164
Directive (EEC) 87/18 on the harmonization of laws, regulations and administrative provisions relating to the application of the principles of good laboratory practice and the verification of their applications for tests on chemical substances ([1987] OJ L15/29) 150
Directive (EEC) 87/102 on the approximation of the laws, regulations and administrative provisions of the Member States concerning consumer credit ([1987] OJ L42/48) 14, 20, 48, 243, 244, 245, 266
Art 1(2)(c) 242
Art 1a 243
Art 2 242
Art 3 243
Art 4(2) 243
Art 6 242, 243, 259
Art 7 243
Art 8 243
Art 9 244
Art 10 244
Art 15 245
Art 17 245
Annex I 243
Directive (EEC) 87/250 on the indication of alcoholic strength by volume in the labelling of alcoholic beverages for sale to the ultimate consumer ([1987] OJ L113/57) 37
Art 3 211
Directive (EEC) 87/302 adapting to technical progress for the ninth time Council Directive 67/548/EEC on the approximation of the laws, regulations and administrative provisions relating to the classification, packaging and labelling of dangerous substances ([1988] OJ L133/1) 164
Directive (EEC) 87/357 on the approximation of the laws of the Member States concerning products which appearing to be other than they are, endanger the health or safety of consumers ([1987] OJ L192/49) 207, 48
Art 1 207
Art 2 208
Art 5 208

Directive (EEC) 87/432 adapting to technical progress for the eighth time Council Directive 67/548/EEC on the approximation of the laws, regulations and administrative provisions relating to the classification, packaging and labelling of dangerous substances ([1987] OJ L239/1) 164
Directive (EEC) 88/146 on the prohibition of certain hormonal substances in meat ([1988] OJ L70/16) 39, 52
Directive (EEC) 88/314 on indication of prices of non-food products ([1988] OJ L142/19) 204, 212
Directive (EEC) 88/357 on the coordination of the laws, regulations and administrative provisions relating to direct insurance other than life assurance and laying down provisions to facilitate the effective exercise of freedom to provide services and amending Directive 73/239/EEC ([1988] OJ L172/1) 292
Directive (EEC) 88/378 on the approximation of the laws of the Member States concerning the safety of toys ([1988] OJ L187/1) 48, 181
Art 2 182
Art 9 183
Art 10 183, 184
Art 11 182, 184
Art 12 184
Art 13 184
Annex I 182
Annex II 182
Annex III 183
Annex IV 184
Directive (EEC) 88/379 on the approximation of the laws, regulations and administrative provisions of the Member States relating to the classification, packaging and labelling of dangerous preparations ([1988] OJ L187/14) 165, 166
Art 10 171
Directive (EEC) 88/388 on the approximation of the laws of the Member States relating to flavourings for the use in foodstuff and to source material for their production ([1988] OJ L184/61) 92
Art 1 102
Art 6(2) 103
Art 8 103
Art 9 103
Art 9(1)(a) 103
Annex I 103
Annex II 103
Directive (EEC) 88/490 adapting to technical progress for the tenth time Council Directive 67/548/EEC on the approximation of the laws, regulations and administrative provisions relating to the classification, packaging and labelling of dangerous substances ([1988] OJ L259/1) 164
Directive (EEC) 88/667 adapting to technical progress for the fourth time Annex II to Council Directive 76/768/EEC on the approximation of the laws of the Member States relating to cosmetic products ([1988] OJ L382/46) 152
Directive (EEC) 89/48 on a general system for the recognition of higher education diplomas on completion of professional education and training of at least three years' duration ([1989] OJ L19/16)
Art 1 149

Directive (EEC) 89/107 on the approximation of the laws of the Member States concerning food additives authorised for use in foodstuffs intended for human consumption ([1989] OJ L40/27) 52, 96, 97, 98
Art 1 98
Art 1(2) 92
Art 1(3) 92
Art 2 92
Art 3 93, 95, 98, 100
Art 4 93, 94
Art 5 94
Art 6 94
Art 7 94, 95
Art 8 95
Art 9 95
Art 11 93, 95
Art 12 95
Annexes 95
Annex I 92, 94
Annex II 92, 97
Directive (EEC) 89/108 on the approximation of the laws of the Member States relating to quick-frozen foodstuffs for human consumption ([1989] OJ L40/34) 53, 104
Art 1(1) 105
Art 2 106
Art 4 105
Art 5 106
Art 6 106
Art 7 106
Art 8(1)(a) 106
Art 9 107
Art 10 107
Art 11 107
Art 12 106, 107
Directive (EEC) 89/109 on materials and articles in contact with foodstuffs ([1989] OJ L40/38) 53, 72, 82
Art 1 83
Art 2 83, 87
Art 3 83
Art 4 84, 89
Art 5 84
Art 6 84
Art 6(5) 91
Art 7 85
Art 8 83, 85
Art 9 84, 85
Annex I 83
Annex II 83
Directive (EEC) 89/197 ([1989] OJ L40/27) on colours 98
Directive (EEC) 89/397 on the official control of foodstuffs ([1989] OJ L186/23) 53, 75

Directive (EEC) 89/398 on the approximation of the laws of the Member States relating to foodstuffs intended for particular nutritional uses ([1989] OJ L186/27) 122, 206
Art 1 123
Art 4 124
Art 13 124
Annex I 123, 124
Directive (EEC) 89/552 on the coordination of certain provisions laid down by law, regulation or administrative action in Member States concerning the pursuit of television broadcasting activities ([1989] OJ L298/23) 53, 191, 227, 228, 266
Art 10 228
Art 11 228
Art 12 229
Art 13 192, 229
Art 14 229
Art 18 230
Art 18(1) 230
Art 19 230
Directive (EEC) 89/646 on the access to and exercise of activities of credit institutions ([1989] OJ L386/1) 53
Directive (EEC) 89/654 concerning the minimum safety and health requirements for the workplace ([1989] OJ L393/1) 187
Directive (EEC) 89/677 amending for the eighth time Council Directive 76/769/EEC on the approximation of the laws, regulations and administrative provisions of the Member States relating to restrictions on the marketing and use of certain dangerous substances and preparations ([1989] OJ L398/19) 175, 177, 178
Directive (EEC) 89/678 amending Council Directive 76/769/EEC on the approximation of the laws, regulations and administrative provisions of the Member States relating to restrictions on the marketing and use of certain dangerous substances and preparations ([1989] OJ L398/24) 173
Directive (EEC) 89/679 adapting to technical progress for the fifth time Annex II to Council Directive 76/768/EEC on the approximation of the laws of the Member States relating to cosmetic products ([1989] OJ L398/25) 152
Directive (EEC) 90/35 defining in accordance with Article 6 of Directive 88/379/EEC the categories of preparations the packaging of which must be fitted with child-resistant fastenings and/or carry a tactile warning of danger ([1990] OJ L19/14) 155
Directive (EEC) 90/128 relating to plastics materials and articles intended to come into contact with foodstuffs ([1990] OJ L349/26) 83
Directive (EEC) 90/220 on the deliberate release into the environment of genetically modified organisms ([1990] OJ L117/15) 119, 121, 122
Directive (EEC) 90/239 establishing a maximum tar yield of cigarettes ([1990] OJ L137/36) 187, 188
Directive (EEC) 90/314 on package travel, package holidays and package tours ([1990] OJ L158/59) 11, 14, 20, 36, 48, 266, 275, 283
Art 3 276
Art 4 277
Art 5 278
Art 7 278, 279
Art 8 279

Annex 277
Directive (EEC) 90/496 on nutrition labelling for foodstuffs ([1990] OJ L276/40) 53, 205
Art 1(4)(a)(ii) 206
Art 4 206
Art 6 206
Art 7 206
Art 9 207
Art 10 206, 207
Directive (EEC) 90/517 adapting to technical progress for the eleventh time Council Directive 67/548/EEC on the approximation of the laws, regulations and administrative provisions relating to the classification, packaging and labelling of dangerous substances ([1990] OJ L287/37) 164
Directive (EEC) 91/71 completing Council Directive 88/388/EEC on the approximation of the laws of the Member States relating to flavourings for use in foodstuffs and to source material for their production ([1991] OJ L42/25) 102
Directive (EEC) 91/155 defining and laying down the detailed arrangements for the system of specific information relating to dangerous preparations in implementation of Article 10 of Directive (EEC) 88/379 ([1991] OJ L76/39) 171
Art 1 171
Art 3 171, 172
Annex 171
Directive (EEC) 91/157 on batteries and accumulators containing certain dangerous substances ([1991] OJ L78/38) 155
Directive (EEC) 91/173 amending for the ninth time Council Directive 76/769/EEC on the approximation of the laws, regulations and administrative provisions of the Member States relating to restrictions on the marketing and use of certain dangerous substances and preparations ([1989] OJ L398/19) ([1991] OJ L85/34) 178
Directive (EEC) 91/321 on infant formulae and follow-on formulae ([1991] OJ L175/35) 123
Directive (EEC) 91/325 adapting to technical progress for the twelfth time Council Directive 67/548/EEC on the approximation of the laws, regulations and administrative provisions relating to the classification, packaging and labelling of dangerous substances ([1991] OJ L180/1) 164
Directive (EEC) 91/326 adapting to technical progress for the thirteenth time Council Directive 67/548/EEC on the approximation of the laws, regulations and administrative provisions relating to the classification, packaging and labelling of dangerous substances ([1991] OJ L180/79) 164
Directive (EEC) 91/410 adapting to technical progress for the fourteenth time Council Directive 67/548/EEC on the approximation of the laws, regulations and administrative provisions relating to the classification, packaging and labelling of dangerous substances ([1991] OJ L228/67) 164
Directive (EEC) 91/442 on dangerous preparations the packaging of which must be fitted with child-resistant fastenings ([1991] OJ L 238/25) 155
Directive (EEC) 91/632 adapting to technical progress for the fifteenth time Council Directive 67/548/EEC on the approximation of the laws, regulations and administrative provisions relating to the classification, packaging and labelling of dangerous substances ([1991] OJ L338/23) 164
Directive (EEC) 91/659 adapting to technical progress Annex I to Council Directive 76/769/EEC on the approximation of the laws, regulations and administrative

provisions of the Member States relating to restrictions on the marketing and use of certain dangerous substances and preparations ([1991] OJ L363/36) 176
Directive (EEC) 91/692 standardizing and rationalizing reports on the implementation of certain Directives relating to the environment ([1991] OJ L377/48) 137, 140
Directive (EEC) 92/28 on the advertising of medicinal products for human use ([1992] OJ L113/13) 266, 267
Directive (EEC) 92/32 amending for the seventh time Council Directive 67/548/EEC on the approximation of the laws, regulations and administrative provisions relating to the classification, packaging and labelling of dangerous substances ([1992] OJ L154/1) 164
Directive (EEC) 92/37 adapting to technical progress for the sixteenth time Council Directive 67/548/EEC on the approximation of the laws, regulations and administrative provisions relating to the classification, packaging and labelling of dangerous substances ([1992] OJ L154/30) 164
Directive (EEC) 92/49 on the coordination of the laws, regulations and administrative provisions relating to direct insurance other than life assurance and amending Council Directive (EEC) 73/239 and Council Directive 88/357 ([1992] OJ L228/4) 53, 292
Art 31 293
Art 42 293
Art 43 293
Directive (EEC) 92/59 on general product safety ([1992] OJ L228/24) 49, 61, 66, 67, 68, 70, 71, 80
Directive (EEC) 92/69 adapting to technical progress for the seventeenth time Council Directive 67/548/EEC on the approximation of the laws, regulations and administrative provisions relating to the classification, packaging and labelling of dangerous substances ([1992] OJ L383/113) 164
Directive (EEC) 92/75 on the indication by labelling and standard product information of the consumption of energy and other resources by household appliances ([1992] OJ L297/16) 215
Art 2(3) 215
Art 10 216
Directive (EC) 92/85 on the introduction of measures to encourage improvements in the safety and health at work of pregnant workers and workers who have recently given birth or are breastfeeding ([1992] OJ L348/1) 187
Directive (EC) 92/96 on life insurance (third generation of directives in the field of life insurance) ([2002] OJ L345/1) 53
Directive (EC) 93/10 relating to materials and articles made of regenerated cellulose film intended to come into contact with foodstuffs ([1993] OJ L93/27)
Art 4 90
Art 5(1) 89
Annex I 90
Annex II 90
Directive (EC) 93/13 on unfair terms in consumer contracts ([1993] OJ L95/29) 11, 14, 20, 36, 40, 49, 253, 255, 266, 267
Art 2(c) 256
Art 3 259
Art 3(1) 256, 257
Art 3(2) 257

Art 4(2) 258
Art 5 258, 259
Art 7 259
Art 9 262
Annex 259, 260, 262
Directive (EC) 93/21 adapting to technical progress for the eighteenth time Council Directive 67/548/EEC on the approximation of the laws, regulations and administrative provisions relating to the classification, packaging and labelling of dangerous substances ([1993] OJ L110/20) 162, 164
Directive (EC) 93/35 adapting to technical progress for the sixth time Annex II to Council Directive 76/768/EEC on the approximation of the laws of the Member States relating to cosmetic products ([1993] OJ L151/32) 143, 146, 148, 149, 152
Directive (EC) 93/72 adapting to technical progress for the nineteenth time Council Directive 67/548/EEC on the approximation of the laws, regulations and administrative provisions relating to the classification, packaging and labelling of dangerous substances ([1993] oJ L258/29) 164
Directive (EC) 93/73 on the methods of analysis necessary for checking composition of cosmetic product ([1993] OJ L231/34) 154
Directive (EC) 93/77 on fruit juices ([1993] OJ L244/23) 74
Directive (EC) 93/99 on additional measures concerning the official control of foodstuffs ([1993] OJ L290/14) 75
Directive (EC) 93/101 adapting to technical progress for the twentieth time Council Directive 67/548/EEC on the approximation of the laws, regulations and administrative provisions relating to the classification, packaging and labelling of dangerous substances ([1993] OJ L13/1) 164
Directive (EC) 93/105 laying down Annex VII D, containing information required for the technical dossier referred to in Article 12 of the seventh amendment of Council Directive 67/548/EEC ([1993] OJ L294/21) 164
Directive (EC) 93/151 on package travel, package holidays and package tours ([1993] OJ L121/20) 275
Directive (EC) 94/11 on the approximation of laws, regulations and administrative provisions of Member States relating to the labelling of material used in main components of footwear for sale to consumers ([1994] OJ L100/37) 212
Annex I 212
Annex II 212
Directive (EC) 94/19 on deposit guarantee schemes ([1994] OJ L135/5) 53
Directive (EC) 94/35 on sweeteners for use in foodstuffs ([1994] OJ L237/3) 97
Art 1 96
Art 1(3) 96
Art 2(1)(a) 97
Art 2(3) 97
Art 3 96
Art 4 96
Art 5 97
Art 6 97
Art 7 97
Annex 96
Directive (EC) 94/36 on colours for use in foodstuffs ([1994] OJ L237/13) 98
Art 1 100, 101

Art 3 101
Art 5 101
Annexes 101
Annex I 101
Annex II 101
Annex III 101
Annex IV 101
Annex V 101
Directive (EC) 94/47 on the protection of purchasers in respect of certain aspects of contracts relating to the purchase of the right to use immovable properties on a timeshare basis ([1994] OJ L280/83) 11, 13, 20, 36, 49, 238, 240, 266, 275, 279
Art 3 259, 280
Art 4 281
Art 5 281
Art 7 281
Annex 280, 281
Directive (EC) 94/55 on the approximation of the laws of the Member States with regard to the transport of dangerous goods by road ([1994] OJ L319/7) 155
Directive (EC) 94/69 adapting to technical progress for the twenty-first time Council Directive 67/548/EEC on the approximation of the laws, regulations and administrative provisions relating to the classification, packaging and labelling of dangerous substances ([1994] OJ L381/1) 164
Directive (EC) 95/2 on food additives other than colours and sweeteners ([1995] OJ L61/1) 98
Art 1(1) 98, 241
Art 1(3) 99
Art 1(4) 99
Art 1(5) 98
Art 2 99
Art 3 99
Art 5 99
Art 6 99
Art 7 99
Annex I 99
Annex II 99
Annex III 99
Annex IV 99
Annex V 99
Directive (EC) 95/32 on the methods of analysis necessary for checking composition of cosmetic product ([1995] OJ L178/20) 154
Directive (EC) 95/45 laying down specific purity criteria concerning colours for use in foodstuffs ([1995] OJ L226/1) 91, 93
Directive (EC) 95/46 on the protection of individuals with regard to the processing of personal data and on the free movement of such data ([1995] OJ L281/31) 270
Directive (EC) 96/22 concerning the prohibition on the use in livestock farming of certain substances having a hormonal or thyrostatic action and of beta-agonists ([1996] OJ L125/3) 117

Directive (EC) 96/45 on the methods of analysis necessary for checking composition of cosmetic product ([1996] OJ L123/8) 154
Directive (EC) 96/54 adapting to technical progress for the twenty-second time Council Directive 67/548/EEC on the approximation of the laws, regulations and administrative provisions relating to the classification, packaging and labelling of dangerous substances([1996] OJ 248/1) 164
Directive (EC) 96/56 amending for the eighth time Council Directive 67/548/EEC on the approximation of the laws, regulations and administrative provisions relating to the classification, packaging and labelling of dangerous substances ([1996] OJ L236/35) 164
Directive (EC) 96/74 on textile names ([1997] OJ L32/38) 213
Art 8 214
Art 9 214
Art 10 214
Annex I 214
Annex II 214
Directive (EC) 96/77 laying down specific purity criteria on food additives other than colours and sweeteners ([1996] OJ L339/1) 91, 93
Directive (EC) 96/83 amending Directive 94/351 EC on sweeteners for use in foodstuffs ([1996] OJ L48/16) 96
Directive (EC) 96/84 amending Directive 89/398/EEC on the approximation of the laws of the Member States relating to foodstuffs for particular nutritional uses ([1997] OJ L48/20) 122
Directive (EC) 96/85 amending Directive 95/2/EC on food additives other than colours and sweeteners ([1997] OJ L86/4) 99
Directive (EC) 97/5 on cross-border credit transfers ([1997] OJ L43/25) 50, 285
Art 3 286
Art 4 286
Art 5 286
Art 7 287
Art 8 287
Directive (EC) 97/7 on the protection of consumers in respect of distance contracts ([1997] OJ L144/19) 11, 20, 32, 49, 234, 246, 251, 314
Art 4 248
Art 4(2) 259
Art 5 249, 259
Art 14 250
Annex I 247
Directive (EC) 97/36 amending Council Directive (EEC) 89/552 on the coordination of certain provisions laid down by law, regulation or administrative action in Member States concerning the pursuit of television broadcasting activities ([1997] OJ L202/60) 228
Directive (EC) 97/37 adapting to technical progress Annexes I and II to Directive 96/74/EC of the European Parliament and of the Council on textile names ([1997] OJ L169/74) 214
Directive (EC) 97/66 concerning the processing of personal data and the protection of privacy in the telecommunications sector ([1998] OJ L24/1) 270
Directive (EC) 98/6 on consumer protection in the indication of the prices of products offered to consumers ([1998] OJ L80/27) 10, 37, 47, 67, 204, 212

Art 2 204
Art 3 205
Art 3(1) 204
Art 5 205
Art 7 205
Art 8 205
Art 10 205
Directive (EC) 98/27 on injunctions for the protection of consumers' interests ([1998] OJ L166/51 20, 50, 51, 57, 234, 251
Art 4(2) 267
Annex 246, 266
Directive (EC) 98/73 adapting to technical progress for the twenty-fourth time Council Directive 67/548/EEC on the approximation of the laws, regulations and administrative provisions relating to the classification, packaging and labelling of dangerous substances ([1998] OJ L305/1) 164
Directive (EC) 98/83 on the quality of water intended for human consumption ([1998] OJ L330/320) 133
Directive (EC) 98/98 adapting to technical progress for the twenty-fifth time Council Directive 67/548/EEC on the approximation of the laws, regulations and administrative provisions relating to the classification, packaging and labelling of dangerous substances ([1999] OJ L293/1) 164
Directive (EC) 99/4 on coffee and chicory extracts ([1999] OJ L66/26)
Art 5 116
Art 8 116
Annex 116
Directive (EC) 99/34 amending Council Directive 85/374/EEC concerning liability for defective products ([1999] OJ L141/20) 62
Directive (EC) 99/41 amending Directive 89/398/EEC on the approximation of the laws of the Member States relating to foodstuffs for particular nutritional uses ([1999] OJ L172/38) 122
Directive (EC) 99/44 on certain aspects of the sale of consumer goods and associated guarantees ([1999] OJ L171/12) 14, 262, 266
Art 2 263
Art 3(1) 263
Art 3(2) 263
Art 4 264
Art 6 264
Directive (EC) 99/45 concerning the approximation of the laws, regulations and administrative provisions of the Member States relating to the classification, packaging and labelling of dangerous preparations ([1999] OJ L200/1) 52, 155, 165, 171, 173
Art 1 166
Art 1(5) 166
Art 3 167
Art 4 167
Art 5 167, 171
Art 5(2) 167
Art 6 167, 171
Art 7 167, 171

Art 8 168
Art 9 168
Art 10 167, 169
Art 10(3) 169
Art 10(4) 169
Art 11 169
Art 12 170
Art 13 170
Art 14 171
Art 15 170
Art 17 168
Art 19 170
Annexes 167
Annex I, Pt B 167
Annex II 167
Annex III 167
Directive (EC) 99/94 relating to the availability of consumer information on fuel economy and CO2 emissions in respect of the marketing of new passenger cars ([2000] OJ L12/16) 214
Directive (EC) 99/144 on consumer sales ([1999] OJ L171/12) 20
Directive (EC) 2000/13 on the approximation of the laws of the Member States relating to the labelling, presentation and advertising of foodstuffs for sale to the ultimate consumer ([2000] OJ L109/29)50, 108, 109, 110, 111, 112, 123, 126, 141, 200, 206, 221
Art 1.3(a) 200
Art 2 200
Art 3 200
Art 5 201
Art 6 201
Art 6(6) 209
Art 7 202
Art 8 202
Art 18 203
Art 19 202, 203
Art 20(2) 203
Annex I 201
Annex II 201
Annex III 201
Annex IV, Pt B 204
Directive (EC) 2000/26 on the approximation of the laws of the Member States relating to insurance against civil liability in respect of the use of motor vehicles and amending Council Directives (EEC) 73/239 and (EEC) 88/357
Art 3 295
Art 4 295
Art 4(1) 2, 296
Art 5 296
Art 6 296
Art 7 296

Art 12 297

Directive (EC) 2000/31 on certain legal aspects of information society services, in particular electronic commerce, in the Internal Market (Directive on electronic commerce) ([2000] OJ L178/1) 20, 266, 270, 271

Art 3 273

Art 3(4)–(6) 273

Directive (EC) 2000/32 adapting to technical progress for the twenty-sixth time Council Directive 67/548/EEC on the approximation of the laws, regulations and administrative provisions relating to the classification, packaging and labelling of dangerous substances ([2000] OJ L136/1) 164

Directive (EC) 2000/33 adapting to technical progress for the twenty-seventh time Council Directive 67/548/EEC on the approximation of the laws, regulations and administrative provisions relating to the classification, packaging and labelling of dangerous substances ([2000] OJ L136/900) 164

Directive (EC) 2000/36 on cocoa and chocolate products intended for human consumption ([2000] OJ L197/19)

Art 2 114

Art 2(2) 114

Art 3(2) 114

Art 3(3) 114

Art 3(4) 114

Art 3(5) 114

Art 6(2) 115

Art 8 115

Annex I 113, 114, 115

Directive (EC) 2000/113 relating to fruit jams, jellies and marmalades and sweetened chestnut puree intended for human consumption ([2000] OJ L109/29)

Art 1 109

Art 2 109

Art 6(2) 110

Art 8 109

Annex I 109

Annex II 109

Directive (EC) 2001/5 amending Directive 95/2/EC on food additives other than colours and sweeteners ([2001] OJ L55/59) 99

Directive (EC) 2001/18 on the deliberate release into the environment of genetically modified organisms ([2001] OJ L106/1) 119, 121, 122

Annex I B 121

Directive (EC) 2001/37 on the approximation of the laws, regulations and administrative provisions of the Member States concerning the manufacture, presentation and sale of tobacco products ([2001] OJ L194/26) 188

Art 3 188

Art 5 188, 220

Art 5(5) 189

Art 5(6) 189

Art 5(7) 189

Art 6 189

Art 8 189

Art 9 189

Art 10 189
Art 11 189
Art 13 189
Annex I 188
Directive (EC) 2001/54 repealing Directive (EEC) 79/1066 laying down Community methods of analysis for testing coffee extracts and chicory extracts ([2001] OJ L191/42 116
Directive (EC) 2001/59 adapting to technical progress for the twenty-eighth time Council Directive 67/548/EEC on the approximation of the laws, regulations and administrative provisions relating to the classification, packaging and labelling of dangerous substances ([2001] OJ L225/1) 164
Directive (EC) 2001/83 on the Community code relating to medicinal products for human use ([2001] OJ L311/67) 125, 217
Title V 231
Title VIII 231
Arts 54–69 217, 219
Art 54 217, 219
Art 55 217
Art 59 219
Art 59(1) 217, 219
Art 62 219
Art 68 219
Art 69 220
Art 86 231
Art 87 231
Art 87(1) 231
Art 88(2) 232
Art 89 232
Arts 91–96 233
Art 91 233
Art 92 233
Art 93 233
Art 94 233
Art 95 233
Art 96 233
Art 97 234
Annex II, Pt B 220, 234
Directive (EC) 2001/90 adapting to technical progress for the seventh time Annex I to Council Directive 76/769/EEC on the approximation of the laws, regulations and administrative provisions of the Member States relating to restrictions on the marketing and use of certain dangerous substances and preparations ([2001] OJ L283/41) 179
Directive (EC) 2001/91 adapting to technical progress for the eighth time Annex I to Council Directive 76/769/EEC on the approximation of the laws, regulations and administrative provisions of the Member States relating to restrictions on the marketing and use of certain dangerous substances and preparations ([2001] OJ L286/27) 179
Directive (EC) 2001/95 on general product safety ([2002] OJ L11/4)11, 29, 54, 61, 66, 67, 71, 80, 194, 195

Art 2 67, 68
Art 3(2) 67, 68
Art 6 69
Art 7 69
Art 8 69
Art 8(1)(b)–(f) 195
Art 8(b)–(f) 70
Art 3(3) 68
Art 10 69, 196
Art 11 70
Art 12 70, 83
Art 13 70
Art 16 71
Art 19(2) 71
Art 20 71
Annex II 70, 195

Directive (EC) 2001/110 relating to honey ([2002] OJ L10/53
Art 2 111
Art 7(2) 111, 112
Art 9 111
Annex I 111
Annex II 111

Directive (EC) 2001/111 relating to certain sugars intended for human consumption ([2002] OJ L10/53)
Art 2 110
Art 2(3) 110
Art 2(4) 110
Art 2(5) 110
Art 5(2) 110
Art 7 110
Annex 110

Directive (EC) 2001/112 relating to fruit juices and certain similar products intended for human consumption ([2002] OJ L10/58)
Art 1 107
Art 2 107
Art 8(2) 108
Art 10 108
Annex I 107, 108
Annex III 108

Directive (EC) 2001/114 relating to certain partly or wholly dehydrated preserved milk for human consumption ([2002] OJ L15/19)
Art 6(2) 113
Annex I 112, 113
Annex II 112, 113

Directive (EC) 2002/45 amending for the twentieth time Council Directive 76/769/EEC relating to restrictions on the marketing and use of certain dangerous substances and preparations (short-chain chlorinated paraffins) ([2002] OJ L177/21) 175

Directive (EC) 2002/46 on the approximation of the laws of Member States relating to food supplements ([2002] OJ L183/52) 124, 126
Art 2 124
Art 6(3) 126
Art 13(2) 125
Annexes 126
Annex I 125, 126
Annex II 125
Directive (EC) 2002/58 concerning the processing of personal data and the protection of privacy in the electronic communications sector ([2002] OJ L201/37) 53
Directive (EC) 2002/62 adapting to technical progress for the ninth time Annex I to Council Directive 76/769/EEC on the approximation of the laws, regulations and administrative provisions of the Member States relating to restrictions on the marketing and use of certain dangerous substances and preparations ([2002] OJ L183/58) 179
Directive (EC) 2002/65 concerning the distance marketing of consumer financial services ([2002] OJ L271/16) 11, 38, 50, 246, 266
Art 3 251, 252
Art 3(3) 252
Art 4 252
Art 9 253
Art 10 253
Directive (EC) 2002/83 concerning life assurance ([1998] OJ L80/27) 293
Art 2 294
Art 32 294
Art 33 294
Art 35 294
Art 36 294
Annex III(A) 294
Annex III(B) 294
Directive (EC) 2003/2 relating to restrictions on the marketing and use of arsenic ([2003] OJ L4/9) 179
Directive (EC) 2003/3 relating to restrictions on the marketing and use of 'blue colourant' ([2003] OJ L4/12) 179
Directive (EC) 2003/15 banning animal experiments for cosmetics ingredients or combinations of ingredients ([2003] OJ L66/26) 144, 146, 152
Directive (EC) 2003/33 on the approximation of the laws, regulations and administrative provisions of the Member States relating to the advertising and sponsorship of tobacco products ([2003] OJ L152/16) 187, 190
Art 3 190
Directive (EC) 2003/36 amending for the 25th time Council Directive 76/769/EEC on the approximation of the laws, regulations and administrative provisions of the Member States relating to restrictions on the marketing and use of certain dangerous substances and preparations ([2003] OJ L156/26) 175
Directive (EC) 2003/801 establishing a symbol indicating the durability of cosmetic products in Annex VIIIa to Council Directive (EEC) 76/768 152

Energy Information (Dishwashers) Regulations 1999 (SI 1999/1676) 216
Energy Information (Refrigerators and Freezers) Regulations 1994 (SI 1994/3076) 216

Flavourings in Food Regulations 1992 (SI 1992/1971) 103
Food Imitation (Safety) Regulations 1989 (SI 1989/1291) 208
Food Labelling (Amendment) Regulations 1994 (SI 1994/804) 207
Food Safety Act 1990 85
Food Safety (Exports) Regulations 1991 (SI 1991/1476) 85
Footwear (Indication of Composition) Labelling Regulations 1995 (SI 1995/2489) 213

General Agreement on Tariffs and Trade 1994 (GATT 1994) 122
General Product Safety Regulations 1994 (SI 1994/2328) 71
Glazed Ceramic Ware (Safety) Regulations (Northern Ireland) 1975 (SR (NI) 1975/313) 86

Materials and Articles in Contact with Food Regulations 1987 (SI 1987/1523) 85
Materials and Articles in Contact with Food (Amendment) Regulations 1992 (SI 1992/1927) 91
Medicines (Control of Substances for Manufacture) Order 1997 (SI 1997/1728) 117
Medicines (Stilbenes and Thyrostatic Substances Prohibition) Revocation Order 1997 (SI 1997/1727) 117,
Miscellaneous Food Additives Regulations 1995 (SI 1995/3187) 96, 100, 102
Montreal Convention (1999) 284

Natural Mineral Waters Regulations 1985 142
Novelties (Safety) (Amendment) Regulations 1985 (SI 1985/128) 179

Package Travel, Package Holiday and Package Tours Regulations 1992 (SI 1992/3228) 279
Packaging and Labelling of Dangerous Substances Regulations 1978 (SI 1978/209) 164
Passenger Car (Fuel Consumption and CO2 Emissions Information) Regulations 2001 (SI 2001/3523) 215
Plastic Materials and Articles in Contact with Food Regulations 1992 (SI 1992/3145) 89
Plastic Materials and Articles in Contact with Food (Amendment) (England) Regulations 2002 (SI 2002/2364) 89, 113
Portuguese law of 1985
  preamble 258
  Art 16 257
Pricing Order 1999 (SI 1999/3042) 205
Private Water Supplies Regulations 1991 (SI 1991/2790) 137

Quick-frozen Foodstuffs Regulations 1990 (SI 1990/2615) 107

Recommendation (EEC) 87/598 laying down general principles relating to the contract between issuers (banks) and traders or consumers ([1987] OJ L365/72) 289
Recommendation (EEC) 88/590 concerning payment systems and in particular the relationships between card issuers and card holders ([1988] OJ L31 7/55) 51, 287
  preamble 288
  Annex 287

Recommendation (EEC) 90/109 concerning the transparency of banking conditions applicable to cross-border financial transactions ([1990] OJ L67/39) 53
Recommendation (EEC) 92/295 on codes of conduct for the protection of consumers in the field of contracts negotiated at a distance ([1992] OJ L156/21) 51, 247, 259
Recommendation (EC) 97/489 concerning transactions by electronic payment instruments and in particular the relationship between issuer and holder ([1997] OJ L208/52) 51, 289
Recommendation (EC) 97/618 concerning the scientific aspects and the presentation of information necessary to support applications for the placing on the market of novel foods and novel food ingredients and the preparation of initial assessment reports under Regulation (EC) No 258/97 of the European Parliament and of the Council ([1997] OJ L253/1) 120
Recommendation (EC) 98/257 on the principles applicable to the bodies responsible for the out-of-court settlement of consumer disputes ([1998] OJ L 115/31) 18, 57, 265, 269
Recommendation (EC) 2001/310 on the principles for out-of-court bodies involved in the consensual resolution of consumer disputes ([2001] OJ L109/56) 18, 57, 269
Regulation (EEC) 1576/89 on the definition, description and presentation of spirit drinks ([1989] OJ L160/1)
Art 1(2) 210
Regulation (EEC) 295/91 establishing common rules for a denied-boarding compensation scheme in scheduled air transport ([1991] OJ L36/5) 53, 282
Regulation (EEC) 1601/91 on the description and presentation of aromatized wines, aromatized wine-based drinks and aromatized wine-product cocktails ([1991] OJ L149/1) 210
Art 8 211
Regulation (EC) 2092/91 on organic production of agricultural products and indications referring thereto on agricultural products and foodstuffs ([1991] OJ L198/1) 127
Art 2 127
Art 5 127
Regulation (EC) 2081/92 on the protection of geographical indications and designations of origin for agricultural products ([1992] OJ L208/1) 129, 130, 131
Art 2.2(a) 129
Art 2.2(b) 129
Art 3 130
Arts 4–7 130
Art 17 130
Annex I 129
Annex II 129
Regulation (EC) 2082/92 on certificates of specific character for agricultural products and foodstuffs ([1992] OJ L208/9) 129, 130, 131
Annex 131
Regulation (EC) 2232/96 setting out rules for the use of flavouring substances in or on foodstuffs in the EU ([1996] OJ L299/1) 103
Regulation (EC) 258/97 concerning novel foods and novel food ingredients ([1997] OJ L43/1) 118, 119, 121
Art 1 119
Art 4 120
Art 6 120

Art 7 120
Art 8 120
Art 13 119, 121
Art 14 121
Regulation (EC) 2027/97 on air carrier liability in the event of accidents ([1997] OJ L285/1)
Art 3(3) 284
Regulation (EC) 257/98 on jurisdiction and the recognition and enforcement of judgments in civil and commercial matters (Brussels Regulation) ([2001] OJ L12/1) 17, 21
Regulation (EC) 1139/98 on the labelling of GM soy and maize varieties ([1998] OJ L159/4) 120
Regulation (EC) 1804/99 supplementing Regulation (EEC) No 2092/91 on organic production of agricultural products and indications referring thereto on agricultural products and foodstuffs to include livestock production ([1999] OJ L222/1) 127
Regulation (EC) 178/2000 laying down the general principles and requirements of food law ([2002] OJ L31/1) 50, 55
Ch II 76
Regulation (EC) 331/2000 amending Annex V to Council Directive (EEC) 2092/91 on organic production of agricultural products and indications referring thereto on agricultural products and foodstuffs ([2000] OJ L48/1) 128
Regulation (EC) 1980/2000 on a revised Community eco-label award scheme ([2000] OJ L237/1)
Art 3 216
Art 4 216
Annex I 216
Annex II 216
Annex III 217
Regulation (EC) 44/2001 on jurisdiction and the recognition and enforcement of judgments in civil and commercial matters (Brussels Regulation) ([2001] OJ L12/1) 21, 36
Regulation (EC) 178/2002 laying down the general principles and requirements of food law ([2002] OJ L31/1) 73, 74, 75, 80, 84, 97, 126, 199
Art 1(2) 74
Art 2 76
Art 7 77
Art 9 77
Art 10 77
Art 14 76
Art 15 76
Art 16 76
Art 19 78, 241
Art 20 78
Arts 25–28 79
Art 50 80, 81, 196
Art 53 81
Art 55 81
Art 58(2) 81

Regulation (EC) 304/2003 concerning the export and import of dangerous chemicals ([2003] OJ L169/27) 155
Resolution of 14 April 1975 on a preliminary programme for the European Community for a consumer protection and information policy ([1975] OJ C92/1) 1, 6
Resolution of 19 May 1981 on a second programme of the European Community for a consumer protection and information policy ([1981] OJ C133/1) 25
Resolution of 12 March 1982 on the campaign against smoking ([1982] OJ L87/118) 187
Resolution of 7 May 1985 on the new approach to technical harmonisation ([1985] OJ C136/1) 26
Resolution of 23 June 1986 on the future orientations of the Community consumer policy ([1986] OJ C167/1) 28
Resolution of 7 July 1986 on a programme of action of the EC against cancer ([1986] OJ C184/21) 187
Resolution of 11 February 1988 on stepping up action against smoking ([1988] OJ C68/84) 187
Resolution of 10 March 1988 on the implementation of European Community legislation relating to water ([1988] OJ C94/155) 134
Resolution of 10 March 1988 on lead in drinking water ([1998] OJ C94/158) 134
Resolution of 9 November 1989 on the future priorities for the relaunching of a Community consumer policy ([1989] OJ C294/1) 28, 29, 48
Resolution of 11 March 1992 on access to the law for consumers ([1992] OJ C94/217) 44
Resolution of 13 July 1992 on the future priorities for the development of a consumer protection policy ([1992] OJ C186/1) 30, 48
Rome Convention (19 June 1980) 17, 34, 36

Sale and Supply of Goods to Consumers Regulations 2002 (SI 2002/3045) 265
Single European Act 1986 2, 7, 8
Sweeteners in Food Regulations 1995 (SI 1995/3123) 98

Timeshare Regulations 1997 (SI 1997/1081) 281
Tobacco Products (Manufacture, Presentation and Sale) (Safety) Regulations 2002 (SI 2002/3041) 189
Toy Safety Regulations 1995 (SI 1995/204) 185
Treaty of Amsterdam (2 October 1997) 1, 10
Treaty of Rome (25 March 1957) (EEC Treaty) 5
preamble 6
Art 2 2, 6
Art 94 2, 6
Art 95 2, 8
Art 308 6
Treaty on the European Economic Area (EEA) (1992) 58
Treaty on the European Union (7 February 1992) (EC Treaty) 12, 13, 14, 46, 66, 68, 125, 203, 205, 222, 250, 265, 282
Art 3 9, 241
Art 28 13, 15, 40, 115, 219, 221, 223, 241
Art 29 130
Art 30 13
Art 33(e) 5

Art 61 19
Art 81(3) 5
Art 82 5
Art 94 239
Art 95 11, 143, 188, 211, 237
Art 100a 9
Art 129a 245
Art 133 188
Art 149 9
Art 150 9
Art 151 9
Art 152 9
Art 153 1, 2, 9, 10, 11, 14, 30, 48, 59
Art 247 9
Protocols 20

Unfair Competition Act (Germany) 40
Unfair Contract Terms Act 1977 261
Unfair Terms in Consumer Contracts Regulations 1999 (SI 1999/2083) 261
Sch 1, Pt I 261

Vitreous Enamel-Ware (Safety) Regulations 1976 (SI 1976/454) 86
Vitreous Enamel-Ware (Safety) Regulations (Northern Ireland) Regulations 1976 (SR (NI) 1976/328) 86

Water Industry Act 1991
ss 67–86 137
Water Resources Act 1991 140
s 5(2) 140
Water Supply (Water Quality) (Amendment) Regulations 1991 (SI 1991/1837) 137

1

INTRODUCTION

Although no common policy on consumer protection was adopted by the European Community at its inception, public health issues were identified early on as a major factor of other Community policies, particularly agriculture. In 1975, a preliminary programme was drawn up by the European Community for a consumer protection and information policy.[1] Since then, an increasing number of legislative measures and initiatives, mainly geared towards establishing a single internal market within the Community, have been adopted which take account of and have regard to consumer interests, including safety. Since the Treaty on the European Union, which contains provisions giving an explicit legal basis for European Community action in this field,[2] we can now expect more Community intervention and initiatives specifically aimed at protecting consumer health and safety and extending consumers' interests. The Treaty of Amsterdam reaffirms the importance of such objectives and recommends that consumer protection requirements are also taken into account in defining and implementing other Community policies and activities.

It is clear from an analysis of relevant directives in the area of consumer safety, one of the key areas identified in the first programme on consumer protection, that the development of the internal market policy of the Community has had a dramatic influence on the promotion of consumer interests. The promotion of the internal market has meant lifting barriers and restrictions on trade throughout Member States and this has been achieved to a large extent by the adoption of harmonisation provisions by Member States so as to eliminate any distortions in the market. Obviously, as a result, any policies or initiatives undertaken by Member States or even the Community in the area of consumer safety have to be balanced and checked against the fundamental principle laid down in the EC Treaty of free movement of goods and services. In theory, the establishment and development of the single internal market should benefit consumers by giving rise to a wider choice of products at lower prices. In addition, for the market to be successful, there should be consumer confidence and this means that, politically, the Community has to be seen to be of benefit not just to business but to citizens as well, and therefore consumer protection is of great importance.

It is, however, necessary to ask how the single internal market actually works, in practice, to benefit the consumer. It is possible that standardisation of the regulatory framework throughout Member States, due to the harmonisation provisions, could mean a loss of some elements of consumer

1 Council Resolution of 14 April 1975 ([1975] OJ C92/1).

2 See EC Treaty, Art 153 (ex 129a).

protection where certain Member States have more stringent protection measures in place. As a result, on the whole, harmonisation has proceeded on the basis of the minimum level required to maintain good protection for the consumer, but with sufficient flexibility for Member States to adopt more stringent measures or maintain their status quo. This raises the problem of how far the harmonisation objective of the Community can be achieved. Flexibility means allowing for different provisions and levels of protection, different interpretations of Community legislation and means of redress for consumers. However, the fundamental problem with tying in consumer protection to the internal market is that consumer issues, whether of health, safety, economic interests, representation or redress, have only been dealt with as an extension to the single market, rather than as priority areas in their own right.

One of the major problems in promoting issues related to consumer protection has been the lack of a legal basis in this field for Community institutions to take initiatives on their own merit. The EEC Treaty did not provide Community institutions with competence to act. Those directives adopted prior to the Single European Act 1986 had to rely on Article 2 dealing with improvements of conditions of living or Article 94 (ex 100) dealing with the functioning of the common market. This lack of an appropriate legal base is reflected in what those directives aimed to achieve.

Since the Single European Act 1986, a legal base has, to a certain extent, been provided by Article 95 (ex 100a). This provides for harmonisation measures for the establishment and functioning of the internal market, but in the adoption of such measures, where they concern health, safety, environmental and consumer protection, a high level of protection must be taken as a base. In addition, the ability of Community institutions to act by qualified majority instead of unanimously has opened up more possibilities when considering related consumer protection issues. There is, however, still no legal basis for dealing with consumer policy as a legitimate area unconnected with the internal market, and this restricts the scope of measures taken in this area.

The Treaty on the European Union has eventually introduced, with Article 153 (ex 129a), an express legal basis for consumer policy which is partially independent of the internal market. The structures for consumer participation in the Community decision-making process, on the other hand, remain weak.

The Consumer Committee,[3] which is composed of representatives of national and European consumer organisations, is under used, and its opinions are not binding. More effective use of this body and better consumer representation in any consultative procedures would help to strengthen

3 The Consumer Committee, set up by Decision (EC) 2000/232 ([2000] OJ L111/30), replaces the Consumer Committee set up by Commission Decision (EC) 95/260 ([1995] OJ L162/37), now repealed.

measures impinging on consumer health and safety. Also, consumer participation and active involvement with the work of both national and European standardisation institutes, which have had a significant role in defining technical safety standards in many sectors since the introduction of the 'new approach' doctrine, would make a major contribution to laying down safety standards at acceptable levels for consumers.

The provision of sufficient information to make it possible for the consumer to make more effective choices is an important component of any consumer policy in a market economy. In fact, when linked to areas of health, safety and quality of goods and services, access to adequate information is an essential tool in promoting consumers' interests. Although this is already reflected in many measures taken by directives requiring more disclosure of information in the marketing of goods and services, too often the labelling requirements, whether in relation to nutritional matters, quality or as indications of origin and geographical designation, seem to constitute promotional tools for the producers of such products and services. Greater consultation of consumers' interests would improve and promote issues related to consumer protection.

This section is primarily concerned with those legislative measures and initiatives taken by the European Community which affect consumers. Although it discusses certain areas of consumer interest such as pharmaceuticals, textiles, motor vehicles and animal health, they, together with the issue of food generally, are only discussed insofar as the measures taken relate specifically to consumer issues. Implementing English legislation is briefly mentioned.

2
THE DEVELOPMENT OF EC CONSUMER PROTECTION

A. NO REFERENCE TO CONSUMER PROTECTION IN THE TREATY OF ROME

Consumer protection was not considered an objective of the 1957 Treaty of Rome. Under the Treaty of Rome, protection of consumers' interests appeared to be a mere by-product of more fundamental Community policies and of the application of rules designed to serve wider purposes such as the creation of a fully competitive environment in the market. Therefore, there was no common consumer policy for the European Community.

In the same years, however, the first national consumers' representative groups emerged and at domestic level Member States were notoriously engaged in pursuing interventionist policies favouring the weak parties, including consumers.

Nevertheless, the notion of 'consumer' appeared in the EC Treaty in several Articles:

(a) Article 33(e) (ex 39(e)), relating to the common agricultural policy, explicitly listed among the aims of the latter to 'ensure that supplies reach consumers at reasonable prices';

(b) Article 81(3) (ex 85), relating to the competition policy, empowers the Commission to exempt agreements between undertakings subject to four cumulative conditions, one of which being that the consumer will receive a fair share of the resulting benefit;

(c) Article 82 (ex 86), also relating to the competition policy, and specifically abuse of dominant positions, identifies as an example of unfair practices 'limiting production, markets or technical development to the prejudice of consumers'.

Even if the need to protect the consumer was not explicitly recognised, several directives adopted during the first decade of existence of the Community were of interest to consumers, especially in the fields of foodstuffs, animal health and nutrition, pharmaceuticals, textiles, detergents, motor vehicles, etc. Indeed, public health issues, which today overlap with those of consumer protection, were identified very early on as being a major component of the common policies, for example the common agricultural policy.

On the other hand, although it did not make any specific mention of the direct protection of the interests of the consumer, the Treaty of Rome contained several provisions which made it possible to integrate measures taken to promote the interests of the consumer into the more general framework of the improvement of living and working conditions, creating in some respects the forerunner of a people's Europe:

(a) in its preamble, the Treaty proclaimed that one of the basic aims of the Community is 'the constant improvement of the living and working conditions' of its peoples;

(b) Article 2 identified, as one of the objectives of the common market, the promotion of 'harmonious development of economic activities, a continuous and balanced expansion, an increase in stability, an accelerated raising of the standards of living'.

1. The Paris summit of 1972

The European summit which met in Paris in 1972 officially decided that the improvement of living conditions implies the protection of the health and safety of consumers, as well as the protection of their economic interests. The heads of State and of government invited the Community institutions to coordinate actions taken in favour of consumer protection and to present a programme for the beginning of 1974.

This summit constituted the starting point of the EC initiatives oriented specifically towards the promotion of the interests of the consumer.

In spite of the absence of a focused reference to a Community consumer policy, two provisions of the Treaty of Rome have been used over the years to serve as the legal basis for specific Community action in the field of consumer protection:

(a) Article 94 (ex 100), which stated, at the time, that 'the Council shall, acting unanimously on a proposal from the Commission, issue directives for the approximation of such provisions laid down by law, regulation or administrative action in Member States as directly affect the establishment or functioning of the common market'.

(b) Article 308 (ex 235), which provides that 'if action by the Community should prove necessary to attain, in the course of the operation of the common market, one of the objectives of the Community and this treaty has not provided the necessary powers, the Council shall, acting unanimously on a proposal from the Commission and after consulting the European Parliament, take the appropriate measures'.

2. The recognition of consumer rights at EC level

The notion of specific rights for consumers at EC level was first introduced into EC law and policy by a Council resolution of 14 April 1975 on a preliminary programme of the European Economic Community for a consumer protection and information policy.[4] This programme laid the

4 Council Resolution of 14 April 1975 ([1975] OJ C92/1).

foundations for an important framework of legislative protection for the consumer at EC level.

The preliminary programme explicitly acknowledged that the time had come to implement a Community policy for consumer protection and summed up the five basic consumer rights as:

(a) the right to protection of health and safety;

(b) the right to protection of economic interests;

(c) the right of redress;

(d) the right to information and education;

(e) the right of representation (the right to be heard).

The preliminary programme contained the basic principles of consumer policy and described the priority measures to be taken, structured in accordance with the five consumer rights identified.

3. The contribution of the *Cassis de Dijon* case

The *Cassis de Dijon* judgment[5] introduced the principle of mutual recognition, according to which goods marketed legally in one Member State are to be accepted on the market of another Member State, even if they do not comply with the regulatory framework in force in this Member State and applicable to its domestic goods. The case had dramatic consequences on free movement of goods in terms of promoting the circulation of national products, thus securing wider choice for the consumers, and of decreasing the Commission's workload in the area of positive harmonisation by reducing the need to adopt common rules.

The case also had landmark importance for the recognition of consumers as economic partners, whose needs and welfare had to be taken into account as much as producers' needs. According to the European Court of Justice (ECJ), obstacles to the free movement of goods within the Community resulting from disparities between national laws must be accepted in so far as those laws may be recognised as being necessary in order to satisfy mandatory requirements relating to the defence of the consumer. Accordingly, by including consumer protection among the grounds on which a measure restrictive of trade can be upheld, the ECJ made a sharp turn towards the conferral of citizenship on the consumer in the European Community.

4. The Single European Act 1986

The adoption in 1986 of the Single European Act 1986 (SEA), which represented the first amendment to the Treaty of Rome, could have filled in the gap left by the latter in the field of consumer protection. However, the authors of the SEA did not go so far as to introduce a specific provision into the Treaty regarding the competence of the Community in the field of the promotion of consumer interests. Nevertheless, the SEA did introduce two

5 Case120/78 Rewe-Zentral v Bundesmonopolverwaltung für Branntwein [1979] ECR 649.

modifications into the Treaty of Rome which had an important impact on the capacity of the EC institutions to adopt measures designed to protect consumers, described below.

Article 95 (ex 100a), introduced by the SEA, concerns the adoption of measures for the completion and functioning of the internal market. In paragraph 3, it states that the Commission, in its proposals concerning consumer protection, will take as a base a high level of protection. The reference to consumer protection in Article 95 (ex 100a) may be considered to constitute an implicit recognition of the competence of the EC institutions to adopt measures in the field of consumer policy. However, as Article 95 (ex 100a) is devoted to the completion of the internal market, it has been construed to mean that consumer protection measures may only be taken by the EC in so far as they are linked to the functioning of the internal market. On the other hand, this Treaty provision represents a political sign rather than an effective means of ensuring that EC measures taken in the field of consumer protection afford a high level of protection. Indeed, careful reading of paragraph 3 shows that only the Commission is obliged to take a high level of consumer protection as a basis: if the Council, in adopting the final text of a directive, does not take account of this high level of protection, there is no means provided in the Treaty for attacking the validity of the directive.

The SEA introduced qualified majority voting by the Council of Ministers into the EC decision-making process, principally for the measures related to the completion and functioning of the internal market, whereas previously unanimity was required. The qualified majority voting procedure allows more flexibility in the carrying out of the legislative work of the Council and, in the field of consumer policy, makes it possible to adopt legislative measures much more quickly than in the past.[6] However, as there is no need for all Member States to agree on certain provisions, measures adopted are potentially less watered down than those adopted under the previous voting procedure.

B. THE CONSOLIDATION OF EC CONSUMER PROTECTION POLICY: THE TREATY ON THE EUROPEAN UNION

During the discussions concerning the Treaty on the European Union, signed in 1992, the question of a specific provision concerning EC competence in the field of consumer protection was raised at a very early stage. In spite of scepticism expressed in the course of the debates by several Member States on the need to introduce such a provision, the Treaty on the European Union contained an explicit legal basis for EC action in the field of consumer policy. This can be found in two provisions:

6 For example, Council Directive (EEC) 85/374 on product liability ([1985] OJ L210/29) was adopted after 12 years of discussions.

(a) Article 3, stating the various actions of the Community to achieve the objectives laid down in Article 2, lists, in its points: 'a contribution to strengthening of consumer protection'.

(b) Article 153 (ex 129a) stated that:

1. The Community shall contribute to the attainment of a high level of consumer protection through:

(a) measures adopted pursuant to Article 100a (now 95) in the context of the completion of the internal market;

(b) specific action which supports and supplements the policy pursued by the Member States to protect the health, safety and economic interests of consumers and to provide adequate information to consumers.

2. The Council, acting in accordance with the procedure referred to in Article 189b (now 247) and after consulting the Economic and Social Committee, shall adopt the specific action referred to in paragraph 1(b).

3. Action adopted pursuant to paragraph 2 shall not prevent any Member State from maintaining or introducing more stringent protective measures. Such measures must be compatible with this treaty. The Commission shall be notified of them.

Some difficulties of interpretation have arisen since the adoption of these provisions by the authors of the Treaty on the European Union. The distinction between the measures listed in (a) and the actions referred to in (b) has led some to question whether the second category allows the Community to take legislative measures. However, a careful reading of the total text of the Treaty reveals that every time the authors wanted to limit the Community's legislative competence, they indicated it clearly.[7] On the other hand, Article 153 (ex 129a) makes no specific reference to consumer redress. It does, however, seem that given its horizontal nature, the right of access to justice is included in the list of other rights recognised in (b).

In spite of these difficulties of interpretation, the Treaty on the European Union put an end to the controversies arising from the lack of an explicit legal basis for Community initiatives to promote consumer interests. It also established a distinction between consumer protection initiatives linked with the completion of the internal market and other consumer protection measures, and therefore freed consumer policy from internal market policy. In addition, the application of the co-decision procedure provided for in Article 247 (ex 189b), which implies much more active participation from the European Parliament, must be considered as an important step towards a more active consumer policy at EC level.

7 See, for example, EC Treaty, Art 149 (ex 126) on education; Art 150 (ex 127) on vocational training; Art 151 (ex 128) on culture; Art 152 (ex 129) on public health.

As yet, however, only Directive 98/6 on consumer protection in the indication of the prices of products offered to consumers [8] has been adopted on the legal basis of Article 153(2) (ex 129a).

C. THE TREATY OF AMSTERDAM AND CONSUMER PROTECTION

The amendments made to Article 153 (ex 129a) by the Treaty of Amsterdam aim at further reinforcing the idea of a high level of consumer protection as an explicit Community objective in its own right. Article 153 (ex 129a) sets out the Community objectives in terms of protection of health, safety and economic interests of the consumers and promotion of their right to information, education, and to organise themselves in order to safeguard their interests. Health, safety and economic interests of consumers still have the status of 'interests' and objectives of consumer policy, without being recognised as 'rights'.

The Treaty does not set out in detail the priorities for action and the measures to be taken, thus leaving to the Commission the task of translating those provision into practice.

Article 153 (ex 129a) also integrates consumer protection in Community action by obliging the Community institutions to take consumer requirements into account in the definition and implementation of other Community policies and activities. In practice, it is difficult to understand how to determine the acts of the Community in which consumers interests should be considered, since potentially these could be taken into account in respect of every policy.

Besides the measures adopted within the framework of the internal market objective, the Community is now required to take measures (as opposed to the 'specific actions' mentioned in the pre-Amsterdam version of Article 153 (ex 129a)) which support and supplement the policy pursued by the Member States. This seems to clarify that Community initiatives in the consumer field not primarily aimed at completing the internal market can nevertheless be of a legislative nature. In view of the possibility for the Community to adopt consumer protection measures in the context of the completion of the internal market, it is expected that the impact of this amendment will be low.[9]

In addition, the Community is now entitled to take measures which monitor the policy of the Member States, but it is unclear what in practice this provision may entail.

8 Parliament and Council Directive (EC) 98/6 ([1998] OJ L80/27).

9 J Stuyck, 'European Consumer Law after the Treaty of Amsterdam: Consumer Policy in or beyond the Internal Market?' (2000) 37 Common Market Law Review 347.

D. INTERNAL MARKET POLICY AND CONSUMER POLICY

1. Internal market policy as a way to introduce consumer protection measures

The implementation of the internal market policy provided for in Article 95 (ex 100a) of the EC Treaty has led to several legislative initiatives specifically oriented towards the improvement of consumer protection. Examples of these initiatives include the Package Travel Directive,[10] the Unfair Contract Terms Directive,[11] the Timeshare Directive,[12] the Distance Sales Directive,[13] the Consumer Sales Directive,[14] the General Product Safety Directive,[15] the Directive on distance marketing of financial services.[16]

This approach is largely justified because the functioning of the internal market is at least in part linked to the approximation of conditions of consumer protection in the various Member States. In other words, differing national consumer protection legislation creates barriers to trade and distorts competition in a way which is incompatible with the completion of the internal market.

However, the essential link established in the late eighties and the nineties between internal market policy and consumer policy had one major drawback: consumer policy was instrumental to internal market policy. Initiatives in the former policy area were given priority only insofar as they contributed to the development of the latter policy area. Consumer policy measures which were not linked to the abolition of trade barriers and the promotion of free movement of goods or services (such as social measures in the field of under-privileged consumers or measures to improve small claims redress procedures) were not put on the EC agenda, as is well illustrated in the first three-year action plan on consumer policy, adopted by the Commission in 1990.[17] This means that EC consumer policy was not recognised as a specific and independent Community policy, but rather had to justify itself (prior to the adoption of Article 153 (ex 129a)) on the grounds of its links with the internal market policy.

Although most consumer protection directives after the insertion of Article 153 (ex 129a) are still based on Article 95 (ex 100a), the Commission Communication on Consumer Policy strategy for the years 2002–2006[18]

10 Council Directive (EEC) 90/314 ([1990] OJ L158/59).
11 Council Directive (EEC) 93/13 ([1993] OJ L95/29).
12 Parliament and Council Directive (EC) 94/47 ([1994] OJ L280/83).
13 Parliament and Council Directive (EC) 97/7 ([1997] OJ L144/19).
14 Parliament and Council Directive (EC) 99/144 ([1999] OJ L171/12).
15 Parliament and Council Directive (EC) 2001/95 ([2002] OJ L11/4).
16 Parliament and Council Directive (EC) 2002/65 ([2002] OJ L271/16).
17 COM(90)98 final.
18 COM(2002)208 final.

establishes a clear connection not only between consumer policy and the internal market, but also between consumer policy and the improvement of the quality of life. Accordingly, together with the adoption of internal market related measures for the achievement of a high level of consumer protection, the new policy strategy aims to promote effective enforcement of consumer protection rules and to encourage involvement of consumer organisations in Community policies.

At the same time, the relationship between internal market and consumer policy changed after the Treaty on the European Union as the consumer is no longer seen as a passive beneficiary of market integration: the 'active' consumer seeks to profit from the removal of barriers by obtaining products or services abroad. In this perspective, the establishment of common consumer protection rules throughout Europe would give consumers the confidence necessary to conduct transactions anywhere in the internal market and to reap significant benefits from a well-designed internal market policy, which would provide him with a greater choice of products and services in a more competitive market.

2. Gaps in the internal market policy from the point of view of consumer protection

The practical conditions of marketing for suppliers and the conditions of protection for consumers sometimes still differ considerably by virtue of national legal and cultural traditions and by differing control and penalty practices. Also, cross-border commercial movements require cooperation between the competent national authorities if they are to be efficiently controlled and, to date, the cooperation mechanisms have not yet been properly installed in all sectors, in spite of the opening up of the markets concerned.

A market is only coherently integrated if it offers redress to its economic agents. Experience has shown that, in the field of cross-border complaints, and especially consumer complaints, the internal market simply collapses and gives way to 15 judicial systems which consumers and undertakings may have to confront in order to have their rights respected.

The shortcomings of the present internal market policy have been a constant issue of concern for the Commission. In June 1993, for example, the Commission issued a Communication to the Council and the European Parliament on 'Reinforcing the Effectiveness of the Internal Market'.[19] In it, it proposed to increase the transparency and consistency of application of EC laws, notably by publishing the national implementing measures by sector, selecting those where directives leave the greatest margin of discretion to the

19 COM(93)256 final.

Member States,[20] and by making greater use of regulations. This should minimise national disparities as regulations are directly applicable and do not require national implementation measures to be effective. The Commission also recognised the specific difficulties of access to justice in cross-border disputes in a 1993 Green Paper on access to justice[21] that proposed to improve dissemination of information on rights under EC laws and to increase transparency of national sanction systems. In their 2000 Review of the Internal Market Strategy,[22] the Commission stated that the internal market should be made as effective as possible in economic terms, but also admitted that many EU citizens often find attempts to exercise their internal market rights a frustrating and dispiriting experience. Accordingly, the Commission emphasised the need to develop effective, rapid and simple solutions for citizens by enabling them to seek redress in cross-border disputes. In this respect, the most remarkable initiative has been the launch of the pilot project, EEJ-net (the European extra-judicial network), aimed at facilitating out-of-court dispute settlement.

More fundamentally, however, the harmonisation of the law applying to the marketing of products and services often implies a levelling of existing national provisions, as it does in the field of consumer protection. Consumers in some countries therefore face a diminution of the protection they enjoyed before the process of harmonisation. From the point of view of consumer protection, this approach is not acceptable, as harmonisation is, for the consumer, not an end in itself. The EC institutions have acknowledged the difficulties faced in the harmonisation process by Member States whose consumers already benefit from advanced protection, and have introduced the principle of minimum harmonisation. According to the principle of minimum harmonisation, a Member State may, in areas covered by a Community directive, maintain or introduce more stringent consumer protection measures, as long as they are compatible with the EC Treaty, and especially with Articles 28 (ex 30) and 30 (ex 36). This principle constitutes an important means of achieving progress in discussions on the scope and content of EC initiatives in the field of consumer protection, as Member States which already have advanced protection in the relevant sector will be more willing to accept a levelling down of the content of the EC measure if they are allowed to keep their domestic protection mechanisms, and are not obliged to dismantle them.

The principle of minimum harmonisation was explicitly used for the first time during the adoption of the Misleading Advertising Directive, where it is

20 For example, the Product Liability Directive, Council Directive (EEC) 85/374 ([1985] OJ L210/29), provides for optional harmonisation and permits Member States to set a maximum compensation ceiling and to introduce or maintain a development risks defence.

21 See Commission Green Paper COM(93)509, published at the end of 1993.

22 Communication from the Commission to the European Parliament, the Council, the Economic and Social Committee and the Committee of the Regions – 2000 Review of the Internal Market Strategy, COM(2000)257 final.

contained in Article 7.[23] Among the directives which refer to the principle are the Doorstep Selling Directive,[24] the Consumer Credit Directive,[25] the Package Travel Directive,[26] the Unfair Contract Terms Directive,[27] the Distance Sales Directive[6] and the Consumer Guarantees Directive.[28]

The possibility to include a minimum harmonisation formula in consumer protection legislation is, since the Treaty on the European Union, embedded in the third paragraph of Article 153 (ex 129a).

In cases where a minimum harmonisation formula is included, the relevant directive would only be aimed at partial harmonisation. In those cases, the relationship between market integration and consumer protection can be expressed in the following steps: (1) partial negative integration: deregulation does not occur in cases where the ECJ identifies a need to protect consumers. In those instances, domestic regulation stands and market fragmentation persists; (2) re-regulation and positive integration: EC law is adopted in order to achieve harmonisation in the field where market fragmentation persists by setting common rules and standards; (3) adoption of the minimum harmonisation formula in re-regulating the market: because of the minimal character of EC legislation, Member States are allowed to maintain their own regulations. In those cases, market fragmentation would once again persist. Thus, it is possible to imagine cases where the market would not be subject to any variation from stage 1 to stage 3: a domestic measure restrictive of trade would be entitled to stand on the basis of *Cassis'* mandatory requirements first, on the basis of the minimum harmonisation formula once positive integration has occurred. In practice, however, the ECJ's attitude to admitting exceptions based on the mandatory requirements has been quite restrictive; justification under the minimum harmonisation formula, on the other hand, would probably enhance remarkably the chances of a domestic measure being upheld. Rather than being simply tolerated, the measure would be fully legitimised under the provisions of a related, 'minimal' directive.[29]

On the other hand, where directives are aimed at total harmonisation and do not include a minimum harmonisation formula, Member States that enact implementing measures that are more protective of consumers would be considered to be in breach of the obligations under Community law.[30]

As far as the promotion of the interests of the consumer in the Community is concerned, the recourse to the principle of minimum harmonisation has been welcomed as a pragmatic solution to blocked decision-making

23 Council Directive (EEC) 84/450 ([1984] OJ L250/17).
24 Council Directive (EEC) 85/577 ([1985] OJ L372/31).
25 Council Directive (EEC) 87/102 ([1987] OJ L42/48).
26 Council Directive (EEC) 90/314 ([1990] OJ L158/59).
27 Council Directive (EEC) 93/13 ([1993] OJ L95/29).
28 Parliament and Council Directive (EC) 99/44 ([1999] OJ L171/12).
29 See Case 328/87 Buet v Ministère Public [1989] ECR 1235.
30 See, for example, Case C-52/00 Commission v France and Case C-154/00 Commission v Greece.

procedures, though it has repeatedly been stressed that Community initiatives in the field of consumer protection should be progressive and stimulating and should therefore be adopted at the highest level of consumer protection existing in the Community. Only this way will a high level of consumer protection be achieved at EC level. The fact that Member States are given the opportunity to maintain or introduce more stringent measures does not constitute a guarantee that they will do so effectively.

Another principle that may be, in some cases, detrimental to consumer protection is that of mutual recognition. Mutual recognition is designed to promote the free movement of goods and services and to dismantle barriers to trade. It gives rise, however, to criticism that it creates the possibility for undertakings to engage in 'home country shopping'. This is where the Member State with the least stringent marketing obligations is identified and exports are made from there into the other EU countries.

Also, the principle of mutual recognition contains the danger that national consumer protection provisions will be levelled down. Indeed, industries submitted to more stringent domestic provisions than those which export to the Member State concerned will be tempted to enter into lobbying activities aimed at eliminating the distortion of competition existing, to their disadvantage, between them and foreign undertakings.

Another aspect of the internal market policy which may be subject to some criticism from the point of view of the promotion of the interests of the consumer is the concept of 'average consumer' elaborated by the Court.

This has been developed in a number of cases concerning the extent to which domestic measures allegedly aimed at protecting consumers could be justified on the grounds of the mandatory requirements or were to be considered as an unlawful barrier to trade, contrary to Article 28 (ex 30) of the EC Treaty. In several cases, domestic legislation for the protection of consumers was found by the ECJ to be exceedingly strict in that it was aimed at protecting even the weakest and more vulnerable consumers. So, for example, the use of the word 'Clinique' on a cream may lead the more gullible consumer to believe that it has permanent effects, but may not mislead an average, well informed consumer. Accordingly, a domestic law that prevents the marketing of cream under that name may be found to be overprotective and contrary to Article 28 (ex 30).[31] In many cases, the ECJ has restrained itself to setting out the guidelines of the test, and has left its application to the domestic court which is placed in a better position to assess the specific conditions of a domestic market. It is nevertheless clear that the concept of 'average consumer' no longer allows States to determine the level of protection they want to ensure.

31 See C-315/92 Verband Sozialer Wettbewerb eV v Clinique Laboratoires SNC and Estée Lauder Cosmetics GmbH [1994] ECR I-317.

Finally, from the point of view of the consumer, promotion of the free movement of goods is not enough to ensure the implementation of a genuine European market without internal frontiers. There is a danger that public frontiers, eliminated by the internal market policy, will be substituted by private barriers to trade, such as joint ventures, mergers, or other agreements by undertakings. Therefore, the internal market policy must be supplemented by a pro-active competition policy in order to guarantee an effective area of free movement and choice for the consumer.

3. Legal problems linked to cross-border consumer complaints

In a perfect market without internal frontiers, the consumer should have access to equivalent redress procedures wherever in the market a dispute has originated. From a judicial point of view, the internal market should, to be perfect, be considered as a large domestic jurisdiction. However, the internal market policy has not yet led to the elimination of judicial frontiers nor to a satisfactory legal environment for consumer redress in cross-border situations. Cross-border consumer transactions, ie, transactions between a consumer and a supplier who do not reside in the same country, are expected to increase with the completion of the internal market and due to the increasing number of transactions carried out through the Internet. Many of these transactions are, and will be, completed to the satisfaction of the parties concerned. Some, however, will give rise to disputes. Consumers already face specific difficulties when confronted with disputes in domestic transactions; experience has shown that they face even greater difficulties if the transaction which is at the source of the dispute is characterised by one or several cross-border elements. Many of the difficulties faced by the consumer or his advisers are of a practical nature: language difficulties, geographical distance, ignorance of the foreign legal system or of the content and construction of legal provisions, lack of information about rights, costs of international phone calls, etc. However, some fundamental legal problems also play a major deterrent role in the handling of cross-border consumer complaints, as described below.

The EC harmonisation process does not totally eliminate differences in national legislation and it is therefore necessary to identify which Member State or States has or have jurisdiction over a dispute, even if the issues are already covered by EC legislation. For example, Council Directive (EEC) 85/374[32] on product liability provides for optional harmonisation in the field principally of the so-called development risks: a Member State may decide whether or not the state of scientific and technical knowledge at the time of marketing a product constitutes a defence for the producer of a product which at a later period turns out to be defective. Luxembourg has not allowed this defence for the producer, while Belgium has. So, if a Belgian consumer buys a product in Luxembourg which gives rise to a dispute under product liability

32 [1985] OJ L210/29.

law, it will be important to define the legislation applicable to the dispute. However, the definition of the law applicable to consumer disputes constitutes the subject of complex rules of international private law, some of which are to be found in the Rome Convention of 19 June 1980 on the law applicable to contractual obligations.[33] Others are to be found in other international conventions or even in laws of the individual Member States. It is extremely difficult, then, not only for the consumer, but also for those who are to provide legal advice, be they solicitors or employees of private or public consumer advice centres, to identify the appropriate law.

The question of which legislation is applicable to a cross-border dispute is decided in the last instance by the court which has to judge the dispute. This court is not necessarily the court of the country of residence of the consumer nor that of the country of residence of the supplier, and the rules it applies in order to define the law applicable to the dispute are not necessarily the ones which would be applied in the domestic courts. This implies that the identification of the appropriate court also constitutes a key difficulty in the preliminary steps of the handling of cross-border consumer disputes. Some rules concerning jurisdiction may be found in the so-called Brussels Regulation on jurisdiction and judgements in civil and commercial matters,[34] which defines the conditions under which courts are competent to handle disputes. However, in several Member States, some provisions of consumer law are of a criminal nature and therefore do not come within the ambit of the Brussels Regulation.

The enforcement of consumer protection law, even if originating in EC legislation, lies with national enforcement authorities. In the case of malpractice originating in another EC Member State, those consumer protection agencies face lack of jurisdiction and are not allowed to undertake action abroad against the foreign supplier. Thus, UK trading standards officers have no jurisdiction over disputes where British legislation is not applicable; the Danish consumer ombudsman may only take up complaints submitted to Danish law and only before Danish courts. The only means of improvement of public action against cross-border malpractice is to be found in intensified cooperation between the concerned national agencies, but this cooperation at present only exists in limited sectors and is still in its early stages.

New initiatives, however, have recently been taken in this respect. In 1998 the Commission adopted Recommendation (EC) 98/257[35] on the principles applicable to the bodies responsible for the out-of-court settlement of consumer disputes.

33 This Convention came into force on 1 April 1991.

34 Council Regulation (EC) 44/2001 of 22 December 2000 on jurisdiction and the recognition and enforcement of judgments in civil and commercial matters ([2001] OJ L12/1), formerly the Brussels Convention on Jurisdiction and the Recognition and Enforcement of Judgments in Civil and Commercial Matters of 27 September 1968.

35 [1998] OJ L115/31.

The initiative started from the consideration that out-of-court settlement mechanisms available to consumers in the Member States vary remarkably from State to State: they may be the fruit of public initiatives both at central level (such as the consumer complaints boards in the Scandinavian countries) and at local level (such as the arbitration courts in Spain), or they may spring from private initiatives (such as the mediators/ombudsmen of the banks or insurance companies). Because of this diversity, the status of the decisions adopted by these bodies differs greatly: some are mere recommendations (such as in the case of the Scandinavian consumer complaints boards and most of the private ombudsmen), whereas others are binding only on the professional (as in the case of most of the bank ombudsmen), yet others are binding on both parties (arbitration). Although cheaper, faster and informal, those different out-of-court methods mechanisms are not always – in particular when they are the result of private initiatives – supplied with adequate guarantees.

The Commission adopted Recommendation (EC) 98/257 in order to ensure that these procedures offer the parties a minimum number of quality guarantees such as independence, transparency, efficiency and the respect of law.

The bodies listed in a database kept by the Commission are those which the Member States consider as being in conformity with the Commission's Recommendation. Hence, persons who have recourse to these bodies may and should expect that the principles enshrined in the Recommendation are respected.

Recommendation (EC) 2001/310[36] on the principles for out-of-court bodies involved in the consensual resolution of consumer disputes makes similar provisions for consensual settlement procedures (such as mediation) where a third party facilitates the resolution of a consumer dispute by bringing the parties together and assisting them in reaching a solution by common consent. The Recommendation establishes common criteria that these consensual procedures should meet in order to give consumers and business confidence that their disputes will be handled with rigour and efficiency. The criteria do not prescribe how such procedures should operate but identify a set of principles that such procedures should follow in order to ensure a common minimum standard, such as impartiality, transparency, fairness and effectiveness.

Member States have been asked to notify the Commission of such procedures meeting the common criteria for inclusion on this database.

A further step has been taken by setting up the European extra-judicial network (EEJ-net). This is a communication and support structure made up of national contact points (or 'clearing houses') established by each Member State. In practice, the 'clearing house' in the consumer's home State will help him with information and support in making a claim in the out-of-court

36 [2001] OJ L109/56.

alternative dispute resolution system in the country where the business from which the relevant product or service was acquired. A list of clearing houses by country is maintained by the Commission on its website.

The launch of the pilot phase of the EEJ-net took place in October 2001: accordingly, the practical effect of the initiative cannot at present be adequately estimated.

Another limit to cross-border consumer claims is in the fact that, while many Member States have instituted free legal advice or legal aid schemes for court actions, these systems most often only apply in domestic situations. Consumers who have to submit their case to a foreign court will not benefit from foreign legal aid schemes, nor will they benefit from their domestic legal aid system. A Council of Europe agreement on the transmission of applications for legal aid, signed in Strasbourg in 1977, provides for limited possibilities for non-residents to apply for legal aid. However, this agreement has not been signed by all EC Member States and has not given rise to much practical application due to poor dissemination of information by the national authorities concerned.

In February 2000, the Commission tackled the issue by adopting a Green Paper, 'Legal aid in civil matters: the problems confronting the cross-border litigant',[37] which has been followed in 2002 by a proposal for a Council Directive to improve access to justice in cross-border disputes by establishing minimum common rules relating to legal aid and other financial aspects of civil proceedings.[38]

According to the proposed Directive (based on Article 61 (ex 73i) of the EC Treaty), legal aid shall be granted to all persons involved in a civil dispute who do not have sufficient resources. Legal aid should be granted by the Member State in which the court adjudicating over a certain dispute is sitting and should cover the costs directly related to the cross-border nature of the dispute, including interpretation, translation and travel costs where the physical presence of the persons concerned in court is mandatory. The Member State in which the legal aid applicant resides, on the other hand, shall grant legal aid to cover costs incurred by the recipient in that State and, in particular, the cost of consulting a local lawyer.

The proposed Directive contains additional provisions ensuring that the cross-border litigant will be treated in the same way as if he resided in the Member State of the forum and that the difficulties inherent in the cross-border nature of the dispute will not preclude the grant of legal aid. In the same spirit, the proposal provides for cooperation and information mechanisms between the Member States to facilitate the formalities to be performed by people engaging in cross-border litigation.

37 COM(2000)51 final.
38 COM(2002)13 final.

The Directive shall not be addressed to Denmark, United Kingdom and Ireland pursuant to the Protocols annexed to the Treaty on the European Union, although the latter two countries have indicated their will to 'opt in'.

Remarkable steps have also been taken to reinforce the use of collective actions both for domestic and cross-border disputes.

Until recently, collective actions were not available for cross-border complaints because some of the Member States did not recognise this collective right in their domestic legislation and could not be forced to apply it on behalf of a foreign organisation pleading before their courts. Also, in those countries where collective action was recognised, several conditions had to be met by consumer organisations in order to ascertain their right of representation, such as registration with the national authorities, individual membership numbers, etc. Those conditions were very difficult for foreign consumer organisations to meet and constituted a major limitation to cross-border collective actions.

Directive 98/27[39] approximates Member States' laws relating to actions for injunctions aimed at the protection of consumers' interests. The Directive entitles 'qualified entities' (bodies responsible for the protection of consumers, constituted in accordance with each Member State's law) to seek in the competent court injunctions requiring the cessation or prohibition of any act contrary to the directives listed in an Annex to Directive 98/27, which include the Directives on misleading advertising, doorstep selling,[40] consumer credit,[41] package travel,[42] unfair contract terms,[43] distance sales,[44] timeshare,[45] consumer sales[46] and electronic commerce.[47]

In relation to cross-border actions, Directive 98/27 requires each Member State to ensure that, in the event of an infringement originating in that State, qualified entities in another State, where the interests protected by that qualified entity are affected by the infringement, may seize the court or administrative authority. Inclusion of a given entity in a list drawn up by the Commission and published in the Official Journal of the European Communities will serve as a basis for a court to decide that an entity enjoys *locus standi.*

Surprisingly, the scope of the Directive seems to be limited to the enforcement of the 'contract directives'; other important measures, such as the

39 [1998] OJ L166/51.
40 Council Directive (EEC) 85/577 ([1985] OJ L372/31).
41 Council Directive (EEC) 87/102 ([1987] OJ L42/48).
42 Council Directive (EEC) 90/314 ([1990]OJ L158/59).
43 Council Directive (EEC) 93/13 ([1993] OJ L95/29).
44 Parliament and Council Directive (EC) 97/7 ([1997] OJ L144/19).
45 Parliament and Council Directive (EC) 94/47 ([1994] OJ L280/83).
46 Parliament and Council Directive (EC) 99/144 ([1999] OJ L171/12).
47 Parliament and Council Directive (EC) 2000/31 ([2000] OJ L178/1).

Directive on product safety or on labelling, presentation and advertising of foodstuff, are not included in the list of directives covered.

Difficulties persist where a court decision has been adopted in the country of residence of the consumer against a foreign supplier and the decision must be enforced abroad. The Brussels Regulation mentioned above also provides the fundamental rules of cooperation between the national authorities to ensure smooth enforcement of court decisions abroad, but its scope is limited, as explained above, to civil and commercial matters, and the practical procedures are very complex and time consuming.

These specific difficulties linked to cross-border consumer disputes constitute a significant gap in the internal market policy. Consumer confidence in the internal market can only be achieved by more adequate consideration of their redress possibilities within the European Community. The tackling of the problems linked to the co-existence in one single market of 15 or even more judicial systems will continue to represent a major challenge for the EC legislator in forthcoming years.

E. THE EC CONSUMER PROTECTION PROGRAMMES

1. The preliminary programme: 1975

On the basis of the Council resolution of 14 April 1975, the EC Commission published a preliminary programme of the European Economic Community for a consumer protection and information policy.[48] This programme laid down the general principles and objectives of an EC consumer protection policy and defined the priority measures to be taken at EC level. This programme was very comprehensive and embraced all the major aspects of consumer protection. Some of the measures proposed as a priority were adopted some 20 years later, such as the Directive on unfair terms in consumer contracts.[49]

The preliminary programme identified the general principles underlying the EC consumer protection policy, as well as the priority actions to be undertaken, with regard to the five basic consumer rights it recognised:

(a) the right to protection of health and safety;

(b) the right to protection of economic interests;

(c) the right of redress;

(d) the right to information and education;

(e) the right of representation.

However, because of the lack of recognised EC competence in this field, especially in the field of consumer redress, the measures proposed were not necessarily of a regulatory nature and were limited to studies, dissemination of

48 [1975] OJ C92/1.
49 Council Directive (EEC) 93/13 ([1993] OJ L95/29).

information and to the setting up of procedures for cooperation between Member States.

The measures proposed in the field of protection of consumer health and safety were as follows:

(a) goods and services offered to consumers must be such that, under normal or foreseeable conditions of use, they present no risk to the health and safety of consumers;

(b) consumers should be informed in an appropriate manner of any risk liable to result from a foreseeable use of goods and services;

(c) consumers should also be protected against the consequences of physical injury caused by defective products and services supplied by manufacturers of goods and providers of services;

(d) substances or preparations added to foodstuffs should be defined and their use regulated. Any processing which foodstuffs may undergo should also be defined and their use regulated where this is required to protect the consumer; foodstuffs should not be adulterated or contaminated by packaging or other materials with which they come into contact, by their environment, by the conditions in which they are transported or stored or by persons coming into contact with them;

(e) categories of products, such as machines, appliances and electrical equipment which may prejudicially affect the health and safety of consumers either in themselves or by their use, should be covered by special rules and be subject to a procedure recognised or approved by public authorities to ensure that they are safe for use;

(f) certain categories of new products which may prejudicially affect the health or safety of consumers should be made subject to special authorisation procedures harmonised throughout the Community.

With regard to these objectives, the preliminary programme provided for the Community to implement the programmes relating to the free movement of goods with a particular emphasis on consumer priorities in the following fields: foodstuffs, cosmetics and detergents, utensils and consumer durables, cars, textiles, toys, dangerous substances, materials coming into contact with foodstuffs, medicines, fertilizers, pesticides and herbicides, veterinary products and animal foodstuffs.

In the field of the protection of the economic interests of the consumer, the programme proposed the following priorities:

(a) purchasers of goods and services should be protected against the abuse of power by the seller, in particular against one-sided contracts, the unfair exclusion of essential rights in contracts, harsh conditions of credit, demands for payment for unsolicited goods and high pressure selling methods;

(b) the consumer should be protected against damage to his economic interests caused by defective products or unsatisfactory services;

(c) the presentation and promotion of goods and services, including financial services, should not be designed to mislead, either directly or indirectly, the person to whom they are offered or by whom they are requested;

(d) no form of advertising may mislead the consumer. An advertiser should be able to justify the validity of any claims he makes;

(e) all information on labels at the point of sale or in advertisements must be accurate;

(f) the consumer is entitled to reliable after-sales service for consumer durables including the provision of spare parts required to carry out repairs;

(g) the range of goods available to the consumer should offer him an adequate choice.

In this context, the preliminary programme set out several priority measures to be adopted:

(a) harmonisation of the general conditions of consumer credit, including those relating to hire-purchase;

(b) protection of consumers by appropriate means against false or misleading advertising;

(c) protection of consumers from unfair commercial practices;

(d) harmonisation of the law on product liability so as to provide better protection for consumers;

(e) improvement of the range and quality of services provided for consumers.

In the field of consumer advice, help and redress, the preliminary programme stressed that consumers should receive advice and help in respect of complaints and of injury or damage resulting from purchase or use of defective goods and unsatisfactory services. Consumers were also considered to be entitled to proper redress for such injury or damage by means of swift, effective and inexpensive procedures.

To this end, the preliminary programme provided for the Commission to study the various systems of consumer assistance and redress existing in Member States, to submit, where necessary, appropriate proposals for improving the existing systems and putting them to better use, and to study the feasibility of a procedure for exchanging information on the outcome of action for redress relating to products mass-marketed in all or several Member States.

As regards consumer information, sufficient information should be made available to the purchaser of goods or services to enable him:

(a) to assess goods and services;

(b) to make rational choices between competing products and services;

(c) to use these products and services safely and to his satisfaction;

(d) to claim redress for any injury or damage resulting from the product supplied or service received.

To this end, the preliminary programme stressed the following priorities:

(a) the establishment of rules on information on products and services through labelling and product information requirements;

(b) the promotion of the cooperation between bodies which carry out comparative tests;

(c) the conducting of regular consumer surveys in order to learn more about the needs and behaviour of consumers within the Community;

(d) the giving of information to consumers about measures taken at national and Community level which may directly or indirectly affect their interests;

(e) the carrying out of surveys of retail prices and informing the public as soon as possible of price differences within the Community.

In the field of consumer education, children and young people and adults should be educated to act as discriminating consumers, capable of making informed choices about goods and services, and conscious of their rights and responsibilities. To this end:

(a) the Commission should determine methods and suggest materials for the encouragement of consumer education in schools, universities and other educational establishments;

(b) the Commission should encourage training of instructors;

(c) the Commission should encourage the exchange and dissemination of information on topics of interest to consumers, in cooperation with national authorities and bodies concerned with consumer affairs.

In the field of consumer consultation and representation, the preliminary programme stated that consumers should be consulted and allowed to express their views when decisions which concern them are prepared. To this end:

(a) the Commission will encourage organisations representing consumers to study certain matters of particular importance for consumers, to make known their views and coordinate their efforts;

(b) the Commission will promote exchanges of information between Member States on the most appropriate way of providing consumers with consultation channels.

The principles laid down, as well as the measures identified as priorities for Community action in the preliminary programme, have constituted the basis for several of the subsequent consumer programmes issued by the EC institutions.

The preliminary programme was established for a four-year period, and it was necessary to pursue and to deepen the actions identified by this programme.

2. The second programme: 1981

In 1981, the second programme of the European Economic Community for a consumer protection and information policy, designed for a five-year period, was published.[50] This programme retained in its entirety the basic principles of the preliminary programme and confirmed the basic consumer rights to be recognised in the market place. However, in the light of the context of adoption of the second programme – the difficult economic climate of the late 1970s – special emphasis was put on two questions which have assumed considerable importance for the consumer: the price of goods and services as well as the quality of services. A shift may thus be identified concerning the focus put on consumer rights, away from the question of the consumer's health and safety, and towards his economic interests; also, services have been recognised as counting for a growing share of household expenditure.

Another characteristic of the second programme lies in the emphasis put on the need to promote dialogue between consumers and manufacturers and retailers. In this context, there is also a reference to the advantages of non-legislative means of consumer protection, namely the conclusion of agreements, which the Commission should encourage. The programme stresses, however, that the use of voluntary means of consumer protection should in no case prejudice the application of existing laws and regulations, nor exclude further adoption of statutory or administrative provisions at either national or Community level.

The detailed provisions of the second programme largely stemmed from the preliminary programme and constituted in part a report on the achievements of the latter. It completed and updated the measures listed in the 1975 programme. In this respect, the following elements are to be highlighted:

(a) it announced specific works on unfair terms in consumer contracts;

(b) it acknowledged the need to identify the specific problems faced by underprivileged consumers;

(c) it referred to the need to take consumer interests into account within the framework of the common agricultural policy;

(d) it announced the intention of the Commission to tackle the problem of the quality of after-sales service, in particular as regards the guarantee

50 Council Resolution of 19 May 1981 on a second programme of the European Economic Community for a consumer protection and information policy ([1981] OJ C133/1).

period, especially in the sectors of motor vehicles and electrical household appliances;

(e) it identified the need to ensure consumer representation in the field of public or quasi-public services and announced the preparation of a report on this question for services of an international character.

The second programme may therefore be considered as continuing the line drawn in 1975 by the preliminary programme. The subsequent programmes illustrate more important changes in the concept of consumer policy.

3. A new impetus for consumer protection policy: 1985

In 1985, the Commission agreed a Communication to the Council of Ministers designed to give a new impetus to the Community's consumer protection policy.[51] This Communication recognised that the achievements of the two previous programmes fell far short of their intentions as only a few proposals had gone through the total legislative process. It also identified the reasons for this inadequacy: the deep economic recession, the discussions on the lack of Community competence, the unanimous voting procedure at Council level, and the practice of vertical harmonisation, prescribing detailed rules for a restricted range of goods or ingredients.

To counter these problems, the programme referred in its introduction to the Council resolution of 7 May 1985 on the new approach to technical harmonisation.[52] The new approach 'doctrine' is based on the following principles. Essential safety and other mandatory requirements are laid down in Council directives for categories of products, such as toys, machines, etc. Detailed specifications of product characteristics are not to be dealt with in the directives, as their definition paralyses the legislative adoption process and as directives are difficult to adapt to new technical or scientific developments. Instead, they are left to the European standardisation bodies (CEN – Comité européen pour la normalisations, the European Standardisation Committee; CENELEC – Comité européen de normalisation électro-technique, the European Committee for electro-technical standardisation; ETSI – the European Telecommunications Standards Institute), which are to prepare common standards to satisfy the mandatory requirements set in the directives. Pending the completion of European standards, existing national standards which comply with the mandatory requirements will be granted Community-wide recognition on the basis of the principle of mutual recognition.

The adoption of the new approach doctrine implies, in the context of consumer protection, the limitation of legislative intervention to the definition of essential requirements and the transfer to the standardisation bodies of the responsibility for specifying the detailed characteristics which products and

51 COM(85)314 final.
52 [1985] OJ C136/1.

services have to present in order to comply with those essential requirements. From a legislatively technical point of view, the new approach doctrine represents a shift of legislative power from the legislator (the EC institutions) towards private bodies – the standardisation institutes gathered at EC level into CEN, CENELEC and ETSI. This shift calls into question the democratic representativeness of the standardisation bodies with regard to their role in the legislative decision-making process.

On the other hand, the 1985 Communication explicitly recognised for the first time that it is not sufficient to develop EC consumer legislation to improve consumer protection, but that particular attention must be granted to its proper enforcement by Member States. The increasing importance of the development of closer consultation and cooperation between national authorities responsible for enforcement has been clearly acknowledged and given some concrete application in the programme itself.

The 1985 programme distinguished three main objectives of EC consumer policy:

(1) *Products traded in the Community should conform to acceptable health and safety standards*

The Commission therefore considered that the Community objective should be to establish a comprehensive product safety policy with the following essential components: a legislative programme concerning the safety requirements for products, a programme of cooperative actions between national authorities responsible for the safety of consumer products designed to facilitate proper enforcement of safety laws, the creation of Community facilities for surveillance, and control of health and safety risks posed by the use of consumer products and information and education campaigns for consumers concerning the safe use of products in the home and leisure activities. In the programme, reference is made to the assessment of the need to impose at Community level a general obligation on manufacturers to produce and market products which are safe.

(2) *Consumers must be able to benefit from the common market*

It must be made easier for consumers to buy goods in other countries, to use them at home, to have them repaired in the same way as domestically purchased products and to see complaints handled effectively. The programme acknowledged that, in order to create this positive economic environment for the consumer, several measures had to be taken in order to inform the consumer of the possibilities of cross-border bargains and to protect his economic interests. While reference is made to several measures already listed in the previous programmes, such as measures on unfair contract terms, consumer credit, guarantees and warranties, price information and advertising, the programme also listed the issue of new information technologies among the problems to be dealt with at EC level. The Commission intended to publish guides on the consumer's rights to buy goods in other Community countries and on regular information on prices.

(3) *Consumer interests should be taken more into account in other Community policies*

This aspect of the Commission Communication constitutes a major recognition of the need to engage in horizontal policy-making in order to promote the interests of the consumer. Indeed, the extent and efficiency of measures to promote the interests of the consumer depend not only on specific initiatives taken to promote the interests of the consumer, but also upon the manner in which the latter are taken into account when formulating and enforcing other Community policies, such as competition policy, transport policy, common agricultural policy, internal market policy, tourism policy, external trade policy, etc. In 1985, the Commission extended to all Community policies the reference made in 1981 to the need for more integration of the interests of the consumer in the management of the common agricultural policy. It acknowledged the need for the consultation of consumer representatives on Community measures that significantly affect their interests, in order to ensure interpenetration of consumer protection and other policies.

The Communication of the Commission on the new impetus for the Community consumer policy was taken over by the Council resolution of 23 June 1986 on the future orientations of the Community consumer policy,[53] which reiterated the principles of the new approach doctrine and approved the objective to better integrate consumer policy into other common policies, especially in the field of completion of the internal market, the common agricultural policy, competition and transport. This specific issue of the integration of consumer policy into the other common policies led to the Council resolution of 15 December 1986.[54]

F. COMMUNITY CONSUMER POLICY IN THE INTERNAL MARKET

1. The first three-year action plan: 1990–1992

On 9 November 1989, the Council adopted a resolution on the future priorities for the relaunching of a Community consumer policy, on the basis of which in the early 1990s the Commission prepared a three-year action plan.[55] This plan was largely influenced by the emphasis put during this period on the completion of the internal market by the end of 1992. Indeed, the philosophy underlying the programme refers to the need to ensure that the consumer can

53 [1986] OJ C167/1.
54 [1987] OJ C3/1.
55 [1989] OJ C294/1.

actively play his role in the internal market. As already indicated above, consumer policy has become instrumental to the internal market policy rather than an end in itself, and major attention is paid to those measures which are needed to promote the free movement of goods and services. For example, consumer transactions are only taken into consideration in so far as they contain a cross-border element, linked therefore to the internal market, while, in the perspective of consumer protection, every consumer transaction should benefit from specific protection.

The following principal initiatives were (re)introduced by the Commission:

(a) to assist more systematically in the development of consumer organisations, particularly in Southern Europe and Ireland, with a view to promoting the development of balance between producer and consumer representation;

(b) to support local initiatives of three pilot projects of European consumer information and advice centres for frontier regions, in order to enable consumers to obtain information and advice about cross-border purchases;

(c) to engage in research on product labelling in order to increase transparency;

(d) to propose action to assure transparency in cross-border financial transfers and payments;

(e) to stimulate comparative testing and to introduce legislation to encourage comparative advertising;

(f) to extend the scope of the rapid exchange of information system and to finalise the adoption of the General Product Safety Directive;

(g) to analyse the need for a proposal on liability for physical damage in services;

(h) to examine possible initiatives to simplify cross-border consumer contracts, guarantees and after-sales services;

(i) to propose directives on unfair contract terms and distance selling;

(j) to consider means of improving consumer access to justice and redress.

These initiatives, some of which were already listed among the priorities in the 1975 programme, are important to consumers. They are not, however, sufficient to promote the interests of the consumer within the EC and it is surprising, given the development of EC consumer policy, to note that the three-year action plan in no way addressed the question of integration of consumer policy in other common policies. Also, the action plan did not follow up one of the recommendations of the 1989 Council resolution, which proposed carrying out a comprehensive study on the impact of the internal market on the consumer.

2. Post internal market consumer policy: the second three-year action plan: 1993–1995

The Council resolution of 13 July 1992 on the future priorities for the development of a consumer protection policy[56] paved the way for a second three-year plan to be prepared by the Commission before the end of 1992. It took six months more for the Commission to publish, on 28 July 1993, the second three-year action plan.[57]

In spite of the adoption of the Treaty on the European Union, which introduces Article 153 (ex 129a) into the EC Treaty and which allows for an independent consumer policy at EC level, the latest EC consumer programme again put emphasis on the need to put the single market at the service of the consumer. The new possibilities opened up for the EC institutions by the Treaty on the European Union are only referred to in the preliminary paragraphs and are not given any substance. Indeed, from the beginning, the Commission announced its intention to check measures coming under Article 153 (ex 129a) according to the principle of subsidiarity. To this end, the plan tended, on the one hand on the basis of the report on the challenges of the internal market submitted to the Commission in 1992 by the High Level Group chaired by Peter Sutherland,[58] to consolidate existing EC consumer law; on the other hand, to introduce measures in those fields where the protection of the interests of the consumer needed to be improved.

Concerning the first category of measures, the Commission intended to continue to analyse thoroughly the problems related to the effective implementation of EC directives by individual Member States and to develop close cooperation in this area with the competent national authorities. Particular emphasis was put on the assessment of administrative practices, for example in the field of toy safety, and on national case law, for example in the field of misleading advertising.

As regards new measures, the Commission selected four areas of action:

(1) to reinforce consumer information, especially in the field of product labelling and information. To this end, the Commission intended to give priority to multilateral mechanisms of consultation and dialogue between the various economic operators in order to identify the information needs of consumers and establish measures to adequately respond to these needs. Also, the Commission intended to develop its cooperation with consumer information bodies to publish general consumer guides on the internal market, as well as sectoral or national guides linked to the completion of the internal market. The development of cross-border consumer information centres (the so-called 'Euroguichets'), instituted under the previous programme, was considered by the Commission to

56 [1992] OJ C186/1.
57 COM(93)378 final.
58 COM(92)23 final.

constitute an important factor in the improvement of consumer information on cross-border issues;

(2) to increase and extend dialogue: the Commission intended to maintain and reinforce the efficiency of the Consumer Consultative Council in order to allow for more systematic and structured consultation of consumer representatives in the decision-making process;

(3) to promote access to justice and complaints handling: identified as a major problem in the context of EC consumer policy, and especially in the context of cross-border consumer complaints, the question of access to justice still had not been tackled at EC level, due to lack of EC competence. In the action plan, the Commission announced the publication of a Green Paper for the end of 1993 on consumer access to justice, which would examine the various means of giving legal assistance to consumers. The Commission also intended to engage in initiatives with simplified complaints handling mechanisms, in particular in the context of cross-border complaints;

(4) to adapt financial services to consumer needs: in spite of several EC initiatives in the field of financial services, the Commission acknowledged in the action plan that much needed to be done in this area to promote consumer confidence in this sector, especially in the fields of cross-border payments, of transparency of mortgage credit offers and of home-banking. The Commission did not, however, intend to introduce legislative action per se, and it announced its intention to exploit all consultation opportunities with the parties concerned.

3. The third three-year action plan: 1996–1998

In this third plan,[59] the Commission, supported by an opinion of the Economic and Social Committee, indicated some 10 priorities for a consumer action plan for the three years in question.

First, there should be a major effort to improve consumer education and information. Bearing in mind that information and education have always been the cornerstone of consumer policy which forms the basis of consumer choice, the Commission sought to provide for visible, legible and understandable information to be given to the consumer. In particular, it is suggested that the suppliers of both goods and services should improve the quality of sector specific labelling. The programme stresses the obligation of suppliers to inform consumers correctly, the importance of consumer organisations in providing independent advice and the crucial role of each Member State in promoting consumer education. The Economic and Social Committee suggested that consumer education should start in primary school. Arising out of this priority, the Commission proposed Directives on

59 [1996] OJ C295/64.

injunctions for the protection of consumer interest and the proposed action plan on consumer access to justice and the settlement of consumer disputes in the internal market.

Secondly, the Commission sought to ensure that the consumer's interest is fully taken into account in the completion of the single market. It called for the completion review and updating of the framework of the single market. Measures such as the Directive on guarantees and after-sales service, and amendments to the Product Liability Directive to extend its scope to non-processed agricultural products were part of this priority. In addition, it was stressed that the Commission needs to look at the liability of service providers within the wide diversity of practices used to sell services throughout the EU. A review of the common agricultural policy from the consumer's point of view was also called for, as was the need to liberalise the energy market and measures to prevent practices in fixing air fares.

Thirdly, the Commission raised a number of issues relating to the provision of financial services in the EU. Further examination was called for of the consumer credit market and the need to look for a remedy for the exclusion of financial services from the Distance Selling Directive. The need for minimum consumer protection in this area was recognised.

The need to consider giving more legal and binding protection for the holders of bank and non-bank debit cards in the EU was recognised. Given the existence throughout the EU of complicated individual financial services, including savings, insurance and spending elements which often involve long-term contractual obligations, it was stressed that the need for consumers to receive offers on the basis of standard information throughout the EU is of the greatest importance.

Fourthly, the Commission pointed to the need for the protection of consumers' interest in the supply of public utility services. The Commission was concerned that, in most cases, the consumer has no choice of a supplier or a limited one. Moreover, the range, quantity, quality and price of these services are usually not determined by free market forces of supply and demand but rather by political decision makers or regulatory bodies; additionally, a standard of accountability to consumers by providers of such services should be imposed.

Fifthly, the Commission referred to the Information Technology Society and measures which are required to enable consumers to benefit from the opportunities thus provided. The key to the Community's policy in this area was to ensure that large numbers of consumers are not excluded from the benefits of the Information Technology Society because they are less privileged. Technology should be developed so that it is usable by ordinary people performing ordinary tasks. Areas such as quality standards, contractual relations and conditions and security of transactions needed to be addressed.

Sixthly, the Commission called for measures to improve consumer confidence in foodstuffs. This plank of the three-year action plan received a dramatic dimension in the wake of the Community measures taken with respect to the incidence of BSE in the United Kingdom. The need for health concerns in food production and for reform of food labelling provisions in the Community was stressed; it was also made clear that the importance of providing consumers with clear and better information about food should not be underestimated, as well as the requirement of labelling of alcoholic drinks and compulsory nutritional labelling. The Commission's aim in this matter was to review food labelling to make it simpler and better geared to the real needs of consumers for information. The need also to deal with novel foods was identified.

The Commission wished to encourage a practical approach from consumers to sustainable consumption. The aim was to reduce the environmental impact of the consumption of products and services. The awareness of this issue is growing amongst consumers and so, it was thought, is the willingness to play a more active role in contributing towards a more healthy environment (for instance, in the use of waste separate schemes). The use therefore of the EC eco-labelling schemes supports this aim. The Commission therefore wished that consumers should make choices by being provided with the appropriate information which covers both the relevant environmental and performance aspects. It was suggested therefore that there should be coordination of the national bodies involved in eco-labelling schemes with a view to an establishment of an Environmental Assessment Criteria and the need to review Council Regulation (EEC) 880/92[60] was accepted.

The issue of consumer representation was addressed in the plan by the Commission. The establishment of the new Consumer Committee was designed according to the Commission's general model for such a committee. However, it should be noted that the Commission determines membership of the Consumer Committee as well as whether and when it will meet. The Commission restated its intention to support consumer organisations in Southern Europe although, in accordance with the principle of subsidiarity, this is recognised as primarily a task for national governments.

With the possibility of increased membership of the EU and the relationship of the EU to Central and Eastern European countries, the Commission sets as a priority assistance for these countries the development of consumer policies of their own.

60 [1992] OJ L99/1.
61 [1999] OJ C206/1.

4. The fourth three-year action plan: 1999–2001

The 1999–2000 action plan was adopted by the Council[61] shortly after Decision 283/1999[62] established a general framework for Community Activities in favour of consumers, that allocated 112.5 million to the implementation of consumer policies for the period 1999–2003.

Meanwhile, the Commission's Services were restructured, with the concentration of health and consumer protection issues within a single Directorate-General, under the responsibility of a single Commissioner. The Health and Consumer Protection DG was also made, *inter alia,* responsible for food safety along the entire food chain.

The Commission emphasised the profound changes brought by the globalisation of markets and technological development to the products, services, marketing and selling methods. Against these changes, the responsibilities of consumer policy remains relatively unchanged: rather, the relationship between business and consumers, between Member States and the Community, needs to be improved in order to reinforce consumer confidence and institutional responsiveness.

The action indicated the following priorities for the next three years:

(a) Reinforcement of the consumer's voice throughout Europe. This was to be implemented by providing financial support to consumers' organisations in Europe; by enhancing the Euroguichet network and moving the information centres from Member States' borders to the capital or to more central areas; by encouraging effective dialogue between consumers and business; by launching consumer information and education campaigns;

(b) Ensuring a high level of health and safety for consumers. The BSE crisis required that public confidence be restored among consumers by ensuring rapid identification, assessment and response to unforeseen hazards to consumers' health and safety. This included the development of guidelines for a consistent application of the precautionary principle, invoked when there is scientific uncertainty about the level of risk.

(c) Full respect for consumers' economic interests. Particular attention was to be devoted to financial services and problems arising from the transition to the Euro, where the Commission was to implement various actions designed to encourage good practice by business; to maintaining an up-to-date regulatory framework; to improving the enforcement and monitoring of the existing legislation.

61 [1999] OJ C206/1.
62 Parliament and Council Decision 283/1999 of 25 January 1999 establishing a general framework for Community activities in favour of consumers ([1999] OJ L34/1).

G. CONSUMER POLICY STRATEGY 2002–2006

A high common level of consumer protection, effective enforcement of consumer protection rules and the involvement of consumer organisations in Community policies are the three objectives of the new consumer policy strategy which the Commission adopted on 7 May 2002.[63] The objectives are to be implemented through a set of actions over the years 2002 to 2006.

The objectives are designed to maximise the benefits of the internal market for consumers, to help achieve integration of consumer concerns into all other Community policies, and to prepare for enlargement.

The Commission considers that consumers are still unable to fully benefit from the internal market due to a significant lack of confidence about shopping cross-border. It is therefore essential for the Community to ensure that internal market rules and practices promote consumer confidence in cross-border transactions. This implies simpler and more common rules, a similar level of enforcement across the EU, more accessible consumer information and education and effective redress mechanisms.

As well as specific consumer protection rules, consumers are also affected by other important Community policies such as the internal market, environment and sustainable development, transport, financial services, competition, agriculture, external trade and more. The cross-cutting aim of the strategy is therefore to ensure that other Community policies systematically and specifically address consumer interests.

Key factors in the elaboration of the strategy plan were, *inter alia,* the practical introduction of Euro notes and coins; social, economic and technological changes such as e-commerce; the current state of integration of the internal market; the perspective of enlargement.

Under each objective, the strategy presents the main illustrative actions that the Commission intends to present over the period. Those can be summarised as follows:

(a) 'High level of consumer protection': this entails the adoption of measures aimed at harmonising, by whatever means is most appropriate (framework directive, standards, best practices), not only the safety of goods and services, but also aspects of consumer economic and legal interests that give consumers the confidence necessary to conduct transactions anywhere in the internal market. New initiatives are envisaged particularly in the area of fair commercial practices and safety of services

(b) Effective enforcement of consumer protection rules: this means ensuring that consumers are given in practice the same protection throughout the EU. Priority actions, under this objective, are the

63 COM(2002)208 final.

development of an administrative cooperation framework between Member States and of redress mechanisms for consumers.

(c) Involvement of consumer organisations in Community policies: the objective should be pursued by reviewing mechanisms for the participation of consumer organisations in Community policy-making and the setting up of education and capacity-building projects.

H. THE NOTION OF THE CONSUMER IN EC LEGISLATION

Consumer law is commonly considered as a set of rules and principles specifically designed to protect the consumer in his relationship with the enterprise; this includes a range of measures which cover different aspects of market transactions, from advertising, labelling and negotiation to health and safety of products and contractual terms. The target of achieving protection of a specific category of customers or buyers distinguishes directives related to consumer protection from other directives such as on banking and insurance where such a need is not felt. In those cases, even though protection of consumers can be considered as an indirect aim,[64] the subject matter is to lay down obligations for the undertakings and the institutions involved so as to create a fully integrated market.

However, within the set of legislative measures which are commonly considered as 'consumer protection' measures, it is possible to identify different approaches to the notion of consumer.

A number of directives rely on a 'transaction definition' according to which a consumer is a natural person who, in transactions covered by the directive concerned, is acting for purposes which are not within his trade or profession. All the contract directives use this definition (ie, the Directives on doorstep selling,[65] consumer credit,[66] unfair terms,[67] timeshares,[68] distance selling,[69] consumer guarantees,[70] the Rome Convention and the Brussels Regulation), the only exception being the Package Travel Directive,[71] which covers any person who takes or agrees to take the package or any person on whose behalf the purchase of the package is made or to whom the package is transferred, and thus covers, for example, a businessman buying a business trip.

64 For example, Directives 73/239 and 79/267 recognise the necessity of authorisation procedures for the provision of insurance services 'for the protection of the policyholder'; see Case C-205/84 Commission v Germany [1986] ECR 3755.
65 Council Directive (EEC) 85/577 ([1985] OJ L372/31).
66 Council Directive (EEC) 87/102 ([1987] OJ L42/48).
67 Council Directive (EEC) 93/13 ([1993] OJ L95/29).
68 Parliament and Council Directive (EC) 94/47 ([1994] OJ L280/83).
69 Parliament and Council Directive (EC) 97/7 ([1997] OJ L144/19).
70 Parliament and Council Directive (EC) 99/144 ([1999] OJ L171/12).
71 Council Directive (EEC) 90/314 ([1990] OJ L158/59).

In other cases, for example, the directives on labelling (labelling of foodstuff,[72] indication of prices of foodstuff,[73] labelling of alcoholic products,[74] indication of prices of non-food products[75]) the word 'ultimate consumer' or 'final consumer' is used. It is clear here that these directives relate to the consumer in the final stage of the economic process, the person who actually consumes the product, but the directives do not further define the notion of the consumer. The two directives on indication of prices, however, show the idea that protection should be limited to certain types of transactions, as they exclude from their scope of application purchases made for professional or commercial reasons. Those hints have then been developed in the repealing Directive 98/6:[76] in establishing its purpose as that of stipulating indication of the selling price offered by traders to consumers, the Directive defines as a consumer 'any natural person who buys a product for purposes that do not fall within the sphere of his commercial and professional activity'. The scope of application of this Directive is therefore brought in line with that of most of the directives on the protection of the economic interest of the consumer; however, an unjustified distinction remains with the scope of the other 'labelling' directives.

The directives on product liability[77] and product safety,[78] on the other hand, contain a definition of 'product' and 'producer', but not of the other party, which is later referred to as 'the injured person' or 'consumer' (with no further definition). This approach can be justified, however, by the awareness that some measures need to cover wider economic categories so as to include, in contrast with the transaction definition, consumers who act in a professional capacity. The primary focus of those directives is the general responsibility of producers for their products so that there is no need to restrict the obligations of the producer to any particular category of consumers; it would be not only impractical but also morally unacceptable to prescribe different degrees of product safety or liability according to the use the purchaser makes of the product. Damage to property, however, is compensated under the Product Liability Directive only if the product is of the type ordinarily intended for private use or consumption (Article 9).

A similar rationale justifies the choice made by the Misleading Advertising Directive[79] to extend its protection to all persons carrying out a trade or

72 Parliament and Council Directive (EEC) 2000/13 ([2000] OJ L109/29).

73 Council Directive (EC) 79/581 ([1979] OJ L158/19), now repealed by Parliament and Council Directive (EC) 98/6 ([1998] OJ L 80/27).

74 Council Directive (EC) 87/250 ([1987] OJ L113/57).

75 Council Directive (EC) 88/314 ([1988] OJ L142/19).

76 [1998] OJ L90/86.

77 Council Directive (EC) 85/374 ([1985] OJ L210/29).

78 Parliament and Council Directive 2001/95 (EC) ([2002] OJ L11/4).

79 Council Directive (EC) 84/450 ([1984] OJ L250/17).

business or a profession and the interest of the public in general, as well as consumers (once again not defined).

Accordingly, the lack of coherence which appears to underlie consumer law and policy can, in some cases and to some extent, be justified as due to the need to give account of a pluralistic reality: the definition of consumer depends on the object and scope of the protection that one wants to ensure.[80] More precisely, within the general framework of European consumer law, there seem to be different types of measures: the ones which are addressed to the consumer *stricto sensu* and which give a clear definition of their addressee as a natural person acting outside his business or profession; other measures, which are broadly understood to be consumer protection measures (the word consumer is actually mentioned in the text or in the preamble of the measure at issue but not further defined) but which, as a matter of policy choice, are addressed to a wider audience. In this sense, the borders of consumer law are not easy to define and we can almost distinguish between 'pure' and 'impure' consumer legislation.

This uncertainty is somehow emphasised by the 'horizontal' nature of consumer law: the wish to protect the *persona* 'consumer', understood either in a narrow or broad sense, is the only common denominator to a number of measures which draw on a wide range of disciplines and extend across the traditional legal categories and economic policies without being fully integrated in any of these. Intervention is from time to time justified by the subject matter of the contract (eg, consumer credit) or by the use of a particular selling technique (eg, doorstep and distance selling) or by the wish to impose specific duties in relation to the sale of a certain product (eg, labelling, product safety). The presence of one or more of these variables seems to create the need to protect the weaker party to a certain transaction. So, for example, even though the provision of financial services does not appear to have required special provisions to specifically protect the consumer, such a concern arises when those services are supplied through a distance contract.[81]

I. SOME SELECTED ECJ DECISIONS ON CONSUMERS

The ECJ case law constitutes an important contribution to determining the scope and content of Community provisions having a direct or indirect impact on the interests of the consumer. In addition to this, the ECJ has often adjudicated on the compatibility between Community law and domestic

80 F Picod and V Christianos, 'Consommatures', Rép Communautaire Dalloz, April 1996, 1–42, para 45.
81 Parliament and Council Directive 2002/65 ([2002] OJ L271/16) concerning the distance marketing of consumer financial services.

measures of consumer protection. The following paragraphs provide a short summary of a few seminal ECJ decisions.

Questioned about the validity of the controversial Council Directive (EEC) 88/146 on hormones,[82] the court confirmed in 1990 the validity of this Directive by stating that, even if the scientific proof about the toxicity of hormones is controversial, the prohibition of the use of hormones corresponds to repeated requests from consumers.[83] It thereby implicitly acknowledged the need to refer to the interests of the consumer in the law-making process, and also to the adoption of standards, notably in the foodstuffs area, which correspond to consumer expectations.

In principle, when dealing with cases that concern consumers, the ECJ adopts the interpretation which is most favourable to them.[84] When it comes to defining the personal scope of the rules protecting consumers, however, teleological interpretation gives way to literal and more restrictive interpretation, as shown in the cases below.

Several Directives define the consumer as any natural person who acts for purposes which are outside his trade, business or profession. In *Di Pinto*,[85] the ECJ had to adjudicate upon the status of traders in respect of contracts where they agreed to advertise in a periodical published by Di Pinto the sale of their businesses. The Court rejected the argument that such traders could be considered as consumers within the meaning of the Doorstep Selling Directive and established a close connection between the act performed and the subjective state of the person involved. Acts which are preparatory to the sale of a business are managerial acts performed for the purpose of satisfying requirements other than the family or personal requirements of the trader; in relation to such an act, a normal, well-informed trader cannot be under the influence of surprise as he will be aware of the value of his business.

A similar attitude was adopted by the Court in *Benincasa*[86] and *Dietzinger*.[87] In the latter case, focus on the objective element of the transaction is particularly evident since a guarantee given by Mr Dietzinger for the repayment of his father's business debt was considered as made 'in the course of his business'. Mr Dietzinger, nevertheless, had provided the guarantee outside his business or profession; he did not run a financing

82 [1988] OJ L70/16 (as amended).

83 Case C-331/88 R v Minister of Agriculture, ex parte Fédération Européene de la Sante Animale (FEDESA) [1990] ECR 1-4023, [1991] 1 CMLR 507.

84 See, for example, Case C-168/00 Simone Leitner [2002] 2 CMLR 6; Case C-400/00 Club Tour, Viagens e Turismo SA [2002] ECR I-4051; Case C-481/99 Heininger [2001] ECR I-9945.

85 Case C-361/89 Criminal proceedings against Di Pinto [1991] ECR I-1189.

86 Case C-269/95 Francesco Benincasa v Dentalikit Srl [1997] ECR I-3767, concerning the definition of consumer in the Brussels Convention; see also Case C-150/77 Bertrand v Paul Ott [1978] ECR 1431.

87 Case C- 45/96 Bayerische Hypotheken und Wechselbank AG v Edgar Dietzinger [1998] ECR I-1199.

company, nor did the guarantee fall in any other way within his trade or profession; the guarantee was provided *una tantum* to support his father. The Court emphasised the objective elements related to the contract itself and concluded that a contract of guarantee made by a natural person who is not acting in the course of his trade or profession does not come within the scope of the Directive where it guarantees repayment of a debt contracted by another who, for his part, is acting within the course of his trade or profession.

In the *Idealservice* case[88] the ECJ firmly denied that a company can be considered a consumer for the purposes of Directive 93/13.

The ECJ has also encouraged national courts to grant effective protection to consumers by disregarding, if necessary, conflicting domestic rules of procedure. In *Oceano Grupo Editorial v Rocio Murciano Quintero*[89] the ECJ ruled that the protection provided for consumers by Directive (EEC) 93/13 on unfair terms in consumer contracts entails that the national court should be able to determine of its own motion whether a term of a contract before it is unfair when making its preliminary assessment as to whether a claim should be allowed to proceed before the national courts. Similarly, in *Cofidis v Fredout*,[90] the ECJ held that the protection conferred on consumers by the same Directive precludes a national provision which, in proceedings brought by a seller or supplier against a consumer on the basis of a contract concluded between them, prohibits the national court, on expiry of a limitation period, from finding, of its own motion or following a plea raised by the consumer, that a term of the contract is unfair.

In other cases, the ECJ has adjudicated on the relationship between domestic measures of consumer protection and Article 28 (ex 30) of the EC Treaty. In *Gut Springenheide*,[91] for example, the ECJ had to decide over the allegedly misleading nature of certain egg packages sold in Germany. German courts had developed, in their case law, a rule that a promotional practice may be considered as misleading under the Unfair Competition Act (Gesetz gegen den unlauteren Wettbewerb) if at least 10 to 15% of the purchasers (the 'vulnerable' consumers) are misled. The ECJ had to decide whether, upon such interpretation, German law was contrary to Article 28 of the EC Treaty. In answering to the affirmative, the ECJ made reference to the concept of 'average' or 'well informed' consumer developed in previous case law,[92]

88 Case C-542/99 Idealservice Srl and Idealservice MN RE Sas v OMAI Srl [2001] ECR I-9049.
89 Case C-240/98 Oceano Grupo Editorial SA v Rocio Murciano Quintero [2000] ECR I-4941
90 Case C-473/00 Cofidis SA v Jean-Louis Fredout [2002] ECR I-10875.
91 Case C-210/96 Gut Springenheide GmbH v Oberkreisdirektor des Kreises Steinfurt-Amt fur Lebensmilleluberwachung [1998] ECR I-4657.
92 See Case C-470/93 Verein Gegen Unwesen in Handel und Gewerbe Köln eV v Mars GmbH [1995] ECR I-1923; Case C-315/92 Verband Sozialer Wettbewerb eV v Clinique Laboratoires SNC and Estée Lauder Cosmetics GmbH [1994] ECR I-317; Case C-313/94 Fratelli Graffione v Ditta Fransa [1996] ECR I-6039.

according to which consumer law should be interpreted having in mind the mature and critical consumer rather than the gullible, vulnerable one.

The court has adopted a restrictive approach where the integration of consumer policy into other common policies is concerned: questioned by BEUC, the European Consumers' Association, about the validity of a Commission decision not to authorise BEUC to have access to the non-confidential file in an anti-dumping action, the court decided that the Commission, while it may do so, was under no obligation to give access to the file to a consumer organisation. The court based its reasoning on the fact that consumers are not directly affected by anti-dumping measures.[93] If this is, from a strictly legal point of view, true, one must, however, admit that the price increase introduced by anti-dumping measures is, in the final reckoning, to be borne by the consumer, and that he is therefore affected by any such measure.[94]

J. MEANS OF CONSUMER PARTICIPATION IN THE EC DECISION-MAKING PROCESS

One of the five basic consumer rights identified at EC level concerns the right to be heard in the adoption process of EC legislation, not only in the context of consumer policy, but also in the context of other common policies which directly or indirectly affect the consumer. The EC has provided for several structures and procedures which make it possible for representatives to make their voices heard.

1. The consumer movement in the European Union

It is important, in order to understand the functioning of consumer representation at EC level, first briefly to describe the main features of the consumer movement within the EU.

There is no consumer organisation at EC level which relies on membership of individual consumers. Such an organisation would not, for the time being, correspond to a sufficiently strong European feeling of need among consumers and would not attract sufficient membership to be considered politically representative of EU consumer interest. Indeed, when analysing the consumer movement within the EU, one is struck by its diversity, not only from one country to another, but also within one country. Consumer needs and expectations differ according to national traditions, consumer culture, and the state of consumer law. In some Member States, consumer organisations are

93 Case C-170/89 Bureau Européen des Unions de Consommateurs v Commission [1991] ECR I 5709, ECJ.

94 Incidentally, the Commission, which before the decision based its refusal to give access on a supposed prohibition contained under Council Regulation (EEC) 2423/88, thereafter based its refusal on the absence of any obligation.

publicly funded; in others, they are based on private initiatives; and sometimes public and private organisations co-exist and/or are in competition with each other. There are organisations which are solely devoted to the promotion of the interests of the consumers. There are organisations, such as trade unions or family organisations, which, among the interests they defend, also tend to take into account the interests of consumers. There are rich organisations and there are poor ones, especially in Southern European countries. There are the organisations which were created in the 1950s and 1960s and are well established, and there are the newer organisations, whose legitimacy is in the course of being acquired. There are general consumer organisations, whose scope is to promote all consumer interests, and there are specialised consumer organisations, defending one single consumer interest, such as using a car safely and economically. There are national consumer organisations and local ones, etc. The variety is such that it would be wiser to refer to consumer movements than to a single one.

As a result, at EC level, the interests of the consumer are represented by five organisations which constitute federations – umbrella organisations – of Member State-based organisations. These five organisations are: BEUC (Bureau Européen des Unions de Consommateurs – the European Consumers' Association), which represents national consumer organisations from the EU as well as from EFTA countries; COFACE (Confédération des organisations familiales de la Communauté européenne), which represents family organisations from the EU; EUROCOOP (Confederation of European Cooperatives), which represents cooperatives from the EU and EFTA countries; ANEC (European Association for the Coordination of Consumer Representation in Standardisation), which coordinates and represent consumers in the process of technical standardisation; AEC (Association of European Consumers) that brings together 33 consumer organisation from 17 different countries from the EU and Central and Eastern Europe and focuses on social and environmental awareness.

These five organisations are considered by the EC institutions to be the official consumer organisations at EC level, and their representatives are appointed to the Consumer Committee. However, national organisations are not excluded from the consultation process of the EC.

2. EC structures for consumer representation

Several structures within the EC institutional framework allow for the interests of the consumer to be represented. In this respect, a major contribution has been made by the Commission, which has created, *intra muros*, the Health and Consumer Protection Directorate General (DG XXIV), and which has established the Consumer Committee.

The Health and Consumer Protection DG (formerly 'Consumer Policy Service') was added in 1989 to the other services existing within the Commission in order to overcome the problems linked to the dilution of the interests of the consumer among the various services it was concerned with. The Health and Consumer Protection DG has a double function with regard to the other Directorates-General: on the one hand, it is to initiate action within the framework of the EC consumer policy and, on the other hand, it is to contribute to the actions and initiatives of the other Commission services by stressing the impact of the proposed measures on the interests of the consumer.

In practice, the main responsibilities of the Directorate-General are related to food safety activities covering the entire food production chain, ranging from animal health and plant health to the labelling of food products, as well as animal welfare, scientific advice related to both food safety and public health and non-food consumer products and services.

The Health and Consumer Protection DG, which is headed by a Director-General, has only limited human and financial resources at its disposal: the consumer policy budget for the period 1999–2003 amounts to 112.5 million and often intensive discussions within the Council take place, where major cuts in the budget are proposed at some stage of the discussions, and then re-established by the Parliament.

A Consumer Committee was first set up (as the Consumer Consultative Committee) in 1973 by the Commission in order to allow for the consultation of a body representing the interests of the consumer. It is the only structure within the EC which effectively allows for the consumer representatives to be represented in the decision-making process. The other structures analysed in this section are to be considered rather as fora where the interests of the consumer are discussed.

The Consumer Consultative Committee went through a modification process in 1989, which led to the Consumer Consultative Council (CCC); in June 1995[95] the Commission decided to create a Consumer Committee which would supersede the CCC and which was then replaced by a new Consumer Committee in 2000.[96]

It was intended that the Consumer Committee should have a structure and organisation that would be consonant with the Commission's objectives, and that it should be representative of consumers in all Member States of the European Community whether they be organised at national, regional or European level.

The Committee shall be composed of:

(a) 15 members representative of national consumer organisations, one from each Member State;

(b) one member from each of the following European consumer organisation: BEUC, COFACE, EUROCOOP, ANEC, AEC.

95 Decision 95/260 ([1995] OJ L162/37).

96 Commission Decision 2000/323 ([2000] OJ L111/30).

The members are appointed by the Commission and their term of office (renewable) is three years.

The Committee may be consulted by the Commission on all problems relating to the protection of consumer interests at Community level. The discussions in the Committee are based on the requests for opinion made by the Commission. When requesting an opinion, the Commission can fix the deadline within which the opinion should be delivered. The positions taken by the members will appear in the minutes transmitted to the Commission. The opinions adopted will be annexed to the minutes.

The meetings of the Committee shall be chaired by a Commission representative and all meetings shall take place at the Commission.

Within the European Parliament, the Committee on Environment, Public Health and Consumer Protection has major responsibility for protection of consumers against risks to their health and safety, appropriate consultation and representation of consumers during the preparation of decisions which affect their interests, and improvement of consumer information and education, while the Committee on Legal Affairs and the Internal Market is competent for the remaining areas.

The Environment Committee prepares Parliament's work concerning the protection of the consumer. It prepares opinions on legislative proposals submitted by the Commission, initiates own-initiative opinions,[97] and organises public hearings on issues related to consumer protection. This Committee is composed of members of the European Parliament who are often particularly sensitised by the problems faced by consumers within the European Union.

The European Parliament has played an active part in the adoption of progressive consumer protection measures at EC level. Its opinions on legislative proposals, prepared by the Committee mentioned above, have often contributed to the improvement and extension of Commission proposals in this field. Though the opinions of the Parliament are not of a mandatory nature for the Commission, nor *a fortiori* for the Council, they have regularly been taken on board, at least in part, in the course of the adoption process of legislative measures.

However, according to the rules of procedure of the European Parliament, the Committee on Environment, Public Health and Consumer Protection is not automatically designated to prepare opinions on initiatives directly or indirectly concerning the interests of the consumer. Some major proposals, such as the first proposal for a Directive on the liability of providers of services,[98] have been submitted to other Committees, which are not necessarily

97 See, for example, Parliamentary Resolution of 11 March 1992 ([1992] OJ C94/217) on consumer protection and public health standards in the perspective of the achievement of the internal market.

98 [1991] OJ C12/8 (now withdrawn).

as devoted to the promotion of the interests of the consumer. As within the Commission services, there are therefore inconsistencies between approaches taken within the European Parliament on closely related issues.

Within the Economic and Social Committee (ESC), the section for Single Market, Production and Consumption prepares the opinions of the Committee related to consumer affairs.[99] This section also contributes to the legislative process of the Community by adopting opinions on legislative proposals submitted to it by the Commission, as well as organising public hearings on consumer-related themes and adopting own-initiative opinions that are sometimes given a lot of publicity.

At Council level, the decision taken by some presidencies to organise Council of Ministers meetings exclusively devoted to consumer affairs, the so-called Consumer Councils, has led to important progress in the adoption process of several directives, since it has gathered together the members of the national governments who deal, at least in part, with consumer affairs. However, most often, consumer issues are discussed within other Councils, such as the Internal Market Council or the Economic and Financial Affairs Council, bringing together ministers who do not necessarily have consumer affairs among their responsibilities at national level.

The organisation of the Council of Ministers meetings has led in the past to paradoxical situations. For example, in 1992, the Consumer Council meeting in late June established important priorities to be addressed in the action plan to be prepared and put into practice by the Commission; a few weeks later the Budget Council cut the budget available to the Consumer Policy Service for 1993 by 50%. This budget was eventually re-established by the Parliament, but such situations show the lack of integration of consumer policy with other policies at Council level.

As a consequence of the new approach to technical harmonisation adopted from 1985 by the EC, standardisation structures such as CEN, CENELEC and ETSI have been given major responsibilities in the field of the setting of safety standards to comply with the essential requirements set out in the directives. Consumer representatives are only allowed into meetings organised by these bodies as observers, with no voting rights.

Since its establishment in 1995, ANEC has forged strong relations with the European standards bodies and other related organisations. ANEC is directly represented on more than 55 Technical Committees of the European standards bodies (including CEN, CENELEC and ETSI) and coordinates input into the work of some 160 national consumer representatives. ANEC is also represented directly on the Board of the European Organisation for Testing and Certification (EOTC). At international level, ANEC has close links with ISO

99 See, for example, the ESC Opinion of 8 December 1999 on General Product Safety, CES 1131/99.

(International Organisation for Standardisation) and IEC (International Electro-technical Commission).

3. Procedures for consumer participation and representation

There are few means of consumer participation in the EC decision-making process available to individual consumers or to consumer representatives.

Both at individual and at collective level, consumers are only authorised to submit first instance complaints for supposed breach of Community law to the EC Commission. The Commission, however, is under no duty to investigate the alleged breach. While the Commission often engages in such investigations, especially in cases where the complaint concerns a matter of principle,[100] there is no corollary right for the individual to have a quasi-judicial decision from the Commission on his complaint. It might happen that the Commission, which constitutes a political rather than a jurisdictional body, decides not to follow up a complaint because it does not fit into its current priorities. There is no direct access to the ECJ, which anyway only addresses the question of illegal behaviour of EC institutions or Member States. Therefore, the only judicial route for individual consumers to attack breaches of Community law is to bring actions before national courts, in order for them, where appropriate, to submit a preliminary reference to the ECJ.

It is also possible for a party to intervene in disputes before the court involving an individual or an undertaking, but it is not permissible for a private person to intervene in disputes opposing a Community institution and a Member State.

Citizens may bring petitions before the European Parliament. The consequences of the right to petition are currently limited, as the European Parliament adopts own-initiative resolutions on the most important petitions, which act as political signals of areas where action is needed, to the other EC institutions. The Treaty on the European Union reinforced this function of the European Parliament and instituted an ombudsman within the European Parliament. The latter acts as another mouth-piece for consumer expectations and requests.

In the context of the legislative decision-making process, there is no obligation on the Commission to consult interested parties during the preparation of its proposals. More and more frequently, however, the Commission prepares discussion documents, or even organises public hearings on specific topics and invites, among other pressure groups and campaigning bodies, organisations and bodies representing the interests of the consumer.

100 See Joined Cases 25, 26/84 Ford-Werke AG and Ford of Europe Inc v Commission [1985] ECR 2725, [1985] 3 CMLR 528, ECJ, introduced by the Commission on the basis of a complaint by BEUC.

K. LEGISLATIVE ACHIEVEMENTS UNDER EC CONSUMER POLICY: AN OVERVIEW

Many EC regulations and directives have had a major impact on the promotion of the interests of the consumer. However, only a few of them were prepared specifically under the consumer policy programmes established since the 1970s. In the present section, only the latter will be shortly and chronologically described, while brief and inexhaustive reference will be made to the former at page 52.

1. Legislative initiatives within the competence of the Health and Consumer Protection Directorate-General (formerly the Consumer Policy Service)

The directives which come at present under the responsibility of the Health and Consumer Protection Directorate-General are as follows:

(1) Council Directive (EEC) 71/307 on textile names.[101] This Directive is intended to approximate the use of textile names in the different languages.

(2) Council Directive (EEC) 76/768 on cosmetic products.[102] This Directive sets safety requirements to be met by cosmetic products, through positive and negative lists of ingredients;

(3) Council Directive (EEC) 98/6 on price indications for foodstuffs.[103] This Directive stipulates the indication of retail prices on all foodstuffs entering into its scope. It also establishes the obligation to introduce unit pricing for certain types of foodstuffs. Prices must be clear, easily identifiable and legible.

(4) Council Directive (EEC) 84/450 on misleading advertising.[104] This Directive provides for a broad EC-wide definition of misleading advertising and defines the measures which should be put at the disposal of competitors or bodies/organisations representing consumer interests or professional interests. It does not deal with the problem of unfair advertising, nor does it deal with the question of comparative advertising. However, a more recent Directive, the Comparative Advertising Directive[105] enables one trader to advertise his goods or services by reference to those of another trader, provided that the comparative is not misleading and is verifiable.

101 [1971] OJ L185/16 (as amended).
102 [1998] OJ L80/27.
103 [1979] OJ L158/19 (as amended).
104 [1984] OJ L250/17 (as amended).
105 Council Directive (EC) 97/55 ([1997] OJ L290/18).

(5) Council Directive (EEC) 85/577 on doorstep selling.[106] This Directive protects the consumer when he concludes a contract with a trader during an organised excursion, at the consumer's home or working place, if the visit has not been made at the express request of the consumer. The Directive establishes certain rules on the form and content of the contract. It introduces an EC-wide cooling-off period of seven days, starting after receipt by the consumer of written information explaining this cooling-off period. However, the numerous exemptions provided by the Directive, namely in the field of insurance contracts, severely limit its contribution to the improvement of consumer protection in this sector.

(6) Council Directive (EEC) 87/102 on consumer credit.[107] This Directive encourages the provision of information to the consumer by regulating the promotion of credit offers and the form of the contract. It constitutes an interesting, if only partial contribution, to the solution of consumer problems in the area of credit. Council Directive (EEC) 90/ 88[108] amends Council Directive (EEC) 87/102 by approximating the method of calculation of the Annual Percentage Rate (APR).

(7) Council Directive (EEC) 87/357 on dangerous imitation products.[109] This Directive is intended to prevent future accidents relating to non-food products which are sold in such a way as could mislead the consumer, especially a child, as to their nature and could be considered as foodstuffs (eg, erasers with a strawberry taste).

(8) Council Directive (EEC) 88/378 on the safety of toys[110] – the first new approach directive. This Directive defines the essential mechanical, chemical and physical safety requirements to which a toy must conform to be put onto the EC market. Conformity to these essential requirements must be certified by the manufacturer by the placing of the EC mark on the toy or its packaging.

(9) Council Directive (EEC) 90/314 on package holidays.[111] This Directive constitutes an important contribution to the protection of the tourist. It contains obligations regarding the pre-contract information, as well as the form and the content of the contract itself. It also provides for strict liability of the tour organiser/travel agent where the consumer is confronted with losses due to any provider of a service under the package. However, it only provides limited protection for the tourist in the case of the tour operator/travel agent's bankruptcy or insolvency

106 [1985] OJ L372/31.
107 [1987] OJ L42/48 (as amended).
108 [1990] OJ L61/14.
109 [1987] OJ L192/49.
110 [1988] OJ L187/1 (as amended).
111 [1990] OJ L158/59.

between the moment of the down-payment and the beginning of the holiday, or during the course of the holiday.

(10) Council Directive (EEC) 92/59 on general product safety.[112] This Directive places a general obligation on the producer and the suppliers to put only safe products on the market. It also obliges the Member States to take the measures necessary for compliance with the general safety obligation. It applies in specific sectors only where the specific regulations do not contain provisions having the same objective as that of the horizontal Directive.

(11) Council Directive (EEC) 93/13 on unfair terms in consumer contracts.[113] This Directive establishes an EC definition of unfairness in contractual relationships and contains in its Annexes some clauses which illustrate the concept of unfairness and are considered to be, in principle, invalid in contracts concluded between consumers and professional suppliers. It refers to consumer organisations as being the judicial means of redress for consumers who want an end to be put to the use of a contract term considered to be unfair.

(12) Parliament and Council Directive (EC) 94/47 on the protection of purchasers in respect of certain aspects of contracts relating to the purchase of the right to use immovable properties on a timeshare basis.[114] This Directive constitutes a reaction to the numerous cross-border complaints received by the Commission from EU citizens who had bought timeshare property in another Member State and had experienced tremendous difficulties in the performance of the contract. It aims to increase the information given to the consumer, to enable him to benefit from a cooling-off period, to provide him with some financial security by providing a prohibition on advance payments during the cooling-off period, and to regulate the content of the contract. The Directive does not, however, regulate the legal status of timeshare property, which appears to be very different in the various Member States.

(13) Parliament and Council Directive 97/7 on contracts negotiated at a distance.[115] This Directive aims to protect the consumer when being invited to conclude contracts by new means of telecommunication, such as telephone, television, telefax, videotex, etc. In its current version, it provides for mandatory information, as well as for a cooling-off period. It also protects the consumer against unsolicited deliveries, as well as

112 2 [1992] OJ L228/24, repealed with effect from 15 January 2004 by Parliament and Council Directive 2001/95 ([2001] OJ L11/4).2

113 [1993] OJ L95/29.

114 [1994] OJ L280/83.

115 Parliament and Council Directive (EC) 97/7 ([1997] OJ L144/19).

against credit card fraud. It provides for collective means of redress, namely in cross-border situations, and therefore represents an important development of EC consumer law.

(14) Parliament and Council Directive 97/5 on cross-border credit transfers,[116] which is intended to put an end to the long discussion concerning the difficulties faced by consumers when trying to send or receive payments to or from another Member State. The Directive seeks to enhance consumer information on cross-border payments, as well as to set certain minimum obligations as to the speed and guarantee of payment incumbent on financial institutions.

(15) Parliament and Council Directive (EC) 2002/83[117] on consumer protection in the indication of the prices of products offered to consumers.

(16) Parliament and Council Directive (EC) 98/27 on injunctions for the protection of consumers' interests.[118] The aim of the Directive is to approximate Member States' laws relating to actions for injunctions for the protection of collective interests of consumers.

(17) Parliament and Council Directive (EC) 1999/44[119] on certain aspects of the sale of consumer goods and associated guarantees, laying down a common set of minimum guarantees valid no matter where the goods are purchased.

(18) Parliament and Council Directive (EC) 2000/13 on the approximation of the laws of the Member States relating to the labelling, presentation and advertising of foodstuffs for sale to the ultimate consumer.[120]

(19) Parliament and Council Directive (EC) 2000/31[121] on certain legal aspects of information society services, in particular electronic commerce, in the Internal Market ('the E-commerce Directive').

(20) Parliament and Council Regulation 178/2000 laying down the general principles and requirements of food law, establishing the European Food Safety Authority and laying down procedures in matters of food safety.[122]

(21) Directive (EC) 2002/65 of the European Parliament and of the Council of 23 September 2002[123] concerning the distance marketing of consumer financial services and amending Council Directive (EEC)

116 Parliament and Council Directive (EC) 97/5 ([1997] OJ L43/25).
117 [1998] OJ L80/27.
118 [1998] OJ L166/51.
119 [1999] OJ L171/12.
120 [2000] OJ L109/29.
121 [2000] OJ L178/1.
122 [2002] OJ L31/1.
123 [2002] OJ L271/16.

90/619 and Directives (EC) 97/7 and (EC) 98/27, laying down common rules for selling contracts for credit card, investment funds, pension plans, etc, to consumers by fax, phone or internet.

The Commission is currently planning initiatives in two important areas: safety of services[124] and unfair commercial practices.[125]

Apart from legislative initiatives, some recommendations adopted by the EC institutions have also been specifically oriented towards the improvement of consumer protection.

(1) Commission Recommendation of 17 November 1988 concerning payment systems and in particular the relationships between card issuers and card holders.[126] This Recommendation, which in its first draft was intended to become a directive, attempts to ensure a balance of contractual obligations between the card issuer and the consumer. It establishes rules on consumer information, eg, written contracts, use of an easily understood language, etc. It introduces limitation of the card holder's liability in case of loss or theft of the card, unless the consumer was grossly negligent or fraudulent. The non-mandatory status of the recommendation greatly limits its efficiency in terms of consumer protection. Though it stated that the banking sector should comply with its provisions within one year, the Recommendation is still today not sufficiently applied by the financial institutions in the EU.

(2) Commission Recommendation of 7 April 1992 on codes of conduct for the protection of consumers in the field of contracts negotiated at a distance.[127] This Recommendation is addressed to the trade associations in the field of distance selling and encourages them to adopt codes of conduct to detail, for their sector, the rules contained in the directive-to-be. The codes should deal with promotional techniques (premiums, lotteries, contests), financial security, cooling-off periods, presentation of solicitations, etc.

(3) Commission Recommendation of 30 July 1997[128] concerning transactions by electronic payment instruments and in particular the relationship between issuer and holder.

124 Report from the Commission to the European Parliament and the Council on the safety of services for consumers, COM(2003)313 final.

125 Proposal for a Directive of the Parliament and Council on Unfair Commercial Practices, COM(2003)356 final.

126 Commission Recommendation (EEC) 88/590 ([1988] OJ L317/55).

127 Commission Recommendation (EEC) 92/295 ([1992] OJ L156/21).

128 Commission Recommendation (EC) 97/489 ([1997] OJ L208/52).

2. A selection of initiatives outside the scope of the Health and Consumer Protection Directorate-General but still relevant in terms of consumer protection

There are a number of initiatives outside the scope of the Health and Consumer Protection Directorate-General which are highly relevant in the terms of consumer protection. In this volume we will deal with the main initiatives which are of the greatest importance to the protection of consumers. They constitute an important framework aimed in part or in whole at promoting the interests of the consumer within the European Union. However, the adoption of the legislative measures at the EC level is far from sufficient to ensure that effective improvement of the consumer's position in the market place has in fact taken place.

Among the EC initiatives which fall under the competence of other EC services, the following are of the greatest importance:

(1) Council Directive (EEC) 67/548 on the classification, packaging and labelling of dangerous substances;[129]

(2) Council Directive (EEC) 85/374 on product liability.[130] This Directive constitutes a major instrument for the protection of the consumer confronted with the consequences of defective products. Such situations, due to sometimes non-transparent reasons linked to the attribution of competence within the Commission, do not fall within the ambit of the Consumer Policy Service. It introduces a strict liability regime within the European Community: if a consumer is a victim of a defective product, its producer is held to be liable, even if he proves that he has not been at fault. However, the Directive leaves three matters to the Member States to decide: whether non-processed agricultural, fishery and game products should be covered by the strict liability regime, whether the state of scientific and technical knowledge at the time of putting the product on the market constitutes a valid defence for the producer (development risk defence) and whether a financial ceiling should be foreseen for mass accidents caused by the same product;

(3) Council Directive (EEC) 88/146 on the prohibition of certain hormonal substances in meat;[131]

(4) Council Directive (EEC) 1999/45 on the classification, packaging and labelling of dangerous preparations;[132]

(5) Council Directive (EEC) 89/107 on additives;[133]

129 [1967] OJ L196/1 (as amended).
130 [1985] OJ L210/29 (as amended).
131 [1988] OJ L70/16 (as amended).
132 [1999] OJ L200/1 (as amended).
133 [1989] OJ L40/27 (as amended)

(6) Council Directive (EEC) 89/108 on quick-frozen foodstuffs;[134]

(7) Council Directive (EEC) 89/109 on materials and substances in contact with foodstuffs;[135]

(8) Council Directive (EEC) 89/397 on the official control of foodstuffs;[136]

(9) Council Directive (EEC) 89/552 on trans-border television;[137]

(10) Council Directive (EEC) 89/646 on the access to and exercise of activities of credit institutions;[138]

(11) Commission Recommendation (EEC) 90/109 concerning the transparency of banking conditions applicable to cross-border financial transactions;[139]

(12) Council Directive (EEC) 90/496 on nutrition labelling;[140]

(13) Council Regulation (EEC) 295/91 on compensation for passengers who are denied boarding on regular air transport services;[141]

(14) Council Directive (EEC) 92/49 on insurance other than life insurance (third generation of directives in the field of non-life insurance);[142]

(15) Council Directive (EEC) 92/96 on life insurance (third generation of directives in the field of life insurance);[143]

(16) Council Directive (EC) 94/19 on deposit guarantee schemes;[144]

(17) Directive (EC) 2002/58 of the European Parliament and of the Council of 12 July 2002 concerning the processing of personal data and the protection of privacy in the electronic communications sector ('the Directive on privacy and electronic communications').

The regulatory instruments listed above constitute an important framework aimed at partially or totally promoting the interests of the consumer within the European Union. However, the adoption of legislative measures at EC level is far from sufficient to ensure an effective improvement of the consumer's position in the market place.

134 [1989] OJ L40/34 (as amended).
135 [1989] OJ L40/38 (as amended).
136 [1989] OJ L186/23 (as amended).
137 [1989] OJ L298/23 (as amended).
138 [1989] OJ L386/1 (as amended).
139 [1990] OJ L67/39.
140 [1990] OJ L276/40.
141 [1991] OJ L36/5.
142 [1992] OJ L228/4 (as amended).
143 [2002] OJ L345/1.
144 [1994] OJ L135/5.

3. The Commission's 2001 Green Paper on Consumer Protection

According to the Commission Green Paper on Consumer Protection of 2 October 2001,[145] the main problem in guaranteeing consumer protection in the internal market lies in the different national laws concerning commercial practices between businesses and consumers. Neither group is currently taking full advantage of the potential of the internal market, now strengthened by the Euro and the increased popularity of e-commerce.

Businesses wishing to offer consumers the option of electronic commerce are faced with discouraging legal uncertainties, which limit the effectiveness of the internal market. This problem is also detrimental to consumers, as it restricts access to various products and to greater selection.

Following an analysis of the relevant services, the Green Paper states that Community rules on consumer protection need simplification and improved effectiveness. In this perspective, the Green Paper puts forward the proposal to adopt either a series of new directives or a framework directive supplemented by targeted directives. The option of a framework directive offers greater advantages, as it would simplify the existing rules applicable throughout the European Union. In addition, it would be easier to negotiate than a series of directives.

The Commission is therefore currently elaborating a proposal for a framework directive that would harmonise national rules on the fairness of commercial practices (advertising, aggressive marketing, after-sales customer assistance) between businesses and consumers.

L. NON-LEGISLATIVE ACHIEVEMENTS UNDER EC CONSUMER POLICY

The European Community has not only contributed to the promotion of the interests of the consumer by adopting legislative or quasi-legislative instruments, but has also undertaken specific actions to address specific consumer problems in the common market.

1. Stimulation of cooperation between national authorities

As from 1984, the Council decided to establish a Community system of rapid exchange of information on the dangers linked to the use of consumer products[146] (RAPEX). This system was incorporated in the later decisions and was finally enshrined in the context of the Directive on general product safety.[147]

This system is intended to establish a rapid information flow between the national competent administrations in order to set in motion an emergency

145 COM(2001)531 final.
146 Council Decision (EEC) 84/133 ([1984] OJ L70/16).
147 Parliament and Council Directive (EC) 2001/95 ([2001] OJ L11/4).

procedure in case a consumer product or a category of products constitutes an important and imminent danger on their territory. The Commission has established in the framework of RAPEX a clearing house which dispatches information to the other Member States. Currently, the rapid exchange of information system comprises two contact points – one network for food products (as per Regulation 178/2000[148]) and one for non-food products. The list of contact points and officials responsible for these networks is disseminated only to the members of the network.

The system applies to all consumer goods, except pharmaceutical products.

In the last two years, the Commission received 98 notifications, including both food and non-food sectors. Although this system has contributed to preventing accidents and enabled dangerous products to be withdrawn from the market, the number of notifications is certainly far below the total number of dangerous situations identified in EU territory; in addition, there are some difficulties concerning the rapid identification of products on the market, since the notifications do not always contain sufficiently detailed information.

For the period 1 January 1999 to 31 December 2003, the Community has also adopted a programme of Community action on injury prevention. The objective of the programme is to create a data collection and information exchange system on injuries, particularly those resulting from home and leisure accidents.

The system relies upon the collection of information from the emergency services of hospitals and other appropriate establishments and services. The collection and transmission of data to the information system will be carried out under the responsibility of the Member States, which should seek to ensure the reliability of sources.

The system is being developed on the basis of the experience acquired with, and the assessment made of, the earlier EHLASS (European Home and Leisure Accident Surveillance System), set up as a pilot project in 1986[149] and extended several times.

2. Consumer information projects

The Commission has, under the different consumer policy programmes, undertaken several schemes intended to promote consumer information. It has granted financial help to consumer organisations to support them in their informational activities and it has financed comparative tests to enable consumers to become aware, for example, of the price differences existing in the EU. It has published information leaflets or has granted financial support to private bodies to publish such leaflets on specific consumer issues (such as child safety, safety in swimming pools, etc).

148 [2002] OJ L31/1.

149 Council Decision (EC) 86/138 concerning a demonstration project with a view to introducing a Community system of information on accidents involving consumer products ([1986] OJ L109/23).

In the context of the completion of the internal market, the Commission set up a network of European Consumer Centres (ECC-Network). Those centres ('Euro-guichets') initially concentrated on consumer information and consumer support related exclusively to cross-border transactions. The offices were mostly located in cities close to the border.

Following an evaluation in 1997, the network was remodelled and given a wider scope. Priority was given to more general information on European consumer issues, and the centres were moved from the border areas to the capital or anyway to more central areas from where a whole Member State could be served.

The Euro-guichets currently provide information on legislation and on case law both at European and Member State level; organise comparative testing and develop cross border studies; and advise and support consumers on problems within the internal market. The ECCs cooperate closely within their network as well as with other European networks such as EEJ-net (the European extra-judicial network), local consumer organisations and national and local authorities.

The Health and Consumer Protection Directorate-General has published, from time to time, consumer guides, brochures and leaflets aimed at promoting consumer confidence in the internal market, providing better information about comparative national consumer protection systems, and making consumers aware of the opportunities and risks linked to cross-border purchases.

Since June 2001, the Directorate also publishes a quarterly trilingual news bulletin, 'Consumer Voice'. The bulletin reports on current consumer affairs and debates, focusing on the EC institutions at work, on personalities related to the consumer world, on consumers' views on particular subjects, on news and developments as well as on forthcoming events. The bulletin is not directly aimed at consumers but rather at 'information multipliers', such as directors and members of consumer organisations, lawyers specialising in consumer law, national ministry employees in charge of consumer affairs, business employees responsible for communication, teachers, journalists, etc.

3. Consumer education programmes

The importance of consumer education, especially in schools, has been acknowledged by the Commission since 1975, when studies were carried out which established that it was possible to integrate a new topic into existing school syllabuses and that it was necessary to provide adequate training as well as appropriate didactic material to teachers. In 1986, the Council adopted a resolution on consumer education in primary and secondary schools[150] which recommended the Member States to promote consumer education in schools and which invited the Commission to promote teacher training as well

150 Council Decision (EEC) 86/138 ([1986] OJ L109/23) (as amended).

as the preparation of adequate material. The Commission has consequently engaged in several such programmes.

4. Consumer access-to-justice projects

The 1993 Green Paper on consumer access to justice[151] identified in detail the problems faced by consumers in cross-border litigation and sought to propose solutions to respond to these difficulties (eg, by providing the right of consumer organisations to bring collective actions in cross-border litigation).

Following the Green Paper, the Commission adopted in 1998 Recommendation (EC) 98/257[152] on the principles applicable to the bodies responsible for the out-of-court settlement of consumer disputes, followed in April 2001 by Recommendation (EC) 2001/310[153] on the principles for out-of-court bodies involved in the consensual resolution of consumer disputes.

Coordination of out-of-court-settlement procedures throughout Europe and support for the solution of cross-border disputes is entrusted to EEJ-net. EEJ-net provides a structure made up of national contact points (or 'clearing houses') established by each Member State which help the consumer with information and support in making a claim to an appropriate out-of-court alternative dispute resolution system.

In May 1998, the Community adopted Directive 98/27[154] which entitles qualified entities to seek in the competent court, internally or across the border, injunctions requiring the cessation or prohibition of any act contrary to one of the directives listed in an Annex to Directive 98/27.

5. Stimulation of research and training

The Commission has granted financial support to several initiatives aimed at in-depth analysis of consumer problems in particular areas. It has also supported numerous conferences and seminars, making it thus possible for consumer experts to exchange their experiences, and training courses on Community consumer law. It is currently engaged in a feasibility study of databases on consumer law, which, if finalised, would, among other things, make it much easier for consumer advisers to identify the legislation applicable to a cross-border consumer dispute.

6. Stimulation of consumer–supplier dialogue

The Commission has also engaged in the examination of the possibilities of promoting consumer–supplier dialogue in order to supplement or even replace regulatory intervention in the market place. In the recent 2002–2006

151 COM(93)576.
152 [1998] OJ L115/31.
153 [2001] OJ L109/56.
154 [1998] OJ L166/51.

consumer policy strategy,[155] the Commission focused especially on the need for more consultation between the interested parties and announced its intention to call for such consultation in several areas, such as financial services.

7. Framework proposal for financing EU activities in favour of consumers

Decision 283/99 of 25 January 1999[156] establishes a legal framework for the financing of the EC's activities in favour of consumers. This is the first time that consumer policy expenditure has been put on a proper footing. It will allow for forward planning until the year 2003 with a global budget of 112.5 million.

The framework will focus on four priority areas, namely:

(1) the health and safety of consumers, especially in respect of product and services;

(2) the protection of the economic and legal interests of consumers, including access to dispute resolution, as regards product and services;

(3) education information of consumers; and

(4) promotion and representation of consumers' interests.

M. EC CONSUMER POLICY IN AN INTERNATIONAL CONTEXT

The Community consumer policy has implications not only within the EU. It also affects the EFTA Member States. On the other hand, external trade policy and EC consumer policy sometimes contradict each other, as will be described below.

1. EC consumer policy and the European Free Trade Association

Since the Treaty on the European Economic Area came into force, EC consumer legislation has been part of the 'acquis communautaire' which the EFTA Member States have to implement, rather undemocratically, as part of their national legislation:

(a) in many cases, EFTA countries have been faster in implementing EC legislation than EU Member States, although they are not obliged to do so;

(b) in some instances, the adoption of EC consumer legislation by EFTA countries results in a deterioration of consumer protection in those countries.

Three of the EFTA Member States (Austria, Finland, Sweden) became full members of the European Union in 1995. From the point of consumer

155 COM(2002)208 final.
156 [1999] OJ L34/1.

protection, this has to be welcomed, as these countries have a long tradition of consumer protection. From 1995, they have been in a position to influence EC decision-making; this was not the case when they were EFTA members.

2. The links between EC consumer policy and EC external trade policy

The Community external trade policy constitutes an interesting illustration of the gaps existing between the definition, at EC level, of the interests of the consumer, and the Community trade policy. The Community decision-making procedures in the field of trade policy do not specifically take into account the interests of consumers and are followed with difficulty by consumer representatives because of their extreme lack of transparency.[157]

N. CONCLUDING REMARKS: FUTURE CHALLENGES FOR EC CONSUMER POLICY

The previous sections have described the achievements of the European Community's consumer policy, as well as the gaps in it which continue to exist and the conflicts which are identified with other policies. The following are the major challenges currently on the EC consumer policy agenda:

(1) To define the scope of future consumer policy under the Treaty on the European Union, it is essential for the EC to free consumer policy from internal market policy, and therefore, it has to take up the challenge of Article 153 of the EC Treaty. It has to define the new actions which may be undertaken in the field of consumer policy, and has to apply the principle of subsidiarity in such a way as it does not oppose any EC initiative which is not linked to the completion of the internal market.

(2) To make the functioning of the internal market effective for consumers. This implies the effective application of Community law by enforcement authorities and the preparation of solutions to cross-border disputes.

(3) To engage in actions to improve the transparency of Community decision-making procedures, as well as that of existing Community law, both for consumer representatives and individuals.

(4) The effective functioning of the internal market for consumers also requires a more proactive policy which will convince both consumers and undertakings to engage in cross-border activities.[158]

157 For example, in the field of anti-dumping policy, Case C-170/89 Bureau Européen des Unions de Consommateurs v Commission [1991] 1 ECR 1-5709, [1992] 1 CMLR 820, ECJ.

158 Experience has shown that even where all relevant legal conditions are met to enable the consumer to engage in cross-border contracts with an undertaking abroad, the latter sometimes refuses to contract for practical reasons; eg, in the field of consumer credit, it is more difficult for a credit institution to recover debts abroad.

(5) To attain the proper involvement of consumer organisations in Community policies, in particular to establish better consumer representation in the standardisation process, in order to contribute to an adaptation of standards to consumer expectations and needs.

(6) To improve and speed up work on access to justice issues, especially in cross-border disputes.

(7) To continue to improve the integration of consumer policy into other common policies, especially in the fields of competition, the internal market and external trade.

3

PRODUCT LIABILITY AND GENERAL PRODUCT SAFETY

1. Introduction

Although improving the quality of life by protecting the health and safety of consumers has long been recognised as one of the tasks of the European Community, most initiatives designed to improve consumer safety were aimed at specific products or substances. It was really only after 1985 when the Commission agreed a communication entitled 'A new impetus for consumer protection policy'[159] to the Council of Ministers, designed to set forth the objectives of the Community's consumer protection policy, that the limitations of setting down detailed rules for a restricted range of goods was recognised. It was in this communication that provision was made for implementing certain measures, including the preparation of a report on a general obligation to place safe products on the market.

During 1985, the Council passed its Directive on approximation of laws, regulations and administration provision of Member States concerning liability for defective products.[160]

To counter the problems setting down detailed rules for a restricted range of goods, the 'new' approach to consumer policy was to be based on laying down essential, broad safety and other mandatory requirements rather than detailed specifications, and leaving the details of technical harmonisation to the European standardisation bodies. This new approach implies limiting legislative intervention to essential but framework requirements and paying more attention to proper enforcement by Member States. The first Council Directive on product safety,[161] repealed and replaced by the second Directive on product safety,[162] is one of those measures which, though not concerned with technical harmonisation in a particular product area, reflects the new approach by dealing with broad requirements and laying down a general legislative framework designed to ensure a high level of protection of safety and health for consumers with adequate enforcement procedures.

159 COM(85)314.
160 Council Directive (EEC) 85/374 ([1985] OJ L210/29), amended by Parliament and Council Directive 1999/34 ([1999] OJ L141/20).
161 Council Directive (EEC) 92/59 ([1992] OJ L228/24).
162 Parliament and Council Directive (EEC) 2001/95 ([2002] OJ L11/4).
163 [1985] OJ L210/29.

2. Council Directive (EEC) 85/374 on the approximation of the laws, regulations and administrative provisions of Member States concerning liability for defective products[163]

(a) Objective: The purpose of this Directive was to harmonise the laws concerning liability for defective products. Approximation of laws concerning the liability of the producer for damage caused by the defectiveness of his products was thought to be necessary because the divergences between Member States could distort competition, and rules on liability varied in severity from State to State and thus led to differing costs for industry. It was thought therefore that this would effect the free movement of goods in the Community.

Approximation was also necessary because, under Member States' laws prior to the Directive, a consumer was protected against damage caused to his health and property by a defective product either in differing degrees or not at all. The Directive was therefore based on the assumption that equal and adequate protection of the consumer could only be achieved through the introduction of liability irrespective of fault on the part of the producer of the article which was defective and caused the damage.

(b) Scope of application: The strict liability regime imposed by Directive 85/374 applies to all products (ie, all movables and electricity). Under the original formulation of Article 2 of Directive 85/374, defective articles which are primary agricultural products or game (ie, the products of the soil, of stock-farming and of fisheries, excluding products which have undergone initial processing) were excluded. However, to respond to consumers' anxiety following the bovine spongiform encephalopathy (BSE) crisis, Article 2 was amended by Directive 1999/34[164] so as to include primary agricultural products and game in the strict liability regime created by the Directive.

Together with addressing consumers' legitimate concerns about the safety of primary agricultural products, Directive 1999/34 resolves difficulties that have sometimes arisen over the dividing line between transformed and primary agricultural products.

(c) Strict liability: Article 1 introduces the principle of strict liability (also called objective liability or liability without fault). According to it, any producer of a defective product must compensate any damage caused by it to the physical well-being or property of individuals, whether or not there is negligence on the part of the producer. The injured person shall be required to prove the damage, the defect and the causal relationship between defect and damage (Article 4), while it is of course not necessary to prove the negligence or fault of the producer (or importer). The fact that the damage may be caused both by a defect in the product and by the act or omission of a third party does

163 [1985] OJ L210/29.
164 [1999] OJ L141/20.

not alter the producer's liability. Also, when the injured person is at fault, the producer's liability may be reduced or disallowed.

The liability arising from the Directive cannot be excluded or limited by the producer.

(d) Producer: Under Article 3, by 'producer', the Directive means the manufacturer of a finished product, the producer of any raw material or the manufacturer of a component part and any person who, by putting his name, trade mark or other distinguishing feature on the product presents himself as its producer. Additionally, any person who imports into the Community a product for sale, hire, lease or any form of distribution in the course of his business shall be deemed to be a producer within the meaning of the Directive and shall be responsible as a producer. If the producer of the product cannot be identified, each supplier of the product shall be treated as its producer unless he informs the injured person, within a reasonable time, of the identity of the producer or of the person who supplied him with the product. The same shall apply, in the case of an imported product, if this product does not indicate the identity of the importer (even if the name of the producer is indicated).

(e) Joint and several liability: According to Article 5, where two or more persons are liable in respect of the same damage, they are jointly and severally liable. Each person retains the right to compensation from the other.

(f) Defective products: Under Article 6, a product is to be regarded as defective when it does not provide the safety which a person is entitled to expect, taking into account all the circumstances, including its presentation, the use to which it could be reasonably be expected to be put, and the time at which it was put into circulation.

The fact that a better product is subsequently put into circulation cannot be taken into consideration in determining the defectiveness of the product in question.

(g) Exceptions: Exceptions to producers' liability are set out in Article 7. The most notable one is the so-called 'state of the art' defence contained in Article 7(e), according to which the producer is freed from all liabilities if he can prove that the state of scientific and technical knowledge at the time when the product was put into circulation was not such as to enable the defect to be discovered. On this point, the Member States were permitted to take measures by way of derogation.

In 1995, the European Commission brought proceedings under Article 226 against the UK for incorrect transposition of Article 7(e) of the Directive. According to the Commission, the wording of s 4(10)(e) in Part I of the Consumer Protection Act 1987 (implementing the Directive in the UK) did not faithfully transpose the Directive in that it allowed a wider defence for the producer than the European measure. According to the Commission, the formulation of Article 7(e) of the Directive in objective terms requires the producer of a defective product to show that the state of scientific and technical knowledge was such that no one would have been able to discover the defect; Article 4(1)(e) of the Act, on the other hand, adopts a more subjective approach and requires that a producer of a defective product shows that neither he nor a producer of similar products could have identified the defect, thus appearing to impose a lighter test than the Directive. The ECJ dismissed the action[165] on grounds, *inter alia,* that, in the absence of any case law on Article 4(1)(e), the Commission could not point at any actual inconsistency with the Directive, and that domestic courts were anyway bound to interpret the Act in the light of the Directive (see in this respect the decision of Burton J in the English case, *A and Others v The National Blood Authority*[166]).

The judgement did not resolve the traditional difficulty of defining the 'state of scientific and technical knowledge' but simply reformulated the wording of the defence by stating that the knowledge must be 'accessible', without further qualifying what 'accessible' means in practice.

(h) Damage: Article 9 of the Directive indicates that 'damage must cover both damage resulting from death or from personal injuries and damage to, or destruction of, an item of property. In the latter case, the damage must be of an amount exceeding 500 whilst the item damaged must be of a type ordinarily intended for private use or consumption and must have been used as such by the injured person.

In two infringement actions brought by the Commission against France and Greece,[167] the ECJ upheld the Commission's claim that Member States were not allowed to disregard, in implementing the Directive, the 500 threshold imposed by Article 9.

In *Veedfald*[168] the ECJ also held that, save for non-material damage, whose reparation is governed solely by national law, full and proper compensation for persons injured by a defective product must be available and a Member State cannot restrict the types of material damage, resulting from death or personal injury, or from damage to or destruction of an item of property, which are to be made good.

(i) Limitation period: For the recovery of damages, the Directive gives a limitation period of three years running from the date on which the claimant became aware of the damage, the defect and the identity of the producer. The producer's liability expires after 10 years from the date on which the producer put into circulation the individual product which caused the damage.

(j) Domestic provisions: Articles 15 and 16 allow Member States not to introduce the 'state of the art' defence in their implementing measures and to set a limit for a producer's total liability for damage resulting from death or

165 Case C-300/95 Commission v UK (1997).
166 [2001] 3 All ER 289.
167 Case C-154/00 Commission v Greece [2002] ECR I-3879; Case C-52/00 Commission v France [2002] ECR I-3827.
168 Case C-203/99 Veedfald v Aarhus Amtskommune [2001] ECR I-3569.

personal injury caused by identical items with the same defect. This limit may not be lower than 70 million.

In addition, Article 13 makes it clear that the system of rules put in place by the Directive does not preclude the application of other systems of contractual or non-contractual liability based on other grounds, such as fault or a warranty in respect of latent defects.

The fact that the Directive provides for certain derogations or refers in certain cases to national law does not mean, however, that in regard to the matters which it regulates harmonisation should not be complete. The ECJ has pointed out in several judgements[169] that the possibility of derogation or different regimes applies only with regard to the matters exhaustively specified and it is narrowly defined.

(k) Implementation: In the UK, Directive 85/374 is implemented by the Consumer Protection Act 1987. All Member States have notified implementing measures.

(l) Follow-up work: The adoption of the Directive was followed by two reports by the Commission. The first one,[170] issued in 1995 and aimed at assessing the application of certain aspects of the Product Liability Directive, concluded that the latter had raised awareness of, and emphasis on, product safety and had made it easier for an injured person to prove his case, without nevertheless increasing the number of claims made or giving rise to large increases in insurance premiums.

The second report, issued in 2001,[171] followed a Green Paper[172] aimed at assessing whether the objectives pursued by the Directive (protecting victims, promoting improved product safety and facilitating trade in goods within the internal market without jeopardising innovation and job creation) were actually being achieved. The report points out that experience with regard to the application of the Directive is still limited and the little information available does not allow the identification of any major problems with its application: accordingly, it appears to be premature to propose any changes to the existing provisions. The Commission intends, however, to take some measures in order to fill information gaps. Those include setting up an expert group as well as launching two more studies aimed at providing the information necessary to assess the need for and the feasibility of developing a strengthened Community liability system for defective products.

169 Case C-154/00 Commission v Greece [2002] ECR I-3879; Case C-52/00 Commission v France [2002] ECR I-3827; Case C-183/00 Sanchez v Medicina Asturiana SA [2002] ECR I-3901.
170 Commission Report of 13 December 1995 on the application of the Council Directive 85/374 on the approximation of the laws, regulations and administrative provisions of the Member States concerning liability for defective products, COM(95)617 final.
171 Commission Report of 31 January 2001, COM(2000)893 final.
172 Commission Green Paper on Liability for Defective Products of 28 July 1999, COM(1999)396 final.

3. Parliament and Council Directive (EC) 2001/95 on general product safety[173]

(a) Objective: The first measure on general product safety, Directive 92/59,[174] was adopted to make it obligatory for all those involved in the design, manufacture and sale of products to comply with a general safety requirement. Some Member States had already introduced legislation imposing a general obligation on economic operators to market only safe products, but the level of protection afforded to individuals varied from State to State, and these disparities were felt to create barriers to trade and to distort competition within the internal market. Given the difficulties and impracticability of introducing Community legislation for every product which exists or is likely to be developed, a broad-based legislative framework to deal with products and ensure a high level of protection of safety and health to individuals was felt to be the most appropriate way forward.

In addition, under the EC Treaty, it is primarily up to Member States to take appropriate measures when dealing with dangerous products. It is recognised that measures may differ from one Member State to another causing unacceptable disparities in consumer protection. However, it is likely that product safety problems could affect all or a large part of the Community, and there are no procedures laid down which would be applicable in such an urgent situation. This Directive, therefore, provides for an adequate mechanism allowing, in the last resort, for the adoption of measures applicable throughout the Community to cope with any emergency situation. It also aims to ensure that rights of redress through competent courts are available in respect of any measures taken which restrict the placing on the market of a product or require its withdrawal.

(b) Repeal of Directive 92/59: In 1998 the application and enforcement of Directive (EEC) 92/59 underwent a planned four-year review by the Health and Consumer Protection Directorate-General. The review suggested several improvements to correct the shortcomings of the Directive; such improvements were then embedded in Directive 2001/95 which replaces Directive 92/59 as from 15 January 2004.

Directive 2001/95 cannot be looked at in isolation but must be seen in relation to other Community directives dealing with particular subjects but all concerned with aspects of health and safety. In particular, they must be seen as a necessary complement to the Directive on product liability.[175] The difference is that the latter is primarily remedial whereas Directive 2001/95 is intended as mainly preventive.

173 [2002] OJ L11/4.
174 Council Directive (EEC) 92/59 ([1992] OJ L228/24).
175 Council Directive (EEC) 85/374 on the approximation of the laws, regulations and administrative provision of the Member States concerning liability for defective products ([1985] OJ L210/29).

The general Product Safety Directive is complemented by more specific directives and by the Directive concerning products which, appearing to be other than they are, endanger the health or safety of consumers.[176] It should also be noted that Directive 2001/95 is only relevant to non-food products as food safety is regulated elsewhere.

The new Directive maintains, in principle, the requirements of Directive 92/59 but reinforces a number of concepts already existing, while others are completely new.

(c) Scope of application: Under Article 2, Directive 2001/95 applies to all products intended for consumers or likely to be used by consumers. It does not apply to second-hand products (antiques and products to be repaired or reconditioned prior to being used), nor does it apply to equipment used by service providers to supply a service; it applies, however, to products that are supplied or made available to consumers in the context of service provision for use by them.

Products intended for use by professionals and subsequently supplied to consumers (the so-called 'migrating products') also come within the scope of the Directive.

(d) General safety obligation: The general obligation imposed by the Directive that manufacturers/distributors shall place only safe products on the market remains the same as in Directive 92/59.

As in Directive 92/59, a product is safe when under normal or reasonably foreseeable conditions of use it presents no risks or only the minimum risks compatible with its use. In assessing whether a product is safe or not, various factors are to be taken into account, such as: the characteristics of the product; its effect on other products; instructions for use; and, most importantly, at whom the product is aimed. For example, children can be at serious risk because they cannot be expected always to follow instructions and may be expected to misuse a product. Dangerous products are those which are not safe within the meaning of this Directive.

The Directive applies as long as there is no specific Community legislation setting out safety requirements covering certain risks or categories of risk. In this case, the general safety requirement of the Directive only applies to the other risks.

(e) Conformity assessment criteria: The conformity assessment criteria imposed by Directive 2001/95 are more articulated than in Directive 92/59.

According to Article 3(2), a product that satisfies the specific rules of national law of the Member States in which it is sold is considered safe in the absence of specific Community provisions governing safety; these rules, however, are supposed to have been drawn up in conformity with the EC

176 Council Directive (EEC) 87/357 on the approximation of the laws of the Member States concerning products which, appearing to be other than they are, endanger the health or safety of consumers ([1987] OJ L192/49).

Treaty. Article 3(2) goes on to say that, where there is no specific legislation, a product that satisfies national, non-compulsory standards implementing European standards is presumed to be safe as far as the risks and categories of risks covered by the relevant national standards are concerned; compliance with these standards, however, does not imply that the products meet the general safety requirement, unlike with legislation. In all other cases, conformity with the Directive is assessed taking into account other circumstances listed at paragraph 3 of Article 3.

The conformity with any of the above criteria, however, does not prevent competent authorities in the Member States from imposing restrictions or requiring the withdrawal or recall of hazardous products despite such conformity. Such measures, however, must be adequately motivated.

The safety standards imposed by Article 3(2) of the Directive require that, for its effective and consistent application, European voluntary standards are drawn up. These are established by European standardisation bodies under mandates set by the Commission assisted by an appropriate Committee.

(f) Other obligations of producers and distributors: Under Article 5, the duty to observe the general safety requirement is supplemented in the Directive by an obligation on producers to supply consumers with relevant information to enable them to assess risks inherent in a product throughout its normal or foreseeable use, particularly when these are not directly obvious, and an obligation to take the necessary measures to avoid such threats (eg, withdraw products from the market, inform consumers and even recall products which have already been supplied to consumers, possibly providing for compensation such as refund or exchange). The Directive makes it clear, however, that provision of a warning will not exempt a producer from meeting the requirements laid down.

Producers are also required to take measures to ensure that they are informed of the risks that a product may pose and that they are able to take appropriate action to avoid these risks. Such actions may include marking and identifying batches, investigating complaints and informing distributors.

Distributors are also required, in proportion to their respective responsibilities, to act with due care to help ensure compliance with the applicable safety requirements.

A relevant innovation in comparison with Directive 92/59 is the introduction by Directive 2001/95 of a wider duty of cooperation for producers and distributors with competent national authorities. This includes not only informing the authorities that an unsafe product has been placed on the market, but also, at the request of the latter, to cooperate on actions taken by them to avoid the risks posed by products which the producers in question supply or have supplied (Article 5(4)).

(g) Producer: Obligations under Directive 2001/95 are placed on the 'producer'. This is defined by Article 2 as 'the manufacturer of the products, when he is established in the Community, and any other person presenting himself as the manufacturer by affixing to the product his name, trade mark or other distinctive mark as the person who reconditions a product'. A producer may also be the manufacturer's representative if the manufacturer is not established in the Community, or even the importer. Other professionals involved in the supply chain are included within the definition if their activities affect the safety properties of a product. Precisely who these other professionals are is not entirely clear. A distributor is defined as 'any professional in the supply chain whose activity does not affect the safety properties of a product'. Accordingly, a carrier could affect the safety of a product because of poor handling or packaging, for instance, even though it had not actually worked on the product; many retailers may fall within the meaning of distributor, but others do affix their brand names to goods and fall within the meaning of a producer.

(h) Powers and enforcement: There is a general obligation on Member States under Article 6 to adopt the necessary laws and regulations to make producers and distributors comply with the Directive. The Directive also requires Member States to nominate authorities charged with the duty of monitoring compliance with the general safety requirement and for those authorities to have the powers to enforce the Directive. Article 7 states that Member States must arrange for the definition of effective, proportionate and dissuasive penalties to be imposed in case of violation of national provisions implementing the Directive.

Article 8 sets out in more detail the powers of enforcement granted to the competent authorities of the Member States. Those include, for all products, organising appropriate checks on their safety properties, requiring information from parties involved, taking samples and subjecting them to safety checks. Other, more specific measures for certain products are listed in paragraphs (b) to (f) of Article 8. In particular, Member States have the power to order or organise the withdrawal or recall of dangerous products, but in all cases measures must be implemented in a manner proportionate to the seriousness of the risks and taking into account the precautionary principle.

(i) The European Product Safety Network: In order to enhance cooperation among Member States' competent authorities, Article 10 introduces the task for the Commission of promoting the setting up of a European Product Safety Network to facilitate, in a coordinated manner with other Community procedures (in particular the RAPEX system), collaboration at operational level on market surveillance and enforcement activities such as risk assessment and testing of products. A structured collaboration at European level has enormous potential to increase consumer protection while saving resources. At the time of writing, preparations for setting up the network are taking place notably with regard to the main operational objectives of the Network such as the establishment of communication means, definition of its modus operandi and the identification of a series of exercises in priority areas corresponding to the different objectives of the Network.

(j) Information exchange: When a Member State restricts the marketing of a product or requires its withdrawal or recall, under Article 11, this must be notified to the Commission. If the measures relate to an event whose effect is limited to that of the Member State, it shall be notified to the extent that the information is likely to be of interest to other Member States. The Commission then forwards the notification to the other Member States, unless it decides that the measure does not conform to Community law.

(k) Emergency situation and action at Community level: For serious product safety problems that need to be addressed in a rapid and efficient manner, the Directive provides for a system for the rapid exchange of information between the Member States and the Commission, the rapid exchange system (RAPEX). This already existed under Directive 92/59 but Directive 2001/95 aims to improve it and additionally to ensure that unsafe products are not exported to third countries.

Under Article 12, where a Member State adopts measures to prevent or limit circulation of products posing a serious threat, it shall immediately notify the Commission through RAPEX. The application procedures for RAPEX are described in Annex II to the Directive.

Any information received by the Commission, whether before or after measures are adopted, is to be checked by the Commission to see if it complies with the Directive, and forwarded to other Member States which, in turn, shall immediately inform the Commission of any measures adopted.

Under Article 13, the Commission can also adopt rapid measures at Community level when it is aware that a certain product poses a serious threat. After consulting the Member States and in certain circumstances a Scientific Committee, the Commission can decide to require Member States to take the measures indicated in Article 8(b) to (f) provided that: (1) Member States are at odds as to the approach to be adopted to cope with the risk; (2) the risk cannot be dealt with effectively under other procedures; and (3) effective action for eliminating the risk and protecting the consumer can only be undertaken at Community level. The Commission's decisions are either permanent or of a one-year duration, with the possibility of extending this by additional periods of the same duration. In certain cases, the product concerned is prohibited from being exported. In any case, the decisions taken in accordance with the Directive and those restricting a product from being put on the market must be justified and may be appealed before the competent courts.

All products intended for consumers or likely under reasonably forseeable conditions to be used by consumers are included within the scope of RAPEX, with the exception of pharmaceutical products.

According to Article 16, if the authorities of the Member States or the Commission are aware of the threat posed by certain products, information must be provided to the public. Professional secrecy is limited to justified cases.

Rapid exchange of information both for monitoring purposes and in everyday situations in respect of the safety of a product is seen as crucial to the successful working of this Directive and the effective supervision of product safety. Notification procedures already established for the provision of information in the field of technical standards and for the improvement of information on safety, hygiene and health will continue to operate.[177]

Past experience with RAPEX does not seem to have been entirely satisfactory in that the number of notifications exchanged was not very high (138 in 2000 and 143 in 2001). It is hoped that the more systematic and structured approach to market surveillance, the newly established framework of cooperation and the revision of RAPEX will result in more effective enforcement of the new Directive.

(l) Implementation: Member States are required to implement Directive 2001/95 by 15 January 2004. The regulations[178] implementing Directive 92/59 in the UK will therefore need to be amended or repealed by a new piece of legislation. At the time of writing, only Belgium had notified implementing measures.

(m) Follow-up work: Article 19(2) requires the Commission to submit a report to the European Parliament and the Council on the implementation of this Directive every three years. In addition, under Article 20, the Commission is to submit to the Parliament and the Council a report identifying the needs, possibilities and priorities for Community action on the safety of services. As part of the preparation of this report, a consultation paper on the safety of services was published on 12 August 2002 on the website of the Health and Consumer Protection Directorate-General.

Directive 2001/95 provides for the establishment of non-binding guidelines for RAPEX, aimed at indicating simple and clear criteria for the application of the definition of serious risks, deadlines for exchanging the information, standards forms, etc. At the time of writing, these guidelines are being drafted.

177 See, eg, Parliament and Council Directive (EC) 98/34 ([1998] OJ L204/37) (as amended) and Commission Decision (EEC) 88/383 ([1988] OJ L183/34) (as amended).
178 General Product Safety Regulations 1994, SI 1994/2328.

4

SAFETY OF AGRICULTURAL PRODUCTS AND FOODSTUFFS

A. INTRODUCTION

The agro-food sector is one of major importance for the European economy as a whole. Agriculture alone has an annual production of about 220 billion, providing 7.5 million jobs; the food and drink industry is a leading industrial sector in the EU, employing over 2.6 million people with an annual production worth almost 600 billion.

Food safety measures taken on a sectoral basis have been central to European legislation since the early days of the Community. Recent development in the food and farming process, however, require a more coordinated, integrated approach than the one so far adopted.

In the last few decades, there have been enormous developments in the methods of food production, in the patterns of handling and distribution and in the level of integration of national economies. At the same time, public confidence in food supply, food law and food control has decreased following dramatic events such as the BSE and the dioxin crisis.

The Commission has undertaken, since the mid-1990s, a range of actions to complement and modernise EC food legislation and to organise food safety in a more coordinated, integrated and flexible way. After a Green Paper on Food Law[179] and subsequent consultations, the Commission adopted on 12 January 2000 a White Paper[180] on food safety setting out new priorities and a new legal framework for food safety, including animal feed production.

The guiding principles throughout the White Paper are that food safety policy must be based on a comprehensive integrated approach, so as to ensure food safety throughout the food chain ('from farm to fork'); that feed and food operators should have primary responsibility for food safety; that adequate procedures to facilitate traceability of feed and food and their ingredients should be introduced. At the same time, surveillance and control of these operators, but also information gathering and analysis, should be ensured by Member States under the supervision of the Commission; where appropriate, the precautionary principle must be applied in risk management decisions.

The aforementioned principles are enshrined in Regulation 178/2002,[181] adopted in January 2002 as the first of the set of legislative initiatives envisaged by the White Paper.

179 COM(1997)176 final.
180 COM(1999)719 final.
181 Parliament and Council Regulation 178/2002 ([2002] OJ L31/1).

Reform according to the guidelines laid down in the White Paper also includes the setting up of a European Food Safety Authority,[182] entrusted with the task of providing scientific advice and support for Community legislation and policies in all fields having a direct or indirect impact on food and feed safety. According to the White Paper, the lack of scientific support for the system of scientific advice, inadequacies in monitoring and surveillance of food safety issues, gaps in the rapid alert system and lack of coordination of scientific cooperation and analytical support constituted serious loopholes in the Community food safety strategy. The EFSA (European Food Safety Authority) has therefore been set up in order to provide to stakeholders, policy makers and the public independent information on food safety issues and to communicate risks in the food chain to the general public.

Risk management, including legislation and control, remains the responsibility of the other relevant European institutions; the tasks of the authority will only concentrate on risk assessment and risk communication.

In addition to Regulation 178/2002, there are measures in this chapter which aim to give consumers more information and knowledge about what they are purchasing, and also dealing with certain restrictions and minimum standards such as Council Directive (EEC) 93/77 on fruit juices[183] and similar products. Other directives deal more exclusively with setting down certain minimum standards and restricting the use of certain products on the basis of hazard assessments to human health, such as Council Directive (EEC) 89/109[184] on materials and articles intended to come into contact with foodstuffs. All are ultimately geared towards improving consumer safety within the European Community.

Another important innovation is the adoption by the Commission[185] of a proposal for a new and integrated approach towards official food and feed control in the European Union in 2003. This proposal establishes a clear EC framework for a control system, in which the respective responsibilities of the Member States and the Commission are systematically set out. It takes into account the general principle that all parts of the food production chain must be subject to official controls. Furthermore, it provides for a common approach with regard to controls on imports of food and feed from third countries.

Although food inspections are outside the scope of this work, it is important to note that the new regime will replace, probably as from January

182 See Regulation 178/2002, Art 1(2).
183 [1993] OJ L244/23 (as amended).
184 [1989] OJ L40/12.
185 COM(2003)52.

2005, several directives on the sampling, analysis and inspection of food and feed.[186]

B. GENERAL PRINCIPLES AND REQUIREMENTS OF SAFETY

1. Introduction

The setting up of EFSA is the cornerstone of the new Community strategy to ensure that the European consumer has access to safe food. Regulation 178/2002 also sets out the guiding principles of EC food legislation: these include the responsibility of food and feed businesses to ensure that only safe food and feed is placed on the market, and that foods and feedingstuffs that are unsafe are withdrawn from the market; rules imposing the traceability of all foodstuffs, animal feed and feed ingredients; procedures for developing food law and dealing with food emergencies.

In addition, the new Regulation sets up a new rapid alert system for feed and food. The system foresees obligatory notification of any direct or indirect risk to human health, animal health or the environment within a network consisting of national competent authorities, the EFSA and the European Commission. It builds upon the existing rapid alert system (already used for food), extending it to include the feed sector and feed and food imports from outside the EU. The European Commission is in charge of managing the system and ensuring immediate transmission of information to all contact points.

2. Regulation 178/2002 laying down the general principles and requirements of food law, establishing the Food Safety Authority and laying down procedures in matters of food safety[187]

(a) Objective: As one of the main pillars of the new approach to food safety, the Regulation's primary aims are to set out the general principles of food law, to establish the European Food Safety Authority (EFSA) and to lay down procedures in matters of food safety, particularly in emergency cases.

In line with the 'farm to fork' strategy, the Regulation promotes principles which are sometimes applicable not only to food, but to animal feed as well.

In combination with the general objectives of a high level of protection of human life and health and of the protection of consumers' interests, the Regulation also seeks to achieve the free movement in the Community of food and feed manufactured and marketed according to the general principles of Community food law. To enhance the safety and confidence of consumers in

186 Such as Council Directive 89/397 on the official control of foodstuffs ([1989] OJ L186/23) and Council Directive 93/99 on additional measures concerning the official control of foodstuffs ([1993] OJ L290/14).
187 Parliament and Council Regulation 178/2002 ([2002] OJ L31/1).

third countries and to facilitate food exports, the Regulation also encourages compliance with the developing international food standards.

(b) Scope of application: In order to ensure that a comprehensive and integrated approach to food safety is taken, Article 2 adopts a broad definition of food, so as to comprise any substance, including water, intentionally incorporated into the food during its manufacture, preparation or treatment. The Regulation excludes, *inter alia,* medicinal and cosmetic products, tobacco and tobacco products, and animal feed. Several provisions of the Regulation, however, deal specifically with feed.

It is important to note that the Regulation applies to all stages of production, processing and distribution of food and feed. It does not apply to primary production and preparation of food for private domestic consumption.

(c) General food law: Chapter II of the Regulation contains the Community principles, obligations and requirements of food law. The most notable of these are as follows.

(i) Safety requirement: The basic idea underlying the Regulation is that only safe food and feed should be placed in the market. According to Article 14, food shall be deemed to be unsafe if it is considered to be injurious to health or unfit for human consumption. In determining whether any food is unsafe, regard shall be had to the normal conditions of use of the food by the consumer and to the information provided to the consumer, including information on the label, or other information generally available to the consumer. In determining whether any food is injurious to health, regard shall be had not only to the probable immediate and/or short-term and/or long-term effects of that food on the health of a person consuming it, but also on subsequent generations; to the probable cumulative toxic effects; to the particular health sensitivities of a specific category of consumers where the food is intended for that category of consumers. In determining whether any food is unfit for human consumption, regard shall be had to whether the food is unacceptable for human consumption according to its intended use, for reasons of contamination, whether by extraneous matter or otherwise, or through putrefaction, deterioration or decay.

Parallel requirements are laid down by Article 15 in relation to feed safety.

Article 16 also requires that the labelling, advertising and presentation of food or feed is not such as to mislead consumers.

(ii) Risk analysis: Measures adopted by Member States and the Community to ensure food and feed safety should be based on risk analysis, save where this is inappropriate to the circumstances of the case. Risk analysis consists of three interconnected components: risk assessment (scientific advice and information analysis), risk management (regulation and control) and risk communication (interactive exchange of information). The organisation of independent, high quality and transparent scientific advice shall fall within

the tasks of the EFSA. Risk analysis should provide a systematic methodology for the determination of effective, proportionate and targeted actions to protect health. In particular, risk assessment should be undertaken in an independent, objective and transparent manner but a decision on risk management shall also be based on other factors such as societal, economic, traditional, environmental and ethical factors, and the feasibility of controls.

(iii) Precautionary principle: Where appropriate, the precautionary principle should be applied in risk management decisions. This principle has been successfully invoked by Member States to ensure health protection, thus giving rise to barriers to the free movement of food or feed. The Regulation therefore seeks to provide a uniform basis for its use throughout Europe. According to Article 7, when a risk to life or health exists but no scientific certainty as to the risk presented by the product exists, provisional measures can be adopted pending further scientific evidence. Application of this principle, however, should comply with the proportionality principle.

(iv) Transparency: To ensure consumers' and trading partners' confidence, food law should be developed in a open and transparent manner. Under Article 9, openness and transparency shall be achieved by public consultation, directly or through representative bodies, at the time of preparation, evaluation and revision of food law; under Article 10, ensuring consumers' and trading partners' confidence also requires that public authorities take appropriate steps to inform the public when there are reasonable grounds to suspect that a food may present a risk to health.

(v) Traceability: A successful food policy demands the traceability of feed and food and their ingredients. Adequate procedures to facilitate traceability must therefore be introduced so that targeted and accurate withdrawals can be undertaken or information given to consumers or control officials. This includes the obligation for food and feed business to ensure that adequate records are kept, not only suppliers of raw materials and ingredients but also those to whom the product has been supplied.

(vi) Food trade: Food and feed imported into the Community must comply with the relevant food law or with conditions recognised by the Community to be at least equivalent or with the terms of a specific agreement existing with the exporting country. Food and feed exported from the Community must comply with Community law or the requirements set up by the importing country. Outside those cases, food or feed can be exported only with the express agreement of the country of destination, provided that they are not injurious to health or unsafe.

The Community and the Member States shall contribute to developing international standards and trade agreements.

(vii) Food and feed business operators' responsibilities: Feed manufacturers, farmers and food operators have the primary legal responsibility for ensuring food safety: competent authorities monitor and

enforce this responsibility through the operation of national surveillance and control systems; the Commission concentrates on evaluating the ability of competent authorities to deliver these systems through audits and inspections at national level.

Under Article 19, a food business operator who becomes aware that an unsafe food has been put on the market is under a duty to immediately initiate procedures to withdraw it. If the product has already reached the consumer, the operator must inform the consumer for the reasons of the withdrawal. This responsibility lies not only on producers, but also on retailers and dealers who must participate in contributing to safety.

If food injurious to human health is put into circulation, competent authorities must immediately be informed by food operators who shall also collaborate with the actions taken by the authorities.

Similar principles apply to feed business operators (Article 20).

(d) European Food Safety Authority (EFSA): One of the most remarkable innovations brought by Regulation 178/2002 is the setting-up of the EFSA. The EFSA is a Community body with its own legal identity, funded from the Community budget but operating independently of the Community institutions. It will not therefore be managed by the Commission but by an Executive Director who in turn will be answerable to a Management Board.

The EFSA is entrusted with a number of key tasks embracing independent scientific advice on all aspects relating to food safety, operation of rapid alert systems, communication and dialogue with consumers of food safety issues as well as networking with national agencies and bodies. It is primarily a scientific risk assessment body, the responsibility for risk management or decision making remaining with the EC's political institutions.

(i) Scientific advice and support: The system for the provision of scientific advice to the Commission is currently based on the existence of eight sectoral Scientific Committees (of which five cover, directly or indirectly, food and feed areas), plus a Scientific Steering Committee providing advice on multi-disciplinary matters, including BSE and harmonised risk assessment procedures. The recent food crises have shed light on the incapacity of the system to cope with the increase in demands placed upon it and on the delays this has created for the Commission's ability to respond to problems.

The EFSA has been set up with the purpose of addressing this problem. The EFSA should take up the role of several Scientific Committees attached to the Commission and is entrusted with the task of providing independent scientific advice and support and to promote coherence between the risk assessment, risk management and risk communication functions. The EFSA can issue scientific opinions at the request of the Commission, the European Parliament or a Member State and also by its own initiative. The EFSA may also be requested by the Commission to provide scientific or technical assistance, in particular for the establishment or evaluation of technical criteria.

The task of advising and supporting the Commission may be carried out by means of the following activities: scientific evaluation of risks, collection and analysis of scientific data, commissioning of scientific study, safety evaluations of dossiers put forward by industry for Community level approval of substances or processes, identification of emerging risks, scientific support to the Commission, particularly in the case of a food safety crisis.

The EFSA can carry out scientific assessment on any matter that may have a direct or indirect effect on the safety of the food supply, including matters relating to animal health, animal welfare and plant health and can give scientific advice on non-food and feed GMOs, and on nutrition in relation to Community legislation.

The EFSA also has extensive responsibilities for communicating scientific and technical information directly to the public in a coherent and consistent manner.

(ii) Rapid alert system and European networking of organisation: Any messages exchanged under the rapid alert system set up by the Regulation shall be forwarded to the EFSA, which shall analyse it in order to provide the Commission and the Member States with any information required for the purposes of risk analysis.

The EFSA is in charge of promoting scientific cooperation among European organisations operating in the field within the EFSA's mission.

(iii) Organisation: To gain and preserve the confidence of the Community institutions and of the public in the EFSA it is necessary that, in its organisation independence, high scientific quality, transparency and efficiency are ensured.

The EFSA comprises a Management Board, an Executive Director, an Advisory Forum, a Scientific Committee and Scientific Panels. Their respective tasks are set out in Articles 25 to 28.

The Management Board is responsible for ensuring that the Authority functions effectively and efficiently. Within this objective, it is responsible for establishing the Authority's draft budget and work programmes, monitoring their implementation, and agreeing to internal rules and regulations. It is also responsible for appointing the Executive Director of the Authority and the members of the Scientific Committee and Panels.

The Executive Director is responsible for the day-to-day management of the Authority and is answerable to the Management Board. The Executive Director is responsible for the appointment of the Authority's technical, scientific, administrative and communications personnel.

The Executive Director will be assisted by an Advisory Forum composed of representatives from the competent bodies in the Member States, which undertake tasks similar to those of the Authority, on the basis of one representative per Member State. These bodies will most probably be national agencies performing risk assessments in the food sector where they exist in a Member State. Their close involvement is essential, for example, to ensure efficient networking with national scientific organisations as a mechanism for exchanging information on potential risks and for pooling knowledge.

A Scientific Committee and several Scientific Panels will be responsible for the scientific opinions of the Authority.

A Scientific Committee will be responsible for the general coordination necessary to ensure the consistency in the scientific opinions of the different panels. This Committee will be composed of the chairpersons of the Scientific Panels and six independent experts who do not belong to any panel. The Scientific Panels will be composed of independent scientific experts selected following an open call for expressions of interest and appointed by the Management Board. They will be selected on the basis of criteria of competence, knowledge, independence and experience.

In accordance with the Regulation, until these Committee and Panels are established, scientific advice on matters falling within the competence of the Authority will continue to be provided by the existing scientific committees established by Commission Decisions and supported by the Commission's civil servants.

(e) RAPEX: A system for rapid alert already exists in the framework of Directive 92/59[188] (now Directive 2001/95[189]) on general product safety (the so-called RAPEX). The scope of this system includes food and industrial products but not feed. Various other systems of notification exist in different areas, such as transmissible diseases in human and animals or animal products stopped at the borders of the EU. However, integrated use of the information is difficult because of the difference in objectives and scope of these systems. Regulation 178/2002 seeks to achieve the creation of a comprehensive and harmonised legal framework for all food and feed and also to ensure that an appropriate link with other information systems is made.

The functioning of this system is similar to the one laid down in Directive 92/59 (now Directive 2001/95) for defective products.

Under Article 50, the network is managed by the Commission. The Member States, the Commission and the Authority designate each a contact point, which shall be a member of the network. Where a member of the network has any information relating to the existence of a serious direct or indirect risk to human health deriving from food or feed, this information shall be immediately notified to the Commission. The Commission shall transmit this information immediately to the members of the network, and the Authority may supplement the notification with any scientific or technical

188 [1992] OJ L228/24.
189 [2002] OJ L11/4.

information, which will facilitate rapid, appropriate risk management action by the Member States.

Member States shall then immediately notify the Commission of any measure they adopt aimed at preventing, restricting or imposing specific conditions on the placing on the market or use of food or feed.

The Commission shall immediately transmit to the members of the network the notification and all supplementary information received. Member States must, in turn, immediately inform the Commission of the action implemented or measures taken following receipt of the notifications, and the Commission shall immediately transmit this information to the members of the network.

It is planned that participation in the rapid alert system will be be opened up to applicant countries, third countries or international organisations, on the basis of agreements between the Community and those countries or international organisations

As yet, the measures for implementing Article 50 have not been adopted.

(f) Emergency measures and crisis management: As with defective products, for serious food or feed safety problems that need to be addressed in a rapid and efficient manner, Article 53 provides for an emergency system whereby the Commission, acting in accordance with Article 58(2), is entitled to adopt rapid measures at Community level when it is aware that a certain product poses a serious risk to human or animal health or the environment. Those measures include suspension of the placing on the market or of the imports of the food or feed in question or subjecting placing on the market or imports to special conditions.

The measures taken shall be confirmed, amended, revoked or extended within 10 working days; any delay shall be adequately justified.

In parallel with this procedure, Article 55 envisages the creation of a plan for crisis management. The objective is to make it possible to improve coordination of effort and to determine the most effective measures on the basis of the best scientific information. In situations involving a serious, direct or indirect risk to human health deriving from food or feed and where the risk cannot be managed by way of the other procedures, the Commission shall set up a crisis unit, responsible for collecting and evaluating all relevant information. The EFSA shall participate in the crisis unit and if necessary provide scientific and technical assistance.

(g) Implementing actions: The EFSA has started its activity only recently. The Management Board and the Executive Director were appointed between 2002 and 2003, while the Members of the Scientific Committee, of the eight Panels and of the Advisory Forum are still to be appointed. Meanwhile, the existing Scientific Committees continue to exist and an interim advisory forum holds informal meetings.

The Authority has temporarily been located in Evere, Brussels.

C. MATERIAL IN CONTACT WITH FOODSTUFFS

1. Introduction

The Community measures in this area seek to ensure that any material or substance (including packaging materials but also cutlery, dishes, processing machines, containers, etc) intended to come into contact, whether directly or indirectly, with foodstuffs, is sufficiently stable to avoid contamination of the foodstuffs when this would be likely to endanger health or provoke any similar change in composition or deterioration of the foodstuffs.

The contamination, transfer of constituents of the food contact materials into the food, is called migration. To ensure the protection of the health of the consumer and to avoid adulteration of the foodstuff, two types of migration limits have been established in the area of plastic materials: an overall migration limit (OML) that applies to all substances that can migrate from the food contact material to the foodstuff, and a specific migration limit (SML) which applies to individual authorised substances and is fixed on the basis of the toxicological evaluation of the substance. The SML is generally established according to the acceptable daily intake (ADI) or the tolerable daily intake (TDI) set by the Scientific Committee on Food (SCF).

Food contact materials and articles are regulated by three types of Directives: (a) framework Directive (EEC) 89/109, that lays down general requirements for all food contact materials; it also establishes that to achieve its objective specific directives have to be implemented laying down various types of limitations tailored to the technological characteristics peculiar to each group of materials and articles; (b) specific directives covering groups of materials and articles coming into contact with food; (c) specific directives on substances used in the manufacture of materials and articles intended for food contact. The latter directives are outside the scope of this work.

2. Council Directive (EEC) 89/109 on the approximation of the laws of the Member States relating to materials and articles intended to come into contact with foodstuffs[190]

(a) Objective: This Directive was adopted to replace Council Directive (EEC) 76/893 on the approximation of the laws of the Member States relating to materials and articles intended to come into contact with foodstuffs.[191] Council Directive (EEC) 76/893[192] was originally adopted to harmonise national laws relating to such materials and articles to help the free movement of goods and the establishing and functioning of the common market. As Directive 76/893 had been substantially amended on numerous occasions, this Directive not only makes further amendments but takes the opportunity to consolidate the existing provisions, thus ensuring legal clarity.

190 [1989] OJ L40/38.
191 [1976] OJ L340/19 (repealed).
192 Ibid.

(b) Scope of application: Article 1 lays down the scope of the Directive, stating that it shall apply to materials and articles which, in their finished state, are intended to be in contact with or to come into contact with foodstuffs. This includes those materials and articles in contact with water intended for human consumption, for example, plastic and glass containers for still mineral water.

Antiques are excluded under Article 1, as are covering and coating substances such as cheese rinds, prepared meat products or fruit, which actually form part of the foodstuffs or may be consumed with them. With such substances, account must be taken of possible direct consumption by consumers, and different rules would be necessary.

Under Article 12, the Directive is not intended to apply to materials and articles intended for export.

(c) Basic principle: Article 2 states the basic principle behind this Directive. Materials and articles must be manufactured in accordance with good manufacturing practice so that under normal and foreseeable conditions of use they do not contaminate foodstuffs in quantities which could either:

(i) endanger human health; and/or

(ii) bring about an unacceptable change in the composition of the foodstuffs or a deterioration in their characteristics.

Article 3 sets out those provisions which are to be covered by specific directives adopted under the procedure laid down in Article 8. Annex I lists those groups of materials and articles to be covered by specific directives, for example, plastics, paper and board, ceramics, glass, and metals.[193]

Specific directives already adopted are: Council Directive (EEC) 84/500[194] on ceramics; Commission Directive (EC) 93/10[195] on regenerated cellulose film; Commission Directive (EEC) 2002/72[196] on plastic.

Provisions to be covered by specific directives include:

(i) lists of authorised substances;

(ii) purity standards;

(iii) special conditions;

(iv) specific and overall migration limits;

(v) hazard provisions;

(vi) rules for checking compliance, for sampling and methods of analysis.

Any provisions relating to public health must fulfil the criteria set out in Annex II.

193 See paras [357] to [398].
194 [1984] OJ L277/12.
195 [1993] OJ L93/27; repealing Council Directive (EEC) 83/229 ([1983] OJ L123/31).
196 [2002] OJ L220/18; repealing Commission Directive (EEC) 90/128 ([1990] OJ L349/26.

(d) Authorisation of substances: Article 4 provides for limited authorisation of substances not included in any list of authorised substances provided it is for not more than two years, is subject to an official check and bears a distinctive indication. Within this two-year period, a Member State may submit to the Commission a request together with supporting documents to include any such substance in its authorised list. The Commission must make a decision within 18 months after consulting with the Scientific Committee on Foods,[197] during which time the temporary authorisation remains in force. If certain provisions need to be laid down in relation to any such substance, they must be adopted in accordance with the procedure laid down in Article 9.

Article 5 grants Member States the authority to temporarily bar or restrict any substance if, in the light of new information or after a reassessment of existing information, there are grounds to show it would endanger human health. Any such action must be informed to other Member States and the Commission. After consultation with the Standing Committee on Foodstuffs,[198] the Commission will initiate the appropriate procedure to consider any amendments to the specific directives in question in order to remedy difficulties and protect human health. Any safeguards implemented by a Member State may be retained until such amendments are adopted.

(e) Labelling requirements: As labelling is seen as the key to informed use of such materials and substances, general provisions are laid down in this Directive, although the methods used for such labelling may vary according to the user. The labelling provisions of this Directive are not intended to apply to products which are not designed to come into contact or be in contact with foodstuffs.

Unless there are exceptions under specific directives, Article 6 sets out the general labelling requirements for all materials and articles intended to come into contact or be in contact with foodstuffs when placed on the market. They must be accompanied by:

(i) the words 'for food use' or a specific indication of use such as coffee machine, or a symbol to be determined in accordance with the appropriate procedure;

(ii) any special conditions;

(iii) the name or trade name and address or registered office or the registered trade mark of the manufacturer, processor or seller.

These particulars must be conspicuous, legible and indelible and, at the retail stage, must be on the materials, articles or packaging or on labels affixed

197 The Scientific Committee on Foods was set up by Commission Decision (EEC) 74/234 ([1974] OJ L136/1) (repealed); see now Commission Decision (EC) 97/579 ([1997] OJ L237/18).

198 Set up by Council Decision 69/414 ([1969] OJ L291/9) and to be repealed by Parliament and Council Regulation 178/2002 ([2002] OJ L31/1).

or on a notice in the immediate vicinity. At other marketing stages these particulars must be on accompanying documents, on the labels or packaging or on the materials or articles themselves. These particulars are not compulsory for materials and articles which by their nature are intended to come into contact with foodstuffs. These particulars are intended to be confined to those materials and articles subject to this Directive and with any specific directives. An obligation is also placed on Member States to ensure that articles and materials are banned if the particulars required are not given in a language which can be understood by purchasers.

(f) Freedom to trade: Under Article 7, if materials and articles comply with this Directive or with any specific directives, no restrictions should be placed by Member States in the trade or use of such materials and articles.

(g) Amendments: By virtue of Article 8, any amendments to this Directive or to any specific directives to bring them into line must be adopted in accordance with the procedure laid down in Article 9, which involves consultation of the Standing Committee on Foodstuffs by the Commission.

(h) Implementation: Member States were to take measures to prohibit, from 21 December 1991, trade in and use of materials and articles not complying with this Directive.

There are no specific regulations implementing this Directive at present. However, there are regulations in place which deal with some of the specific directives envisaged under this Directive, for example:

(i) the Materials and Articles in Contact with Food Regulations 1987;[199]

(ii) the Food Safety Act 1990; and

(iii) the Food Safety (Exports) Regulations 1991.[200]

All Member States except Ireland have notified implementing measures.

3. Council Directive (EEC) 84/500 on the approximation of the laws of the Member States relating to the ceramic articles intended to come into contact with foodstuffs[201]

(a) Objective: Council Directive (EEC) 84/500 was adopted as a reflection of the varying provisions within the Community for protecting human health. The Directive is concerned with the limits for extractable quantities of lead and cadmium, both constituents of ceramic articles which, when in a finished state, are used in the preparation, cooking and storage of foodstuffs.

Whilst there is no disagreement amongst Member States that lead and cadmium are substances which can endanger human health in certain quantities and that there is a possibility they can migrate from finished

199 SI 1987/1523 (as amended by the Materials and Articles in Contact with Food (Amendment) Regulations 1987, SI 1994/979).
200 SI 1991/1476.
201 [1984] OJ L277/12.

ceramic articles and thereby contaminate food if in contact, the provisions relating to these substances vary from one Member State to another.

The Directive seeks therefore to approximate the laws of Member States relating to the extractable quantities of lead and cadmium in ceramic articles, thereby eliminating some of the obstacles to the establishment and functioning of the common market. It intends that the harmonisation of limits and test and analysis methods for such articles will lead to more uniformity in the type of ceramic articles being placed on the Community markets.

(b) Scope of application: The Directive applies to ceramic articles, ie, those which are manufactured from a mixture of inorganic materials with an argillaceous or silicate content to which small quantities of organic materials may have been added, which are then shaped and fixed before being glazed, enamelled or decorated.[1] It is only meant to cover those types of articles intended to come into contact with foodstuffs.

(c) Limits: The quantities of lead and cadmium transferred to ceramic articles must not exceed specific limits laid down in Article 2. The limits vary according to the capacity of the article and according to whether it is used for cooking. The limits for articles with lids are the same as those for the vessel alone.

It should be noted that where the limits for lead and cadmium in a ceramic article are exceeded, but only by no more than 50%, that article will still be regarded as having satisfied the requirements provided three other articles with the same shape, dimensions, decoration and glaze do not exceed the set limits.

(d) Test and analysis: The conditions and tests for ensuring that the levels of cadmium and lead do not exceed the limits set are laid down in Annex I and Annex II of the Directive. Annex I lays down the basic rules for determining the migration of lead and cadmium and Annex II sets out the accepted methods of analysis for making those determinations.

(e) Implementation: This Directive is implemented throughout the United Kingdom by the Ceramic Ware (Safety) Regulations 1988.[202] They are implemented under powers granted to the Secretary of State under the Consumer Protection Act 1987 following consultation with representative organisations with interests substantially affected by these regulations. Previous regulations relating to requirements for vitreous enamel-ware under the 1975 and 1976 regulations have been revoked.[203]

All Member States have notified implementing measures.

202 SI 1988/1647.

203 The Glazed Ceramic Ware (Safety) Regulations 1975, SI 1975/1241; the Glazed Ceramic Ware (Safety) Regulations (Northern Ireland) 1975, SR (NI) 1975/313; the Vitreous Enamel-Ware (Safety) Regulations 1976, SI 1976/454; and the Vitreous Enamel-Ware (Safety) Regulations (Northern Ireland) Regulations 1976, SR (NI) 1976/328.

(f) Follow-up work: It is proposed in Article 4 that further limits will be determined by the Council in relation to the migration of lead and cadmium from those areas or parts of ceramic articles intended to come into contact with the mouth. To date, no specific directive has been issued to deal with this aspect.

It was also contemplated, once more technological and toxicological data had been collected, that the limits set would be re-examined with a view to reducing them further. No new limits have been set.

4. Commission Directive (EC) 2002/72 relating to plastics materials and articles intended to come into contact with foodstuffs[204]

(a) Objective: The Directive aims to consolidate the provisions of Directive 90/128,[205] amended several times. It is concerned with the constituents of plastics materials and articles intended to come into contact with foodstuffs. Directive 90/128 was issued as a specific directive to achieve the objectives laid down in Council Directive (EEC) 89/109[206] whose general provisions also apply. This states that materials and articles, in their finished state, must not transfer their constituents to foodstuffs in quantities which could endanger human health or bring about an unacceptable change in the composition of the foodstuffs.

The Directive seeks to harmonise the laws of the Member States and ensure that the constituents of plastics materials and articles do not contaminate foodstuffs, thereby protecting consumer health.

(b) Scope: Article 1 lays down that articles and materials consisting exclusively of plastics or made up of two or more layers, each consisting exclusively of plastics and bound together with adhesives or some other way, and which in their finished state are intended to come into contact with foodstuffs are covered by the Directive. It also contains a description of plastics for the purposes of the Directive.

Certain materials are not to be regarded as plastics. These include varnished or unvarnished regenerated cellulose film, elastomers and natural and synthetic rubber, paper and paperboard whether modified or not by the addition of plastics, surface coatings obtained from paraffin waxes and mixtures, ion-exchange resins and silicones. Articles composed of layers which did not consist exclusively of plastics, even though the layer intended to come into contact with foodstuffs is plastic, are also excluded.

(c) General principles: The Directive establishes in the Annexes lists of approved substances and additives which, subject to restrictions, may be used in the manufacture of plastic materials and articles. This is accompanied by limits on overall migration so as to avoid any contamination. These limits are a

204 [2002] OJ L220/18.
205 [1990] OJ L75/19 (as amended). The text of this Directive has been replaced: see [1990] OJ L349/26.
206 Council Directive (EEC) 89/109 ([1989] OJ L40/38), Art 2.

measure of the inertness of the material and prevent an unacceptable change in the composition of the foodstuffs. Council Directive (EEC) 82/711[207] lays down the basic rules necessary for testing migration of the constituents of plastics materials and articles and Council Directive (EEC) 85/572[208] establishes the list of stimulants to be used in migration tests, both of which are applicable to this Directive. It also recognises that there are still areas of difficulty so that it is not yet possible to permit adoption of a complete list of authorised substances applicable to all types of plastics materials and articles, but that this will happen in due course. This does mean that substances currently used in some Member States can continue for the moment.

As this Directive relates to plastics, it is also subject to Council Directive (EEC) 78/142[209] laying down limits for the quantity of vinyl chloride present and the amount of this substance that may be released in such materials.

(d) Contamination limits: Article 2 sets down the migration limits permissible from the constituents of plastics to foodstuffs. Two different ways of assessing migration limits are set according to whether the articles are containers of specific capacity or of a type for which it is impracticable to estimate the surface area in contact with foodstuffs or are types of sealing devices.

Under Article 8, these migration limits must be verified in accordance with the provisions of Annex I and those rules specified in earlier directives dealing with the problem of contamination.[210] However, if it can be established that the articles comply with the limits set by Article 2, no further verification is required. Also, the verification of compliance is not compulsory if it can be established that, by assuming complete migration of any residual substance, the specific limit of migration is not exceeded.

The purpose of setting such overall limits is two-fold. First, to prevent contamination and therefore unacceptable changes in foodstuffs. Secondly, it reduces the need for many specific limits and still gives effective control.

Article 7 clarifies the units used in Annex II for specifying migration limits.

(e) Authorised substances: Under Article 3(1), only those monomers and other starting substances listed in Annex II, sections A and B may be used for the manufacture of plastics materials and articles subject to the restrictions specified. Annex II sets out in section A those authorised monomers and other starting substances which are authorised, while section B lists monomers and other starting substances which may continue to be used until December 2004, pending evaluation by the Scientific Committee on Food. Under Article 3(3), section A may be amended by adding substances listed in section B or by

207 [1982] OJ L297/26 (as amended).
208 [1985] OJ L372/14.
209 [1978] OJ L44/15.
210 Council Directive (EEC) 82/711 ([1982] OJ L297/26) (as amended) and Council Directive (EEC) 85/572 ([1985] OJ L372/14).

including new substances, but no new substances can be authorised excepted under the procedure in Article 4 of Council Directive (EEC) 89/109.[211]

Certain types of monomers and other starting substances listed in Article 3(5) are not yet included in the lists of Annex II.

Additives which may be used for the manufacture of plastic materials and restrictions to their use are, according to Article 4, listed in Annex III.

(f) Other matters: Under Article 9, at the marketing stage (except the retail stage), those plastics and articles intended to be placed in contact with foodstuffs must be accompanied by a suitable declaration.

The symbol that may accompany any material and article intended to come into contact with foodstuffs including plastics is determined under Commission Directive (EEC) 80/590.[212]

(g) Implementation by Member States: Member States are in the process of adapting their legislation to the new Directive.

At the time of writing, the following countries have already taken measures to implement the Directive: Belgium, Denmark, Finland, France, Greece, Spain, and the UK.

To implement the Directive, the UK has adopted the Plastic Materials and Articles in Contact with Food (Amendment) (England) Regulations 2002.[213]

5. Commission Directive (EEC) 93/10 relating to materials and articles made of regenerated cellulose film intended to come into contact with foodstuffs[214]

(a) Objective: This Directive is intended to replace Council Directive (EEC) 83/229[215] which was originally adopted in the light of the varying provisions within the Community for protecting public health but has since been changed many times.[216]

The Directive is issued as a specific directive by the Commission to achieve the objective laid down in Directive 89/109,[217] whose general provisions are also applicable, which states that materials and articles must not transfer their constituents to foodstuffs in quantities which could endanger human health or bring about an unacceptable change in the composition of the foodstuffs.[218]

The Directive seeks to approximate the laws of Member States relating to materials and articles made of regenerated cellulose film, and lays down,

211 [1989] OJ L40/38.
212 [1980] OL L151/21.
213 SI 2002/2364, amending the Plastic Materials and Articles in Contact with Food Regulations 1992, SI 1992/3145.
214 [1993] OJ L93/27.
215 [1983] OJ L123/31.
216 Directive 93/10 was amended by Commission Directive (EC) 93/111. This Directive amended the second sentence of Art 5(1) by prohibiting as from 1 January 1994 the trading and use of regenerated cellular film which did not comply with the Directive.
217 [1989] OJ L40/38.
218 See Directive 89/109, Art 2.

accompanied by limits to the quantities to be used, a list of approved substances, the purpose of which is to protect the health of the consumer.

(b) Scope of application: The Directive is concerned with the substances used in the manufacture of regenerated cellulose film and effectively consolidates Directive 83/229 and the subsequent amendments made to it.

The Directive is intended to cover regenerated cellulose film which is either a finished product itself or is part of a finished product intended to come into contact with foodstuffs. It is not designed to include regenerated cellulose film which has a suitable coating on the side intended to come into contact with foodstuffs or which are synthetic casings of regenerated cellulose.

Annex I describes regenerated cellulose film as thin sheet material obtained by refining cellulose derived from unrecycled wood or cotton. Suitable substances may be added in the mass or to the surface to meet technical requirements and it may be coated on one or both sides.

The use of substances as colouring matters or as adhesives used in the manufacture of regenerated cellulose film may continue, provided there is no possible migration of the substances into or onto foodstuffs detectable by a validated method. The method for determining the absence of migration is to be fixed at a later date. Until criteria of purity and methods of analysis have been drawn up, national provisions will remain in force. Likewise, synthetic castings of regenerated cellulose are to be the subject of specific provisions.

(c) General principles: The Directive establishes a list of approved substances and prohibits direct contact between printed regenerated cellulose film and foodstuffs. It also recognises that there are still some areas of difficulty, including the drawing up of criteria of purity and methods of analysis and the method for determining the absence of migration of colouring matters, which will require more input and consultation before provisions can be drawn up.

(d) Authorised substances: Annex II sets out the list of substances authorised in the manufacture of regenerated cellulose film. It includes the denominations of all authorised substances together with the restrictions imposed on each substance. Certain of the authorised substances are still subject to the restrictions laid down in national legislation pending the adoption of Community provisions.

It should be noted that substances not included in this Annex may be used when such substances are employed as colourings or adhesives provided there is no trace of migration into or onto foodstuffs, detectable by a method determined by an already established procedure.

(e) Other matters: The Directive prohibits direct contact between printed surfaces of regenerated cellulose film and foodstuffs. Article 4 requires a suitable written declaration to accompany all materials and articles made of regenerated cellulose film intended to come into contact with foodstuffs at the marketing stages but other than the retail stages for such products, unless that is their prime purpose. This written declaration must be in accordance with Article 6(5) of Council Directive (EEC) 89/109. If special conditions of use are indicated, the article or material must be labelled accordingly.

(f) Implementation: The Directive is implemented in England, Wales, Scotland and Northern Ireland by the Materials and Articles in Contact with Food Regulations 1987[219] as amended by the Materials and Articles in Contact with Food (Amendment) Regulations 1992.[220]

All Member States have notified implementing measures.

D. FOOD ADDITIVES

1. Introduction

Additives are substances which are neither normally consumed as food nor used as a characteristic ingredient, but which are added intentionally for a technological purpose in the course of manufacture, processing, preparation, treatment packaging or storage of food.

Divergence in national laws regulating food additives and the conditions for their use may hinder the free movement of foodstuffs and distort competition. Accordingly, Community action in this area has sought to harmonise national laws, taking into account of public health concerns.

Additives were meant to be dealt with in a comprehensive directive to be drawn up in stages. This, however, is yet to be done and at present a general framework for food additives is provided by Directive 89/107,[221] followed by a number of more specific measures within Directive 89/107 on sweeteners, colours, and additives which are not colours or sweeteners that contain more extensive lists of permitted additives.

These directives are based on the principle that only those additives that are explicitly authorised may be used. Most food additives may only be used in limited quantities in certain foodstuffs. If no quantitative limits are foreseen for the use of a food additive, it must be used according to good manufacturing practice, ie, only as much as necessary to achieve the desired technological effect.

Furthermore, all authorised food additives have to fulfil purity criteria which are set out in detail in three Commission directives.[222]

219 SI 1987/1523.

220 SI 1992/1927.

221 Directive 89/107 ([1989] OJ L40/27).

222 Commission Directive 95/31 (EC) laying down specific criteria of purity concerning sweeteners for use in foodstuffs (as amended) ([1995] OJ L178/1); Commission Directive 95/45 (EC) laying down specific purity criteria concerning colours for use in foodstuffs ([1995] OJ L226/1) (as amended); Commission Directive 96/77 (EC) laying down specific purity criteria on food additives other than colours and sweeteners ([1996] OJ L339/1).

Flavourings are excluded from the scope of Directive 89/107 and are regulated separately by Directive 88/388.[223]

2. Council Directive (EEC) 89/107 on the approximation of the laws of the Member States concerning food additives authorised for use in foodstuffs intended for human consumption[224]

(a) Objective: Differing national laws relating to food additives and the conditions for their use hinder the free movement of foodstuffs and may distort fair competition directly affecting the establishment of an effective common market. This Directive seeks to harmonise national laws to remove this problem but also to take account of public health matters.

(b) Scope of application: The Directive applies to food additives used or intended to be used as ingredients in the manufacture and preparation of foodstuffs and remaining present in the final product. The various categories of foodstuffs are given in Annex I.

Article 1(2) defines food additive as any substance not normally consumed as food in itself and not normally used as a characteristic ingredient of food and which is added intentionally for a technological purpose at any stage in manufacture, processing, preparation, treatment, packaging, storage and as a result becomes a component of food. There are, however, certain exceptions under Article 1(3) of the Directive including:

(i) processing aids;

(ii) substances conforming to Community rules on plant health and used to protect plants and plant products;

(iii) flavourings for use in foodstuffs covered by Council Directive (EEC) 88/3881;[225]

(iv) substances such as minerals and vitamins added to foodstuffs as nutrients.

(c) Authorised additives: Under Article 2, only those additives listed in Annex I may be used in the manufacture and preparation of food and only under the conditions of use specified. The basis for inclusion of any additive in one of the listed categories is its principal function and it is quite possible that a given additive may be authorised for several functions. The general criteria for inclusion on the list of authorised additives is set down in Annex II. These criteria include:

(i) demonstration of a reasonable technological need;

(ii) no health hazard to the consumer on the scientific evidence available;

(iii) no misleading of the consumer;

223 [1988] OJ L184/61.
224 [1989] OJ L40/27.
225 [1988] OJ L184/61.

(iv) evidence of benefit to the consumer, for example, by preserving the nutritional quality of food, enhancing the quality or stability of food or providing necessary ingredients for consumers with special dietary needs.

These criteria are designed to keep consumer health and safety matters in consideration and to allow for continuous evaluation.

Under Article 3, it was intended that particular provisions in respect of the additives in the categories listed in Annex I, in particular purity criteria, shall be laid down in a comprehensive directive which will include relevant specific directives. This comprehensive directive shall cover, once a proposal has been submitted to Council, the following:

(i) a list of authorised additives to the exclusion of all others;

(ii) a list of foodstuffs to which they can be added and the conditions under which they can be added;

(iii) other rules when additives are used as solvents or carrier substances, including where necessary purity criteria.

In the meantime, measures on purity criteria,[226] methods of analysis and sampling and any other relevant rules to ensure compliance will be adopted by the Commission acting on a qualified majority basis in accordance with the cooperation procedure laid down in Article 11.

Since its adoption, this Directive has been amended so that the rules for harmonisation in relation to food additives should not affect national provisions of Member States existing on 1 January 1992 which prohibit the use of certain additives in certain specific products considered as traditional in their territories and so that these products can be distinguished by appropriate labelling.[227] Member States will have to provide the Commission with a list of foodstuffs they consider traditional with their reasons, as well as their relevant legislative provisions for criteria to be drawn up to be applied in such cases for consideration by the Council.[228]

(d) Public health measures: Under Article 4, Member States may temporarily suspend or restrict the application of any provision in their territory if, as a result of new information, they have detailed grounds for considering that one additive may endanger human health even though it complies with this Directive or may comply with the comprehensive directive referred to in Article 3. In the event of such steps being taken by any Member

226 See Commission Directive 95/31 (EC) laying down specific criteria of purity concerning sweeteners for use in foodstuffs ([1995] OJ L178/1) (as amended); Commission Directive 95/45 (EC) laying down specific purity criteria concerning colours for use in foodstuffs ([1995] OJ L226/1 (as amended); Commission Directive 96/77 (EC) laying down specific purity criteria on food additives other than colours and sweeteners ([1996] OJ L339/1).

227 Parliament and Council Directive (EC) 94/34 ([1994] OJ L237/1) amending Council Directive (EEC) 89/107 by adding Art 3a.

228 Ibid.

State, the Commission must examine the grounds given so that appropriate measures can be taken, including amending this Directive or the comprehensive directive, to resolve the difficulties and protect human health.

In addition to these provisions in Article 4, Article 6 requires consultation with the Scientific Committee on Food before any general provisions which may have an effect upon public health are adopted.

(e) Scientific and technological developments: Under Article 5, Member States may provisionally authorise the marketing and use of an additive in one of the categories listed in Annex I provided that certain conditions are satisfied, including:

(i) authorisation for a limited period up to a maximum of two years;

(ii) monitoring of any foodstuffs containing the additive;

(iii) special indication that a foodstuff contains the additive.

Authorisation of any additives in such circumstances must be communicated to other Member States and to the Commission within two months. Any requests to have the additive included in the relevant list under this Directive must be made within two years and, in the light of such a request, the Commission, on the basis of the evidence provided, must decide whether to submit a proposal to the Council for adoption. If no proposal is submitted or if the Council does not act on any proposal, any authorisations for such an additive must be cancelled.

(f) Labelling: Under Article 7, food additives for use in manufacturing and not intended for sale to the ultimate consumer may be marketed only if their packaging or containers bear the following information in conspicuous, legible and indelible form:

(i) the name and EEC number of each additive, or a description enabling it to be identified in descending order of proportion by weight;

(ii) when other substances are incorporated into the additives, the name of the additive and an indication of each component in descending order of the proportion by weight;

(iii) a statement saying 'for use in food' or 'restricted use in food' or some other specific reference to intended use;

(iv) directions for use;

(v) an identifying batch or lot mark;

(vi) the name and address of manufacturer or packager or seller established in the Community;

(vii) indication of the percentage of any component which is subject to quantitative limits or adequate compositional information to enable a purchaser to comply with Community provisions;

(viii) the net quantity; and

(ix) any other information provided in the comprehensive directive referred to in Article 3.

Some of this information may appear only on the relevant documents, for example, batch marks, names and addresses, provided it is stated conspicuously on the package or container that it is intended for the manufacture of foodstuffs and not for retail sale.

Under Article 8, where the food additives are intended for sale to the ultimate consumer, any packaging or containers must bear in a form which is conspicuous, clearly legible and indelible the following information:

(i) all the information required for manufacture as stated in Article 7 with the exception of the indication of the percentage of any component subject to a quantitative limit;

(ii) the name under which the product is sold plus its EEC number or a description; or

(iii) its date of minimum durability as laid down in Council Directive (EEC) 79/112.[229]

By virtue of Article 9, the labelling requirements of Articles 7 and 8 are not intended to affect more detailed or extensive provisions relating to weights and measures or to affect the provisions on dangerous substances or their transport. There is no need for more detailed requirements than those contained in Articles 7 and 8, but any particulars on labelling must be in a language readily understood by the purchaser.

(g) Amendments: Article 11 lays down the procedure for adopting amendments to this Directive in the future. Draft measures are to be submitted to the Standing Committee on Foodstuffs for an opinion. Voting is by qualified majority and measures are adopted in accordance with the cooperation procedure. Any measures to bring existing Community directives into line with this Directive shall be adopted in accordance with this procedure.

(h) Member States' obligations: Article 12 places a general obligation on Member States to ensure that food additives may only be marketed if they conform to this Directive and its Annexes. Member States may not place restrictions on the marketing of food additives, food or food ingredients on grounds relating to additives if they comply except in the circumstances already mentioned in the Directive.

(i) Implementation: This Directive is addressed to all Member States, who should have taken measures to comply with this Directive by 21 June 1990. These measures should have included authorising the marketing and use of food additives complying with this Directive by 21 December 1990, and prohibiting the marketing and use of food additives not complying by 21 December 1991.

229 [1979] OJ L33/1 (as amended).

In the UK, the Directive was implemented by the Food Additives Labelling Regulations 1992[230] and the Miscellaneous Food Additives Regulations 1995.[231]

All Member States have notified implementing measures.

(j) Follow-up work: Commission Decision 2002/247(EC)[232] has recently suspended the placing on the market and import of jelly confectionery containing the food additive E 425 konjac.

3. Council Directive (EC) 94/35 on sweeteners for use in foodstuffs[233]

(a) Objective: This Directive should be considered in conjunction with Council Directive (EEC) 89/107 on the approximation of the laws of the Member States concerning food additives authorised for use in foodstuffs intended for human consumption.

The purpose of the Directive is to lay down harmonised rules on sweeteners and conditions for their use which protect and inform the consumer.

(b) Scope: The Directive on sweeteners does not affect rules relating to functions other than the sweetening properties of these substances. The rules laid down by this Directive apply when sweeteners are used to replace sugar in a wide range of products, including energy-reduced foods, those without added sugar, where sugar is replaced by sweeteners to extend shelf life and for dietetic products.

More specifically, under Article 1, the Directive applies to food additives used to impart sweet taste to foodstuffs or used as table-top sweeteners and referred to as 'sweeteners'. It does not apply to foodstuffs with their own sweetening properties. As a result of the amending Council Directive (EC) 96/83,[234] a provision was added to Article 1 that the Directive applied to corresponding foodstuffs used for particular nutritional purposes within the meaning of Council Directive (EEC) 89/398.[235]

Terms such as 'no added sugar' and 'energy-reduced' are used in the Annex to describe the kinds of foodstuffs in which sweeteners can be used and are defined for clarification in Article 1(3). By virtue of Articles 3 and 4, this Directive is not intended to apply to other specific directives permitting those additives listed in the Annex and used for purposes other than sweetening nor to other Community provisions governing the composition and description of foodstuffs.

230 SI 1992/1978.
231 SI 1995/3187.
232 [2002] OJ L84/69.
233 [1994] OJ L237/3 (as amended).
234 Parliament and Council Directive (EC) 96/83 ([1997] OJ L48/16).
235 Council Directive 89/398 on the approximation of the laws of the Member States relating to foodstuffs intended for particular nutritional uses ([1989] OJ L186/27).

(c) Authorised substances: According to Article 2(3) of Directive (EC) 94/35, as amended, sweeteners are forbidden in food for infants and young children as referred to in Council Directive (EEC) 89/398[236] including food for infants and young children who are not in good health.

In cases where the Annex to the Directive makes it clear that no maximum level of sweetener is specified, the Directive provides that sweeteners should be used in accordance with good manufacturing practice at a dose level not higher than necessary to achieve the purpose and on the strict undertaking that the consumer is not misled.

Article 2a permits the presence of sweeteners in compound foodstuffs with no added sugar or energy reduced, in compound dietary foodstuffs intended for low calorie diets and in compound foodstuffs with long shelf life, insofar as the sweetener is permitted in one of the ingredients of the compound foodstuff or if the foodstuff is intended to be used solely in preparation of a compound foodstuff.

(d) Labelling and descriptions for sweeteners: Under Article 5, and in order to comply with the terms of Directive 89/107, the sales description of a table top sweetener must include the term 'based table-top sweetener' using the name of the authorised substance. The labelling of table-top sweeteners containing polyols, and/or aspactame, must include suitable specified warnings.[237]

General provisions concerning the details which must appear on the labelling to make their presence clear and any other relevant warnings are, according to Article 6, to be adopted in accordance with the procedure laid down in Article 7.

(e) Procedure: The procedures to be adopted in relation to any measures relevant to this Directive is for draft measures to be submitted by the Commission to the Standing Committee on Foodstuffs for an opinion, decided by vote if necessary.[238] Each Member State shall have the right to have their position recorded. The Commission will then be under an obligation to take account of the opinion but no provisions are made for following the standard cooperation procedure.

(f) Monitoring systems: By virtue of the Directive, under the terms of Annex II of Directive 89/107 dealing with the general criteria for the use of food additives, Member States will be under an obligation to establish a system of consumer surveys to monitor consumption.[239] These surveys are to be used as a basis for a report on changes in the market, the level of use of sweeteners, and whether there is a need to restrict conditions of use including

236 [1989] OJ L186/27.

237 These are set out in Council Directive (EC) 96/83 ([1997] OJ L48/16), Art 5(2).

238 The Committee was set up by Council Decision 69/414 ([1969] OJ L291/9), now to be repealed by Parliament and Council Regulation 178/2002 ([2002] OJ L31/1).

239 Council Directive (EC) 94/36 ([1994] OJ L237/13), Art 6 and Council Directive (EC) 94/ 35 ([1994] OJ L237/3), Art 8.

warnings. If necessary, the report should be accompanied by proposals to amend this Directive. The time scale proposed for this is five years from notification of the Directive.

(g) Implementation: The Directive is implemented in the UK by the Sweeteners in Food Regulations 1995.[240]

All Member States except Germany and Greece have notified implementing measures.

4. European Parliament and Council Directive (EC) 95/2 on food additives other than colours and sweeteners[241]

(a) Objective: This Directive is for food additives other than colours and sweeteners and is a specific directive forming part of the more comprehensive Directive 89/197 applying to additives. The Directive seeks to approximate the laws between Member States and to remove conditions of unfair competition taking into account the need to protect the consumer.

(b) Scope: Article 1(1) provides that this Directive is to be a specific directive forming part of a comprehensive directive within the meaning of Article 3 of Council Directive (EEC) 89/107.[242] The Directive is not intended to affect rules relating to sweeteners and colours,[243] nor to enzymes other than those mentioned in the Annexes.

By virtue of Article 1(5) and following the application of Article 1 of Directive 89/107, certain substances are not considered as food additives. These are, for example, substances used for the treatment of drinking water and certain starches.

(c) General principles: Certain principles underpin the provisions laid down in the Directive. These include the following:

(i) that a food additive should only be used when there is evidence that its use provides an advantage for the consumer;

(ii) that unprocessed foodstuffs and certain others should be free from food additives.

Where additives may be used, the latest scientific and toxicological information is to be used to determine which substances are permitted and under what conditions. However, strict rules will need to be applied to their use, particularly in respect of infant formula and weaning foods.

Modifications and adaptations to the Directive whether relating to existing purity criteria on food additives (other than colours and sweeteners) or new specifications where no purity criteria exist will be adopted in accordance with procedures laid down in Directive 89/107.

240 SI 1995/3123.
241 [1995] OJ L61/1.
242 [1989] OJ L40/27.
243 These are covered in Council Directive (EC) 94/35 ([1994] OJ L237/3) and Council Directive (EC) 94/36 ([1994] OJ L237/13).

(d) Authorised substances: Under Article 2, only those substances listed in Annexes I,[244] III, IV[245] and V[246] may be used in foodstuffs for the purposes mentioned in Article 1(3) and (4). Food additives listed in Annex I are permitted, with the exception of the foods listed in Annex II, following the 'quantum satis' principle (ie, in accordance with good manufacturing practice, at a level no higher than it is necessary to achieve the intended purpose and provided they do not mislead the consumer). This, however, does not apply to unprocessed foods and honey, virgin oils, butter, pasteurised and sterilised milk and cream, mineral waters, coffee, unflavoured tea leaves, sugars, dry pasta, food for infants and young children.

Additives listed in Annex III and IV can only be used in the foodstuffs referred to in the Annexes and under the conditions there specified. Annex V lists those additives which may be used as permitted carriers or carrier solvents and their conditions of use.

(e) Permissible uses: Article 3 lays down the general circumstances where the presence of a food additive is permitted. This is generally not in unprocessed foods but:

(i) in compound foodstuffs to the extent that the additive is permitted in the separate ingredients making up the compound, and

(ii) if the foodstuff is intended to be used solely in the preparation of another foodstuff and to the extent that the compound foodstuff conforms to this Directive.

(f) Adaptation to progress: Articles 5 and 6 lay down the circumstances and the procedure when this Directive may need to be adapted to progress. Article 5 specifies that the procedure may need to be followed when any substance needs to be considered for authorisation or its criteria for use needs to be changed or whether it should be considered as an additive within the terms of this Directive. Article 6 describes the procedure that is to be followed. Where the measures envisaged are in accordance with the opinion of the Standing Committee for Foodstuffs, the Commission shall adopt them. Where the measures are not in accordance with the opinion of the Committee, or where no opinion is delivered, the Commission shall, without delay, submit to the Council a proposal relating to the measures to be taken. The Council shall act by a qualified majority. If the Council does not act within three months of referral, the proposed measures shall be adopted by the Commission.

(g) Monitoring: Under Article 7, Member States have three years to establish systems which will monitor the consumption and use of food additives and report their findings to the Commission. The Commission is under an obligation to report within five years to the European Parliament on

244 As amended by Parliament and Council Directive 96/85 ([1997] OJ L86/4) and, more recently, by Parliament and Council Directive (EC) 2001/5 ([2001] OJ L55/59).
245 As amended by Parliament and Council Directive (EC) 2001/5.
246 Ibid.

the changes which have taken place in the food additives market, their levels of use and consumption. The Commission is also under an obligation to review and propose modifications where necessary within five years.

(h) Implementation: This Directive is implemented in the United Kingdom by the Miscellaneous Food Additives Regulations 1995.[247]

All Member States except Belgium, France and Germany have notified implementing measures.

(i) Follow-up work: A proposal for a directive amending Directive (EC) 95/2[248] was adopted by the European Commission on 29 November 2002, with the aim of harmonising the regulations in the EU for additives necessary for the storage and use of flavourings. The proposal envisages the authorisation only of those additives which present no hazard to the health of consumers and which are strictly necessary for the storage and use of flavourings.

5. European Parliament and Council Directive (EC) 94/36 on colours for use in foodstuff[249]

(a) Objective: The Directive is a specific directive forming a part of the comprehensive directive within the meaning of Article 3 of Directive 89/107.[250]

It seeks to lay down uniform rules for the use of colours in foodstuffs, taking into account the need to protect and inform the consumer.

(b) Scope: The Directive applies to colours for use in foodstuffs. According to Article 1, 'colours' are substances which add or restore colour in a food, and include natural constituents of foodstuffs and natural sources which are normally not consumed as foodstuffs as such and are not normally used as characteristic ingredients of food.

Preparations obtained from foodstuffs and other natural source materials obtained by physical and/or chemical extraction resulting in a selective extraction of the pigments relative to the nutritive or aromatic constituents are colours within the meaning of this Directive.

The following substances shall not be considered colours for the purposes of this Directive:

(i) foodstuffs, whether dried or in concentrated form and flavourings incorporated during the manufacturing of compound foodstuffs, because of their aromatic, sapid or nutritive properties together with a secondary colouring effect, such as paprika, turmeric and saffron,

247 SI 1995/3187, as amended by the Miscellaneous Food Additives (Amendment) Regulations 1997, SI 1997/ 1413 to take account of amendments brought about by Council Directive (EC) 96/85.
248 COM(2002) 662 final.
249 [1994] OJ L237/13.
250 [1989] OJ L40/27.

(ii) colours used for the colouring of the inedible external parts of foodstuffs, such as cheese coatings and sausage casings.

(c) General principles: Certain principles underpin the provisions of the Directive. Those can be summed up as follows.

A food additive may only be used when there is evidence that it is technologically necessary and that its use is not harmful to health; what 'technologically necessary' means is not clear, but the Directive suggests that colours shall be used to restore the original appearance of food whose colour has been affected by processing, storage, packaging and distribution, to make food more visually appealing and to help identify flavours normally associated with particular foods and to give colour to food otherwise colourless.

Unprocessed foodstuffs and certain other basic foodstuffs should be free from food additives.

According to the most recent scientific and toxicological information on additives, some of these shall be permitted only for certain foodstuffs and under certain conditions of use.

(d) Authorised substances and permitted uses: The rules on the authorised substances and their permitted use are to be found in the Annexes to the Directive.

Only the substances listed in Annex I may be used as colours in foodstuffs. Some colours are permitted for certain uses only and are listed in Annex IV.

Colours may be used only in the foodstuffs listed in Annexes III, IV and V and under the conditions specified therein; colours may not be used in the foodstuffs listed in Annex II except where specifically provided for in Annex III, IV or V.

Under Article 3, the presence of a colour in a foodstuff is permissible:

(i) in a compound foodstuff other than one mentioned in Annex II to the extent that the colour is permitted in one of the ingredients of the compound foodstuff; or

(ii) if the foodstuff is destined to be used solely in the preparation of a compound foodstuff and to such an extent that the compound foodstuff conforms to the provisions of this Directive.

It may be decided by a procedure laid down in Article 5 whether a particular foodstuff belongs to a category of foods mentioned in the Annexes, and whether substances are colours within the meaning of Article 1.

(e) Maximum levels: The Annexes indicate maximum levels of quantities of colouring principle contained in the colouring preparation permitted in relation to ready-to-eat foodstuffs.

In the Annexes, 'quantum satis' means that no maximum level is specified. However, colouring matters shall be used according to good manufacturing practice at a level not higher than is necessary to achieve the intended purpose and provided that they do not mislead the consumer.

(f) Monitoring systems: Member States were obliged, within three years of the adoption of this Directive, to establish systems to monitor the consumption and use of colours and report their findings to the Commission. This report would be used by the Commission to report to the European Parliament on changes which have taken place in the colours market, the levels of use and consumption.

In accordance with the general criteria of point 4 of Annex II to Directive 89/197, within five years from the adoption of this Directive, the Commission was to review the conditions of use mentioned in this Directive, and propose modifications where necessary.

(g) Implementation: The measure was implemented in the UK by the Miscellaneous Food Additives Regulations 1995.[251]

All Member States except France and Germany have notified implementing measures.

6. Council Directive (EEC) 88/388 on the approximation of the laws of the Member States relating to flavourings for the use in foodstuff and to source material for their production[252]

(a) Objective: The Directive, as completed by Commission Directive 91/71,[253] seeks to approximate national laws relating to flavourings in order to enhance the free movement of foodstuffs and create conditions of equal competition, while taking into account human health requirements but also, within the limit required for the protection of health, economic and technical needs.

The Directive aims to provide a framework on general purity criteria, definitions, labelling, and the principles on the basis of which legal differences may subsequently be eliminated, while leaving it to the Council to adopt at a later stage appropriate provisions concerning individual categories of flavourings and source materials and any necessary measures concerning their use and methods of production.

(b) Scope: The Directive applies to 'flavourings' used or intended for use in or on foodstuffs to impart odour and/or taste, and to source materials used for the production of flavourings. 'Flavouring' is understood as including any flavouring substances, flavouring preparations, process flavourings, smoke flavourings or mixtures, as defined in Article 1.

The Directive does not apply to:

(i) edible substances and products intended to be consumed as such, with or without reconstitution,

(ii) substances which have exclusively a sweet, sour or salt taste,

(iii) material of vegetable or animal origin, having inherent flavouring properties, where they are not used as flavouring sources.

251 SI 1995/3187.
252 [1988] OJ L184/61.
253 [1991] OJ L42/25.

The Directive applies to flavouring intended for use in foodstuffs, and to foodstuffs, imported into the EU, but not to flavourings or foodstuffs intended for export outside the EU.

(c) General principles: Member States are under a duty to take all measures necessary to ensure that:

(i) flavourings do not contain any element or substance in a toxicologically dangerous quantity;

(ii) subject to any exceptions provided for in the specific criteria of purity referred to in Article 6 (2), third indent, they do not contain more than 3 mg/kg of arsenic, 10 mg/kg of lead, 1 mg/kg of cadmium and 1 mg/kg of mercury;

(iii) the use of flavourings does not result in the presence in foodstuffs as consumed of undesirable substances listed in Annex I in quantities greater than those specified therein;

(iv) the use of flavourings and of other food ingredients with flavouring properties does not result in the presence of substances listed in Annex II in quantities greater than those specified therein.

Under Article 8, however, should the use in a flavouring of a substance or material authorised on the basis of this Directive or provisions adopted at a later stage or the presence of one of the substances listed in Annex II appear to constitute a health risk, Member States should be authorised to suspend or limit such use, or to reduce the maximum limits provided, pending a decision at Community level

(d) Marketing of flavourings: Flavourings not intended for sale to the final consumer may not be marketed unless their packaging or container bear the information listed in Article 9, which should be easily visible, clearly legible and indelible. This includes the name or business name and address of the manufacturer or packer and the sales description.

Flavourings intended for sale to the final consumer may not be marketed unless their packaging or container bears the information listed in Article 9a.

(e) Implementation: The measure was implemented in the UK by the Flavourings in Food Regulations 1992.[254]

All Member States except Greece have notified implementing measures.

(f) Follow-up work: Parliament and Council Regulation (EC) 2232/96 sets out some more rules for the use of flavouring substances in or on foodstuffs in the EU. It furthermore lays down a procedure for the establishment of a EU-wide positive list of flavouring substances. After its establishment, foreseen by July 2005 at the latest, only those flavouring substances listed may be added to foods.

The flavouring substances authorised for use in foodstuffs at national level have been listed by the Commission in a register of about 2,700 substances.

254 SI 1992/1971.

These are now being evaluated by a Scientific Committee; this process, started in 2000, should be completed within 2005.

In 2002, the Commission also adopted a proposal for a Regulation on smoke flavourings used or intended for use in or on foods.[255] The objective of the proposal is to establish Community procedures for the safety assessment and the authorisation of smoke flavourings intended for use in or on foods.

E. SPECIFIC PRODUCTS

1. Introduction

This part aims to analyse the most significant product-specific legislation concerning both the content and the selling requirements for foodstuffs. Substances which are not strictly considered as 'food' (for example, additives and flavourings), as well as special products such as organic foodstuff and traditional products, are considered in other parts of this section. Other significant legislation, concerned only with labelling requirements, is also analysed elsewhere in this section.

Although legislation concerning meat is considered to be outside the scope of this section, since it mainly involves rules concerning the breeding, feeding and slaughtering of animals, the Directive on hormones is briefly discussed by reason of its importance in the international scene in the context of a WTO dispute, and the consequence that the latter may have on the safety of foodstuffs.

2. Council Directive (EEC) 89/108 on the approximation of the laws of the Member States relating to quick-frozen foodstuffs for human consumption[256]

(a) Objective: The manufacture and trade of quick-frozen foodstuffs intended for human consumption is assuming increasing importance in the Community for two reasons. First, the change in consumers' eating habits and lifestyles has increased demand for such foodstuffs. Secondly, increased demand for such products has implications in relation to problems of quality control, deterioration in the products and health hazards to humans.

The Directive aims to harmonise national laws relating to quick-frozen foods thereby eliminating unequal conditions of competition and improving the functioning of the common market. The Directive lays down the general principles which any quick-frozen food must satisfy. It is envisaged though, at some later stage, that additional provisions may need to be made for certain categories of quick-frozen food.

(b) Scope: The scope of the Directive is wide and intended to cover not just quick-frozen foods going directly to the ultimate consumer but also those

255 COM(2002)400 final.
256 [1989] OJ L40/34 (as amended).

supplied to restaurants, hospitals, canteens, other mass caterers and, in addition, those products that still need further processing or preparation.

Under Article 1(1), the Directive applies to all quick-frozen foodstuffs intended for human consumption. Quick-frozen foodstuffs means all those which have undergone a suitable freezing process known as 'quick- freezing' whereby the resulting temperature of the product is continuously maintained at a level of -18ºC or lower at all points in the foodstuff and is marketed as such. Ice cream and other edible ices are not regarded as quick-frozen foodstuffs.

(c) General principles: The general principles addressed by this Directive include:

(i) the requirement that all new materials are of sound, genuine and merchantable quality and fresh;

(ii) the requirement that the preparation and quick-freezing of products is carried out promptly using appropriate equipment to keep chemical, biochemical and microbiological changes to a minimum;

(iii) the need to maintain a minimum temperature, subject to certain technically inevitable tolerance, to suspend microbiological activity likely to impair the quality of a foodstuff during storage and distribution;

(iv) the need to set toleration levels for certain temperature increases for technical reasons provided no harm is done to the quality of the foodstuffs (such quality to be maintained by good storage and distribution practice).

The Directive recognises that certain technical equipment in use at present may make compliance with this Directive difficult and, therefore, provides for a transitional system allowing for existing equipment to be used for its normal lifetime. But to ensure that this Directive can be complied with, provision is made for Member States to make official checks on equipment in the hope that this will render the need for a system of official certification superfluous.

As well as laying down general principles and systems to check compliance, the Directive provides for the adoption of a list of substances and criteria for their purity and conditions for their use in relation to the possible use of cryogenic fluids in direct contact with foodstuffs. The main concerns in establishing and adopting such a list will be to ensure that such fluids do not import any of their constituents in quantities likely to be a health hazard to humans and that they do not give rise to unacceptable changes or impair the characteristics of such foodstuffs.

(d) Authorised substances: Under Article 4, certain cryogenic media are authorised, to the exclusion of all others, for use in direct contact with quick-frozen foodstuffs. These are:

(i) air;

(ii) nitrogen;

(iii) carbon dioxide.

Until 31 December 1992, provision was made for some derogation from this Article under the national laws of some Member States, but no longer. Purity criteria for such media are to be determined, so far as necessary, under the procedure in Article 12.

(e) Temperature maintenance: Article 5 sets down the provisions for the correct maintenance of temperature levels and any toleration limits. Generally, the temperature must be maintained as stable at -18ºC or lower at all points in the product but upward fluctuations of up to 3ºC are permitted during transport.

Tolerances permitted during local distribution and in retail display cabinets should not exceed 3ºC but may reach 6ºC in retail display cabinets if Member States permit this. The temperature tolerance permitted by the Member State must be notified to the Commission, together with the grounds for this measure. These tolerances are subject to review by the Commission and, in any event, for a period of eight years from 21 December 1988, Member States may authorise tolerances of up to 6ºC for local distribution. These transitional arrangements are designed to allow Member States to comply with this Directive while technical equipment may still need improving.

(f) Member States' obligations: Under Article 6, Member States must ensure that equipment used for quick freezing, storage, transport, local distribution and retail display cabinets is such that compliance can be guaranteed. In addition, Member States must conduct random official checks on the temperature of quick-frozen foodstuffs.

(g) Packaging: Article 7 requires that all quick-frozen foodstuffs intended for supply to the ultimate consumer are packed in suitable pre-packaging which protects against microbiological or other forms of external contamination and against drying.

(h) Labelling: The labelling rules laid down by Parliament and Council Directive (EC) 2000/13[257] are applicable to quick-frozen foodstuffs but there may be a need to lay down particulars specific to quick-frozen foodstuffs or which are applicable to those not intended for the ultimate consumer or restaurants, hospitals, canteens and other mass caterers. The task of implementing any such measures of a technical nature is to be left to the Commission and implemented in accordance with the cooperation procedure established between the Commission and Member States.

Certain additional requirements are also laid down in Articles 2 and 8(1)(a), including provisions for special sales names and description, the period during which quick-frozen foodstuffs may be stored by the purchaser, and the storage temperature and/or the type of equipment required. The labelling must include a batch reference and a message stating, 'do not refreeze after defrosting'.

257 Consolidating and repealing Council Directive 79/112 ([1979] OJ L33/1).

Under Article 9, though, products which are to be further processed or prepared need only contain the mandatory particulars listed in that Article, which must appear on the packaging, wrapping or label. Provided any quick-frozen foodstuff complies with this Directive under Article 10, Member States may not prohibit or restrict its marketing for a reason related to its labelling.

(i) Sampling procedures: By virtue of Article 11, sampling procedures for monitoring the temperature in quick-frozen foodstuffs and in the means of transport, warehousing and storage may all be determined in accordance with the procedure laid down in Article 12. Under Article 12, all measures proposed by the Commission are to go to the Standing Committee on Foodstuffs for an opinion which will be delivered by qualified majority. The measures may then be adopted in accordance with the cooperation procedure established between Member States and the Commission.

Sampling procedures are now laid down in Commission Directive (EEC) 92/2.[258]

(j) Implementation: This Directive is implemented in the United Kingdom by the Quick-frozen Foodstuffs Regulations 1990.[259]

All Member States except Italy have notified implementing measures.

3. Council Directive (EC) 2001/112[260] relating to fruit juices and certain similar products intended for human consumption

(a) Objective: Council Directive (EEC) 75/726[261] was issued to approximate the laws of the Member States governing fruit juices and other similar products. Council Directive (EEC) 93/77[262] was adopted to consolidate the amendments made to Council Directive (EEC) 75/726 thereby rationalising and clarifying it. Directive 2001/112 now seeks to make the rules on manufacturing and marketing conditions for fruit juices and certain similar products more accessible and to bring in line Directive 93/77 with general Community legislation on foodstuffs, particularly legislation on labelling, colouring matter, sweeteners and other authorised additives.

(b) Scope: Article 1 of the Directive, by reference to Annex I, Part 1, defines the range of products it is intended to cover, including fruit juice, fruit juice from concentrate, dried and concentrated fruit juice, fruit nectar. Annex I also defines the characteristics of each of those products.

(c) Authorised substances, ingredients and treatments: Article 2 authorises the addition of vitamins and minerals within certain limits; other substances, ingredients and certain treatments are allowed in accordance with the rules laid down in Annex I, Part 2.

258 [1992] OJ L34/30.
259 SI 1990/2615.
260 [2002] OJ L10/58.
261 [1975] OJ L311/40, repealed by Council Directive 93/77.
262 [1993] OJ L244/23.

(d) Labelling: In principle, the labelling requirements of Directive 2000/13[263] apply to the products defined in Annex I, subject to the condition that the product names, listed in Annex I, are used in trade to designate them. Annex III provides a list of alternative names to the product names referred to in Annex I.

The main additional labelling requirements are as follows:

(1) For products manufactured from two or more fruits (except where lemon juice is used) the product names shall be supplemented by a list of the fruits used, in descending order of the volume of the fruit juices or purées included. However, in the case of products manufactured from three or more fruits, the indication of the fruits used may be replaced by the words 'several fruits' or a similar wording, or by the number of fruits used.

(2) For fruit juices which have been sweetened by the addition of sugars, the sales name shall include the word 'sweetened' or 'with added sugar', followed by an indication of the maximum quantity of sugar added, calculated as dry matter and expressed in grams per litre.

(3) For mixtures of fruit juice and fruit juice from concentrate, and for fruit nectar obtained entirely or partly from one or more concentrated products, the labelling shall bear the words 'made with concentrate(s)' or 'partially made with concentrate(s)', as appropriate. That information shall be entered close to the product name, standing out well from any background, in clearly visible characters.

(4) For fruit nectars, the labelling shall indicate the minimum content of fruit juice, fruit purée or any mixture of those ingredients, by the declaration 'fruit content: ... % minimum'. That information shall be located in the same field of vision as the product name.

(e) Member States' obligations: Under Article 10, it is the responsibility of Member States to authorise the marketing of the products that comply with the Directive and to prohibit the marketing of products that do not. However, the marketing of products that do not comply with the Directive may continue until stocks run out.

(f) Further measures: Measures which are necessary for the implementation of the Directive shall be adopted by the Commission assisted by the Standing Committee on Foodstuffs in accordance with the procedure laid down in Article 8(2).

(g) Implementation: Member States are under a duty to bring into force the necessary implementing measures before 12 July 2003.

At the time of writing, Sweden, the Netherlands, Luxembourg, Ireland, Greece and Finland have notified implementing measures.

263 [2000] OJ L109/29.

4. Council Directive (EC) 2001/113[264] relating to fruit jams, jellies and marmalades and sweetened chestnut puree intended for human consumption

(a) Objective: Council Directive (EEC) 79/693[265] was first adopted to approximate the laws of the Member States governing fruit jams, jellies and marmalades and chestnut puree. Directive 2001/113 now seeks to make the rules on manufacturing and marketing conditions for such products more accessible and to bring them in line with general Community legislation on foodstuffs, particularly Directive 2000/13.[266]

(b) Scope of application: Article 1 of the Directive, by reference to Annex I, defines the range of products it is intended to cover as well as their characteristics. The Directive applies to products such as jams, extra jams, jellies, marmalades, sweetened chestnut puree, but does not apply to products intended for manufacture in fine bakery wares, pastries or biscuits.

(c) Labelling: Article 2 establishes that Directive 2000/13 applies to the products covered in Annex I. The product names listed in Annex I apply only to the products referred to therein and shall be used in trade to designate them. The product names used in Annex I may, however, be used in addition to the name and in accordance with practices used to designate other products which cannot be confused with those defined in Annex I.

Additional requirements imposed by the Directive include, for example:

(i) a duty to indicate the fruit or fruits used, in descending order of weight of the raw materials used. However, for products manufactured from three or more fruits, the indication of the fruits used may be replaced by the words 'mixed fruit' or a similar wording, or by the number of fruits used;

(ii) a duty to indicate the fruit content by including the words 'prepared with ... g of fruit per 100 g' of the finished product;

(iii) a duty to indicate the total sugar content and other relevant detailed information on the sugar content.

(d) Ingredients: Only the additional ingredients listed in Annex II and raw materials which comply with this Annex can be used in the manufacture of products covered by the Directive.

(e) Member States' obligations: Under Article 8, it is the responsibility of Member States to authorise the marketing of the products that comply with the Directive and to prohibit the marketing of products that do not. However, the marketing of products that do not comply with the Directive may continue until stocks run out.

264 [2002] OJ L10/67.
265 [1979] OJ L205/5.
266 [2000] OJ L109/29.

(f) Further measures: Measures which are necessary for the implementation of the Directive shall be adopted by the Commission assisted by the Standing Committee on Foodstuffs in accordance with the procedure laid down in Article 6(2).

(g) Implementation: Member States are under a duty to bring into force the necessary implementing measures before 12 July 2003.

At the time of writing, Sweden, the Netherlands, Luxembourg, Greece and Finland have notified implementing measures.

5. Council Directive (EC) 2001/111[267] relating to certain sugars intended for human consumption

(a) Objective: Directive 73/473[268] harmonised laws concerning certain sugars intended for human consumption by setting out composition characteristics of the various sugars and setting out rules for their labelling and packing. Directive 2001/111 now seeks to make the rules on manufacturing and marketing conditions for such products more accessible and to bring them in line with general Community legislation on foodstuffs, particularly Directive 2000/13.[269]

(b) Scope of application: The Directive applies to the products defined in Part A of the Annex but does not apply to icing sugars, candy sugars, and sugars in loaf form.

(c) Labelling: Article 2 establishes that Directive 2000/13 applies to the products covered in Part A of the Annex. The product names listed in Part A of the Annex apply only to the products referred to therein and shall be used in trade to designate them. The product names used in the Annex may, however, be used to designate other products in accordance with custom provided this is not misleading.

Additional labelling requirements are listed in points (3), (4), (5) of Article 2.

(d) Member States' obligations: Under Article 7, it is the responsibility of Member States to authorise the marketing of the products that comply with the Directive and to prohibit the marketing of products that do not. However, the marketing of products that do not comply with the Directive may continue until stocks run out.

(e) Further measures: Measures which are necessary for the implementation of the Directive shall be adopted by the Commission assisted by the Standing Committee on Foodstuffs in accordance with the procedure laid down in Article 5(2).

(f) Implementation: Member States are under a duty to bring into force the necessary implementing measures before 12 July 2003.

267 [2002] OJ L10/53.
268 [1973] OJ L356/71.
269 [2000] OJ L109/29.

At the time of writing, Denmark, Greece, Sweden, the Netherlands, Luxembourg and Finland have notified implementing measures.

6. Council Directive (EC) 2001/110[270] relating to honey

(a) Objective: Council Directive (EEC) 74/409[271] harmonised the laws of the Member States relating to honey. Directive 2001/110 now seeks to recast such a Directive to make rules on the conditions for the production and marketing of honey more accessible and to bring them in line with general Community legislation on foodstuffs, particularly Directive 2000/13.[272]

(b) Scope of application: The Directive applies to the different types of honey listed in Annex I. These types of honey must comply with the composition criteria for honey set out in Annex II.

(c) Labelling: Article 2 makes Directive 2000/13 applicable to honey products subject to the condition that the term 'honey' is applied only to the product defined in Annex I and is used in trade to designate that product.

Most honey products (those defined in points (2) and (3) of Annex I) can be traded under the simple name 'honey', except in the case of filtered honey, comb honey, chunk honey or cut comb in honey and baker's honey. Special provisions are made for filtered honey and baker's honey.

More importantly, it is compulsory to indicate on the label the country or countries of origin where the honey has been harvested. However, if the honey originates in more than one Member State or third country, that indication may be replaced with one of the following, as appropriate: 'blend of EC honeys', or 'blend of non-EC honeys', or 'blend of EC and non-EC honeys'.

(d) Member States' obligations: Under Article 9, it is the responsibility of Member States to authorise the marketing of the products that comply with the Directive and to prohibit the marketing of the product that do not. However, the marketing of products that do not comply with the Directive may continue until stocks run out.

(e) Further measures: The Commission may adopt methods to permit verification of compliance of honey with the provisions of this Directive. These methods shall be adopted adopted by the Commission assisted by the Standing Committee on Foodstuffs in accordance with the procedure laid down in Article 7(2). Until the adoption of such methods, Member States shall, whenever possible, use internationally recognised validated methods such as

270 [2002] OJ L10/53.
271 [1974] OJ L221/10 (as amended).
272 [2000] OJ L109/29.

those approved by Codex Alimentarius to verify compliance with the provisions of this Directive.[273]

Any other measures which are necessary for the implementation of the Directive shall be adopted by the Commission assisted by the Standing Committee on Foodstuffs in accordance with the procedure laid down in Article 7(2).

(f) Implementation: Member States are under a duty to bring into force the necessary implementing measures before 1 August 2003.

At the time of writing, Greece, Sweden and Finland have notified implementing measures.

7. Council Directive (EC) 2001/114 relating to certain partly or wholly dehydrated preserved milk for human consumption[274]

(a) Objective: Council Directive 76/118[275] attempted to approximate as a first stage some of the laws relating to partly or wholly dehydrated preserved milk. Directive 2001/114 now seeks to recast such a Directive to make rules on the conditions for the production and marketing of honey more accessible and to bring them in line with general Community legislation on foodstuffs, particularly Directive 2000/13.[276]

(b) Scope of application: This Directive shall apply to partly or wholly dehydrated preserved milk as defined in Annex I.

(c) Authorised substances: Member States may authorise the addition of vitamins to the products defined in Annex I.

(d) Labelling: Directive (EC) 2000/13 applies to the products defined in Annex I, subject to the condition that the product names listed in Annex I apply only to the products referred to therein and are used in trade to designate them. As an alternative to the product names referred to in subparagraph (a), Annex II provides a list of particular designations.

Additional requirements impose that:

(i) the labelling states, near the trade name, the percentage of milk fat, expressed by weight in relation to the finished product, subject to certain exceptions.

(ii) in the case of totally dehydrated milk, the label states the recommendations as to the method of dilution or reconstitution, including details of the fat content of the product thus diluted or reconstituted.

273 The Codex Alimentarius was set up in the 1960s as a joint instrument of the United Nations Food and Agriculture Organisation and the World Health Organisation to develop food safety standards which serve as a reference for international food trade. It lays down, inter alia, maximum limits for additives, contaminants, pesticides residues and veterinary drugs.

274 [2002] OJ L15/19.

275 [1976] OJ L24/49.

276 [2000] OJ L109/29.

(iii) where products weighing less than 20g per unit are packed in an outer packaging, the particulars required by this Article appear on the outer packaging only, subject to some exceptions.

(iv) the labelling of totally dehydrated milk states that the product is 'not intended as a food for infants under 12 months'.

(e) Member States' obligations: Member States are precluded from adopting national provisions not provided for by this Directive for the products listed in Annexes I and II.

(f) Further measures: Measures which are necessary for the implementation of the Directive shall be adopted by the Commission assisted by the Standing Committee on Foodstuffs in accordance with the procedure laid down in Article 6(2).

(g) Implementation: Member States are under a duty to bring into force the necessary implementing measures before 17 July 2003.

At the time of writing, Greece, Sweden and Finland and the Netherlands have notified implementing measures.

8. Parliament and Council Directive (EC) 2000/36[277] on cocoa and chocolate products intended for human consumption

(a) Objective: Directive 73/241[278] was the first measure to approximate Member States' legislation relating to cocoa and chocolate. The Directive was amended on a number of occasions and finally replaced by Directive 2000/36 to take account of technological progress and changes in consumer tastes and to take into account general Community legislation on foodstuffs, in particular legislation on labelling, sweeteners and other authorised additives, flavourings, extraction solvents and methods of analysis.

In practice, in the name of free movement, the Directive waters down the 'purity' requirements for cocoa products imposed by certain States by allowing that a percentage of vegetable fat other than cocoa butter is used in chocolate products in all Member States.

(b) Scope: The Directive applies to the cocoa and chocolate products intended for human consumption, as defined in Annex I to the Directive, including:

(i) cocoa butter;

(ii) cocoa and powdered chocolate, including reduced-fat or non-fat;

(iii) chocolate, milk chocolate (including family chocolate), white chocolate, filled chocolate, 'chocolate a la taza' and chocolates or pralines.

(c) General requirements: The Directive defines the composition requirements of the products referred to in Annex I. So, for example, 'chocolate' designates the product obtained from cocoa products and sugars

277 [2000] OJ L197/19.
278 [1973] OJ L228/23.

which contains no less than 35% total dry cocoa solids, including no less than 18% cocoa butter and no less than 14% of dry non-fat cocoa solids.

The minimum contents of the products are calculated either after deduction of flavourings, additional edible matter and/or filling, or according to the total weight of the finished product, as appropriate.

In addition, Article 2 allows that chocolate, milk chocolates (including plain chocolate), white chocolate, as well as 'chocolate a la taza', may contain:

(i) up to 5% vegetable fat other than cocoa butter. The permitted vegetable fats, as well as the characteristics these must have, are listed in Annex II;

(ii) up to 40% of other edible substances. However, this excludes animal fats and preparations not exclusively derived from milk, as well as flour or starch (except 'chocolate a la taza');

(iii) flavourings that do not imitate the natural flavour of chocolate or of milk fat. This provision also applies to cocoas and powdered chocolates.

(d) Labelling: Cocoa and chocolate products must be labelled in accordance with Council Directive 79/112.[279] The sale names listed in Annex I shall apply and can only be used to designate products that comply with Annex I. In exceptional cases, these sale names may be used for other products that cannot be confused with those defined in this Directive in the country of sale.

A few additional requirements are imposed on certain products:

(i) chocolate products containing vegetable fats other than cocoa butter must bear on their label the conspicuous and clearly legible statement 'contains vegetable fat in addition to cocoa butter'. This statement shall be in the same field of vision as the list of ingredients, clearly separated from that list, in letters at least as large and in bold with the sales name nearby (Article 2(2));

(ii) powdered chocolate, of sweetened cocoas, chocolate, milk chocolate, family milk chocolate, chocolate a la taza and chocolate familiar a la taza must indicate in their label the total dry cocoa solids content (Article 3(3)). In addition, the labelling of non-fat and reduced-fat cocoas and powdered chocolate must indicate the cocoa butter content (Article 3(4));

(iii) the sale names for chocolate, white and filled milk chocolates, and chocolates or pralines may be replaced by the sale name 'assorted chocolates' or 'assorted filled chocolates' when sold as assortments. Article 3(2));

(iv) the sale names 'chocolate', 'milk chocolate' and 'couverture' may, in certain cases, be supplemented by descriptions relating to quality criteria (higher cocoa and milk content) (Article 3(5)).

279 Now repealed by Parliament and Council Directive 2000/13 ([2000] OJ L109/29).

(e) Member States' obligations: Member States are precluded from adopting national provisions not provided for by this Directive for the products listed in Annex I.

Under Article 8, it is the responsibility of Member States to authorise the marketing of the products that comply with the Directive and to prohibit the marketing of products that do not. However, the marketing of products that do not comply with the Directive may continue until stocks run out.

(f) Further measures: Measures which are necessary for the implementation of the Directive shall be adopted by the Commission assisted by the Standing Committee on Foodstuffs in accordance with the procedure laid down in Article 6(2).

(g) Implementation: Member States are under a duty to bring into force the necessary implementing measures before 3 August 2003.

To date, Denmark, Finland, Greece, Ireland, Sweden and the Netherlands have notified implementing measures.

(h) ECJ case law: Two interesting cases[280] have arisen in relation to the Directive formerly harmonising laws relating to cocoa and chocolate products. Directive 73/241 allowed Member States to maintain domestic measures authorising or prohibiting the addition of vegetable fats other than cocoa butter to chocolate products. According to Italian law, any food preparation containing cocoa whose texture, consistency, colour and taste are similar to those of chocolate, but to which vegetable fact had been added, had to be marketed as 'chocolate substitute'; similarly, such products could not be marketed in Spain under the name 'chocolate'. The ECJ held, in both cases, that the Italian and the Spanish rules constituted measures having equivalent effect to a quantitative restriction under Article 28 (ex 30) and could not be justified by an overriding requirement relating to consumer protection, since measures existed which were less restrictive of the free movement of cocoa and chocolate products to ensure the protection of consumer interests (such as appropriate labelling).

The judgments raise the issue of the delicate balance between the requirement that measures taken by Member States to protect consumer satisfy the requirement of proportionality and the concern that consumers may not be effectively protected against lower quality products by simple labelling.

9. Parliament and Council Directive 99/4 (EC)[281] on coffee and chicory extracts

(a) Objective: A Directive of 1977[282] laid down rulesconcerning coffee and chicory extracts with regard to the composition of these products and the

280 Case C-14/00 Commission v Italy [2003] ECR I-513; Case C-12/00 Commission v Spain [2003] ECR I-459.
281 [1999] OJ L66/26.
282 Directive 1977/436 ([1977] OJ L172/20).

substances which may be used in their manufacture, their packaging materials and their labelling and the conditions on which specific designations may be used for certain products.

Directive 99/4 aims to simplify and repeal the older Directive.

(b) Scope of application: The Directive applies to the products described in the Annex, ie, 'coffee extracts', 'soluble coffee extracts', 'soluble coffee' or 'instant coffee', with the exception of 'café torrefacto soluble', as well as to 'chicory extracts', 'soluble chicory' or 'instant chicory', which, having been obtained by extraction, using water, from roasted coffee beans or chicory, comply with coffee or chicory based dry matter content requirements and the minimum composition requirements defined in the Annex.

(c) Labelling: Coffee and chicory extracts must be labelled in conformity with the provisions set out in Directive 79/112[283] on the labelling, presentation and advertising of foodstuffs. However, only the descriptions set out in the Annex ('coffee extracts', 'soluble coffee extracts', etc), possibly accompanied by information concerning the form ('paste', 'liquid', 'concentrated', etc), any added substances ('preserved with', 'roasted with', etc), as well as caffeine content ('decaffeinated', etc) of these products may be used. An indication of the minimum coffee or chicory based dry matter content as a percentage by weight of the finished product is also obligatory.

(d) Member States' obligations: Member States are precluded from adopting national provisions not provided for by this Directive for the products listed in Annex I.

Under Article 8, it is the responsibility of Member States to authorise the marketing of the products that comply with the Directive and to prohibit the marketing of products that do not. However, the marketing of products that do not comply with the Directive may continue until stocks run out.

(e) Further measures: Measures which are necessary for the implementation of the Directive shall be adopted by the Commission assisted by the Standing Committee on Foodstuffs in accordance with the procedure laid down in Article 5.

The procedure has been followed by the Commission to adopt Directive (EC) 2001/54[284] repealing Directive (EEC) 79/1066[285] laying down Community methods of analysis for testing coffee extracts and chicory extracts.

(f) Implementation: Member States are under a duty to bring into force the necessary implementing measures before 13 September 2000.

283 [1979] OJ L33/1, now repealed by Parliament and Council Directive 2000/13 ([2000] OJ L109/29).
284 [2001] OJ L191/42.
285 [1979] OJ L327/17.
286 SI 2001/1440.

The Directive was implemented in England by the Coffee Extracts and Chicory Extracts (Wales) Regulations 2001.[286]

All Member States except Germany have notified implementing measures.

10. Hormones in meat: Council Directive (EC) 96/22 concerning the prohibition on the use in livestock farming of certain substances having a hormonal or thyrostatic action and of beta-agonists[287]

(a) The Directive: Since 1988, the EC bans the use of certain hormonal substances to enhance animal growth. The ban, lastly embedded in Directive 96/22, concerned the placing on the market and administering of substances having hormonal effects or beta-antagonist effects to farm or aquaculture animals. Some specific substances were authorised subject to certain conditions and other were authorised for well-defined therapeutic purposes in certain categories of bovine animals and pets.

All Member States had notified implementing measures. In the UK, the Directive was implemented by the Animals and Animal Products (Examination for Residues and Maximum Residue Limits) Regulations 1997;[288] the Medicines (Stilbenes and Thyrostatic Substances Prohibition) Revocation Order 1997;[289] and the Medicines (Control of Substances for Manufacture) Order 1997.[290]

(b) The WTO dispute: The US and Canada had long been contesting such measures and in March 1996 held formal consultations with the EC in the framework of the WTO dispute settlement mechanism regarding EC legislation prohibiting six type of hormones all approved for use in the United States.

In May 1996, the WTO Dispute Settlement Body established a panel to hear the case in response to a US request. Canada later brought a parallel action to challenge the EC ban, and the same panelists were assigned to hear the Canadian case.

The US challenge was based primarily on arguments that the EC import ban breached provisions of the WTO Agreement on the Application of Sanitary and Phytosanitary Measures ('the SPS Agreement'), which requires that food safety measures applied by governments to protect human life and health must in fact be for that purpose and not for protectionist purposes, and must be based on scientific evidence.

In August 1997, the panels ruled against the lawfulness of the ban,[291] but on appeal by the EC the WTO Appellate Body reversed two of three findings of

286 SI 2001/1440.
287 [1996] OJ L125/3.
288 SI 1997/1729.
289 SI 1997/1727.
290 SI 1997/1728.
291 Report of 18 August 1997, WT/DS26/R/USA, WT/DS48/R/C.

the panels.[292] The WTO Appellate Body only upheld the finding that prohibition of imports of meat from hormone-treated animals to the EU did not comply with the requirement that such a measure should be based on a relevant assessment of the risks to human health. In reaction to these findings, the EC carried out a several complementary risk assessments and mandated the Scientific Committee on Veterinary measures relating to Public Health (SCVPH) to evaluate the risks to human health from hormone residues in bovine meat and meat products treated with six hormones for growth promotion. The SCVPH concluded in 1999, in 2000 and again in 2002 that no acceptable daily intake could be established for any of the six hormones evaluated. For oestradiol 17ß it concluded that there is a substantial body of evidence suggesting that oestradiol 17ß has to be considered as a complete carcinogen and that the data available would not allow a quantitative estimate of the risk.

(c) Post-WTO: In the light of the opinion of the SCVPH, the Commission has adopted a proposal for a Directive[293] to ban the use of oestradiol 17ß and its ester-derivaties and to maintain provisionally the prohibition of all other substances having an oestrogenic, gestagenic or androgenic effect until further scientific information is available.

Meanwhile, due to the EC inability to comply with the WTO's recommendation to review its measure, a WTO arbitrator[294] awarded the US and Canada nullification and impairment suspension of concessions to the amount of US$116.8 million per year to the US and of Can$11.3 million per year to Canada.

F. NOVEL FOODS AND GENETICALLY MODIFIED ORGANISMS (GMOs)

1. Introduction

The Novel Foods Regulation 258/97 came into force on 15 May 1997.[295] It relates specifically to new ingredients and novel foods, ie, ingredients that have not been previously used for human consumption to a significant degree within the EU. The instrument, which is directly applicable in all Member States, addresses the concern of consumers over the safety of food products and deals with the issue of labelling.

The Novel Foods Regulation also covers products derived from genetically modified organisms (GMOs), such as pasta from a GMO. GMOs and GMMs (genetically modified micro-organisms) are organisms the genetic material

292 Report of 16 January 1998, WT/DS48/AB/R, WT/DS26/AB/R.
293 Amended Proposal for a Directive of the Parliament and of the Council amending Council Directive (EC) 96/22 concerning the prohibition on the use in stockfarming of certain substances having a hormonal or thyrostatic action and of beta-agonists, COM(2001)131 final.
294 Report of 12 August1999, WT/DS26/ARB.
295 Council Regulation (EC) 258/97 ([1997] OJ L43/1).

(DNA) of which has been modified in a way that does not occur naturally by mating or natural recombination.

It is a matter of fact that the existence and availability on the market of genetically modified products is a cause of serious concern for consumers in the light of the currently unknown consequences that these may have, in the long term, on human health.

It is therefore important that the release on the market of such products is strictly regulated and that consumers should receive adequate information on whether products on the market consist of or contain GMOs.

The legislative framework for GMOs is currently provided by Directive 2001/18[296] authorising experimental release and placing on the market of GMOs and by Regulation 258/97 in relation to labelling. As yet, no Community legislation is in place concerning GMOs in animal feed.

A detailed analysis of the legislation concerning novel food and GMOs is outside the scope of this work; this chapter can, however, provide a brief overview of the information which is essential from the point of view of consumer protection.

2. Parliament and Council Regulation 258/97 concerning novel foods and novel food ingredients

(a) Objective: The Regulation seeks to harmonise national laws relating to novel foods or food ingredients that may otherwise hinder the free movement of foodstuffs and create conditions of unfair competition. The Regulation also aims to protect public health by ensuring that novel foods and novel food ingredients are subject to a single safety assessment through a Community procedure before they are placed on the market within the Community.

(b) Scope of application: Under Article 1, the Regulation applies to a wide range of novel foods and ingredients which have not hitherto been used for human consumption to a significant degree within the Community, including, more significantly, foods and food ingredients containing or consisting of genetically modified organisms or produced from, but not containing, genetically modified organisms; foods and food ingredients with a new or intentionally modified primary molecular structure; foods and food ingredients consisting of or isolated from micro-organisms, fungi or algae; foods and food ingredients consisting of or isolated from plants; and food ingredients isolated from animals.

Where necessary, it may be determined in accordance with the procedure laid down in Article 13 whether a type of food or food ingredient falls within the scope of the Regulation.

The Regulation does not apply to food additives, flavouring and extraction solvents as long as those are regulated elsewhere.

296 [2001] OJ L106/1, repealing Directive 90/220 ([1990] OJ L117/15) as from 17 October 2002.

(c) General principles: Foods and food ingredients falling within the scope of this Regulation must not:

(i) present a danger for the consumer,

(ii) mislead the consumer,

(iii) differ from foods or food ingredients which they are intended to replace to such an extent that their normal consumption would be nutritionally disadvantageous for the consumer.

(d) Placing on the market of a novel ingredient or food: Whoever is responsible for placing on the market a novel food or ingredient must follow the procedure set out in Articles 4, 6, 7 and 8 by submitting an application in accordance with Commission Recommendation (EC) 97/618.[297]

A simplified procedure is also provided for in the case of novel foods and novel food ingredients which are substantially equivalent to existing foods or food ingredients.

(e) Labelling: According to Article 8, additional specific labelling requirements shall apply to novel foodstuff beyond the usual labelling requirements. Those include an indication of :

(i) any characteristic or food property, such as composition, nutritional value or nutritional effects, or intended use of the food, which renders a novel food or food ingredient no longer equivalent to an existing food or food ingredient.

(ii) the presence in the novel food or food ingredient of material which is not present in an existing equivalent foodstuff and which may have implications for the health of certain sections of the population;

(iii) the presence in the novel food or food ingredient of material which is not present in an existing equivalent foodstuff and which gives rise to ethical concerns;

(iv) the presence of an organism genetically modified by techniques of genetic modification.

In the absence of an existing equivalent food or food ingredient, appropriate provisions shall be adopted where necessary in order to ensure that consumers are adequately informed of the nature of the food or food ingredient.

While labelling of GMOs is covered by the Regulation, labelling of GM soy and maize varieties is covered by Regulation 1139/98.[298]

(f) Further measures: Any detailed rules for implementing the Regulation shall be adopted by the Commission with the assistance of the Standing

297 [1997] OJ L253/1.
298 [1998] OJ L159/4 (as amended). Additionally, GM additives and GM flavours have to be labelled according to Regulation 50/2000 on the labelling of foodstuffs and food ingredients containing additives and flavourings that have been genetically modified or have been produced from genetically modified organisms ([2000] OJ L6/15).

Committee for Foodstuffs in accordance with the procedure laid down in Article 13.

(g) Follow-up work: Under Article 14, no later than five years from the date of entry into force of the Regulation and in the light of experience gained, the Commission shall forward to the European Parliament and to the Council a report on the implementation of this Regulation accompanied, where appropriate, by any suitable proposal. Notwithstanding this review, the Commission shall monitor the application of this Regulation and its impact on health, consumer protection, consumer information and the functioning of the internal market and, if necessary, bring forward proposals at the earliest possible date.

3. Parliament and Council Directive 2001/18(EC) on the deliberate release into the environment of genetically modified organisms

(a) Objective: Directive 2001/18 puts in place a step-by-step approval procedure on a case-by-case assessment of the risks to human health and environment before any GMOs are released into the environment and the market.

(b) Scope of application: The Directive applies to genetically modified organisms, ie, organisms, with the exception of human beings, in which the genetic material has been altered in a way that does not occur naturally by mating and/or natural recombination. The Directive shall not apply to organisms obtained through the techniques of genetic modification listed in Annex I B , nor does it apply to the carriage of genetically modified organisms by rail, road, inland waterway, sea or air.

As already mentioned, labelling requirements are dealt with by Regulation 258/97.

(c) Traceability: The Directive requires that Member States ensure traceability at all stages of the placing on the market of GMOs.

(d) Authorisation: This Directive is based on the principle that an independent scientific assessment in respect of impact on human, animal and plant health and the environment should be carried out before any GMO is approved for marketing. Companies intending to market GMOs or foods derived from GMOs in the EU must submit an application to a Member State including a full environmental risk assessment in the case of GMOs or a safety assessment in the case of GM foods. The assessment is sent to the European Commission which circulates it to all other Member States. In case of objections, the European Commission seeks an opinion from the relevant Scientific Committee (the European Food Safety Authority in the future) and then takes a decision.

Up to 29 October 2001, under the previous similar procedure foreseen in Directive (EEC) 90/220, 18 GMOs were authorised. From October 1998 until October 2001, no further authorisations were granted under Directive (EEC)

90/220 and, as of 29 October 2001, 12 applications for authorisation are pending.

(e) The WTO dispute: Failure to deliver any further authorisations in the last few years has resulted in a request by Argentina, Canada and the US for the establishment of a WTO Panel to assess whether the EC's de facto 'moratorium' contravenes the Agreement on Sanitary and Phytosanitary Measures ('the SPS Agreement'), the General Agreement on Tariffs and Trade 1994 ('GATT 1994'), the Agreement on Agriculture ('the Agriculture Agreement'), and the Agreement on Technical Barriers to Trade ('the TBT Agreement'). The request was put forward on 8 August 2003.[299]

(f) Further legislative initiatives: The Commission adopted on 25 July 2001 two further legislative proposals concerning GMOs aimed at setting up a Community system for the traceability, aimed at improving the current system of labelling and authorisation of GMOs, and at introducing rules on GMO feed.[300]

G. DIETETIC FOODS AND FOOD SUPPLEMENTS

1. Introduction

Foodstuffs intended to satisfy particular nutritional requirements of specific groups of the population are so-called 'dietetic foods' or 'dietary foods'. Examples of dietetic foods are foods for infants and young children, foods for weight reducing diets or foods for special medical purposes.

Food supplements, on the other hand, are concentrated sources of nutrients or other substances with a nutritional or physiological effect whose purpose is to supplement the intake of nutrients in the normal diet. They are being increasingly used within the Community and are marketed in 'dose' form, ie, as pills, tablets, capsules, liquids in measured doses, etc.

In both areas, the Community has taken action in order to ensure harmonisation while at the same time maintaining a high level of human health protection by prescribing rules for the composition, marketing and labelling of such products.

2. Council Directive (EEC) 89/398[301] on the approximation of the laws of the Member States relating to foodstuffs intended for particular nutritional uses

(a) Definition: Directive 89/398 harmonises laws relating to foodstuffs for particular nutritional uses by setting out a framework of rules for the

299 DS293 (Argentina); DS 292 (Canada); DS 291 (US).

300 Commission Proposal for a Regulation on traceability and labelling of GMOs and products produced from GMOs, COM(2001)182 final; Commission proposal for a Regulation on GM food and feed, COM(2001)425 final.

301 [1989] OJ L186/23, amended by Council Directive (EC) 96/84 ([1997] OJ L48/20) and by Parliament and Council Directive 1999/41 ([1999] OJ L172/38).

composition, marketing and labelling requirements of dietetic foods. This Directive repeals and replaces Directive 77/94.[302]

(b) Scope of application: 'Dietetic' or 'dietary' does not have the same accepted meaning in all Member States. The Directive lays down in Annex I lists of groups of dietary foods for which specific rules shall be set out by Commission directives. In principle, the products covered by Directive 89/398 are according to Article 1 thus foodstuffs, the composition and preparation of which must be specially designed to meet the particular nutritional requirements of the persons for whom they are mainly intended. A particular nutritional use must fulfil the particular nutritional requirements of certain categories of persons whose digestive processes or metabolism are disturbed or of certain categories of persons who are in a special physiological condition or of infants or young children in good health.

(c) Labelling: In the labelling, presentation and advertising of foodstuffs for normal consumption the following shall be prohibited:

(i) the use of the adjectives 'dietetic' or 'dietary' either alone or in conjunction with other words, to designate these foodstuffs;

(ii) all other markings or any presentation likely to give the impression that one of the products referred to in Article 1 is involved.

Labelling or advertising must not attribute properties for the prevention, treatment or cure of human disease to such products or imply such properties. Particulars must appear on the labels of the products, including the available energy value. Committee procedure was to be used to establish sampling procedures and methods of analysis, and the EC Council acting unanimously on a proposal from the EC Commission was to lay down the purity criteria. The labelling requirements of Directive 79/112[303] also apply.

(d) Composition: The nature or composition of 'dietetic' products must be such that the products are appropriate for the particular nutritional use intended. These products must also comply with any mandatory provisions applicable to foodstuffs for normal consumption, save as regards changes made to them to ensure their conformity with the definitions given in Article 1.

The specific provisions applicable to the groups of foods for particular nutritional uses appearing in Annex I are laid down by means of specific directives. At present, specific directives have been adopted for specific dietary food groups:

(i) food for infants and young children[304] (infant formulae and follow-on formulae; processed cereal-based foods and baby foods);

302 [1997] OJ L26/55.
303 [1979] OJ L327/17, now repealed by Parliament and Council Directive 2000/13 ([2000] OJ L109/29).
304 Commission Directive 91/321 ([1991] OJ L175/35).

(ii) foods intended for use in energy-restricted diets for weight reduction;[305]

(iii) food for special medical purposes.[306]

(e) New foodstuffs: Article 4 of the 1989 Directive, as amended, allows foodstuffs resulting from scientific progress to be placed on the market rapidly. The amendment allows the Commission, after consulting the Scientific Committee for Food and in accordance with the procedures laid down in Article 13, to authorise for a two-year period the placing on the market of foodstuffs which do not comply with the rules as to composition laid down by the specific directives referred to in Annex I. If necessary, the Commission may also add in the authorisation labelling rules relating to the change in the composition.

(f) Implementation: All Member States except the UK have notified implementing measures.

3. Parliament and Council Directive (EC) 2002/46 on the approximation of the laws of Member States relating to food supplements[307]

(a) Objective: An adequate and varied diet provides, under normal circumstances, all necessary nutrients for normal development and maintenance of a healthy life in adequate quantities. Consumers, however, because of their particular lifestyles or for other reasons, increasingly choose to supplement their intake of some nutrients through food supplements.

As a consequence, an increasing number of products containing concentrated sources of nutrients and presented for supplementing the intake of nutrients are marketed in the EU. Those products are regulated in Member States by differing national rules that may impede their free movement, create unequal conditions of competition, and thus have a direct impact on the functioning of the internal market.

In order to facilitate free movement and to ensure a high level of protection for consumers, Directive 2002/46 was adopted. This seeks to ensure that common rules on the safety and labelling of food supplements are in place within the Community.

(b) Scope of application: This Directive concerns food supplements, as defined in Article 2, marketed as foodstuffs and presented as such. These products shall be delivered to the ultimate consumer only in a pre-packaged form.

In particular, the Directive lays down specific rules for vitamins and minerals used as ingredients of food supplements. Food supplements containing vitamins or minerals as well as other ingredients should also be in

305 Commission Directive 96/8 ([1996] OJ L55/22).
306 Commission Directive 1999/21 ([1999] OJ L91/29).
307 [2002] OJ L183/51.

conformity with the specific rules on vitamins and minerals laid down in the Directive.

Specific rules concerning nutrients other than vitamins and minerals or other substances with a nutritional or physiological effect used as ingredients of food supplements will be laid down at a later stage, provided that adequate and appropriate scientific data about them become available. Until such specific Community rules are adopted and without prejudice to the provisions of the EC Treaty, national rules concerning nutrients or other substances with nutritional or physiological effect used as ingredients of food supplements, for which no Community specific rules have been adopted, may be applicable.

The Directive does not apply to medicinal products as defined by Directive (EC) 2001/83.[308]

(c) Manufacture of food supplements: Only vitamins and minerals listed in Annex I, in the forms listed in Annex II, can be used for the manufacture of food supplements. Purity criteria for the substances listed in Annex II are to be adopted in accordance with the procedure referred to in Article 13(2). For those substances listed in Annex II for which purity criteria are not specified by Community legislation, and until such specifications are adopted, generally acceptable purity criteria recommended by international bodies shall be applicable and national rules setting stricter purity criteria may be maintained.

Until 31 December 2009, Member States may allow in their territory the use of vitamins and minerals not listed in Annex I, or in forms not listed in Annex II, provided that the substance in question is used in one or more food supplements marketed in the EU on the date of entry into force of this Directive and the European Food Safety Authority has not given an unfavourable opinion in respect of the use of that substance.

Modifications to the lists referred to in paragraph 1 shall be adopted in accordance with the procedure referred to in Article 13(2).

(d) Maximum amounts: Maximum amounts of vitamins and minerals present in food supplements per daily portion of consumption as recommended by the manufacturer shall be set, taking into account:

(i) upper safe levels of vitamins and minerals established by scientific risk assessment based on generally accepted scientific data, taking into account, as appropriate, the varying degrees of sensitivity of different consumer groups;

(ii) intake of vitamins and minerals from other dietary sources.

To ensure that significant amounts of vitamins and minerals are present in food supplements, minimum amounts per daily portion of consumption as recommended by the manufacturer shall be set, as appropriate.

308 [2001] OJ L311/67.

(e) Labelling In principle, rules laid down by Directive (EC) 2000/13 apply. The name under which products covered by this Directive should be sold is 'food supplement'.

In addition, the labelling shall bear the particulars listed in Article 6(3).

The labelling, presentation and advertising must not attribute to food supplements the property of preventing, treating or curing a human disease, or refer to such properties; nor shall it include any mention stating or implying that a balanced and varied diet cannot provide appropriate quantities of nutrients in general.

The amount of the nutrients or substances with a nutritional or physiological effect present in the product shall be declared on the labelling in numerical form. The units to be used for vitamins and minerals shall be those specified in Annex I. The amounts of the nutrients or other substances declared shall be those per portion of the product as recommended for daily consumption on the labelling.

(f) Further measures: Purity criteria, modifications to the Annexes, maximum and minimum amounts of vitamins and minerals, more detailed rules concerning labelling and any other implementing measure shall be adopted by the Commission assisted by the Standing Committee on the Food Chain and Animal Health[309] in accordance with the procedure referred to in Article 13(2).

(g) Member States' obligations: Member States shall not, for reasons related to their composition, manufacturing specifications, presentation or labelling, prohibit or restrict trade in products which comply with the Directive.

However, where a Member State, as a result of new information or of a reassessment of existing information made since this Directive or since one of the implementing Community acts was adopted, has detailed grounds for establishing that a product endangers human health though it complies with the Directive, that Member State may temporarily suspend or restrict application of the provisions in question within its territory and inform the other Member States and the Commission.

The Commission shall examine the case and consult the Member States within the Standing Committee on the Food Chain and Animal Health, then deliver its opinion without delay and take appropriate measures.

(h) Implementation: Member States must implement the Directive by 31 July 2003. To date, Denmark, the Netherlands and Sweden have notified implementing measures.

309 See Regulation 178/2002 ([2002] OJ L31/1).

H. ORGANIC FOOD

1. Introduction

Organic food is meeting increasing success with European consumers. The raising awareness of environmental and food safety issues has resulted in wider and wider interest in products grown or in animals bred in accordance with sustainable farming and breeding systems. Organic farming is one of the fastest growing agricultural sectors throughout Europe, with a yearly growth rate between 25% and 30%.

EC rules to regulate the labelling, processing and marketing of organic products have been in place since 1992. Although these are, strictly speaking, part of the Community's agricultural policy since they concern farming and breeding methods and inspections, they are also relevant to this section to the extent that they include labelling rules aimed to ensure that organic products offered to consumers meet the requirements of organic methods of farming and breeding.

2. Council Regulation 2092/91 on organic production of agricultural products and indications referring thereto on agricultural products and foodstuffs[310]

(a) Objective and scope of application: The Regulation sets out the legal framework for the production and marketing of organic products. Since its scope was widened by Regulation (EC) 1804/1999,[311] it applies to non-processed crop, livestock products, animal products and animal feed. Genetically modified organisms (GMOs) and products derived from GMOs are explicitly excluded from organic production methods.

Most of the provisions of the Regulation, apart from those on labelling and advertising, are outside the scope of this work. Suffice here to say that Article 2 defines in each language the term considered the most characteristic to describe the products covered by the Regulation (such as 'organic' in English, 'biologique' in French, 'ecológico' in Spanish).

Regulation 2092/91 does not preclude the application of the general Community rules on conventional agriculture, production, preparation, labelling, marketing[312] and inspection that apply to all agricultural products.

(b) Labelling and advertising: Labelling and advertising may refer to organic production methods only where they make it clear that the information relates to a method of agricultural production that complies with the Regulation. According to Article 5, the operator must be subject to the inspection measures laid down in the Regulation and the name/code of the inspecting authority must be indicated.

310 [1991] OJ L198/1 (as amended).
311 [1999] OJ L222/1.
312 Such as, for example, Council Directive 48/450 on misleading advertising ([1984] OJ L50/17).

A product may be described and advertised as organic when it contains at least 95% of the ingredients from organic agricultural origin. The remaining 5% may be produced by conventional methods only where those ingredients are not available or are in very short supply in the EU. Products with an organic content of 70% to 95% may not be labelled as organic, although reference to the organic production methods of certain ingredients can be made in the list of ingredients. Where the organic content of a product is below 70%, no reference to organic production methods is allowed.

A particular indication is available for organic production methods which have been undergoing conversion to organic methods for at least 12 months (this may take from two to three years); such products may bear the words 'product under conversion to organic farming'.

In March 2000, the European Commission introduced a logo bearing the words 'Organic Farming – EC Control System'[313] to be used on a voluntary basis by producers whose systems and products have been found on inspection to satisfy EC requirements. In particular, products bearing this logo fulfil the following conditions:

(i) at least 95% of the product's ingredients have been organically produced;

(ii) the product complies with the rules of the official inspection scheme;

(iii) the product has come directly from the producer or preparer in a sealed package;

(iv) the product bears the name of the producer, the preparer or vendor and the name or code of the inspection body.

I. TRADITIONAL PRODUCTS

1. Introduction

In several European countries, such as France, Italy, Spain and Germany, there is a great deal of interest in the legal protection of products which, having gained an international reputation, often find themselves in competition with products which, being of inferior quality, pass themselves off as the genuine article by taking the same name. This has been the case, for example, with regard to Roquefort and Parmigiano cheeses and Parma and Bayonne hams.

The Council has therefore adopted legislation that aims to offer legal protection, to various degrees, to products which are produced and/or processed and/or prepared in a given geographical area using recognised know-how, or that fulfil certain characteristics traditionally associated with a certain trade name. The relevant provisions are contained in Regulation

313 Commission Regulation 331/2000 ([2000] OJ L48/1).

2081/92[314] on the protection of geographical indications and designations of origin for agricultural products and in Regulation 2082/92 on certificates of specific character for agricultural products and foodstuffs.[315]

2. Council Regulation 2081/92 on the protection of geographical indications and designations of origin for agricultural products and foodstuffs

(a) Objective: Regulation 2081/92 offers protection against the misuse of geographical denominations by manufacturers that are not established in the geographical area to which the name of the product refers. The Regulation distinguishes between Protected Geographical Indications (PGIs) and Protected Designations of Origin (PDIs). Stricter conditions apply to the latter category concerning the connection between the product and the region of origin. To gain protection, a denomination must be registered. Registered PGIs and PDOs are legally protected against any misuse or false or misleading indication.

(b) Scope of application: The Regulation applies to the foodstuffs specified in Annex I to the Regulation, to the agricultural products, whether or not processed, listed in Annex II to the Regulation and to all agricultural products intended for human consumption referred to in Annex II to the Treaty. These include, for example, fresh meat and meat based products, fish, cheeses, oils and fats, products of animal origin such as eggs and honey, beers, bread and pastries, fruits and vegetables, natural mineral waters and spring waters. Wines and spirit drinks are excluded. The Annexes to the Regulation may be amended by Commission with the assistance of a committee composed by the representatives of the Member States and chaired by the representative of the Commission.

(c) Products that qualify for PGIs and PDOs: To qualify for a PGI or PDO designation, a product must comply with a specification containing the following: the name and description of the product; the definition of the geographical area; the methods of preparation; factors relating to the geographic environment; the inspection bodies; details of labelling and any legislative requirements that must be met.

Under Article 2.2(a) , to qualify for a PDO, the quality or characteristics of a product must be essentially or exclusively due to a particular geographic environment (including both the natural and human factor) and the production, processing and preparation which take place in the geographical area defined. The conditions to qualify for a PGI are less stringent (Article 2.2(b)): it is sufficient that a product originates from the region after which the product is named and that a specific quality, reputation or characteristic is attributable to that geographic origin and the production and/or processing and/or preparation that takes place in that geographic area.

314 [1992] OJ L208/1.
315 [1992] OJ L208/9.

In *Consorzio del Prosciutto di Parma e Salumificio Santa Rita v Asda Stores Ltd*[316] the ECJ ruled that Regulation 2081/92 does not preclude the use of a protected designation of origin from being subject to the condition that operations such as the slicing and packaging of the product take place in the region of production, where such a condition is laid down in the specification. Where the use of the protected designation of origin 'Prosciutto di Parma' for ham marketed in slices is made subject to the condition that slicing and packaging operations be carried out in the region of production, this constitutes a measure having equivalent effect to a quantitative restriction on exports within the meaning of Article 29 of the EC Treaty, but may be regarded as justified, and hence compatible with that provision.

(d) Registration: To gain protection, a denomination must be inserted in a register kept by the Commission in accordance with the procedure set out in Articles 4 to 7. An application for a registration (together with a 'product specification' containing a description of the product) can be sent by any group of producers to the Member State in which the geographical area of that product is located. After checking the application, the Member State sends it to the Commission and to the other Member States. Six months after the application has been published on the Official Journal, the denomination is entered in the register provided that no objections are notified. In the latter case, the Commission examines the objection and takes a decision.

A simplified procedure was in place to allow Member States to register names established by usage which they wished to register pursuant to the Regulation within six moths from its entry into force (Article 17).

An inspection body is charged with checking whether products comply with the criteria described in the denomination.

Under Article 3, names that have become generic cannot be registered.[317]

3. Council Regulation 2082/92 on certificates of specific character for agricultural products and foodstuffs

(a) Objective: This regulation aims to provide protection for products bearing the denominations Traditional Speciality Guaranteed (TSG).

Like Regulation 2081/92, this Regulation aims to provide protection against any practice liable to mislead the public. Unlike Regulation 2081/92, however, this Regulation does not refer to the origin of the product but highlights traditional character, either in the composition or means of production. Because of the much less stringent requirements imposed to register TSG denominations, this type of registration is much less sought after. Products that enjoy this type of protection are, for example, 'jamon serrano' and 'mozzarella'.

316 Case C-108/01 [2003] 2 CMLR 21.

317 That was the issue in the 'Feta' case. In Cases C-289/96, C-293/96 and C-299/96 Denmark, Germany and France v Commission [1999] ECR-I 1541 these countries successfully sought the annulment of the provision including the denomination 'Feta' in the PDOs on grounds that the name had become generic.

(b) Scope: The Regulation applies to agricultural products listed in Annex II to the Treaty and intended for human consumption and foodstuffs listed in the Annex to the Regulation.

(c) Products that qualify and registration: To qualify for a TSG denomination, a product must present a feature or set of features which distinguish it clearly from other similar products or foodstuffs belonging to the same category. In other words, a product must either be produced using traditional raw materials or be characterised by a traditional composition or a mode of production and/or processing reflecting a traditional type of production and/or processing.

The presentation of an agricultural product or a foodstuff is not regarded as a feature within the meaning of the first sub-paragraph.

The procedure for the registration of TSG denominations is similar to the one set out in Regulation 2081/92.

5
WATER

1. Introduction

Community measures relating to water have as much to do with the Community programme of action for the environment as they have to do with consumer protection and safety issues. As the measures taken by the Community are essentially to do with providing requirements necessary for the protection of public health, they are considered appropriate for comment within the context of general consumer safety. The measures adopted by the Community reflect the desire to set standards throughout Member States by harmonising provisions in this area and can be regarded, therefore, as an integral part of the functioning of the internal market.

Implementation by Member States of the Community directives on water has been slow and inadequate. This was felt to be due to a number of factors such as practical and technical difficulties in achieving objectives arising from insufficient public investment, poor consultative procedures resulting in low levels of support for Community legislation and lack of public knowledge of requirements and procedures to remedy contravention.

However, in the last 20 years there has been a shift in public awareness of such issues with concern being expressed more and more often on health hazards related both to toxic chemical substances and to harmful bacteria in bathing as well as water for human consumption. Certain factors which give rise to pollution have merited particular attention in recent years. The corrosion of lead piping, laid down often in the last century, in various regions of the EU has given rise to the risk of excessive concentrations of lead in drinking water which research has shown can have particularly harmful effects on some sections of the population in the EU, notably babies, young children and pregnant women. The increased use of chemicals and artificial fertilisers in agricultural activities as well as the problems of disposal of chemical waste and effluent in industrial activities have all underlined the need to set quality standards for bathing and drinking water.

The main directives setting quality standards in this area are Council Directive (EEC) 80/778[318] on drinking water and Council Directive (EEC) 76/160[319] on bathing water. Frustration at the lack of progress being made by Member States on implementation of these Directives except when threatened with legal action has led to resolutions being passed requiring the Commission

318 [1980] OJ L229/11 (as amended). As of 25 December 2003, Directive 80/778 will be repealed and replaced by Council Directive 98/83 on the quality of water intended for human consumption ([1998] OJ L330/320).

319 [1976] OJ L31/1 (as amended).

to take further steps in this area.[320] One such step taken has been the introduction of a requirement to report on progress at regular intervals so as to rationalise and improve on a sectoral basis those provisions dealing with the transmission of information. It must be noted that it is in relation to quality standards for water that the Commission has been forced to take the most legal action through the European Court of Justice against Member States.

2. Council Directive (EEC) 80/778[321] relating to the quality of water intended for human consumption

(a) Objective: The intention of this Directive is to lay down quality standards with which water for human consumption must comply in view of its importance for public health. By setting standards throughout the Community it aims to approximate the laws in this sphere. It was hoped that the approximation of such laws would be accompanied by wider Community action to achieve one of its aims of the improvement of living standards.

Standards are laid down in this Directive by setting values for certain parameters relevant to water for human consumption, including softened water. These values are intended to be taken by Member States as 'guide levels'.

In addition, this Directive provides for rules to be drawn up governing the use of certain substances used in preparing water for human consumption in order to avoid possible harmful effects on public health due to excessive concentrations or quantities of such substances. To ensure standards are met, regular monitoring is provided for in this Directive as well as a procedure for speedy adaptation to technical progress.

Certain specific measures have already been taken in relation to laying down standards for surface water intended for the abstraction of drinking water[322] and for natural mineral waters.[323]

(b) Scope of application: The Directive applies to water intended for human consumption, ie, all water intended for that purpose either in its original state or after treatment whether supplied for consumption or used in a food production undertaking and affecting the wholesomeness of food in its finished form.

Under Article 4, the Directive does not apply to natural mineral water,[324] recognised or defined as such, nor to medicinal waters also so recognised.

320 See, eg, Resolution of 10 March1988 on lead in drinking water ([1998] OJ C94/158); Resolution of 10 March1988 on the implementation of European Community legislation relating to water ([1988] OJ C94/155).

321 [1980] OJ L229/11.

322 See Council Directive (EEC) 75/440 ([1975] OJ L194/26) (as amended).

323 Council Directive (EEC) 80/777 ([1980] OJ L229/1) (as amended).

324 Regulated by Directive 80/777 on the approximation of laws relating to the exploitation and marketing of natural mineral waters ([1980] OJ L229/1).

(c) Quality standards: Annex I sets out the values fixed for different parameters. Under Article 3, values for toxic and microbiological parameters are listed for the competent national authorities of Member States to apply when considering whether water is likely to affect the wholesomeness of foodstuff in its finished form. Under Article 6, Member States are to send to the Commission national values for parameters other than those mentioned above and other appropriate information about industrial sectors in which national authorities consider the wholesomeness of finished foodstuffs is unaffected by the quality of water used. The information obtained is to be used to consider any measures and to draw up a report periodically.

Under Article 7, it is up to Member States to fix values applicable to water for human consumption for the parameters shown in Annex I. The values fixed must be less than or the same as those values shown for maximum admissible concentrations. Guide levels are given. For softened water, the values must not be lower than those giving the minimum required concentration where water is supplied for consumption.[325]

(d) Member States' obligations: Under Article 4(2), Member States are under an obligation to take the necessary steps to ensure that water for human consumption does at least meet the requirements specified in Annex I. Where the quality of water meets the requirements of this Directive, Member States may not restrict the marketing of foodstuffs on grounds of water quality unless there is a hazard to public health.

Under Article 8, Member States are obliged to take measures to ensure that any substances used in the preparation of water for human consumption do not, either directly or indirectly, constitute a public health hazard, and, in particular, do not remain in concentrations higher than the maximum admissible.

In addition, under Article 11, any measures taken should not have the effect of allowing any deterioration in the present quality of water or an increase in the pollution of waters used for drinking water.

Under Article 16, it is open to all Member States to lay down more stringent provisions than those provided for in this Directive.

(e) Derogations: Article 9 provides for Member States to make derogations from the provisions of this Directive to take account of:

(i) specific geographical and geological conditions in the area of the water supply; and

(ii) exceptional meterological conditions.

Any derogations are to be informed to the Commission within two months or 15 days respectively. No derogations may be made relating to toxic or microbiological factors or which may constitute a public health hazard.

325 See Case C-337/89 Commission v United Kingdom [1992] ECR 1-6103.

(f) Emergencies: The Directive accepts that there may be emergency situations arising which may compel national authorities to waive the requirements of this Directive. In such instances, Article 10 provides for maximum admissible concentrations of substances laid down in Annex I to be varied for a limited period of time provided this would not constitute an unacceptable risk to public health and provided there would be no other way of maintaining the supply of water for human consumption. The Commission brought an action against the Federal Republic of Germany for allowing derogations in circumstances not envisaged by this Article and for notifying such derogations which the court upheld.[326]

Article 10 also provides for a waiver of the requirements of this Directive for a limited period when a Member State is obliged to resort to surface water which does not reach the requirements of Council Directive (EEC) 75/440[327] and cannot devise suitable treatment provided there is no unacceptable risk to public health.

The Commission is to be informed of the reasons and length of time during which any such derogations are in place.

(g) Monitoring: Regular monitoring by Member States of the quality of drinking water must take place at the point it is made available to the consumer under Article 12. The Directive is ambiguous here as this phrase is not defined. It could mean either the tap or the connection to the consumer's service pipe. Deterioration of a consumer's own pipes could alter the quality of drinking water being supplied. National authorities will determine the points for sampling. All monitoring must conform with Annex II and the methods of analysis used should, as far as practicable, be those set out in Annex III, or at least the equivalent.

(h) Labelling: Under Article 17, it is open to Member States to adopt special provisions about information to be supplied both on packaging or labels and in advertising concerning a water's suitability for the feeding of infants. If a Member State takes any such measures, the Commission must be informed.

(i) Adaptation to technical progress: As it is anticipated that speedy adaptations may need to be made to the reference methods of analysis, Articles 13–15 provide for a Committee to be set up for this purpose and a procedure laid down to be followed in these circumstances. Where adaptations are necessary, draft measures are to be submitted to the Committee for its opinion within an appropriate timetable having regard to the urgency of the matter. Opinions are adopted by qualified majority.[328] Where measures are in accordance with the opinion, the Commission will adopt them but, if not, they

326 Case C-237/90 Commission v Germany [1992] ECR 1-5973, ECJ.
327 Council Directive (EEC) 75/440 (as amended) lays down standards for surface water intended for the abstraction of drinking water ([1975] OJ L194/26).
328 Article 15(2).

are to be submitted to Council who act on a qualified majority. If the Council does not act, the Commission can proceed to adopt the measures proposed.

(j) Implementation: Measures bringing this Directive into force were to be brought into force by 15 July 1982 and measures to ensure that the quality of drinking water complies with this Directive were to be in place by 15 July 1985. As a result of an amendment made by Council Directive (EEC) 91/692,[329] Article 17a was added whereby Member States are placed under an obligation to send information to the Commission every three years on the implementation of this Directive in the form of a sectoral report also covering other pertinent directives. This amendment was to be implemented by 1 January 1993. The first report is supposed to cover the period from 1993–95 inclusive. However, Article 20 provides for Member States, in exceptional cases and for geographically defined population groups, to submit special requests to the Commission for a longer period for compliance. Any request must set out the grounds, difficulties experienced and an action programme with an appropriate timetable for compliance.

This Directive is implemented in England and Wales by a number of provisions, including the Water Supply (Water Quality) Regulations 1989[330] as amended, ss 67 to 86 of the Water Industry Act 1991 and the Private Water Supplies Regulations 1991.[331]

Although all Member States have now notified implementing measures, in 1988 the European passed a Resolution[332] seeking to condemn those Member States which had taken no measures to implement the Directive and called upon the Commission to use all measures at its disposal to ensure that the Directive is respected.

Furthermore, the European Parliament called upon the Commission to scrutinise any applications under the Directive for extensions on the time limit particularly in relation to the action programmes and timetables which must be submitted. It also called upon Member States to draw up as a matter of urgency programmes and allocation of funds to deal with the very real risk to health posed by corrosion in lead piping. In view of the number of derogations from the Directive and the problems of monitoring its implementation, as there is no obligation on Member States to report back, the European Parliament questioned the effectiveness of the Directive in its current form. Accordingly, certain amendments were made obliging Member States to report back on implementation under Council Directive (EEC) 91/692.[333]

329 [1991] OJ L377/48.
330 SI 1989/1147, as amended by the Water Supply (Water Quality) (Amendment) Regulations 1989 and 1991, SIs 1989/1284 and1991/1837.
331 SI1991/2790.
332 [1988] OJ C94/158.
333 [1991] OJ L377/48.

3. Council Directive (EEC) 76/160 concerning the quality of bathing water[334]

(a) Objective: As part of a wider programme to protect the environment and public health, this Directive aims to reduce the pollution of bathing water and to protect such water from further deterioration by setting out certain standards which relate to the quality of bathing water. The Directive sets up a system of surveillance to help achieve the Community's objective of improving living conditions and lays down limits and values on parameters to attain quality objectives drawn up as part of the programme of action of the European Communities in the environment.

The Directive recognised that there must be some flexibility in its implementation provided requirements essential for the protection of public health were not disregarded, and that there should be certain conditions under which it would be accepted that bathing water would be deemed to conform.

Given the increasing level of public interest in the environment and in the improvement of its quality, this Directive also aims to ensure that the public receives objective information on the quality of bathing water.

(b) Scope of application: The Directive applies to bathing water, defined as all running, still fresh water and/or sea water where bathing is explicitly authorised or alternatively not prohibited and traditionally carried out. A bathing area is any place where such water is found and bathing season means any period during which bathers use such waters either according to local custom or according to other rules which govern bathing and/or weather conditions. The Directive does not apply to water for therapeutic purposes and water in swimming pools.

(c) Quality standards: The Annex to the Directive sets out the physical, chemical and microbiological parameters applicable to bath water.

Under Article 3, Member States are free (within limits) to set for all bathing areas or any individual bathing area, the values applicable to bathing water for the parameters laid down. However, the values set must not be less stringent than those set forth in the Annex and stated to be mandatory.[335] Where guideline values are also given, Member States should endeavour to observe these.

Under Article 7, Member States may fix more stringent values than those provided for in the Annex but any measures taken must not lead, either directly or indirectly, to a deterioration in the current quality of bathing water.

(d) Conformity: Under Article 4 , Member States had 10 years until 8 December 1985 to take measures ensuring that the quality of bathing water conformed to the standards set. In the case of *Commission v United*

334 [1976] OJ L31/1.
335 See Case C-92/96 Commission v Spain (1998).

Kingdom,[336] it was held that works to ensure that bathing water was brought into conformity by 1995 was insufficient to meet the obligations of the United Kingdom under this Directive. However, the mandatory values laid down for standards were to be observed in all bathing areas especially equipped for bathing and created by competent authorities in Member States from the time bathing in them is first permitted.

Where bathing water either in the sea or elsewhere crosses frontiers, common quality objectives were to be determined by collaboration by the riparian Member States concerned.

(e) Deemed conformity: In certain circumstances, water will be deemed to conform to the relevant quality standards under Article 5 . Provided 95% of the samples taken at the same sampling point and at the intervals specified conform to the mandatory values for the parameters set or 90% of the samples in all other cases with the exception of the 'total coliform' and 'faecal coliform' parameters where the percentage may be 80%, bathing water will be deemed to conform. However, those samples which do not conform must not, in general, deviate from the values set by more than 50%, with a few exceptions like pH. Deviations caused by floods or other abnormal weather conditions shall not be taken into account.

(f) Sampling: All Member States are obliged to carry out sampling at intervals laid down in the Annex under Article 6. Samples should be taken at places where there are the most bathers on average, at least two weeks before the bathing season and generally 30cm below the surface of the water. The investigation should include conditions upstream in rivers and other ambient conditions in lakes and sea water and should be done periodically and scrupulously to examine the amount and nature of any pollution. If sampling should reveal any pollution, additional samples should be taken.

(g) Derogations: Under Article 8, in exceptional weather or geographical conditions, the Directive may be amended in the case of certain parameters identified in the Annex and when the quality of bathing water is altered because of changes in soil condition which have nothing to do with human intervention. However, in both these cases, the requirements essential for public health may not be disregarded. All derogations are to be notified to the Commission.

(h) Adaptation to technical progress: Articles 9 to 11 lay down the procedure for adapting the Directive to technical progress for both methods of analysis and the parameters set down. A Committee set up for the purpose shall deliver its opinion by qualified majority on any draft measures proposed within a time limit set according to the urgency of the matter. The Commission shall adopt the measures in accordance with the opinion, otherwise the measures shall be referred to the Council to act by qualified

336 Case C-56/90 Commission v United Kingdom [1993] ECR 1-4109, [1994] 1 CMLR 769.

majority. If the Council does not act, the Commission shall adopt the measures.

(i) Implementation: Regulations to implement this Directive were to be brought into force by December 1977. As a result of an amendment made by Council Directive (EEC) 91/692, Article 13 has been replaced, whereby now every year Member States must send to the Commission a report on the implementation of this Directive in the current year and in sufficient time to inform the public of the quality of bathing water for the most recent period. The first report was to be ready by 31 December 1993.

In England and Wales, this Directive is implemented to some extent by the Water Resources Act 1991 which came into force on 1 December 1991.

The Water Resources Act 1991 is part of the process of consolidation of the legislation relating to water. In general, it relates to the National Rivers Authority (now the Environment Agency) and provides for the general duties of the NRA in relation to the water industry. Although the 1991 Act does not appear to implement in any specific way the provisions of Council Directive (EEC) 76/160, s 5(2) does expressly provide powers to be given to the National Rivers Authority to be used to implement Community obligations. The practice of using Department of Environment circulars to implement Community obligations has been held to be inadequate[337] but nevertheless no provisions or regulations have been made specifically dealing with the provisions of this Directive.

All Member States have notified implementing measures.

4. Council Directive (EEC) 80/777[338] on the approximation of laws relating to the exploitation and marketing of natural mineral waters

(a) Objective: Council Directive (EEC) 80/777 deals with the approximation of laws relating to the exploitation and marketing of natural mineral waters. It concerns in particular the microbiological requirements to be fulfilled and the conditions in which the specific names must be used for certain of the mineral waters.

(b) Scope: The Directive is concerned with waters extracted from the ground of a Member State and recognised by that State as natural mineral waters satisfying the provisions of the Directive, and waters extracted from the ground of a third country imported into the EU and recognised as natural mineral waters by the responsible authority of a Member State.[339]

The Directive does not apply to medicinal products and to natural mineral water used at source for purity purposes in thermal or hydromineral establishments. Nor does it apply to exports from the EU.[340] A Member State is

337 Case 102/79 Commission v Belgium [1980] ECR 1473.

338 [1980] OJ L229/1.

339 Ie, within the meaning of Council Directive (EEC) 65/65, Art 1 (as amended) ([1965] OJ L22/369).

340 Article 14 of the Directive.

obliged to publish grounds for recognition and to inform the Commission about recognised mineral waters.[341]

(c) Marketing: Each Member State is obliged to allow marketing in its territory of natural mineral water recognised as such under the terms of the Directive. In the *Badische Erfrischungs-Getrance GrnbH & Co* case ,[342] the ECJ held that Article 1 of the Directive must be interpreted as precluding a Member State from making the recognition of water as natural mineral water dependent on its possessing properties favourable to health. The Court held that the legislative history of the Directive clearly showed that there was no intention that mineral water should have properties favourable to health and, because the Directive was so detailed in its drafting, it would have made such provision if it was intended so to do. The German legislation on the subject was therefore contrary to EC law.

Member States must take the measures necessary to ensure that only the defined waters which comply with the provisions of the Directive may be marketed as natural mineral waters (Article 2, Annex I), and natural mineral water springs may be exploited and their waters bottled only in accordance with the provisions of the Directive (Article 3, Annex II, Directive (EEC) 90/777 on the approximation of laws relating to the exploitation and marketing of natural mineral waters: Annex II).

(d) Treatment: The Directive lays down in Article 4 the type of treatment that may be afforded to natural mineral water in its state at source and sets out in Article 5 rules relating to protection against contamination. Any containers used for packaging mineral waters must be fitted with closures designed to avoid any possibility of adulteration or contamination (Article 6).

(e) Labelling: Provision is made for sales descriptions and labelling. In particular, any designation or device must not suggest a characteristic which the water does not possess, in particular as regards its origin, the date of authorisation to exploit it, the results of analyses or any similar references to guarantees of authenticity (Articles 7 to 9). Committee procedure is used to establish the sampling procedures and methods of analysis necessary for checking microbiological characteristics and compositional characteristics.

In *Piageme v Peeters NV*[343] the European Court was asked to give a preliminary ruling concerning the labelling of mineral waters under Council Directive (EEC) 79/112.[344] In that case, the plaintiffs imported and distributed various French and German mineral waters in Belgium. It was alleged that the

341 According to Art 1(5), lists of recognised natural mineral waters are to be published in the Official Journal.

342 Case C-17/96 Badische Erfrischungs-Getrdnke GmbH & Co KG v Land Baden-Wiirttemberg [1998] 1 CMLR 341.

343 Case C-85/94 Groupement des Producteurs, Importateurs et Agents Généraux d'Eaux Minérales Etrangeres, VZW (Piageme) v Peeters NV [1991] ECR 1-2971.

344 [1979] OJ L33/1, now repealed and replaced by Parliament and Council Directive 2000/13 ([2000] OJ L109/29).

defendant, which marketed mineral waters in the Flemish speaking region, was infringing Belgian legislation since the bottles it offered for sale were labelled in French or German whereas under Belgian law the labelling should have been in Dutch. The European Court considered that the expression 'a language easily understood' in Article 14 of the Directive was not an equivalent to 'the official language of the Member State' or 'language of the region'. As a result, the court ruled that Article 14 Directive (EEC) 90/777 on the approximation of laws relating to the exploitation and marketing of natural mineral waters: Art 14 of the Directive precluded Belgium from requiring the use of a 'language which is most widely spoken in the area in which the product is offered for sale even if the use at the same time of another language is not precluded'. The court went on to say that all the compulsory particulars specified in the Directive must appear on the labelling in a language easily understood by consumers in the State or region or by other measures such as design, symbols or pictogrammes and that the ease with which the information could be supplied must be assessed in the light of all the circumstances in each individual case.

(f) Implementation: In the UK, the Directive was implemented by the Natural Mineral Waters Regulations 1985.[345]

All Member States have notified implementing measures.

345 SI 1985/71.

6
Cosmetics

1. Introduction

Although the Community provisions relating to the area of cosmetics have been introduced on the legal basis of Article 95, which deals with the functioning of the common market, it is clear that their main objective is to safeguard public health as much as to harmonise provisions within Member States.

One of the major problems in this area, and crucial to safeguarding public health, is delimiting the precise sphere of cosmetic products. There is an area of possible overlap between cosmetic and pharmaceutical products since, under provisions in Member States as well as the Community as a whole, the use of substances and ingredients in pharmaceutical and medical products is by necessity carefully controlled.

Although, in practice, cosmetic products have rarely been associated with health hazards, this does not mean that cosmetics are always safe, especially with regard to possible long-term effects. This has created the need to ensure, as far as possible, the safety of cosmetic products by controlling their ingredients and toxicity.

The drawing up of lists of substances authorised for use in cosmetic products, as well as restrictions on their use, has been an important task within the Community to ensure that such products are not harmful when used under normal or foreseeable conditions. With scientific and technical advances being made all the time in our understanding of the effect of such substances, frequent and continued changes have been made in the Community provisions in this respect, making the law very difficult to grasp comprehensively.

The main point of reference in this area remains, however, Directive (EEC) 76/768)[346] and its six amendments, the most notable of which is probably the last one, Directive (EEC) 93/35.[347]

As with so much of Community legislation, many of the provisions in this sphere are geared towards providing the consumer with adequate information to assess the nature, function and possible harmful effects of any products bought. Provision of this information is seen as an important step to promoting wider consumer protection. Ensuring that false or misleading claims are not made for cosmetic products is an important extension to safeguarding further consumer safety.

One factor which has come to play an important consideration in the production of cosmetics has been increasing public concern about the testing

346 [1976] OJ L262/169 (as amended).
347 [1993] OJ L151/32.

of cosmetics, in their final form as well as any of their ingredients, on animals. Although it is still generally acceptable that it may be necessary to test ingredients and products for the purposes of safeguarding public health in the pharmaceutical and medical industries, it has become much less acceptable in the cosmetic industry. Whole new ranges of products have been built up and marketed successfully on the basis that they are not tested on animals. Directive 2003/15[348] has finally introduced a ban on animal experiments for cosmetics ingredients or combination of ingredients.

2. Council Directive (EEC) 76/768 on the approximation of the laws of the Member States relating to cosmetic products

(a) Objective: At the time this Directive was issued, the rules in Member States relating to composition characteristics of cosmetic products, their labelling and packaging differed from State to State. It was felt that these difficulties effectively hindered trade in cosmetic products and had a direct effect on the establishing and functioning of a common market.

The two-fold objective of this Directive is therefore to ensure that cosmetic products from the different Member States do not hinder trade and the establishment and functioning of the common market and to safeguard public health.

The Directive aims to meet its objectives by essentially drawing up lists of substances which are permitted for use in cosmetic products, or which should be excluded, or which are only permitted and can be used under specific conditions or within well defined limits. These lists of substances relate not only to the chemical composition of cosmetic products, but also include colourings, preservatives, dyes, antioxides and ultraviolet filters.

(b) Scope of application: The Directive only applies to cosmetic products, not to pharmaceutical or medicinal products; it therefore tries to define its scope by reference to cosmetics' application and use.

'Cosmetic products' are defined by Article 1 as any substance or preparation intended for placing in contact with various external parts of the human body or with the teeth or mucous membranes of the oral cavity exclusively or principally to clean, perfume, change their appearance and/or correct body odours and/or protect them or keep them in good condition.

The definition aims to make it clear that the function of such products in cleaning, perfuming or protecting various parts of the human body is not necessarily in order to keep them in good condition, change their appearance or correct body odours. Rather, these latter effects are just some of several possible functions of the products.

Products specifically intended to protect from disease or intended for internal use or consumption are excluded from the ambit of the Directive.

348 [2003] OJ L66/26.

Types of cosmetic products are listed in Annex I. Certain cosmetic products are excluded from the scope of this Directive and it is up to Member States themselves to take appropriate measures with regard to such products. Those excluded are cosmetic products containing the substances listed in Annex VI I.

(c) General obligations: A general obligation is laid down in Article 2 of Directive (EEC) 76/768 on the approximation of the laws of the Member States relating to cosmetic products ([1976] OJ L262/169) to ensure that cosmetic products placed on the market within the Community are not liable to damage human health under normal conditions or reasonably foreseeable conditions of use. Account should also be taken of the possibility of harm occurring to areas of the body which are contiguous to those parts where the product is applied.

This general obligation must be understood taking into account the product's presentation, labelling, any instructions for its use and disposal as well as any other information in this regard provided by the manufacturer or his authorised agent. This should remove ambiguities about what might be normal conditions of use, but the provision of such warnings will not exempt anyone from compliance with other requirements in this Directive. Member States shall take all measures to ensure that neither manufacturers nor importers established in the EU introduce products into the market which do not conform to the provisions of the Directive.

(d) Unauthorised and authorised substances: Article 4 prohibits the marketing of cosmetic products containing various substances or substances beyond certain limits or outside certain conditions; Article 5 sets out which substances are authorised in the marketing of cosmetic products.

Although there are many thousands of different cosmetic products on the market within the EU, they are all derived from a far smaller number of ingredients. This is the basis of the lists of authorised or prohibited substances of the Directive.

The Directive contains a list of chemicals which must not be contained in finished products (Annex II); a list of substances which cosmetic products must not contain except under the conditions and restrictions laid down in Annex III; and a list of authorised substances, which may include colouring agents, preservatives and UV filters (Annexes IV, VI, VII).

The Annexes include a column of data for these substances, colouring agents, preservatives and UV filters when they shall either be:

(i) definitely allowed;

(ii) definitely prohibited;

(iii) manufactured for a given specified period.

These dates and the technical provisions contained in these Annexes are continually being changed according to the latest technological and scientific research and information available by Commission directives. It is only by constant reference to the detailed provisions of the latest amending Commission directive that it is possible to be certain of the precise position.

(e) Animal testing: As a result of increasing public sensitivity to the testing of products on animals, Article 4 now prescribes that the testing of ingredients or combinations of ingredients on animals tested after 1 January 1998 is prohibited by reference to the requirements of Directive (EEC) 86/609[349] on the protection of animals used for experimental and other scientific purposes. Although progress is being made in the development of alternative satisfactory methods for testing cosmetic products, it is possible that, despite all reasonable endeavours, tests offering similar protection to the consumer may not have been scientifically validated. In such cases, a proposal may be presented by 1 January 1997 to Council to defer the entry into force of this provision for a period, but by no more than two years.

In fact, Directive (EC) 97/18[350] postponed the date of 1 January 1998 to 30 June 2000; Directive (EC) 2000/41 [351] further postponed the date after which animal tests are prohibited for ingredients or combinations of ingredients of cosmetic products to 30 June 2002.

Finally, Directive 2003/15 introduced a ban on animal experiments for cosmetics ingredients or combinations of ingredients, and makes it compulsory to use validated alternative methods for the testing of chemicals used in cosmetic products, as soon as such methods become available.

The Directive is to be implemented by Member States before 11 September 2004.

(f) Lists of ingredients: To aid data gathering, Article 5a (as introduced by Directive 93/35) requires that the Commission compiles an inventory of ingredients used in cosmetic products on the basis of information supplied by the industry. The same Article states that 'cosmetic ingredients' are defined as any chemical substance or preparation of synthetic or natural origin except for perfume or aromatic compositions.

The inventory was established in May 1996,[352] together with a common nomenclature of the ingredients employed in cosmetic products. It is updated periodically and its value is merely indicative, ie, it does not constitute a list of authorised substances. It consists of two parts: one for aromatic and perfume ingredients; and one for other ingredients.

The inventory contains information on:

(i) the identity of the ingredient including its chemical name, CTFA name, the European Pharmacopoeia name, the international non-proprietary name recommended by WHO and other organisations, colour index numbers and the common name referred to in Article 7(2)

349 [2003] OJ L159/46.
350 [1997] OJ L114/43.
351 [2000] OJ L145/25.
352 Commission Decision (EC) 96/335 ([1996] OJ L132/1).

Directive (EEC) 76/768 on the approximation of the laws of the Member States relating to cosmetic products ([1976] OJ L262/169): Art 7(2);

(ii) the function of the ingredient in the final product;

(iii) restrictions, conditions and warnings to be printed on labels, where appropriate by reference to the Annexes.

(g) Labelling requirements: Article 6 lays down the labelling requirements for cosmetic products. These requirements were changed in 1988 after experience showed they should be improved and all cosmetic products within the Community were expected to comply with these requirements by 1 January 1992; those that do not may no longer be sold or disposed of to consumers after 31 December 1993.

Cosmetic products may only be marketed if the container or packaging bears the following information in indelible, easily legible and visible lettering:

(i) name or style and address of the registered office of the manufacturer or person responsible for the product. This information may be abbreviated and a Member State may require the country of origin to be specified;

(ii) nominal content at the time of packaging by weight or volume except for small packages of less than 5g, 155mm, free samples or products pre-packaged and sold by number provided the number appears on the packaging;

(iii) the date of minimum durability. This must be indicated by the words 'Best used before the end of ...' followed by the date itself or details of where to find the date on the packaging. This is not mandatory if the minimum durability exceeds 30 months;

(iv) particular precautions to be observed in use and especially those listed in Annexes III, IV, Directive (EEC) 76/768 on the approximation of the laws of the Member States relating to cosmetic products ([1976] OJ L262/169): Annex IV, VI and VII under the column 'Conditions of use and warnings which must be printed on the label'. Where this is impossible for practical reasons, this information may be given on a separate leaflet, if necessary, to which the consumer is referred either by abbreviated information or the symbol given in Annex VIII which must appear on the container or packaging.

(v) the batch number of manufacture or the reference for identifying the goods.

As the prime purpose of the regulations on labelling is to ensure that the ultimate consumer has access to sufficient information about the cosmetic product to assess what is being bought and for what purposes, most of the information must appear on the container and packaging. However, because of the impracticability of this in some instances, information may appear on a separate enclosed leaflet or label or card. Where it is impossible, for reasons of shape or size, for such information to be put on an enclosed leaflet, it must still appear on a label or card enclosed or attached to the product and, if this is difficult on a notice in immediate proximity to the product. Council Directive (EEC) 93/35 amending this Directive for the sixth time also extends the labelling requirements substantially in other ways.

The function of the product, unless clear, is now to be included on the container and packaging. In addition, a list of ingredients in descending order of weight is now to be included for the benefit of the consumer. This list will include perfume and aromatic compositions, colouring agents and substitute ingredients where necessary. If it is impossible for practical reasons for this list to appear on the container or packaging, it must appear on an enclosed card or leaflet in the same way as precautions to be observed. Ingredients must be identified by the common name referred to in Article 7(2) or by one of the names referred to in Article 5(1) and (2). However, certain things are not to be regarded as ingredients:

(i) impurities in raw materials;

(ii) subsidiary technical materials used in preparation but not present in the final product;

(iii) materials used strictly as solvents or carriers for perfume and aromatic compositions.

Member States shall take all measures necessary to ensure that, in the labelling, presentation for sale and advertising of cosmetic products, the wording, use of names, trade marks, images or other signs, figurative or otherwise, suggesting a characteristic which the products in question do not possess, shall be prohibited. [353]

According to Article 7, Member States may not refuse, prohibit or restrict the marketing of any cosmetic products which comply with the requirements of this Directive and the Annexes . They may, however, require that the particulars provided for in Article 6(1)(b), (c) and (d) be expressed at least in their own national or official language or languages.

Furthermore, a Member State may require, for purposes of prompt and appropriate medicial treatment in the event of difficulties, that adequate and sufficient information regarding substances contained in cosmetic products is made available to the competent authority, which shall ensure that this information is used only for the purposes of such treatment.

Where cosmetic products are not pre-packaged or are packaged at the point of sale, Member States must adopt rules to cover these requirements. The onus is also placed on Member States to ensure that the labelling and packaging of

353 See an application in Case C-315/92 Verband Sozialer Wettbewerb eV v Clinique Laboratoires SNC et Estee Lauder Cosmetics GmbH [1994] ECR I-317; Case C-220/98 Estée Lauder Cosmetics GmbH & Co. OHG v Lancaster Group GmbH [2000] ECR I-117.

products do not make unwarranted claims by implication about their characteristics. The labelling requirements may be expressed in Member States' own national or official languages but, so that particulars can be easily understood especially about ingredients, the Commission is to adopt a common ingredients nomenclature in accordance with the procedure in Article 10. It is up to Member States themselves to decide what appropriate information on substances in cosmetic products they require to be notified to the competent authorities should medical treatment be necessary and those authorities shall ensure that the information is used only for the purposes of treatment. Member States must designate a competent authority and send details to the Commission.

(h) Accessibility and monitoring of information: One of the main aims of the latest amendments is to ensure that there can be more effective monitoring of cosmetic products within the EU market, primarily for the benefit of consumer health and safety.

Article 7a, added by Council Directive (EEC) 93/35, places an obligation on the manufacturer or agent or person to whose order a cosmetic product is manufactured or the person responsible for placing an imported product on the market to keep certain information available for the competent authorities for control purposes at the address specified on the label. The information includes:

(i) the qualitative and quantitative composition of the product and name and code number of composition and identity of supplier in the case of perfumes and aromatic compositions;

(ii) physio-chemical and microbiological specifications and purity and microbiological control criteria of the product to assess its quality;

(iii) the method of manufacture complying with good manufacturing practice laid down by either Community law or by the Member State concerned and the person responsible for manufacture on first importation, who must possess an appropriate level of professional qualification or experience;

(iv) assessment of the safety for human health of the finished product taking account of toxicological factors and exposure; this information may be kept at one place if the product is manufactured at several places;

(v) name and address of the qualified person responsible for the assessment and that person must hold a diploma as defined in Article 1 of Council Directive (EEC) 89/48[354] in a relevant field;

(vi) existing data on undesirable effects on human health resulting from use of the product;

(vii) proof of the effect claimed where this is justified.

354 [1989] OJ L19/16.

The assessment of the safety for human health must be carried out in accordance with the principles of good laboratory practice.[355] In *Commission v France*,[356] the Commission applied against France for a declaration that, by requiring a product file to be compiled, lodged and kept up-to-date, outside the framework laid down in Article 7(3) of Council Directive (EEC) 76/768, France had failed to fulfil its obligation under that Directive.

The court held that the Directive had provided exhaustively for the harmonisation of national rules on the packaging and labelling of cosmetic products and a Member State could not subject the movement of cosmetic products to conditions other than those imposed by the Directive.

Furthermore, the court declared that to subject the marketing of cosmetic products to a requirement that a file be kept containing information additional to that required by the Directive was incompatible with the provisions of the Directive itself. The court therefore upheld the complaint by the Commission and made the appropriate declaration.

To help with the monitoring process, the manufacturer or agent or the person responsible for imported goods must notify the competent authorities of the address of manufacture or place of initial importation before the goods are placed on the EU market. Member States must designate the competent authorities and notify the Commission and information about the monitoring authorities will be available in the Official Journal. It is up to Member States to ensure that these authorities continue to cooperate in areas where it is necessary for the smooth application of this Directive.

(i) Adaptation to technical problems: As technical progress relating to cosmetic products necessitates rapid adaptation of the technical provisions, the Directive provides a procedure for establishing close cooperation between Member States and the Commission for these purposes.

It is the responsibility of the Commission to deal with implementing measures determining methods of analysis for checking the composition of cosmetic products and criteria for microbiological and chemical purity. According to Article 8, any amendments for adapting to technical progress are adopted after consultation with the Committee on the Adaptation to Technical Progress of the Directives on the Removal of Technical Barriers to Trade in the Cosmetic Products Sector at the initiative of the Commission or a Member State. The use of this procedure has now been extended with regard to the common nomenclature of ingredients used in cosmetic products and for adapting the provisions within the Annexes to technical progress.

The Committee on the Adaptation to Technical Progress of the Directives on the Removal of Technical Barriers to Trade in the Cosmetic Products Sector, set up by Article 9, is in charge of considering draft measures submitted by the Commission within the time scale set according to the urgency of the matters

355 As defined in Council Directive (EEC) 87/18 ([1987] OJ L15/29).
356 Case C-246/91 [1993] ECR 1-2289.

and deliver its opinion before adoption by the Commission. Matters can be referred to this Committee by Member States or by its Chairman.

As, at any given time, substances may be used in the manufacture of cosmetic products which are not contained in the lists of substances authorised, the Directive allows for Member States to authorise the use of such substances subject to the following conditions:

(i) authorisation for a maximum of three years;

(ii) an official check on the products by the Member State;

(iii) the product must bear a distinctive authorisation.

Any such authorisation must be notified to the Commission within two months. If the substances the subject of the authorisation are to be included in the lists of permitted substances, a request must be made by the Member State to the Commission with supporting documentation. A decision must be made within 18 months of the request on the basis of the latest scientific and technical research and after consultation with the Scientific Committee on Cosmetology in accordance with the procedure laid down.

According to Article 12, it is also possible for a Member State to note that a product, although complying with the requirements of the Directive, represents a health hazard. In such circumstances, it has authority to provisionally prohibit the marketing of the product. Other Member States and the Commission must be immediately informed about such decision and the grounds for taking it. The Commission is under a duty to consult as soon as possible, deliver its opinion without delay and take the appropriate steps. These steps include making the necessary technical adaptations through the procedure laid down and any safeguard measures remain in force until such adaptations are made.

(j) Implementation: This Directive is implemented in the United Kingdom by a number of measures, notably the Cosmetic Products Regulations 1978,[357] the Cosmetic Products (Safety) (Amendment) Regulations 1985,[358] and the Cosmetic Products (Safety) (Amendment) Regulations 1987.[359]

All Member States have notified implementing measures.[360]

(k) Follow-up: As a consequence of the fact that it contains many technical provisions which have required rapid adaptations, there have been a great number of amending directives. There have been seven Council directives amending the substantive Articles of this Directive and 28 Commission directives amending and supplementing the technical provisions in the

357 SI 1978/1354.
358 SI 1985/2045.
359 SI 1987/1920.
360 But see Case C-29/90 Commission v Greece [1992] ECR 1-1917, [1994] 3 CMLR 675; Case C-365/00 Commission v Italy, 7 March 2002; Case C-246-91 Commission v France [1993] ECR 1-2289.

Annexes to this Directive.[361] Further amendments are still expected, especially in order to adapt the Directive to technical progress. Reference will need to be made to each Commission directive to determine the precise nature of the technical change made. Changes are usually either authorising the use of a substance within certain limits or restrictions, changing the nature of the restrictions or warnings or extensively banning the use of a substance..

Commission Directive (EC) 2003/801 establishing a symbol indicating the durability of cosmetic products in Annex VIIIa to Council Directive (EEC) 76/768 imposes the use of a symbol which, as from 11 March 2005, must be displayed on all cosmetic products with a durability of more than 30 months. The symbol (which depicts an open cream jar accompanied by an indication of how long the product will remain suitable for use once opened) is meant to help consumers to identify cosmetic products which, once opened and coming into contact with the outside environment, may become harmful. For cosmetic products the durability of which is less than 30 months, there already was an obligation to indicate the date of minimum durability.

3. Analysis of cosmetic products

(a) The Scientific Committee on Cosmetic Products and Non-Food Products intended for Consumers: The drawing up and amendment of Community rules governing the composition, manufacturing, characteristic packaging and labelling of cosmetic products involve examining scientific and technical problems of complexity. As a result, it was felt that seeking solutions to these problems would require the assistance of highly qualified scientists from a range of disciplines and that the most appropriate way to seek such assistance would be within the context of a permanent advisory committee attached to the Commission.

The role of the Scientific Committee on Cosmetic Products and Non-Food Products intended for Consumers is to deliver opinions to the Commission when consulted on any scientific problem in the field of cosmetic products. It also has authority to draw problems within its competence to the attention of the Commission even when not consulted.

The Committee replaces, since 1997,[362] the Scientific Committee on Cosmetology established in 1978[363] and consists of 16 members drawn from leading highly qualified scientists from a range of disciplines in the field. The members hold office for three years which can be renewed and they are not remunerated for their services. Its chairman is elected from among its

361 The substantive amendments are: Council Directive (EEC) 79/661 ([1979] OJ L192/35); Council Directive (EEC) 82/368 ([1982] OJ L167/1); Council Directive (EEC) 83/574 ([1983] OJ L332/38); Council Directive (EEC) 88/667 ([1988] OJ L382/46); Council Directive (EEC) 89/679 ([1989] OJ L398/25); Council Directive (EEC) 93/35 ([1993] OJ L151/32); Directive (EC) 2003/15 ([2003] OJ L66/26).

362 Commission Decision 97/579 ([1997] OJ L237/18).

363 Commission Decision 78/45 ([1978] OJ L13/24 (as amended).

members for three years and is re-eligible. The Committee can operate in working groups, and meets when convened by the Commission. Commission representatives attend meetings of the Committee and working groups.

When the Committee is consulted for an opinion, the Commission may specify a period within which it is to be delivered. In the event that an opinion is not reached unanimously, the differing positions are drawn up in a report. Members of the Committee are under an obligation not to disclose confidential information.

One of the main actions taken by the Committee has been to recommend a set of guidelines to be taken into account by the cosmetics industry in developing adequate studies to be used in the safety evaluation of cosmetic ingredients.

(b) Methods of analysis necessary for checking the composition of cosmetic products: Under the general Council Directive (EEC) 76/768, as subsequently amended, on the approximation of the laws of the Member States relating to cosmetic products, provision is made for the official testing of cosmetic products with the aim of ensuring that the prescribed conditions concerning their composition are satisfied and consistency in testing achieved.

Accordingly, a number of Directive have been enacted over the years with the purpose of establishing a list of official methods of analysis for checking the composition of domestic products and of adapting them to technical progress.

The first Commission Directive[364] aimed to establish as quickly as possible all the necessary methods of analysis for checking the composition of cosmetic products. It places an obligation on Member States to take all necessary measures to ensure that the official testing of cosmetic products is performed in accordance with the detailed methods described in the Annex. Most of the provisions are highly technical and, therefore, really only meaningful to scientists and technicians involved in the field.

Further methods for analysis are set forth in six other directives, namely:

(1) Second Commission Directive (EEC) 82/434 on the approximation of the laws of the Member States relating to methods of analysis necessary for checking the composition of cosmetic products ;[365]

(2) Third Commission Directive (EEC) 83/514 on the approximation of the laws of Member States relating to methods of analysis necessary for checking the composition of cosmetic products; [366]

364 Directive 80/1335 ([1980] OJ L383/27).
365 [1982] OJ L185/1 (as amended).
366 [1983] OJ L291/9.

(3) Fourth Commission Directive (EEC) 85/490 on the approximation of the laws of the Member States relating to methods of analysis necessary for checking the composition of cosmetic products ;[367]

(4) Fifth Commission Directive (EEC) 93/73 on the methods of analysis necessary for checking composition of cosmetic product;[368]

(5) Sixth Commission Directive 95/32 on the methods of analysis necessary for checking composition of cosmetic product;[369]

(6) Seventh Commission Directive 96/45 on the methods of analysis necessary for checking composition of cosmetic product.[370]

367 [1985] OJ L295/30.
368 [1993] OJ L231/34.
369 [1995] OJ L178/20.
370 [1996] OJ L123/8.

7
Dangerous Substances

1. Introduction

There have been extensive Community provisions concerned with dangerous substances and preparations. These provisions have been aimed not just at protecting the public but in particular for the benefit of workers having to use such substances. They, therefore, constitute a significant contribution to promoting safety within the EU. However, the safety risks attached to these substances either by themselves or in combination in preparations have an impact not just on man but on the environment as well. Community provisions in this area are equally concerned with assessing and limiting the foreseeable risks to the environment as many such substances may pollute and have an adverse affect on the quality of life for all within the EU.

At present, the EC legislation on dangerous substances and preparations consists of three important legal instruments: Council Directive (EEC) 67/548[371] relating to the classification, packaging and labelling of dangerous substances; Directive (EC) 1999/45[372] of the European Parliament and of the Council concerning the approximation of the laws, regulations and administrative provisions of the Member States relating to the classification, packaging and labelling of dangerous preparations; and Directive 76/769[373] relating to restrictions on the marketing and use of certain dangerous substances and preparations.[374]

There are also a few directives aimed at specific products such as aerosol dispensers, batteries and accumulators.[375] Some of those directives (such as Council Directive 78/63 Directive (EEC) 78/63 on the classification, packaging and labelling of pesticides on the classification, packaging and labelling of pesticides, and Directives 90/35 and 91/442 on preparations to be packaged in child resistant fastenings) have been repealed following the enactment of Directive 99/45.

The directives introduced in this area are subject to frequent change and updating in the light of the latest scientific and technological developments

371 [1967] OJ L196/1 (as amended).

372 [1999] OJ L200/1.

373 [1976] OJ L262/201 (as amended).

374 Other pieces of legislation which are relevant to this area but outside the scope of this work are: Council and Parliament Regulation (EC) 304/2003 concerning the export and import of dangerous chemicals ([2003] OJ L169/27); Council Directive 94/55 on the approximation of the laws of the Member States with regard to the transport of dangerous goods by road ([1994] OJ L319/7).

375 See, eg, Council Directive (EEC) 91/157 on batteries and accumulators containing certain dangerous substances ([1991] OJ L78/38); Council Directive (EEC) 75/324 on the approximation of the laws of the Member States relating to aerosol dispensers ([1975] OJ L147/40) (as amended). These specific directives, however, are not considered in the course of this section.

and especially in relation to assessing their impact on man and the environment. It is therefore an area of Community law where consolidation is vital and necessary.

The Commission has reviewed its strategy in a White Paper having as a key objective sustainable development and making the chemical industry accept more responsibility while respecting the precautionary principle.[376]

2. Council Directive (EEC) 67/548 of 27 June 1967 on the approximation of laws, regulations and administrative provisions relating to the classification, packaging and labelling of dangerous substances

(a) Objective: The principal purpose of the Directive is to harmonise the laws, regulations and provisions of the Member States on the classification, packaging and labelling of substances dangerous to man and the environment as well as the notification of substances which are placed on the market in the EU. It also seeks to protect the public and principally workers using dangerous substances by providing for the classification, packaging and labelling of dangerous substances.

In addition, the Directive now seeks to control more effectively the impact and effect of such substances on man and the environment. It seeks to do this by providing for new substances being placed on the market being subjected to prior study by either the manufacturer or importer of the substances and also for notification of all dangerous substances to competent authorities in each Member State. Notification of certain mandatory information and an appropriate procedure for such notification will ensure that all new substances are listed, that a full inventory of dangerous substances can be drawn up and that the use of such substances can be more effectively monitored.

The Directive as amended now has fuller measures and provisions relating to the packaging and labelling of dangerous substances, including those substances not yet officially listed by the Commission. These provisions make indications about safety advice obligatory. The Directive also provides now for an improved system for classifying dangerous substances through the use of better and more precise criteria and for the evaluation of danger to the environment. The Directive, therefore, makes it necessary to enumerate certain characteristics and parameters for assessment and to establish a phased study programme for this purpose.

(b) Scope: To remove trade barriers, the Directive sought initially to harmonise the rules and regulations on classification, packaging and labelling relating to dangerous substances alone. The fact that the Directive applies to substances, not preparations, has been confirmed by the ECJ .[377] In view of the

376 Commission White Paper of 27 February 2001 on the strategy for a future chemicals policy, COM(2001)28 final.
377 Case 187/84 Italy v Caldana [1985] ECR 3013, [1989] 1 CMLR 137.

amount of preparatory work involved in this and still to be done with regard to dangerous preparations only, it was felt that harmonisation provisions relating to dangerous preparations and to the actual use of both substances and preparations would have to follow later.

For the purposes of the Directive, 'substances' are chemical elements and their compounds as they occur in natural state or as produced by industry. 'Preparations' means mixtures or solutions composed of two or more substances.

According to Article 1, certain matters are excluded from the ambit of the Directive. Such matters which would be covered or are intended to be covered by different directives are not appropriate to include within this Directive. The following substances are excluded:

(i) medicinal products, narcotics and radioactive substances;

(ii) the carriage of dangerous substances by rail, road, inland waterway, sea or air;

(iii) munitions and objects containing explosive matter in the form of igniters or motor fuels;

(iv) dangerous substances exported to third countries.

The provisions relating to packaging and labelling are not applicable to containers for gases which are compressed, liquefied or dissolved under pressure.

In addition, the Directive does not apply to the carriage of dangerous substances by rail, road, inland waterway, sea or air and to substances in transit which are under customs supervision, provided they do not undergo any treatment or processing.

(c) Classification and criteria: To aid understanding, Article 2 of the Directive defines certain terms including:

(i) substances;

(ii) preparations;

(iii) notification; and

(iv) placing on the market.

Substances and preparations are classified as dangerous into the following categories:

(i) explosives;

(ii) oxidising;

(iii) extremely flammable;

(iv) highly flammable;

(v) flammable;

(vi) very toxic;

(vii) toxic;

(viii) harmful;

(ix) corrosive;

(x) irritant;

(xi) sensitising;

(xii) dangerous for the environment;

(xiii) carcinogenic;

(xiv) toxic for reproduction; and

(xv) mutagenic.

The basis on which they are classified is given and certain new categories have been included to extend the scope of the Directive.

The criteria to be used in the classification and labelling of dangerous substances and preparations are set out in Annex VI. Annexes VII and VIII set out the characteristics by which real or potential environmental hazards are to be assessed and Annex V specifies the methods by which the physico-chemical properties of such substances and preparations are to be determined as well as their toxicity and ecotoxicity.

The classification of dangerous substances is based on the degree of hazard and specific nature of the risks involved. Those subject to this Directive are listed in Annex I and given a rating, where applicable, enabling the health hazard to be assessed. Annex I is constantly being updated and adapted in the light of scientific and technical knowledge.

(d) General obligations: A general obligation is placed on all Member States to ensure that substances or preparations are not placed on the market unless they:

(i) have been notified to the competent authority;

(ii) are packaged and labelled according to the requirements and criteria of tests laid down.

According to Article 5, substances which are not yet included in the list of dangerous substances but which may reasonably be expected to have dangerous properties must also meet the labelling and packaging requirements of the Directive.

(e) Notification and role of the competent authority: According to Article 6, there is an obligation placed on the manufacturer or importer of a dangerous substance falling within the Directive to submit to the competent authority in a Member State, at least 45 days before the substance is placed on the market, a notification.[378] This notification must include a technical dossier supplying information for evaluating the foreseeable risks to man and the environment and containing information and results of studies for assessing

378 Case 429/85 Commission v Greece [1988] ECR 843.

the environmental hazards with details, full description of studies, methods and bibliographies:

(i) a declaration about its unfavourable effects in terms of its uses envisaged;

(ii) the proposed classification and labelling; and

(iii) proposals for recommended precautions relating to safe use.

If a substance is already notified (reference may be made to results of studies carried out by others if they agree and if it is already listed in Annex I), much of the information need not be supplied, including the technical dossier, if it had been notified at least 10 years previously.

However, where a substance has already been notified, there is an obligation to notify the competent authority of:

(i) changes in the total and/or annual quantities placed on the market;

(ii) new knowledge of the effects on man and environment of which one can reasonably be expected to be aware;

(iii) new uses of which one can reasonably be expected to be aware; and

(iv) any change in properties resulting from modification of the substance.

Results of studies for assessing environmental hazards should also be notified.

This requirement to notify places a larger part of the burden of policing the impact of such substances on man and the environment upon the manufacturer and importer. The competent authorities appointed by Member States remain responsible for receiving this information and examining it to check that it conforms with the Directive. In particular, they must check:

(i) the proposed findings on any foreseeable risk;

(ii) the classification and labelling; and

(iii) the proposals for any recommended precautions for safe use.

Where the need is shown to evaluate a hazard caused by a substance, the competent authority has power to:

(i) ask for further information and/or verification of tests;

(ii) carry out sampling; and

(iii) take appropriate measures relating to the safe use of the substance.

By an amendment, the notification system was also introduced for 'new' substances and, consequently, required the establishment of the list of 'existing' substances. EINECS, the European Inventory of Existing Commercial Chemical Substances, lists all substances that were reported to be on the market on or before 18 September 1981. The substances placed on the market for the first time after this target date are 'new'.

Any information concerning the commercial exploitation or manufacturing of the substance is kept secret.

(f) Exemptions from notification: According to Article 8, substances meeting certain conditions will be considered to be notified. The most important in this category are:

(i) those for research and analysis purposes on the market to determine their properties;

(ii) those placed on the market in very small quantities (less than 1 tonne per year) and intended for laboratory use;

(iii) those placed on the market in very small quantities (less than 1 tonne per year) provided their identity, labelling and quantity is known to the authorities and any conditions imposed are complied with.

If quantities are placed on the market at the research and development stage in small quantities but more than one tonne per year, an exemption period of one year for notification applies provided their identity, quality and labelling data are known and any condition met. Substances at this stage are not to be made available to the general public.

Substances which are considered to be notified must still, however, conform to the Directive's labelling and packaging requirements, but where this is not possible the label must bear a warning stating that the substance has not yet been fully tested.

(g) Circulation of information: According to Article 9, any notification dossier and/or additional information must be passed on to the Commission. The Commission is also under an obligation to pass on the notification dossier or a summary of it and any other relevant information to other Member States (Article 10). It is also open for the competent authority of one Member State to suggest other tests or request further information of other competent authorities. Where agreement cannot be reached between authorities, the Commission may take a decision in accordance with the procedures laid down in the Directive.

(h) Confidentiality: According to Article 11, the manufacturer or importer notifying the authorities may request that certain information regarded as commercially sensitive not be disclosed to anyone other than the Commission and the competent authorities. Full justification must be given in such cases. No claim to commercial or industrial secrecy can be made, for certain information.

It is the responsibility of the competent authority to decide what information is covered by secrecy. Any confidential information received may, however, be disclosed to persons directly involved in proceedings involving sanctions for the purposes of controlling substances placed on the market.

(i) Inventory of substances: The Commission was under an obligation to draw up an inventory of substances placed on the market by 18 September 1981 on the basis of the information provided. However, there is an exemption under Article 13(1) from the provisions on notification for those substances used in other product sectors for which notification procedures exist under Community legislation. The Commission is required to establish a list of such Community legislation.

The inventory required under Article 13 must give the substances' chemical name under an internationally recognised nomenclature. The Commission must also keep a list of all substances notified. The list of substances is contained in Annex J. As frequent adaptations have had to be made to technical progress, this list has been amended and added to many times, the latest change having been made by Commission Directive 2001/59.[379]

(j) Packaging: Article 15, it is the responsibility of Member States to take the necessary measures to ensure that manufacturers and importers do not place dangerous substances on the market unless their packaging satisfies certain requirements:

(i) packages must be designed and constructed so that their contents can not escape unless special safety devices are prescribed instead;

(ii) the materials used must not be liable to attack by the substances or likely to form harmful compounds;

(iii) packages must be strong and solid enough to ensure they will not loosen under the normal stresses of handling;

(iv) containers with replaceable fastening devices must be designed so that the packaging can be repeatedly refastened without the contents escaping.

In addition to these requirements, manufacturers and importers may be obliged to have packages sealed, closed with child-resistant fastenings and carry a warning of danger if products are intended for domestic use. Annex IX contains the technical specifications for such devices.

(k) Labelling: All packages of dangerous substances must also meet the labelling requirements. The requirements are designed not just to give the necessary information about the hazards involved in their use and application, but also for the general protection of the public, people working with the substances and the environment.

According to Article 16, every package must show clearly and indelibly the following information:

(i) the name of the substance;

(ii) the origin of the substance;

(iii) the danger symbol and an indication of the danger involved in its use;

(iv) standard phrases indicating the special risks involved;

379 [2001] OJ L225/1.

(v) standard phrases indicating the relevant safety advice.

The name must either be one of the terms listed in Annex I or in an internationally recognised nomenclature. The indication of origin must include the name and address of the manufacturer, distributor or importer. The symbols used for indications of danger (such as a scull with crossed bones underneath) must conform to those in Annex II and are to be printed in black on an orange-yellow background. The standard phrases for special risks from substances (R-phrases) and for safety precautions (S-phrases) are set out in Annexes III and IV respectively. These Annexes are also subject to frequent updating as substances are added or changed in the list in Annex I and as scientific and technological advances make new phrases necessary or alterations to existing phrases sensible: so, for example, Directive 93/21[380] introduced a symbol for 'dangerous for the environment' in Annex II, new phrases indicating danger to health for substances toxic to reproduction and danger for the environment in Annex III and certain safety advice phrases related to dangers for the environment in Annex IV.

If the advice cannot be included on the label or packaging, it must appear on an accompanying document or paper. If more than one danger symbol is assigned to a substance, the symbol for the most hazardous property must be used. For some of the less hazardous substances, indications of risks and safety advice need not appear in very small packages (less than 125 ml) or if not retailed to the general public.

According to Article 7, the entire surface of the label itself must be firmly affixed to one or more surfaces of the packaging so that it can be read horizontally when the package is set down normally. The dimensions of the label must satisfy certain requirements depending on the size of the package and each symbol must cover 1/10th of surface area of label and be at least 1 cm. Labels may be dispensed with if the required particulars are shown on the package. The colour and presentation of the label must be such that the danger symbol stands out clearly from the background.

If there is an outer package containing an inner package, labelling requirements are satisfied if the inner package satisfies the provisions of this Directive and the outer package is labelled in accordance with international rules on the transport of dangerous substances. If a single package is labelled according to international rules, it will also meet the requirements of this Directive provided the label also includes the name of the substance, an indication of its origin and specifies the special risks and safety advice. If such packages do not leave a Member State, they need only comply with the national rules for transporting such substances.

(l) Derogations: According to Article 18, labelling may be applied to packages in some other suitable form if they are too small or unsuitable or if the substances are not explosive, toxic or very toxic. They may be unlabelled or

380 [1993] OJ L110/20.

labelled in some other way provided the packages contain such small quantities that there is no reason to fear any danger.

(m) Restrictions: According to Article 23, although there is a general obligation to allow substances to be placed on the market which satisfy the requirements of this Directive, where a Member State has detailed evidence that, notwithstanding compliance, a substance constitutes a hazard for man or the environment, it may provisionally prohibit the sale of the substance or subject it to special conditions. The Commission must be informed and other Member States consulted within six weeks. The Commission must give its view without delay and take the appropriate measures which may involve making further adaptations to the Directive. In this case, the Member State which has adopted safeguard measures may maintain them until the adaptations come into force.

(n) Adaptation to technical progress: The nature of this Directive means that a great many adaptations to technical progress have to be made in the light of the latest scientific and technological knowledge. In accordance with Articles 20 and 21, a Committee has been set up for this purpose. Reference may be made to it by the chairman on his own initiative or at the request of a Member State. When draft measures are submitted by the Commission, the Committee must give its view within the time limit set according to the urgency of the matter. The procedures it follows are the same as those of other similarly constituted committees monitoring and advising on directives, and decisions are made by a qualified majority.

381 Council Directive (EEC) 69/81 ([1969] OJ L68/1); Council Directive (EEC) 70/189 ([1970] OJ L59/33) amending for the second time; Council Directive(EEC) 71/144 ([1971] OJ L74/15) amending for the third time; Council Directive (EEC) 73/146 ([1973] OJ L167/1) amending for the fourth time; Council Directive (EEC) 75/409 ([19975] OJ L183/22) amending for the fifth time; Council Directive (EEC) 79/831 ([1979] OJ L259/10) amending for the sixth time; Council Directive (EEC) 92/32 ([1992] OJ L154/1) amending for the seventh time; Parliament and Council Directive (EC) 96/56 ([1996] OJ L236/35) amending for the eighth time.

At the time of writing, the Directive has been amended nine times by Council directives[381] and adapted to technical progress by Commission (more rarely Council) directives 28 times.[382]

The lack of any consolidating directive makes this piece of legislation rather difficult to use, particularly the Annexes.

(o) Implementation: Most of the substantive provisions of this Directive as amended were due to be implemented by 18 September 1981. The subsequent directives adapting the Directive to technical progress all have different implementation dates and there are usually adaptations with which to be complied each year. Only by constant reference to the directives adapting to technical progress can one keep abreast of all the up-to-date time limits on implementation.

This Directive as amended for the sixth time by Council Directive (EEC) 79/831[383] is implemented in Great Britain insofar as the provisions of these directives relate to the classification, packaging and labelling of dangerous substances by the Classification, Packaging and Labelling of Dangerous Substances Regulations 1984.[384] They came into operation on 12 September 1984 and revoked and re-enacted with minor modifications the Packaging and Labelling of Dangerous Substances Regulations 1978 (as amended).[385]

All Member States have notified implementing measures.

381 Council Directive (EEC) 69/81 ([1969] OJ L68/1); Council Directive (EEC) 70/189 ([1970] OJ L59/33) amending for the second time; Council Directive(EEC) 71/144 ([1971] OJ L74/15) amending for the third time; Council Directive (EEC) 73/146 ([1973] OJ L167/1) amending for the fourth time; Council Directive (EEC) 75/409 ([19975] OJ L183/22) amending for the fifth time; Council Directive (EEC) 79/831 ([1979] OJ L259/10) amending for the sixth time; Council Directive (EEC) 92/32 ([1992] OJ L154/1) amending for the seventh time; Parliament and Council Directive (EC) 96/56 ([1996] OJ L236/35) amending for the eighth time.

382 Commission Directive (EEC) 76/907 ([1976] OJ L360/1); Commission Directive (EEC) 79/370 ([1979] OJ L88/1); Commission Directive (EEC) 81/957 ([1981] OJ L351/5); Commission Directive (EEC) 82/232 ([1982] OJ L106/18); Commission Directive (EEC) 84/449 ([1984] OJ L251/1); Commission Directive (EEC) 86/431 ([1986] OJ L247/1); Commission Directive (EEC) 87/302 ([1988] OJ L133/1); Council Directive (EEC) 87/432 ([1987] OJ L239/1); Commission Directive (EEC) 88/490 ([1988] OJ L259/1); Council Directive (EEC) 90/517 ([1990] OJ L287/37); Commission Directive (EEC) 91/325 ([1991] OJ L180/1); Commission Directive (EEC) 91/326 ([1991] OJ L180/79); Commission Directive (EEC) 91/410 ([1991] OJ L228/67); Commission Directive (EEC) 91/632 ([1991] OJ L338/23); Commission Directive (EEC) 92/37 ([1992] OJ L154/30); Commission Directive (EEC) 92/69 ([1992] OJ L383/113); Commission Directive (EEC) 93/21 ([1993] OJ L110/20); Commission Directive (EEC) 93/72 ([1993] oJ L258/29); Commission Directive (EEC) 93/101 ([1993] OJ L13/1); Commission Directive (EC) 93/105 ([1993] OJ L294/21); Commission Directive (EC) 94/69 ([1994] OJ L381/1); Council Directive (EC) 96/56 ([1996] OJ 236/35); Commission Directive (EC) 96/54 ([1996] OJ 248/1); Commission Directive (EC) 98/73 ([1998] OJ L305/1); Commission Directive (EC) 98/98 ([1999] OJ L293/1); Commission Directive (EC) 2000/32 ([2000] OJ 2000 L136/1); Commission Directive (EC) 2000/33 ([2000] OJ L136/900); Commission Directive (EC) 2001/59 ([2001] OJ L225/1).

383 [1979] OJ L259/10.

384 SI 1984/1244.

385 SI 1978/209.

3. Commission Decision (EEC) 85/71 concerning the list of chemical substances notified pursuant to Council Directive (EEC) 67/548 on the approximation of laws, regulations and administrative provisions relating to the classification, packaging and labelling of dangerous substances[386]

Council Directive (EEC) 67/548 is concerned with the harmonisation of the laws in Member States relating to the classification, packaging and labelling of dangerous substances. Under Article 13 of that Directive, the Commission has responsibility for keeping a list of substances notified to it with the objective of protecting man and the environment against risks which could arise from the placing on the market of new substances.

The list of chemical substances is to be prepared and maintained by the Commission on the basis of the information supplied to it by the competent authorities of the Member States. The list must contain, in respect of each substance, the number of its notification, its identity and if dangerous, and its classification according to the Directive. Its identity must be recorded under its trade name and its chemical name in the IUPAC Nomenclature. A request may be made to record a substance under its trade name alone but, if the substance is dangerous, only until it is added to Annex I of the Directive.

The list of these chemical substances is updated each year and published in the Official Journal not later than 31 December for the period covering 1 July of the previous year to 30 June of the year of publication.

4. Parliament and Council Directive 1999/45 concerning the approximation of the laws, regulations and administrative provisions of the Member States relating to the classification, packaging and labelling of dangerous preparations

(a) Objective: While Directive 67/548 set out harmonised rules for classification, packaging and labelling of dangerous chemical substances, Directive 88/379[387] sought to extend these rules to dangerous preparations.

In 1999, Directive 88/379 was replaced, with effect from 30 July 2002 for the majority of preparations and with effect from 30 July 2004 for plant protection products and biocides, by Directive 99/45.[388]

Directive 99/45 extends the scope of the 1988 Directive to pesticides and introduces a requirement to classify and label preparations for environmental hazards. It also revises the text of the 1988 Directive to make it easier to use and understand.

The overall aim of both Directive 99/45 and Directive 88/37 is help eliminate the barriers to trade and establishment of the single market such differences caused and to ensure the protection of the general public and

386 [1985] OJ L30/33.
387 [1988] OJ L187/14.
388 [1999] OJ L200/1.

especially those who come into contact with such dangerous preparations through work or a hobby as well as consumers, notably children and the visually handicapped and also the environment.

(b) Scope of application: The aim of this Directive is laid down in Article 1 as the harmonisation of legislation on the classification, packaging and labelling of preparations which are dangerous to man and the environment when they are placed on the market within the Community. It applies to all preparations containing a dangerous substance as defined and classified by the provisions laid down in Council Directive (EEC) 67/548, but also to those which may present hazards, whether or not they are classified as dangerous within the meaning of the Directive.

According to Article 1(5), there are a wide range of products to which this Directive does not apply provided that they are in finished state, intended for the final user. These include products covered by other specific directives such as medicinal and veterinary products, cosmetics and waste, as well as foodstuffs, feedingstuffs, preparations containing radioactive substances and medical devices which are invasive or used in direct physical contact with the human body. In addition, the Directive does not apply to the carriage of dangerous substances by rail, road, inland waterway, sea or air; and preparations in transit, under customs supervision not undergoing any processing or treatment.

(c) Classification: On the model of Directive 67/548, Directive 1999/45 lays down the following classification criteria for dangerous substances and preparations:

(i) explosives;

(ii) oxidising;

(iii) extremely flammable;

(iv) highly flammable;

(v) flammable;

(vi) very toxic;

(vii) toxic;

(viii) harmful;

(ix) corrosive;

(x) irritant;

(xi) sensitising;

(xii) dangerous for the environment;

(xiii) carcinogenic;

(xiv) toxic for reproduction; and

(xv) mutagenic.

As this Directive is intended to harmonise within the framework Directive (EEC) 67/548, Article 4 stipulates that the general principles of the classification and labelling of preparations must be applied according to the criteria laid down in Annex VI to Council Directive (EEC) 67/548, save where the alternative criteria referred to in Article 5, 6, 7 or 10 and the relevant Annexes to this Directive apply However, alternative criteria are also laid down which may be applicable under Article 3 of this Directive.

Physio-chemical properties to be used on a basis for classification are determined though by the methods laid down in Annex V of Council Directive (EEC) 67/548. Whether a preparation is regarded as explosive, oxidising, extremely flammable, highly flammable or flammable is determined if the requirements listed at Article 5(2) are fulfilled.

For certain cases where the methods laid down in Annex V to Directive (EEC) 67/548 are not appropriate, alternative calculation methods are laid down in Part B of Annex I to this Directive.

(d) Assessment of health hazards: Article 6 sets out two possible methods for the assessment of health hazards:

(a) a conventional method described in Annex II;

(b) by determining the toxicological properties of the preparation necessary for appropriate classification in accordance with the criteria in Annex VI to Directive (EEC) 67/548. These properties shall be determined by means of the methods laid down in Part B of Annex V to Directive (EEC) 67/548.

Where a toxicological property has been established on the basis of both methods (a) and (b), the results from method (b) shall be used for classifying the preparation, except in the case of carcinogenic, mutagenic or toxic effects for reproduction for which only method (a) shall be used. Any of the toxicological properties of the preparation which are not assessed by method (b) shall be assessed in accordance with method (a). When it can be shown that the effect on man differs from that suggested by either assessment, a preparation must be classified according to its effects on man. Any other effects such as antagonism or potentiation must also be taken into account.

New health hazard assessments must be performed whenever there is a change of composition either because of a change in initial concentration by weight or percentage or because of a substitution of one or more of the constituents of the preparation.

(e) Assessment of environmental hazards: Article 7 sets out two possible methods for the assessment of environmental hazards:

(a) a conventional method described in Annex III to this Directive;

(b) by determining the hazardous properties of the preparation for the environment necessary for appropriate classification in accordance with the criteria set out in Annex VI to Directive (EEC) 67/548. These properties shall be determined by means of the methods laid down in Part C of Annex V to Directive (EEC) 67/548 unless, in the case of plant protection products, other internationally recognised methods are acceptable in accordance with the provisions of Annexes II and III to Directive (EEC) 91/414.

Where the environmental hazards have been assessed in compliance with both the procedures mentioned above, the results of method (b) shall be used for classifying the preparation.

New environmental hazard assessments must be performed whenever there is a change of composition involving the substitution or addition of one or more constituents.

(f) Obligations on Member States: According to Article 8, Member States have a general obligation to ensure that dangerous preparations cannot be placed on the market unless they comply with this Directive.

In order to ensure compliance with this Directive, the authorities of the Member States may request information on the composition of the preparation and any other pertinent information from any person responsible for placing the preparation on the market.

Member States shall take all necessary measures to ensure that those responsible for placing the preparation on the market hold at the disposal of the authorities of the Member States: the data used for the classification and labelling of the preparation; any pertinent information relating to packaging requirements; the data used for establishing the safety data sheet.

Member States and the Commission shall exchange information concerning the name and full address of the national authority (authorities) responsible for communicating and exchanging information relating to the practical application of this Directive.

Under Article 17, Member States are responsible for appointing the bodies responsible for receiving information and for ensuring compliance of such bodies with the principles laid down in Article 17.

(g) Packaging: All dangerous preparations placed on the market must satisfy the packaging requirements laid down in Article 9. This means, in practice, that the packaging of preparations covered by this Directive must satisfy the following requirements:

(i) be so designed and constructed that its contents cannot escape;

(ii) the materials constituting the packaging and fastenings must not be susceptible to adverse attack by the contents, or liable to form dangerous compounds with the contents;

(iii) packaging and fastenings must be strong and solid throughout to ensure that they will not loosen and will safely meet the normal stresses and strains of handling;

(iv) containers fitted with replaceable fastening devices shall be so designed that the packaging can be refastened repeatedly without the contents escaping.

Containers which contain preparations covered by this Directive offered or sold to the general public should not have either a shape and/or graphic decoration likely to attract or arouse the active curiosity of children or to mislead consumers, or a presentation and/or a designation used for foodstuffs or animal feedingstuffs or medicinal or cosmetic products.

Containers which contain certain preparations offered or sold to the general public covered by Annex IV should be fitted with child-resistant fastenings and/or carry a tactile warning of danger. The technical specifications of such fastenings are laid down in Annex IX to Council Directive (EEC) 67/548.

(h) Labelling: Article 10 stipulates that the following information must be clearly and indelibly marked on any package:

(i) the trade name or designation of the preparation;

(ii) the name, address and telephone number of the person responsible for placing the preparation on the market;

(iii) the chemical name of the substance or substances present in accordance with certain detailed rules laid down in Article 10;

(iv) the danger symbols and indications of the dangers in accordance with Annexes II and IV to Council Directive (EEC) 67/548;

(v) the risk phrases (R-phrases) conforming to the wording in Annex III and VI to Council Directive (EEC) 67/ 548;

(vi) the safety advice (S-phrases) conforming to the wording in Annex IV and VI to Council Directive (EEC) 67/548;

(vii) the normal quantity of the contents in the case of preparations sold to the general public.

Certain derogations are provided for by Article 10(3) and (4).

No statements such as 'non toxic' or 'not harmful' indicating that a preparation is not dangerous may appear on the packaging or labelling of any preparations to which this Directive applies.

Article 11 goes on to stipulate that the label required must be firmly affixed to one or more surfaces of the package or container so that it can be read horizontally when set down normally. The dimensions of the label are laid down in Annex VI to Directive 67/584. A label is not required if the necessary particulars appear on the package itself. The danger symbol and its background must stand out clearly. Outer packages containing several inner packages will satisfy this Directive if the outer package is labelled in accordance with the international rules of transport in dangerous substances and the inner package in accordance with this Directive. Single packages labelled in accordance with those international rules will also satisfy the Directive but must include certain particulars.

Member States may make the placing on the market of preparations covered by this Directive within their territories subject to use of their official language or languages in the label.

According to Article 12, if the package is too small to be labelled as required, Member States can permit that some other appropriate manner can be used, and likewise if the quantities are very small and there is no danger in the handling of it provided the preparation is extremely flammable, highly flammable, flammable, irritant or oxidising harmful.

(i) Distance selling: According to Article 13, any advertisement for a preparation within the meaning of this Directive which enables a member of the general public to conclude a contract for purchase without first having sight of the label for that preparation must make mention of the type or types of hazard indicated on the label.

(j) Safety data sheet: The safety data sheet information is principally intended for use by professional users and must enable them to take the necessary measures as regards the protection of health, safety and the environment at the place of work.

The person who is responsible for placing on the market a preparation covered by the Directive is responsible for providing the safety data sheet for that preparation.

A safety data sheet providing proportionate information must also be supplied, on request of a professional user, by the person responsible for placing on the market a preparation which, although not classified as dangerous within the Directive, contains certain amounts of substances which pose health or environmental hazards of for which there are Community workplace exposure limits.

(k) Confidentiality: According to Article 15, derogations to the rules laid down in the Directive for confidentiality reasons are only allowed, under certain conditions, for substances which are classified as irritant or harmful.

(l) Restrictions: Member States may restrict or prohibit the marketing of any preparation even though it satisfies the requirements of this Directive if there is detailed evidence that it still constitutes a hazard. In such cases the Commission and other Member States are to be informed immediately.[389] It is up to the Commission to take the appropriate measures after delivering its opinion. Any technical adaptations to this Directive necessary as a result shall be adopted in accordance with the procedure laid down Council Directive (EEC) 67/548.

(m) Adaptation to technical progress: The amendments required to adapt the nine annexes to technical progress are adopted by the Commission with

389 Article 19 of the Directive.

the assistance of a regulatory committee made up of representatives of the Member States and chaired by a representative of the Commission.

(n) Implementation: Directive 1999/45 was to be implemented by 30 July 2002. At the time of writing, not all Member States have implemented the Directive. In the UK, it has been transposed by the Chemicals (Hazard Information and Packaging for Supply) Regulations 2002.[390]

5. Commission Directive (EEC) 91/155 defining and laying down the detailed arrangements for the system of specific information relating to dangerous preparations in implementation of Article 10 of Directive (EEC) 88/379

(a) Objective: The labelling formerly required by Directive (EEC) 88/379 (now by Directive 1999/45) provides a basic source of information for users of dangerous preparations by giving them a clear, concise indication of the potential dangers. This Directive is intended to supplement that by providing for a more detailed information system for industrial users. In particular, Article 10 of Directive (EEC) 88/379 (now Article 14 of Directive 1999/45) provides for the setting up of an information system in the form of safety data sheets relating to dangerous preparations primarily for industrial users to ensure the protection of health and safety in the workplace. Directive 91/155, amended by Directive 2001/58[391] so as to bring it in line with Directive 1999/45, makes detailed arrangements for the provision of such data sheets.

(b) The supply of a safety data sheet: Under Article 1, the person who is responsible for placing a chemical substance or preparation on the market, whether the manufacturer, importer or distributor, shall supply the recipient, who is a professional user of the substance or preparation, with a safety data sheet containing the information set out in Article 3 and the Annex to this Directive, if the substance or preparation is classified as dangerous according to Directive (EEC) 67/548 or Directive (EC) 1999/45.

In addition, any person who is responsible for placing a preparation on the market shall supply, on request of a professional user, a safety data sheet providing proportionate information as set out in Article 3 and the Annex to this Directive, if the preparation is not classified as dangerous according to Articles 5, 6 and 7 of Directive (EC) 1999/45, but the preparation contains, in an individual concentration of > = 1% by weight for non-gaseous preparations and > = 0.2% by volume for gaseous preparations, at least one substance posing health or environmental hazards, or one substance for which there are Community workplace exposure limits.

The sheet must be supplied free of charge at the latest when the substance or preparation is first supplied and afterwards a revision is to be supplied when any significant changes are made. There is no need to supply a safety

390 SI 2002/1689.
391 [2001] OJ L212/24.

data sheet to general users of dangerous substances or preparations when furnished with sufficient information to take the necessary measures on health and safety.

Under Article 3 the safety data sheet must contain the following obligatory information:

(i) identification of the substance/preparation and of the company/undertaking;

(ii) composition/information on ingredients;

(iii) hazards identification;

(iv) first-aid measures;

(v) fire fighting measures;

(vi) accidental release measures;

(vii) handling and storage;

(viii) explosive controls/personal protection;

(ix) physical and chemical properties;

(x) stability and reactivity;

(xi) toxicological information;

(xii) ecological information;

(xiii) disposal considerations;

(xiv) transport information;

(xv) regulatory information; and

(xvi) other relevant information.

The Annex to this Directive sets out explanatory notes for the compilation of the safety data sheet.

(c) Implementation: The Directive, as amended in 2002, was implemented in the UK by the Chemicals (Hazard Information and Packaging for Supply) Regulations 2002.[392]

All Member States have notified implementing measures.

6. Council Directive (EEC) 76/769[393] on the approximation of the laws, regulations and administrative provisions of the Member States relating to restrictions on the marketing and use of certain dangerous substances and preparations

(a) Objective: All the rules concerning the placing on the EU market of dangerous substances and preparations are aimed at protecting the public and, in particular people using or working with such substances and preparations. In addition, it is felt that all of these rules should contribute not only towards

392 SI 2002/1689.
393 [1976] OJ L262/201.

protection of the environment especially when considering those substances and preparations which have characteristics of ecotoxicity or may pollute but also play their part to restore, preserve or improve the quality of human life in the EU.

There are already directives which cover the labelling, packaging and classification of dangerous substances and preparations.[394] However, this Directive addresses the need for special restrictions to be laid down relating to certain substances and preparations especially in respect of those already subject to restrictions decided upon by international organisations. The restrictions laid down in this Directive cover a variety of different substances, all of which over the years have been shown to have a particularly dangerous effect on human health or are especially destructive of the environment. This means that this Directive has been amended piecemeal, often with each amendment covering a different or new substance or preparation, as more scientific and technological knowledge and research has revealed the harmful nature of its characteristics.

Furthermore, the differing provisions in the Member States are considered to be an obstacle to trade and hinder the establishment of a fully functioning common market. There is, therefore, a need to harmonise the laws and regulations between Member States in relation to the restrictions placed on such dangerous substances and preparations.

(b) Scope of application: The Directive is concerned with restricting the marketing and use in the Member States of the dangerous substances and preparations listed in the Annex. According to Article 1(3), substances are chemical elements and their compounds occurring in their natural state or as produced by industry; preparations are mixtures or solutions of two or more substances.

According to Article 1(2), the Directive does not apply to:

(i) the carriage of dangerous substances and preparations by rail, road, inland waterway, sea or air;

(ii) those substances and preparations exported to non-Member State countries;

(iii) those substances and preparations in transit and under customs supervision and not undergoing any processing.

(c) General obligations: Member States must ensure that dangerous substances and preparations are only placed on the market or used subject to the relevant conditions and restrictions laid down in the Annex. According to Article 2(a),[395] these restrictions do not apply to the marketing and use of such

394 Council Directive (EEC) 67/548 ([1967] OJ L196/1) (as amended); Parliament and Council Directive 1999/45 ([1999] OJ L200/1).

395 As added by Council Directive (EEC) 89/678 ([1989] OJ L398/24).

substances and preparation for the purposes only of research and development or analysis.

(d) Adaptation to technical progress: Substances falling under the Limitations Directive are listed in the Annex I, which also specifies the restrictions on marketing and use applying in each particular case.

Where a substance is not already listed in Annex I, the name of the substance and the desired limitations on marketing and use are added using proposals to the Council and the Parliament to amend the Directive. Where a substance is listed and the requirement is to change the limitations already in place, this is done by a Commission Directive adapting the existing limitations to technical progress.

As yet, there have been 26 adaptations and 12 amendments to the Directive. The lack of a consolidated version makes the Directive rather difficult to understand and apply.

(e) Dangerous substances and preparations subject to restrictions: The Annex, as amended, deals with a great number of individual substances and preparations which are subject to restrictions and conditions. In addition, they also deal with particular uses of substances which have caused grave concern both to human health and the environment. In a commentary of this nature, it is not possible to highlight each substance or preparation or product but the most important of these which have frequently merited attention because of their dangerous properties are considered here.

(f) Substances classified as carcinogens, mutagens or substances toxic to reproduction (CMR): Annex I of Council Directive (EEC) 67/548 deals with classification of all notifiable dangerous substances. Those substances classified as carcinogens category 1 or category 2 may cause cancer. To improve health protection it is proposed that these substances and preparations containing them should not be placed on the market for use by the general public in concentrations equal or greater than that specified by Annex I of Council Directive (EEC) 67/548 and must be labelled as 'restricted to professional users'. There are derogations listed and these cover circumstances when their use is covered by other relevant directives, for example, medicinal or veterinary products, cosmetics, motor fuels and waste.

Substances classified as mutagens in Annex I of Council Directive (EEC) 67/548, category 1 or category 2, may cause heritable genetic damage and are similarly restricted as are those substances so classified by Annex I of Council Directive (EEC) 67/548 (as amended), as toxic for reproduction, category 1 or category 2 which may cause birth defects.

396 [2003] OJ L156/26.

Recent amendments in this area are contained in Directive 2003/36,[396] Directive 2003/34[397] and Directive 2002/45.[398]

(g) PCBs and PCTs: The Directive first addressed the problem of placing restrictions on the use of PCBs and PCTs, being products in respect of which the international community had already decided upon restrictions. Their use was prohibited from January 1978 originally, except in certain specialised uses, for example, closed system electrical equipment, large condensers, hydraulic fluids in underground mining equipment. It was found, however, that certain PCTs were of fundamental importance in the manufacture and maintenance of certain products such as gas turbine components, nuclear reactors and the construction of ship and aircraft frames so temporary authorisation was granted for such purposes until 31 December 1984.[399] Constant assessment of the use of these substances revealed that, notwithstanding the restrictions imposed, pollution of the environment by PCBs and PCTs had not lessened significantly. Highly toxic substances are emitted by these products in the event of fire and, therefore, the thresholds for their use were lowered substantially. In addition, as substitutes had been developed which were considered less dangerous to human health and the environment, the marketing of PCBs and PCTs was no longer considered justified except in exceptional circumstances where there was no danger to human health.[400] These further restrictions were implemented with effect from 30 June 1986.

(h) Dangerous liquid products: Certain liquids ranging from flammable to corrosive to toxic had been used in glass containers in types of lamps and other ornamental objects. As these objects are not always stable and easily broken by children causing fatalities, it was decided to prohibit the marketing and use of such liquids in such objects from July 1980.[401] The use of such dangerous liquids in other objects such as games, tricks and jokes, presenting similar hazards, was also subsequently banned from June 1990.[402]

(i) Fire retardant products: A number of fire retardant products have been used to fireproof textiles and garments, especially children's clothing, which have been shown to present a health hazard by coming into contact with the skin. Restrictions were placed on the use of tris-phosphate from July 1980[403] and on the use of tris-phosphinoxide and PBBs from November 1984.[404]

396 [2003] OJ L156/26.
397 [2003] OJ L156/14.
398 [2002] OJ L177/21.
399 Council Directive (EEC) 82/828 ([1982] OJ L350/34).
400 Ibid.
401 Council Directive (EEC) 79/663 ([1979] OJ L197/37).
402 Council Directive 89/677 ([1989] OJ L398/19).
403 Council Directive (EEC) 79/663 ([1979] OJ L197/37).
404 Council Directive (EEC) 83/264 ([1983] OJ L147/9).

(j) Benzene: Benzene is recognised as a substance which is highly toxic, affects the central nervous system and is carcinogenic. It was used in certain toys and could, therefore, be absorbed by children by inhalation, ingestion or through the skin. Maximum concentration limits and the use of benzene have been fixed to exclude these health hazards from occurring and to harmonise the rules on benzene as between Member States. These limits were to be implemented by November 1983. Later provisions reducing these concentration limits further were introduced with effect from June 1990.[405]

(k) Substances and preparations used in jokes and hoaxes: Certain products used in sneezing powders, jokes and hoaxes, all of which are mainly used by children, who are particularly sensitive and require special protection, constitute health hazards. These products include dimethoxybenzidine which, with its close affinity to benzidine, has a carcinogenic effect and is prohibited in jokes and hoaxes. Certain plant-based sneezing powers are banned, as is ammonium polysuiphide which has a corrosive effect particularly harmful to the eyes, and the volatile esters of bromacetic acid used in stink bombs. All these preparations are prohibited from use in jokes and hoaxes from November 1984.[406]

(l) Asbestos: It has long been recognised that the use of asbestos can release fibres and dusts which are detrimental to human health and cause asbestosis and cancer. It was felt that the most effective way to protect human health as well as the environment is to prohibit the use of those types of asbestos which are particularly dangerous, notably crocidolite, known as blue asbestos, with effect from July 1988.[407] However, there was no effective possibility of imposing a total ban immediately on such products, not only because the withdrawal and disposal of them can lead to the release of harmful fibres but also because certain products containing blue asbestos such as asbestos cement pipes could not be wholly replaced by satisfactory substitutes. This is no longer the case and there is now a total ban on the use of crocidolite with effect from July 1993.[408]

To help control the use of other asbestos fibres pending Community restrictions, provisions have been introduced to harmonise the labelling requirements between Member States on asbestos. All products containing asbestos on their packaging must bear a label conforming to certain standards and setting out specific information. The labelling provisions are set out in what is now Annex II to the Directive. The label must:

(i) be of certain minimum dimensions;

(ii) consist of two parts containing a symbol for asbestos and be of specified colouring and wording to ensure the symbol stands out clearly;

405 Council Directive (EEC) 83/264 ([1983] OJ L147/9).
406 Council Directive (EEC) 83/264 ([1983] OJ L147/9).
407 Council Directive (EEC) 83/478 ([1983] OJ L263/33).
408 Commission Directive (EEC) 91/659 ([1991] OJ L363/36).

(iii) state whether it contains asbestos or crocidolite;

(iv) be fixed or printed directly on the packaging or on the product on the smallest units supplied or on the components unless this is impossible, in which case it must be accompanied by a handout;

(v) contain particulars clearly and indelibly inscribed including the relevant symbol, indications of danger and the safety instructions.

Improved monitoring of the marketing and use of dangerous asbestos fibres has revealed that there are substitution products for certain uses which are less dangerous than asbestos fibres. Further restrictions have been placed on the use of other asbestos fibres, in addition to crocidolite. Most of these other dangerous asbestos fibres were prohibited from use in certain products from December 1987 including:

(i) toys;

(ii) finished products retailed to the public in powder form;

(iii) items for smoking, eg, pipes;

(iv) paints and varnishes;

(v) materials for spraying;

(vi) catalytic filters and insulation devices.[409]

Since July 1993, with the greater availability of less dangerous substitutes, all dangerous asbestos fibres have been prohibited from use in:[410]

(i) road surfacing material;

(ii) mortars, protective coatings, fillers, sealants, mastics, glues;

(iii) insulating or soundproofing materials;

(iv) air filters;

(v) underlay for plastic floor and wall coverings;

(vi) roofing felt.

(m) Environmental and aquatic pollutants: Certain products, the most important of which are mercury compounds, arsenic compounds and organostannic compounds, are now prohibited from use with effect from June 1990 because they are harmful and dangerous to man and the environment, particularly the aquatic environment.[411]

These products are generally prohibited when intended to be used:

(i) to prevent the fouling by micro-organisms, plants or animals of the hulls of boats, cages, floats, nets and any other totally or partly submerged equipment;

409 Council Directive (EEC) 85/610 ([1985] OJ L375/1).

410 See, eg, Directive 99/77 (EC) ([1999] OJ L 207/18) (ban on the marketing of the chrysotile type of asbestos fibres).

411 Council Directive (EEC) 89/677.

(ii) in the preservation of wood;

(iii) in the treatment of industrial waters.

In addition, pentachlorophenol and its compounds are also to be considered as falling within this category and restrictions on its concentration limits are applicable from July 1992.[412] This product and its compounds are, however, used for wood preservation and whilst a coordinated Community strategy is being developed on the use of chemical products for this purpose, there are exceptions, as long as they are not sold to the general public, for the treatment of wood, in fibres and heavy duty textiles not for clothing or decorative purposes, for timber and masonry in historic buildings and as a processing agent in industry.

(n) Cadmium: As part of the Community action programme to combat environmental pollution, specific measures have been introduced to restrict the use of cadmium as advances in knowledge and techniques suggest that there are less harmful substitutes which could be used. Most of these restrictions are to take effect from December 1992. Cadmium and its compounds may not be used to give colour to finished products manufactured from polyvinyl chloride (PVC) and similar preparations. This list is to be extended to include other finished products including paint from December 1995. Restrictions are imposed on the use of cadmium as a stabiliser from June 1994 in a wide range of finished products including: packaging materials; office and school supplies; fittings for furniture; clothing accessories; imitation leather; and road transport vehicles amongst others. However, where it is used for colouring or as a stabiliser for safety reasons these restrictions do not apply. In addition, cadmium plating metallic products or components are not to be used in equipment and machinery for food production, agriculture, cooking and freezing, printing and book binding, household goods, furniture, sanitary ware and central heating or air conditioning plant. These restrictions are extended from June 1995 to equipment and machinery for paper and board, textiles and clothing as well as rolling stock, vessels and road and agricultural vehicles.

(n) Other dangerous substances: There are a number of other carcinogenic substances, some of which may be present as impurities in products such as benzidine which have concentration limits placed on them and are restricted to professional users.[413]

These restrictions have been introduced to prevent the incidence of cancer at work and to protect consumers. In addition, lead compounds, especially lead salts readily soluble in the stomach, are still used as pigment for certain decorative paints and are to be prohibited except for the restoration of historic works of art and buildings.

412 Council Directive (EEC) 91/173 ([1991] OJ L85/34).
413 Council Directive (EEC) 89/677.

(o) Recent adaptations: Recent adaptations of Annex I include measures concerning: blue colourant/azo-dye (12th adaptation);[414] arsenic (10th adaptation);[415] organostannic compounds (9th adaptation);[416] hexachloroethane (8th adaptation);[417] creosote (7th adaptation)[418].

(p) Implementation: The nature of this Directive, dealing with constant changes as the dangers of any particular substance or preparation become apparent, means that there is no single implementation date. New implementation dates are added continually as amendments are made to the Annexes to the Directive.

This Directive as amended is implemented in the United Kingdom by various different regulations, including: the Dangerous Substances and Preparations (Safety) (Consolidation) Regulations 1994;[419] the Dangerous Substances and Preparations (Safety) (Consolidation) (Amendment) Regulations 1996;[420] the Novelties (Safety) (Amendment) Regulations 1985;[421] the Asbestos Products (Safety) Regulations 1985.[422]

All Member States have notified implementing measures.

414 Commission Directive (EC) 2003/03 ([2003] OJ L4/12).
415 Commission Directive (EC) 2003/02 ([2003] OJ L4/9).
416 Commission Directive (EC) 2002/62 ([2002] OJ L183/58).
417 Commission Directive (EC) 2001/91 ([2001] OJ L286/27).
418 Commission Directive (EC) 2001/90 ([2001] OJ L283/41).
419 SI 1994/2844.
420 SI 1996/2635.
421 SI1985/128.
422 SI 1985/2402.

8
TOYS

1. Introduction

In 1985, the Commission agreed a communication to the Council of Ministers designed to give a new impetus to the Community's consumer protection policy.[423] This communication recognised that under the two previous programmes, many of their objectives had not been adequately realised or achieved. Among the problems identified was that in the past the Community had tried to proceed by prescribing detailed rules for a restricted range of goods or services. This meant that few had gone through the whole legislative process.

To counter this problem, a 'new approach' to technical harmonisation was introduced. This approach was based on the principles that only essential safety and other mandatory requirements are laid down in the Council directives and detailed specifications are to be drawn up by European standardisation bodies thus removing the difficulties of adapting to technical change and defining characteristics.

Council Directive (EEC) 88/378[424] on the safety of toys was the first new approach directive. It defined essential mechanical, chemical and physical safety requirements to which a toy must conform but left the details to be drawn up by European standardisation bodies. Apart from the problem of adequate consumer representation on the European standardisation bodies, another problem which has emerged is that there is no checking of toy safety by independent bodies, since it may be the manufacturers and importers themselves who stamp the toys with the appropriate CE marking.

As a result of this new approach directive on toys, earlier proposals for Council directives on common technical safety standards have not been adopted.

2. Council Directive (EEC) 88/378 on the approximation of the laws of the Member States concerning the safety of toys[425]

(a) Objective: This Directive was adopted in the light of the differing provisions between Member States relating to safety characteristics of toys. These differences between provisions were felt to be a barrier to trade and also gave rise to unequal conditions of competition within the Community without necessarily giving sufficient protection to consumers, especially children, from any hazards arising.

423 COM(1985)314 final.
424 [1988] OJ L187/1 (as amended).
425 [1988] OJ L187/1.

The Directive therefore attempts to remove these obstacles by laying down conditions for an internal market in which only sufficiently safe toy products should be sold.

(b) Scope of application: The Directive applies to 'toys', defined as any product or material designed or clearly intended for use in play by children of less than 14 years of age. This definition hopes to capture the wide diversity of products on the market but there are a number of products listed in Annex I which are not intended to be covered by this Directive. It is likely that this is not a complete list and there may be other products which will be included in the future.

(c) Mandatory safety requirements: As a general rule, under Article 2, toys shall be placed on the market only if they do not jeopardise the safety and health of users or third parties and if they meet the health and safety requirements laid down in the Directive.

Annex II lays down the essential safety requirements which toys must meet during manufacture and before being placed on the market. These criteria cover general risks (protection against health hazards or physical injury) and particular risks (physical and mechanical, flammability, chemical properties, electrical properties, hygiene, radioactivity).

Under Article 2, these requirements are laid down bearing in mind the intended use of the products with allowance being made for foreseeable use and bearing in mind the normal behaviour of children and the fact that the standard degree of care would not be the same as that of an adult. In addition, it would be necessary to ensure that this standard would be maintained throughout the foreseeable and normal period of use.

The degree of risk also has to take into account the ability of the user (children). If appropriate, the toy must contain a label that specifies a minimum age.

(d) Harmonised safety standards: The European standardisation bodies (CEN, CENLEC) have drawn up, in accordance with the procedure laid down in Council Directive (EEC) 83/189,[426] non-mandatory, harmonised European standards on the basis of the essential requirements set out in the Directive.

The references of those standards are published in the Official Journal of the European Communities.[427]

Compliance with the national standards that transpose such harmonised standards automatically raises a presumption of compliance with the safety requirements of the Directive.

(e) Conformity assessment: Article 11 provides for a CE marking and all toys bearing this mark are presumed to comply with the essential requirements of this Directive. This mark implies that the relevant standards have been met. However, toys are also presumed to satisfy the essential

426 [1983] OJ L109/8.
427 [2003] OJ C62/4.

requirements, where the relevant standards have not been applied or have been, but only in part, or where none exist, if they receive an EC type examination certificate. In practice, there are two forms of conformity assessment:

(i) The manufacturer itself can apply the standards. He draws up a design dossier and describes the means whereby he ensures conformity of the production. Then, he affixes the CE marking, his name and address on the toy or on the packaging before placing the toy on the market.

(ii) The manufacturer submits the model of the toy as well as a design dossier to the notified body. The notified body issues a EC type examination certificate. The manufacturer has the means to ensure the conformity of his production with the approved model. Then, he affixes the CE marking on each toy, or its packaging, when it conforms to the approved mode.

In the first case, the manufacturer of the toy product or an authorised representative, or the person placing the product on the market, must keep certain information for inspection including:

(i) a description of the means such as a report or file by which compliance with the harmonised standards is ensured;

(ii) an EC type certificate;

(iii) copies of documents submitted to the approved body;

(iv) addresses of the places of manufacture and storage;

(v) detailed information about the design and manufacture.

In the second case, the manufacturer, or his authorised representative or the person placing the product on the market, must keep certain information for inspection including the following:

(i) a detailed description of manufacture;

(ii) a description of the means (test report or technical file) whereby conformity with the approved model is ensured;

(iii) addresses of the places of manufacture and storage;

(iv) copies of documents submitted to the approved body;

(v) test certificate for the sample as a certified copy.

(f) Approved bodies: Approved bodies for carrying out the procedures and checking that the essential requirements are met are appointed under Article 9 of the Directive and notified to the Commission. The minimum criteria to make an appointment are listed in Annex III.

(g) Examinations and marks: EC type examination is the procedure by which an approved body finds out and certifies that a model of a toy satisfies the essential requirements of the Directive.[428] Application for such an examination must be lodged by the manufacturer or his authorised

428 Article 10 of the Directive.

representative within the Community. The precise elements which an application and an examination must include are listed in Article 10.

If a model meets the essential requirements, a certificate is drawn up by the approved body and notified to the applicant indicating conditions attached. Copies of the certificate are available on request and any refusal of a certificate shall be informed to a Member State with reasons.

Under Article 11, CE marking indicating compliance with the essential requirements of this Directive together with the name and/or trade mark and/or name and address of the manufacturer, his authorised representative or importer has to be affixed generally to the toy or packaging in a visible, legible and indelible form. If the toys are small, these particulars must be affixed to the packaging or to a label or leaflet and the consumer's attention drawn to them. The CE marking consists of the symbol 'CE' and other symbols likely to be confused with this are prohibited. Certain toys require warnings or precautions to be taken during use. These are listed in Annex IV and may be given in national languages if Member States so require. Examples of such toys include:

(i) those not intended for children under 36 months;

(ii) slides, swings and rings, trapezes, etc;

(iii) functional toys that are used in the same way as appliances intended for adults;

(iv) those containing something inherently dangerous, such as chemistry sets;

(v) skates and skateboards;

(vi) toys for use in water.

(h) Checks: Under Article 12, Member States may take measures to carry out sample checks to verify that toys conform with the Directive. In carrying out such checks, the authority responsible for inspection will require access, on request, to the place of manufacture, storage and to the information required for an EC type examination or may ask for such information within a specified period and may take a sample away to test and examine. In such checks, confidentiality is to be maintained and Member States must make a report every three years to the Commission.

(i) Communication of information: All activities carried out in pursuance of the Directive are to be regularly informed to the Commission so that the Commission can ensure procedures are properly implemented.[429] All decisions taken involving restrictions, together with reasons, are to be notified to all parties concerned.

429 Article 13 of the Directive.

(j) Implementation: In the UK, the Directive was implemented by the Toy Safety Regulations 1995.[430]

All Member States have notified implementing measures.

430 SI 1995/204.

9
Tobacco Products

1. Introduction

Community measures relating to tobacco products, although concerned with the establishment of suitable conditions for the operation of the single internal market, also have as much to do with the introduction of provisions necessary to guarantee public health.

Campaigns against the smoking of tobacco products have been operative not just at national levels within Member States over a number of years but also at Community level. The European Parliament and the Council have since the 1980s backed a programme of action against cancer[431] and called for further measures at Community level to step up the action against smoking within the EU.[432] Current initiatives against tobacco include the setting up of a Community Tobacco Fund[433] (granting financial support to projects improving public awareness of the harmful effects of tobacco consumption in any form) and two networks (ENYPAT: European Network for Young People and Tobacco; ENSP: European Network for Smoking Prevention) financed by the Commission in 2002 under the cancer programme.

The first specific Community measures adopted were Council Directive (EEC) 89/622[434] on the labelling of tobacco products and Council Directive (EEC) 90/239[435] dealing with the maximum tar yield of cigarettes, but these were recently repealed by Directive 2001/37.[436] A first directive restricting the advertising of tobacco products was notoriously annulled by the ECJ and has now been replaced by Directive 2003/33.[437]

The panorama is completed by two directives on safety and health requirements for workplaces[438] and on TV advertising.

431 Council Resolution of 7 July 1986 on a programme of action of the EC against cancer ([1986] OJ C184/21).
432 See, for example, the Resolution on the campaign against smoking of 12 March 1982 ([1982] OJ C87/118), and the Resolution on stepping up action against smoking of 11 February 1988 ([1988] OJ C68/84).
433 Council Regulation 2075/92 ([1992] OJ L21/70).
434 [1989] OJ L359/1 (as amended).
435 [1990] OJ L137/36.
436 [2001] OJ L194/26.
437 [2003] OJ L152/16.
438 Council Directive 92/85(EC) on the introduction of measures to encourage improvements in the safety and health at work of pregnant workers and workers who have recently given birth or are breastfeeding ([1992] OJ L348/1) and Council Directive 89/654 concerning the minimum safety and health requirements for the workplace. These are, however, outside the scope of this section.

2. Parliament and Council Directive (EEC) 2001/37 on the approximation of the laws, regulations and administrative provisions of the Member States concerning the manufacture, presentation and sale of tobacco products

(a) Objective: This Directive recasts and repeals Council Directive 89/622 (establishing a warning to be carried on tobacco products) and Council Directive 90/239 (establishing the maximum tar yield of cigarettes), which had undergone several amendments since their enactment.

As the legal basis relied upon for introducing any measure for the establishment of the internal market is Article 95 (together with Article 133) of the EC Treaty, this Directive's primary aim is to harmonise provisions within Member States on the content of tar, nicotine and carbon monoxide of cigarettes and on the labelling and ingredients of tobacco products, whilst taking into account a high level of health protection.

(b) Scope of application: The Directive makes separate provisions for cigarettes, tobacco products in general and tobacco for oral use (ie, all products for oral use, except those intended to be smoked or chewed, made wholly or partly of tobacco, in power of in particulate form of in any combination of those forms).

(c) Cigarette content: Article 3 sets out the maximum yield of tar (10mg per cigarette); nicotine (1mg per cigarette); carbon monoxide (10mg per cigarette). Special provisions are made for cigarettes which are exported from the EC and for Greece.

Measurement of the above ingredients must be made or verified according to the methods set out in Article 3 by testing laboratories approved and monitored by the individual Member States, who can also require manufacturers or importers to carry out any other tests prescribed by the competent national authorities. The data and information which the national competent authorities obtain through the tests must be adequately disseminated to the Member States, with a view to informing consumers, and communicated to the Commission.

(d) Labelling: By virtue of Article 5, all cigarette packets of tobacco products must bear the tar, nicotine and carbon monoxide content in the official language(s) of the State where the product is marketed.

In addition, each packet of tobacco product (except tobacco for oral use and other smokeless tobacco products) must carry on the most visible surface and rotated in a way that ensures its regular appearance a general warning stating 'Smoking kills/Smoking can kill,' or 'Smoking seriously harms you and others around you'.

An additional warning taken from those listed in Annex I must also be affixed.

Tobacco products for oral use, where their marketing is permitted under Article 8, and smokeless tobacco products shall carry the following warning: 'This tobacco product can damage your health and is addictive'.

Article 5(5), (6) and (7) lays down the specific requirements (size, font type, background colour) for the general warning.

Since 30 September 2003, any sign or writing suggesting that a particular tobacco product is less harmful (such as the denomination 'light') than others is prohibited.

(e) Product information: In order to increase transparency and to assess the toxicity of tobacco products, Article 6 states that Member States shall require manufacturers and importers of tobacco products to submit to them yearly a list of all ingredients and their quantities used in the manufacture of tobacco products by brand name and type.

This list shall be accompanied by a statement setting out the reasons for the inclusion of such ingredients in those tobacco products, together with their function and category and the relevant toxicological data available. This information shall be disseminated appropriately in order to inform consumers.

(f) Tobacco for oral use: The placing on the market of tobacco for oral use is forbidden.

(g) Adaptation to technical progress: Technical and scientific progress in the field of tobacco products requires that the Directive is regularly re-evaluated. Under Article 9, this can be done by the Commission with the assistance of the Committee mentioned in Article 10.

(h) Member States' obligations: Member States cannot prohibit or restrict the import, sale or consumption of tobacco products that conform to the Directive. By the minimum harmonisation formula contained in Article 13, however, they are entitled to introduce more restrictive rules on the manufacture, import, sale and consumption of tobacco products for the protection of public health.

(i) Implementation: Member States were required to implement the Directive by 30 September 2002. Products not complying with the Directive can be marketed for one more year since that date.

In the UK, the Directive is implemented by the Tobacco Products (Manufacture, Presentation and Sale) (Safety) Regulations 2002.[439]

All Member States except Luxembourg, Ireland and Austria have notified implementing measures.

(j) Follow-up work: The Commission (assisted by scientific and technical experts) is to submit a report to the Parliament, Council and the Economic and Social Committee indicating, among the detail listed in Article 11, the features which should be reviewed in the light of development in scientific and technical knowledge and in particular of the development of internationally applicable standards for tobacco products (which are one of the subjects of the

439 SI 2002/3041.

negotiations for the drafting of a World Health Organisation Framework Convention on Tobacco Control).

To ensure the proper functioning of the internal market, the Commission shall include in its report a proposal containing a common list of ingredients authorised for tobacco products, taking into account, *inter alia*, their addictiveness. Pending the establishment of such a list, Member States can provide for the prohibition of the use of ingredients that increase the addictive properties of tobacco products.

Further reports have to be submitted every two years.

3. Parliament and Council Directive 2003/33 (EC) on the approximation of the laws, regulations and administrative provisions of the Member States relating to the advertising and sponsorship of tobacco products

(a) Objective: Directive 2003/33 aims to replace Parliament and Council Directive 376/98 annulled by the ECJ in 2000[440] on the grounds that it exceeded the legal basis on which it was adopted. Quite extraordinarily, the ECJ had in its judgment laid down the conditions upon which a Directive prohibiting certain forms of advertising and tobacco sponsorship could have been adopted. Directive 2003/33 duly takes into account the comments of the Court and the Advocate General.

The Directive seeks to harmonise existing regulations on tobacco advertising in Member States with a view to reinforcing the internal market, but excludes provisions in those areas the Court had indicated as not contributing to facilitate trade in the Community, such as cinema advertising, poster advertising and indirect advertising.

(b) Scope of application: The Directive covers advertising of tobacco products and their promotion in the press and other printed publications; in radio broadcasting; in information society services; and through tobacco related sponsorship, including the free distribution of tobacco products. The Directive that was annulled, on the other hand, applied to (and banned) all forms of advertising and sponsorship of tobacco products.

(c) Advertising in printed media and information society services: The circulation in the internal market of publications such as periodicals, newspapers and magazines is subject to a risk of obstacles to free movement as a result of Member States' divergence in the laws, regulations and administrative provisions which prohibit or regulate tobacco advertising in those media. In order to ensure free circulation throughout the internal market for all such media, Article 3 prohibits advertising in the press and other printed publications, save for those publications which are intended exclusively for professionals in the tobacco trade or which are printed and

440 Case C-376/98 Germany v Parliament and Council [2000] ECR I-8419.

published in third countries, where those publications are not principally intended for the EU market.

The Directive seeks to prevent use of the Internet to carry tobacco advertising by extending the same principle to advertising in information society services.

(d) Radio advertising and sponsorship: All forms of radio advertising for tobacco products are prohibited, as well as the sponsoring of radio programmes by undertakings whose principal activity is the manufacture or sale of tobacco products.

(e) Sponsorship of events: The laws, regulations and administrative provisions of the Member States relating to certain types of sponsorship for the benefit of tobacco products with cross-border effects give rise to an appreciable risk of distortion of the conditions of competition for this activity within the internal market. In order to eliminate these distortions, sponsorship of cross-border events involving tobacco promotion is banned, but national or local events sponsored by tobacco companies would not be covered by the Directive. In order to avoid circumvention, the Directive also prohibits the free distribution of tobacco products as a means of promotion in the context of sponsorship events.

(f) Member States' obligations: It is up to Member States to lay down rules for effective, proportionate and dissuasive penalties applicable to infringements of the Directive. The Directive also provides for the possibility that persons or organisations with a legitimate interest in the suppression of activities that do not conform with the Directive can take legal action against such infringements.

(g) Implementation: Member States must implement the Directive by 31 July 2005 at the latest.

All Member States had transposed Directive 89/552 which prohibited the TV advertising of tobacco products. All Member States already restricted advertising of tobacco products, but certain States, such as Sweden, Spain, Greece, Germany, only did that to a limited extent; other States, for example the UK, France and Italy already operate a total ban on tobacco advertising.

(h) Follow-up work: By 2008, the Commission should draw up a report on the implementation of this Directive together, if necessary, with a number of proposals for amendments to the Directive.

4. Council Directive (EEC) 89/552 of 3 October 1989 on the coordination of certain provisions laid down by law, regulation or administrative action in Member States concerning the pursuit of television broadcasting activities[441]

(a) Objective: This Directive, as is apparent from its title, regulates a whole host of television broadcasting activities.

441 [1989] OJ L298/23.

(b) Relevant provisions: Article 13 of the Directive prohibits all form of television advertising for cigarettes and other tobacco products. The ban includes all direct forms of advertising which do not mention the tobacco product but seek to circumvent the ban by using brand names, symbols or other distinctive features.

10

COMMUNITY WARNING AND INFORMATION SYSTEMS

1. Introduction

The European Community has, in addition to measures on product safety, undertaken other specific actions to meet and address consumer problems. Among these, and of particular concern to this area of consumer safety, have been the projects and systems set up to stimulate cooperation between Member States on accidents arising from the use of consumer products, including food.

Two systems were originally set up. First, a Community system for the rapid exchange of information on dangers arising from the use of consumer products, known as RAPEX, was set up. This system was intended to establish a rapid information flow between Member States allowing for emergency procedures to be set in motion when changes arose from consumer products.

Secondly, a project was designed (and first set up as a pilot project[442] for establishing an information system on accidents linked to consumer products, known as EHLASS[443] (the European Home and Leisure Accident Surveillance System). The project was applied to accidents which occur in the house or its immediate surroundings and which are followed by medical treatment. The basic information was to be obtained from casualty departments of selected hospitals, but Member States might provide additional information from other sources such as family doctors, fire brigades, insurance companies, for example, as the project progresses. Additionally, Member States had to collect and to submit annual reports to the Commission containing a summary and evaluation of the data collected. The Commission was in turn in charge of ensuring that the project was coherent, coordinated and implemented by Member States, of drawing up guidelines for the harmonisation of reports and of ensuring that they were exploited

Although it produced some positive results, the system had several drawbacks, such as the fact that Member States had different collection methods, different classifications and databases. A new system (the Injury Prevention Programme, IPP) was therefore created in 1999[444] with the purpose of bringing together those activities that were undertaken in relative isolation at national level and to enable them to complement one another.

One of the main goals was to create a common database (ISS – Injury Surveillance System within EUPHIN– European Union Public Health

442 Council Decision 81/623 ([1981] OJ L229/1).
443 See Council Decision 3092/94 ([1994] OJ L331/1).
444 Council Decision 372/1999 ([1999] OJ L46/1).

Information Network) with quality data collected using a common classification and comparable methods.

These initiatives have now been superseded by the Commission Programme of Community action in the field of public health (2003–2008)[445] having a broader scope that previous initiatives in improving health information and ensuring rapid reaction.

2. RAPEX

(a) Objective: The RAPEX system was originally set up by Council Decision (EEC) 84/133 introducing a Community system for the rapid exchange of information on dangers arising from the use of consumer products.[446] The system was later incorporated in other decisions, then in Directive 92/59 Directive (EEC) 92/59[447] and, upon repeal of the latter as from January 2004, will now be embedded, with some variations here considered, in Directive 2001/95.[448]

Since the first preliminary programme of the Community for a consumer protection and information policy, it was established that goods offered to consumers should present no risk to health and safety under normal or foreseeable conditions of use. Should risks exist in products, there ought to be measures available to inform consumers, improve the conditions of use or withdraw them from the market.

Accordingly, it was felt that a system should exist for the rapid exchange of information at Community level in the case where unsafe products are placed on the market. To assess how such an information system should be operated, Council Decision (EEC) 84/133 set up an experiment over an initial period to look at products other than those intended solely for professional use or which are already subject to similar procedures. The system has then been continued until present.

(b) Scope of application: The RAPEX system applies to products which are intended for consumers or likely, under reasonably foreseeable conditions, to be used by consumers even if not intended for them, and are supplied or made available, whether for consideration or not, in the course of a commercial activity, whether new, used or reconditioned, with the exception of pharmaceuticals.

(c) Exchange of information: Where a Member State takes measures which restrict the placing on the market of products – or require their withdrawal or recall – it shall inform the Commission of the measures and of the reasons for adopting them. If the risk presented does not or cannot go beyond its territory, the Member State shall notify the measure to the Commission in so far as it involves information likely to be of interest to

445 Council Decision 1786/2002 ([2002] OJ L271/1).
446 [1984] OJ L70/16.
447 [1992] OJ L228/24.
448 [2002] OJ L11/4.

Member States from the product safety standpoint, and in particular if they are in response to a new risk which has not yet been reported in other notifications.

The Commission shall then forward the notification to the other Member States unless, having examined the information contained in the notification, it concludes that the measure does not comply with Community law, in which case it shall immediately notify the Member State which adopted the measure.

(d) Rapid intervention: The detailed procedure for the application of RAPEX and guidelines for notification are laid down in Annex II of Directive 2001/95 . The Commission shall prepare and update further guidelines on the management of RAPEX .

Where a Member State takes steps to restrict, prevent or imposes specific conditions on the marketing or use of a product that presents a serious risk, it shall immediately notify the Commission. If the effects of the risk do not or cannot go beyond its territory, the Member State shall notify the measure to the Commission in so far as it involves information likely to be of interest to Member States.

The information transmitted to the Commission must contain certain details, such as information enabling the product to be identified; a description of the risk involved; the nature and the duration of the measures or action taken or decided on, if applicable; information on supply chains and distribution of the product, in particular on destination countries.

On receiving such notification, the Commission checks in the shortest possible time whether the measures taken comply with the Directive and forwards the information to the other Member States. The Commission may also carry out an investigation of its own initiative when it considers it necessary.

The other Member States must in turn inform the Commission of whether the product has been marketed in their territory, of what measures they may be adopting in the light of their own circumstances, stating the reasons, and of any other relevant information they have obtained on the risk involved, including the results of any tests or analyses carried out. They shall also immediately notify the Commission of any modification or lifting of the measures in question.

Since its amendment by Directive 2001/95, RAPEX now enables exchange of rapid alert notifications with international organisations and third countries, and in particular with candidate countries, subject to reciprocity.

(e) Initiative of the Commission: The Commission itself, if it becomes aware of a serious risk from certain products to the health and safety of consumers in various Member States, may, after consulting the Member States and in some cases the relevant Scientific Committee, adopt a decision requiring Member States to take measures ranging from among those listed in Article 8(1)(b) to (f) of Directive 2001/95 provided that:

(i) it emerges from prior consultations with the Member States that they differ significantly on the approach adopted or to be adopted to deal with the risk;

(ii) the risk cannot be dealt with, in view of the nature of the safety issue posed by the product, in a manner compatible with the degree of urgency of the case, under other procedures laid down by the specific Community legislation applicable to the products concerned;

(iii) the risk can be eliminated effectively only by adopting appropriate measures applicable at Community level, in order to ensure a consistent and high level of protection of the health and safety of consumers and the proper functioning of the internal market.

The decision of the Commission is valid for a period not exceeding one year and may be confirmed, under the same procedure, for additional periods none of which shall exceed one year. However, decisions concerning specific, individually identified products or batches of products shall be valid without a time limit.

The effect of the Commission's decision is also that export from the EU of the relevant dangerous products is prohibited.

(f) Food products: Under the previous regime, the RAPEX system comprised one network for food products and one for non-food products. Food safety , however, is now regulated by Regulation 178/2002.[449] Upon entry into force of this Regulation, the RAPEX food procedure covered by the former General Product Safety Directive ceases to apply and the system is instead called the Rapid Alert System for Food and Feed (RASFF). The legal basis of the RASFF is to be found in Article 50 of Regulation (EC) 178/2002. Practically, nothing will change, except the legal basis and the fact that the alert procedure will be extended to include animal feed.

(g) Market surveillance: Under Article 10 of Directive 2001/95, the Commission is under a duty to promote and take part in the operation of a European network (European Product Safety Network) of the authorities of the Member States competent for product safety, in particular in the form of administrative cooperation. This network operation is to be developed in a coordinated manner with the other existing Community procedures, particularly RAPEX. Its objective shall be to ensure that the provisions of European legislation are complied with across the EU, by taking measures to check that products meet the applicable safety requirements, that action is taken to bring products into compliance, and that sanctions are applied when necessary.

In particular, the network shall facilitate:

449 [2002] OJ L31/1.

(i) the exchange of information on risk assessment, dangerous products, test methods and results, recent scientific developments as well as other aspects relevant for control activities;

(ii) the establishment and execution of joint surveillance and testing projects;

(iii) the exchange of expertise and best practices and cooperation in training activities;

(iv) improved cooperation at Community level with regard to the tracing, withdrawal and recall of dangerous products.

Member States must nominate or establish authorities having the necessary powers and resources for market surveillance. At the time of writing, preparations for the setting up of the network are taking place.

There already exists, at present, an informal organisation for cooperation between market surveillance authorities of the Member States, PROSAFE, established in 1990 by enforcement officers with the aim of building links in operational understanding and mutual trust when working together to enforce Community law. More specifically, PROSAFE aims to encourage liaison between enforcement practitioners by providing, collecting and exchanging information of value to them; to enable discussion and exchange of ideas on the improvement of the enforcement function; to develop a closer understanding of common problems, mutual confidence and more effective working relations contributing to a wide range of European product safety law enforcement matters.

3. Information and reaction to public health problems: Council Decision (EC) 1786/2002

(a) Objective: The programme is part of the Community health strategy. The objectives that are relevant to the present work are to improve information and knowledge on public health issues and to boost the ability to respond rapidly and coherently to health threats.

(b) Scope of application: The programme aims to replace the Community initiatives focusing on individual health issues with a broader programme intended to run for five years. Accordingly, programmes such as EHLASS continue to run under the wider umbrella of the programme.

(c) Community actions: Article 3 of the programme prescribes a number of actions and activities to be pursued by the Community in relation, *inter alia*, to the monitoring and rapid reaction systems. This includes not only maintaining or setting up network activities operated through structures designed by the Member States and other activities of Community interest for public health monitoring and information, but also preparation, establishment and operation of appropriate structural arrangements coordinating and integrating networks for health monitoring and for rapid reaction to health threats. Also, activities related to consultation, knowledge and information must be deployed, such as: information and consultation at Community level on health and health related matters; sharing of experience and exchange of information; development and dissemination to competent authorities in the Member States, stakeholders and, where appropriate, the general public, of health information including statistics, reports, reviews and advice.

(d) Implementation of the programme: The Community is under a duty to ensure the implementation, in cooperation with the Member States, of the actions set out in the programme and, together with the Member States, shall take appropriate action to ensure the efficient running of the programme and to develop mechanisms, at Community and national level, to achieve its objectives. It shall also ensure the transition between the actions previously undertaken within the public health programmes and those to be implemented under the new programme.

(e) Injury prevention: The Community injury data collection and information exchange system first set up as EHLASS and later continued under Decision 372/1999 is to be continued.

Its objective is to collect information on injuries, particularly those resulting from home and leisure accidents, and it has been implemented by recourse principally to telematic means, in particular to the telematic network, EUPHIN (the European Union Public Health Information Network). Member States are under a duty to collect data relating to home and leisure accidents from hospitals and/or other appropriate establishments and services and to transmit them, as a report, to the Commission. The data must be codified using an approach based on the common criteria of the coding manual of the earlier EHLASS system.

The Commission is then in charge of processing, summarising, publishing and diseminating the data received by the Member States.

11
INFORMATION

A. INTRODUCTION

An effective information strategy requires not only truthfulness of the information that the trader gives; it also requires that certain information is given.

Community rules on labelling address both issues in an attempt to inform and protect consumers in connection with the many day-to-day purchases that they undertake. Labelling is actually perceived within the EU as one of the cornerstones of the rights of consumers informing them as to the contents, pricing and unit pricing of products and services,[450] although sometimes the Community appears to go too far in assuming that a consumer who is informed is necessarily protected.

This chapter deals with the Community measures on labelling and price indication of a general nature, but also takes into account a few product-specific directives that appear to be of particular importance for consumers' everyday life. Food and non-food related measures are examined in separate parts. The last part is then devoted to the issue of the language in which consumers should receive information.

B. PRESENTATION AND LABELLING OF FOODSTUFFS

1. Introduction

Community rules on the labelling of foodstuffs are aimed at enabling European consumers to get comprehensive information on the contents and the composition of food products, thus making an informed choice while purchasing their foodstuffs.

In the more recent years, following several food crises, rules on labelling of products have also been aimed at restoring consumer confidence in the origin and quality of food products. The policy on traceability of meat introduced by Regulation 178/2000 is just one example.

To gain a full picture of the Community framework on the presentation and labelling of foodstuffs, however, reference must also be made to product-specific measures which, as they also lay down rules on product content, have already been dealt with in Chapter 4 of this section.

450 As held in Case C-39/90 Denkavit Futtermittel GmbH v Land Baden-Wurttemberg [1991] ECR I-3069, labelling is one of the means that least restrict the free movement of products within the EU.

2. Parliament and Council Directive (EC) 2000/13 on the approximation of the laws of the Member States relating to the labelling, presentation and advertising of foodstuffs for sale to the ultimate consumer[451]

(a) Objective: The Directive consolidates and repeals Council Directive (EC) 79/112[452] on the labelling, presentation and advertising of foodstuffs and its subsequent amendments.

It aims to enact Community rules on the labelling, presentation and advertising of foodstuffs so as to inform and protect consumers and prevent different national legislation impeding the free movement of foodstuffs.

(b) Scope of application: The Directive applies to pre-packaged foodstuffs to be delivered as such to the ultimate consumer or to restaurants, hospitals, canteens and other similar mass caterers.

It does not apply to products intended for export outside the Community.

(c) Labelling: Article 2 lays down general rules concerning 'labelling', understood as any words, particulars, trademarks, brand names, pictorial matters or symbols relating to the foodstuffs and placed on any packaging, document, notice, label, ring or collar accompanying or referring to the foodstuffs (Article 1.3(a)).

Labelling must not:

(i) be such as could mislead the purchaser to a material degree:

– as to the nature, identity, properties, composition, quantity, durability, origin, or method of manufacture or production of foodstuffs;

– by attributing to the foodstuff effects or properties which it does not possess;

– by suggesting it possesses special characteristics when in fact all similar products possess them;

(ii) attribute to the foodstuff, or refer to, any property of preventing, treating or curing a human disease.[453]

In addition, the Council is to draw up an non-exhaustive list of misleading claims, the use of which shall be prohibited or restricted.

These prohibitions also apply to the presentation of foodstuffs, in particular their shape, appearance, packaging materials, their arrangements and settings in which they are displayed or in any advertisement.

(d) Compulsory indications: Under Article 3 , labelling of foodstuffs must include:

451 [2000] OJ L109/29.

452 [1979] OJ L33/1.

453 The provision prohibits, however, a national system which lays down a general prohibition, subject to prior authorisation, of all health-related information on the labelling and presentation of foodstuffs; see Case C-421/00 Criminal Proceedings against Sterbenz [2003] ECR I-1065.

(i) Name under which the product is sold. According to Article 5, this is constituted by the name laid down for the product by any relevant Community provisions or, in the absence of such provisions, in the legislative provisions of, or as generally used in, the Member State where the product is sold. The name under which the product is sold in the producing Member State may also be used, except where, despite the other compulsory particulars and the addition of other descriptive information, it could create confusion in the Member State in which it is sold. The name under which the product is sold must also include particulars as to the physical condition of the foodstuff or the specific treatment which it has undergone (powdered, freeze-dried, deep-frozen, concentrated, smoked, etc) in all cases where omission of such information could lead to confusion. Ionising treatment must always be mentioned.

(ii) List of ingredients. According to Article 6, this must be preceded by the word 'Ingredients'. An 'ingredient' is any substance, including additives, used in the manufacture or preparation of a foodstuff and still present in the finished product, even in an altered form. In certain circumstances, ingredients need not be listed for fresh fruit and vegetables, carbonated water, fermentation vinegars, cheese, butter, fermented milk and cream, and products comprising a single ingredient where the name under which the product is sold is identical with the ingredient name or enables the nature of the ingredient to be clearly identified. The list of ingredients must show all ingredients in descending order of weight (except in the case of mixtures of fruit or vegetables) and designated by their specific name, subject to certain derogations (to be soon amended) laid down in Annex I (Categories of ingredients which may be designated by the name of the category rather than the specific name, eg, 'oil', 'cocoa butter', 'cheese', 'vegetables'), Annex II (Categories of ingredients which must be designated by the name of their category followed by their specific name or EC number, eg, colouring, acidifier, emulsifier) and Annex III (Designation of flavourings).

(iii) Additives which are contained in an ingredient of a foodstuff but serve no technological function in the finished product and additives used as processing aids need not be mentioned on the labelling of the foodstuff. A recent amendment is proposing to abolish the possibility that ingredients of a compound ingredient which constituted less than 25% of the foodstuff need not be listed, thus making it compulsory to list all sub-ingredients. Further detailed rules on ingredients are laid down in Article 6.

(iv) Quantity of an ingredient or category of ingredients expressed as a percentage and in accordance with the detailed rules laid down in Article 7. The indication shall appear in or next to the name under which the foodstuff is sold or in the list of ingredients.

(v) Net quantity. Under Article 8, this must be expressed in units of volume in the case of liquids, and units of mass in the case of other products. For certain foodstuffs, Community provisions or, if none, domestic provisions are applicable provided they are notified in accordance with the procedure laid down in Article 19. Specific provisions are made for certain pre-packaged foodstuffs, foodstuffs sold by number or subject to considerable losses in volume and solid foodstuffs presented in a liquid medium.

(vi) Date of minimum durability, ie, the date until which the foodstuff retains its specific properties if properly stored. The date, consisting of the day, month and year, shall be preceded by the words 'best before'. For foodstuffs which will not keep for more than three months, the day and month are sufficient; for foodstuffs which will not keep for more than 18 months, the month and year are sufficient; for foodstuffs which will keep for more than 18 months, the year is sufficient. The durability date is not required for fruit and vegetables which have not been peeled, cut or anyway processed, beverages containing 10% or more by volume of alcohol, soft drinks, fruit juices, fruit nectars and alcoholic beverages in individual containers of more than 5 litres intended for supply to mass caterers, bakers' or pastry cooks' wares, vinegar, cooking salt, solid sugar, chewing gums and individual portions of ice-cream. In the case of highly perishable foodstuffs, a special 'use by' indication must be used, given the danger that these foodstuffs may constitute for human health.

(vii) Any special storage conditions or conditions of use.

(viii) Name or business name and address of the manufacturer or packager or of a vendor established in the EU.

(ix) Place of origin or provenance, where the omission of such information might mislead the consumer.

(x) Instructions for use, when it would be impossible to make proper use of the foodstuff in the absence of such instructions.

(xi) For beverages containing more than 1.2% by volume of alcohol, the actual alcoholic strength by volume.

(e) Presentation of particulars: The particulars listed above must be easy to understand and marked in a conspicuous place, so as to be easily visible, clearly legible and indelible. Special provisions are made for re-usable glass bottles and small packaging items or containers, foodstuffs offered for sale without pre-packaging and foodstuffs packaged on the sales premises at the consumer's request and pre-packaged foodstuffs. In particular, when the goods are pre-packaged, these particulars must appear on the pre-packaging or on a label attached to it, but where these are marketed at a stage prior to sale to the ultimate consumer or are supplied to mass caterers for processing, the particulars need appear only on the commercial documents.

The particulars must also be indicated in a language easily understood by the consumer, unless the consumer is in fact informed by means of other measures to be determined in accordance with Article 20(2). Labelling may be in several languages.

(f) Member States' obligations and derogations: According to Article 18, Member States cannot forbid the marketing of foodstuffs which comply with the Directive, save in the case of non-harmonised national provisions which are justified on particular grounds, such as the protection of public health, prevention of fraud or the protection of industrial or commercial property.

(g) National provisions: Member States retain competence to regulate, in compliance with the rules of the EC Treaty, the following important matters:

(i) they may impose language requirements;

(ii) they may retain national provisions which require indication of the factory or packaging centre in respect of home production;

(iii) in the absence of Community rules of a specific nature, they retain the right to lay down national provisions to be added to the general provisions of the Directive subject to the procedure laid down in Article 19. This involves notification to the Commission and to the other Member States of the measure adopted and of the reasons justifying it. Member States can take the envisaged measure only three months after the notification and provided the Commission does not express a negative opinion; in this case, it may suggest appropriate modifications.

(iv) they retain the right, depending on local practical conditions and circumstances, to lay down rules in respect of the labelling of foodstuffs sold in bulk provided that information is given to the consumers.

(h) Further measures: The Commission is in charge of adopting implementing measures of a technical nature with the assistance of the Standing Committee on Foodstuff.

(i) Proposal for a Parliament and Council Directive amending Directive (EC) 2000/13 as regards indication of the ingredients present in foodstuffs, COM(2001)433: The proposal, which at the time of writing has received Council's approval on second reading, aims to ensure that consumers receive complete information on the content of foodstuff, particularly in consideration of the increasing proportion of the EU population suffering from allergies or intolerances.

The amending Directive abolishes the 25% rule according to which it is not obligatory to label components of compound ingredients that make up to 25%

of the final food product. The rationale of the rule was to avoid exceedingly long lists of ingredients, on the assumption that the consumer would be able to deduce the composition of compound ingredients. Nowadays, however, a different approach is needed since food production is becoming increasingly complex, food is increasingly processed and the lack of detailed information is detrimental to the confidence of consumers suffering from allergies and intolerances.

The amending Directive also eliminates labelling exceptions that made it possible to declare ingredients only as a category (eg, 'vegetable oil') and makes it compulsory to identify the source for all allergenic ingredients (eg, 'peanut oil'). The source of a natural flavour (currently indicated simply as 'natural flavour') must also be indicated.

Finally, alcoholic beverages, previously exempt from ingredient labelling, must now bear an indication of all allergenic ingredients (eg, sulphites).

(j) Implementation: Annex IV, Part B lays down detailed provisions and deadlines for the transposition of the Directive into national law. To date, the following countries have notified implementing measures: Denmark, Germany, Luxembourg, Ireland, Italy, the Netherlands and Spain.

3. Parliament and Council Directive (EC) 98/6 on consumer protection in the indication of the prices of products offered to consumers[454]

(a) Objective: The Directive seeks to reform the system of price indication previously established by Directives 79/581 (for foodstuff prices) and 88/314[455] (for non-foodstuff prices), which had proven to be overly complex to apply. The Directive therefore introduces a new, simplified system which is easier for the consumer to understand. The Directive seeks to ensure that the obligation to indicate both selling price and the unit price contributes substantially to improving consumer protection.

(b) Scope of application: The Directive applies to all food and non-food products offered to consumers. However, Member States may decide not to apply the rule laid down in Article 3(1) to products supplied in the course of the provision of a service and to sales by auction and sales of works of art and antiques.

(c) Indication of selling price and unit price: According to Article 2, 'selling price' is the final price for a unit of the product, or a given quantity of the product, including VAT and all other taxes; unit price is the final price, including VAT and all other taxes, for one kilogramme, one litre, one metre, one square metre or one cubic metre of the product or a different single unit of quantity which is widely and customarily used in the Member State concerned in the marketing of specific products.

454 [1998] OJ L80/27.
455 [1988] OJ L142/19.

The general rule laid down in Article 3 is that both the selling price and the unit price must be indicated in an unambiguous, easily identifiable and clearly legible way for all products offered by traders to consumers. The unit price need not be indicated if it is identical to the selling price.

Where national or Community provisions require the indication of the net weight and the net drained weight for certain pre-packed products, it shall be sufficient to indicate the unit price of the net drained weight.

For products sold in bulk, only the unit price must be indicated.

(d) Advertising: Any advertising which mentions the selling price must also indicate the unit price.

(e) Member States' powers: According to Article 5, Member States may waive the obligation to indicate the unit price of products for which such indication would not be useful or would be liable to create confusion; in the case of non-food products, Member States shall establish a list of the products to which the obligation to indicate the unit price will remain applicable.

(f) Member States' obligations: Under Articles 7 and 8, Member States must take appropriate measures to inform all persons concerned of the national law transposing this legislation; they shall also lay down, and provide information on, the system of penalties for infringements of the national provisions adopted in application of this Directive.

Member States may also provide for a transitional period during which small retail businesses will not be subject to the obligation to indicate the unit price of products other than those sold in bulk if the obligation to indicate the unit price was found to be an excessive burden for such businesses.

(g) Minimum harmonisation: According to Article 10, the Directive shall not prevent Member States from adopting or maintaining provisions which are more favourable as regards consumer information and comparison of prices, without prejudice to their obligations under the EC Treaty.

(h) Implementation: The Directive must be implemented by the Member States no later than 13 March 2000. In England, the Directive was implemented by the Price Marking Order 1999.[456]

All countries, except Finland, Italy and the Netherlands, have notified implementing measures.

4. Council Directive (EEC) 90/496 of 24 September 1990 on nutrition labelling for foodstuffs[457]

(a) Objective: The purpose of the Directive is to ensure that the consumer can make a choice with knowledge of the basic principles of nutrition and with nutrition labelling. For the benefit of the consumer it was decided that labelling should be presented in a standardised form and foodstuffs not conforming with the Directive should be banned. The Directive is limited

456 SI 1999/3042.
457 [1990] OJ L276/40.

solely to nutritional issues, since the broader framework on labelling is provided by Directive 2000/13.

(b) Scope of application: Unlike other labelling directives, this one also applies to foodstuffs intended for supply to restaurants, hospitals, canteens and mass caterers. It does not apply to natural mineral waters or diet integrators or food supplements. The Directive applies without prejudice to the labelling provisions of Council Directive (EEC) 89/398 on the approximation of the laws of the Member States relating to foodstuffs intended for particular nutritional uses.[458]

(c) General rules: Nutrition labelling is compulsory only if a nutrition claim is made on the label or in advertising material. 'Nutrition labelling' means 'any information appearing on the labelling relating to: (1) energy value; (2) nutrients; and (3) nutrition claims'.

The only permissible claims under the Directive relate to energy and nutrients listed in Article 1(4)(a)(ii) and to substances which belong to or which are components of a category of those nutrients. Further measures restricting or prohibiting nutrition claims may be adopted by the Commission following the procedure in Article 10.

(d) Content of labelling: According to Article 4, where nutrition labelling is provided, the information given shall be that contained in either of the following groups, depending on the labelling:

(i) Group 1, which shall state the energy value and the amount of protein, carbohydrate and fat; or

(ii) Group 2, which shall state the energy value and the amount of protein, carbohydrate, sugar, fat, saturated fatty acids, dietary fibre and sodium.

Member States shall not introduce nutrition labelling specifications that are more detailed than those contained in this Directive.

(e) Presentation and form of the information: Article 7 provides that the information covered by the Directive must be presented in one tabular form with legible and indelible characters. The information must be provided in a language understood by consumers.

According to Article 6, the declared energy value and amount of nutrients shall be given in figures using specific units of measurement. The information shall be expressed per 100g or per 100ml per package. Information on vitamins and minerals must, in addition, be expressed as a percentage of the recommended daily allowance (RDA), which may also be given in graphic form.

(f) Non-pre-packaged foodstuffs: In the case of foodstuffs put up for sale to an ultimate consumer or mass caterers or foodstuffs prepared at the point of sale, the extent of the information referred to and the manner in which it is

458 [1989] OJ L186/27.

communicated may be determined by national provisions until the eventual adoption of Community provisions.

(g) Further measures: Articles 9 and 10 provides that any measures likely to have effect on public health and any further measures implementing the Directive must be adopted after consultation with the Scientific Committee for Food and Article 10 sets down the procedure.

(h) Commission proposal for a Regulation on nutrition and health claims made on foods, COM(2003)424: The proposal aims to introduce more restrictive rules on health and nutrition claims by specifying their conditions of use, prohibiting certain claims and scientifically evaluating the use of certain claims in relation to certain foodstuffs.

More specifically, the new Regulation would first of all regulate and lay down conditions for the use of certain claims, such as 'low fat' or 'high fibre', which are currently not regulated (so, eg, 'high fibre' must relate to a certain minimum amount of fibre in the product). Secondly, the Regulation would require that claims the truthfulness of which is controversial (eg, 'whole grain reduces the risk of heart disease') should be subject to scientific evaluation and used only upon approval. Thirdly, vague claims referring to general physical or psychological well-being (eg, 'reduces stress') will be forbidden. Finally, the Regulation prescribes the carrying out of nutritional profiles of certain foods in order to restrict the claims that can be made in relation to the nutritional properties of such foods.

(i) Implementation: The Directive was implemented in the UK by the Food Labelling (Amendment) Regulations 1994.[459]

All Member States have notified implementing measures.

5. Council Directive (EEC) 87/357 on the approximation of the laws of the Member States concerning products which, appearing to be other than they are, endanger the health or safety of consumers[460]

(a) Objective: The Directive aims where necessary to prohibit the marketing, import, production and export of products which, because they can be confused with foodstuffs, jeopardise the health and safety of consumers. To do this, some dangerous products will have to be withdrawn from the market. The Directive, therefore, makes provision for controls to be carried out by competent authorities of Member States and for discussing and examining the measures taken by Member States to ban or withdraw such products from the market to ensure uniform application of the principles of this Directive throughout the Community.

(b) Scope of application: The Directive applies to products that, according to Article 1, by appearing to be other than they are, endanger the health and safety of consumers. To clarify the type of product intended to be affected by

459 SI 1994/804.
460 [1987] OJ L192/49.

this Directive, they are more precisely defined as those which, although not foodstuffs, look like them in form, colour, appearance, packaging and labelling to such an extent that they can confuse consumers and especially children. Children are particularly vulnerable because they place them in their mouths, suck them and, for example, can suffocate or be poisoned by them.

(c) Member States' obligations: Under Article 2, Member States must take all the necessary measures to prohibit the marketing, import, manufacture or export of such products. In addition, checks must be carried out on products on the market to ensure that no product falling within the Directive is marketed and, if so, measures must be taken to withdraw such products.

Member States that take any specific measures must inform the Commission, give a description of the product and of the grounds for the decision. The Commission then forwards the information to the other Member States at the earliest opportunity. However, no further notification is required of details if these have already been supplied under Council Decision (EEC) 84/133.[461] The Advisory Committee set up under this Decision may be requested to consider views on any question relating to this Directive.

(d) Adjustments: Under Article 5, two years after implementation, the Council may take a decision on the possible adjustment of this Directive with a view to extending its scope or evaluating its procedures on the basis of a report from the Commission based on experience gained. To date, no adjustment has been made.

(e) Implementation: This Directive is implemented in the United Kingdom by the Food Imitation (Safety) Regulations 1989.[462]

All Member States have notified implementing measures.

6. Specific products

Several measures concerning both the labelling and the content of specific foodstuffs have already been examined in Chapter 4 (Safety of agricultural products). A few other relevant measures concerning product labelling are here briefly summarised.

(a) Labelling of foodstuffs containing quinine and caffeine: Quinine and caffeine are substances that, if consumed at moderate levels, are unlikely to pose any health risks for most consumers. Some consumers, however, may suffer adverse effects from these substances, in some cases even if consumed in very small quantities. Quinine, used as flavouring in some soft drinks (such as tonic water), should be avoided by persons with certain metabolic disorders, or with a hypersensitivity to the substance. High caffeine consumption may trigger temporary behavioural changes, particularly in children, and is also not recommended for pregnant women.

461 [1984] OJ L70/16.
462 SI 1989/1291.

Directive 2002/67[463] aims to alert consumers of the presence of these substances and, in the case of caffeine, indicate where the level exceeds a certain limit.

In particular, Directive 2002/67 prescribes that when quinine and caffeine are used in the preparation of foodstuff as flavouring they must be specifically indicated by derogation to Article 6(6) of Directive 2000/13.[464] When a beverage contains caffeine in excess of 150 mg/l, the message 'high caffeine content' must visibly appear on the label followed by an indication of the caffeine content.

Member States must implement the Directive by 30 July 2003. To date, Austria, Denmark, Finland, Greece, Luxembourg, Portugal, Spain and Sweden have notified implementing measures.

(b) Labelling of beef: Commission Regulation (EC) 1825/2000[465] lays down detailed rules for the application of Regulation (EC) 1760/2000[466] as regards the labelling of beef and beef products in accordance with the principle of product traceability.

As from January 2002, in order to give consumers more detailed information on the beef on sale, the beef label has to include the following information: an indication of the Member State or third country of birth; an indication of all Member States or third countries where fattening took place; a reference number ensuring the link between the meat and the animal or animals; and indication of the State where the animal was slaughtered and of the cutting plant. Where the beef is derived from animals born, raised and slaughtered in the same Member State, the indication may be given as: 'Origin: (name of Member State)'. Where the beef is derived from animals born, raised and slaughtered in the same third country, the indication may be given as 'Origin: (name of third country)'. For minced beef, the label must contain: traceability code; Member State of slaughter; Member State of preparation; Member State or Member States of origin, if they are different from the Member State of preparation.

After receiving permission from Member State authorities, operators are free to decide to give further information, such as the indication of the meat categories.

(c) Products containing meat: Commission Directive 2001/101 (EC)[467] establishes a harmonised method for determining the meat content of foodstuffs containing meat as an ingredient by laying down maximum limits for the fat and connective tissue content of products which may be designated by the category name 'meat'.

463 [2002] OJ L191/20.
464 [2000] OJ L109/29.
465 [2000] OJ L216/8.
466 [2000] OJ L204/1.
467 [2001] OJ L310/19.

(d) Definition, description and presentation of spirit drinks: Council Regulation (EC) 1576/89[468] lays down general rules on the definition, description and presentation of spirit drinks.

A 'spirit drink' for the purposes of the regulation is an alcoholic liquid intended for human consumption, having particular organoleptic qualities and, except in some listed cases, a minimum alcoholic strength of 15% by volume and fulfilling certain requirements of content and method of production listed in Article 1(2) .

The Regulation lays down definitions of several terms used to market spirits, such as 'rum', 'whisky or whiskey', 'grain spirit', 'wine spirit', 'brandy or Weinbrand', 'grape marc', 'fruit marc spirit', 'raisin spirit or raisin brandy', 'fruit spirits', 'cider spirit, cider brandy or perry spirit', 'gentian spirit', 'fruit spirit drinks', 'juniper-flavoured spirit drinks', etc. In order to be marketed under such names, spirits must comply with the description given in the Directive.

The Directive also defines general terms including 'spirit drink', 'sweetening', 'mixing', 'blending', etc. Spirit drinks marketed for human consumption may not be described by associating words such as 'style', 'type' or 'flavour'.

Water may be added to spirit drinks, provided it fulfils the quality requirements of water intended for human consumption. Except in a few cases, only natural aromatic substances and preparations may be used as flavourings. The ethyl alcohol used in the preparation of spirit drinks may not be of any origin other than agricultural. Annexes set out the characteristics of ethyl alcohol of agricultural origin as well as geographical designations for different categories of products.

The Regulation also lays down rules concerning the labelling and presentation of spirit drinks, with particular reference to origin and method of manufacture, eg, the alcoholic strength must be expressed to the nearest half per cent.

Member States are responsible for preventing under certain conditions the unlawful use within the EU of geographical designations protected by a third country which is a member of the World Trade Organisation.

(e) Definition, description and presentation of aromatized wines, aromatized wine-based drinks and aromatized wine-product cocktails: Council Regulation (EEC) 1601/91[469] lays down general rules on the description and presentation of aromatized wines, aromatized wine-based drinks and aromatized wine-product cocktails. The Regulation distinguishes between three categories of drinks: aromatized wines, aromatized wine-based drinks and aromatized wine-product cocktails. Classification of drinks in one of these categories depends on their wine content, their alcoholic strength and

468 [1989] OJ L160/1.
469 [1991] OJ L149/1.

whether they contain any added alcohol. The Regulation also applies to exported products.

The Regulation lists several designations of aromatized drinks which shall be reserved exclusively for the drinks complying with the description. Aromatized drinks which do not comply with the Regulation may not be marketed using terms such as 'style', 'type', 'flavour' or similar indications associating them with one of the designations laid down in the Regulation.

Since the reputation of certain drinks is closely linked with their traditional place of origin, it is compulsory to indicate the place of origin in cases where the drink does not originate in the region where it is traditionally produced.

The use of water in the preparation of these drinks is authorised provided that provided it fulfils the quality requirements of water intended for human consumption. The ethyl alcohol used to dilute or dissolve authorised additives must be of agricultural origin and its use must be limited to a strict minimum.

The labelling of aromatized drinks is subject to the general Community labelling rules. However, because of the special characteristics of such drinks, additional provisions are included in Article 8.

Member States are responsible for ensuring that the provisions of these Regulations are complied with and must appoint one or more monitoring agencies.

(f) Commission Directive 87/250[470] on the indication of alcoholic strength by volume in the labelling of alcoholic beverages for sale to the ultimate consumer: This Directive supplements Community rules on the definition of alcoholic strength by volume[471] and on labelling of foodstuffs. It applies to beverages containing more than 1.2% by volume of alcohol.

According to the Directive, alcoholic strength should be determined at 20°C and the corresponding figure is given to not more than one decimal place. It is followed by the symbol '% vol.' and preceded by the word 'alcohol' or the abbreviation 'alc.'.

The margins of tolerance allowed in respect of the indication of the alcoholic strength by volume are indicated in Article 3.

C. PRESENTATION AND LABELLING OF NON-FOOD PRODUCTS

1. Introduction

This Part analyses a wide variety of measures concerning the labelling of non-food products, ranging from textiles to footwear, to medicinal products and to other goods. Like the ones on food products, these measures are often based on Article 95 of the EC Treaty in an attempt to pursue the two-fold objective of ensuring uniformity of regulatory regimes throughout the EU

470 [1987] OJ L113/57.
471 See Directive (EEC) 76/766 ([1976] OJ L262/149).

while at the same time providing consumers with sufficient information to make informed choices.

2. Price indication

Price indication, previously regulated by a specific non-food product Directive,[472] is now covered by Directive 98/6[473] on consumer protection in the indication of the prices of products offered to consumers (dealt with in Part B of this chapter) that applies to both food and non-food products.

3. Components of footwear: Council and Parliament Directive (EC) 94/11 on the approximation of laws, regulations and administrative provisions of Member States relating to the labelling of material used in main components of footwear for sale to consumers[474]

(a) Objective: The purpose of this Directive is to remove disparity of regulations of Member States on footwear labelling which were designed to protect and inform the public as well as to secure legitimate interests of industry.

The Directive is part of the Council's wish to improve consumer information and to introduce a system reducing the risk of fraud by indicating the exact nature of materials used in the main components of footwear. The Directive accepts that labelling is one of the important means of providing better information and transparency to the consumer.

(b) Scope of application: The Directive applies to the labelling of materials used in the main components of footwear for the sale to the consumer. For these purposes, footwear means all articles with applied soles designed to protect or cover feet, including parts referred to in Annex I . A list of the sort of products covered are contained in Annex II to the Directive. This Annex goes through a list of the sort of shoes that one would expect to be covered by the definition, to include everything from flat or high-heeled shoes through to orthopaedic footwear.

Excluded from the Directive are second-hand footwear, protective footwear covered by Council Directive (EEC) 89/686[475] and footwear covered by Council Directive (EEC) 76/769.[476]

(c) Labelling: Information on the composition of footwear shall be by means of labelling which must specify information relating to the upper, the lining and sockwear and the outer sole. The labelling shall provide information on the material determined in accordance with Annex 1 of the Directive which constitutes 80% of each part of the footwear. The information shall be conveyed on the footwear either by pictogramme or written indication in at

472 Council Directive 88/314 ([1988] OJ L142/19).
473 [1998] OJ L80/27.
474 [1994] OJ L100/37.
475 [1989] OJ L399/18 (as amended).
476 [1976] OJ L262/201 (as amended).

least the languages which may be determined by the Member States. The labelling shall involve fixing the required information onto at least one article of footwear in each pair, either printing, sticking, embossing or using an attached label. The labelling must be visible, securely attached and accessible. The manufacturer or his agent in the Community is responsible for the supply of the label and the accuracy of the information on it. If neither the manufacturer or the agent is established in the EU, the obligation falls upon the person responsible for placing the footwear on the EU market. The retailer remains responsible at all times to ensure that the footwear sold by him bears the appropriate labelling.

(d) Implementation: The measure was implemented in the UK by the Footwear (Indication of Composition) Labelling Regulations 1995.[477]

All Member States have notified implementing measures.

(e) Follow-up work: The Commission issued in 2000[478] a report on the application of the Directive based on information gathered from the Member States, the footwear industry associations and consumer associations. It concludes that, in most Member States, the national transposition measures, which often follow very closely the text of the Directive, are sufficient to guarantee proper application of the Directive and ensure better information and increased transparency for consumers. The objectives of the Directive have therefore been achieved.

4. Textile names: Parliament and Council Directive 96/74 on textile names[479]

(a) Objective: The Directive seeks to harmonise the names, composition and labelling of textile products in order to ensure adequate information for consumers and prevent differences in national legislation from impeding the free movement of these products.

(b) Scope of application: For the purposes of the Directive, 'textile product' means any raw, semi-worked, worked, semi-manufactured, manufactured, semi-made up or made up products which are exclusively composed of textile fibres regardless of the mixing or assembly process employed.

The Directive applies to textile products exclusively composed of textile fibres; products containing at least 80% by weight of textile fibres; furniture, umbrella and sunshade coverings; floor coverings, mattresses and camping goods; warm linings of footwear, gloves, mittens and mitts, provided that the textile parts of such products constitute at least 80% by weight of the complete article; textiles incorporated into other products.

477 SI 1995/2489.
478 COM(2000)812 final.
479 [1997] OJ L32/38.

The Directive does not apply to textile products which are intended for export to third countries; which enter Member States, under customs control, for transit purposes; which are imported from third countries for inward processing; which are contracted out to persons working in their own homes or to independent firms that make up work from materials supplied.

(c) Names of textiles: The names and descriptions of the fibres are listed in Annex I . These names may not be used for any other fibres but can be used, subject to certain conditions, to describe fibre mixtures. In this case, the full percentage composition must be given.

(d) Description: No textile product may be described as '100 per cent pure' unless exclusively composed of the same fibre. A textile product may contain up to 2% of weight of other fibres provided the quantity is justified on technical grounds. There are detailed provisions as to wool products and designation of mixed fibres.

(e) Labelling: Article 8 deals with labelling. It provides that textile products should be labelled or marked whenever they are put on the market for production or commercial purposes. Where these products are not being offered for sale to the end consumer, or where they are being delivered in performance of an order placed by the State, labelling or marking may be replaced by accompanying commercial documents.

With the exception of trade marks or the name of the undertaking, information other than that required by this Directive must be quite separate.

Member States may require that their national language be used for the labelling and marking required by the Directive. More detailed rules on labelling are contained in Articles 8, 9 and 10.

(f) Adaptation to technical progress: The Directive has been adapted to technical progress in Annexes I and II by Commission Directive (EC) 97/37.[480]

(g) Implementation: To date, Spain, Finland and Belgium have notified implementing measures.

5. Parliament and Council Directive (EC) 1999/94 relating to the availability of consumer information on fuel economy and CO2 emissions in respect of the marketing of new passenger cars

(a) Objective: The Directive is part of the Community strategy to reduce emissions of greenhouse gases by 8% between 2008 and 2012 in accordance with that undertaken at the December 1997 Kyoto Conference on climate change.

The purpose of the Directive is to ensure that information relating to the fuel economy and CO2 emissions of new cars is given to consumers.

(b) Scope of application: The Directive applies to new passenger cars offered for sale or lease in the EU.

(c) Consumer information: Consumer information on fuel economy and CO2 emissions of new cars must be ensured in the following four ways:

480 [1997] OJ L169/74.

(i) labelling of fuel consumption and CO2 emissions attached to the windshield of all new passenger cars at the point of sale and clearly visible;

(ii) the production of a fuel consumption and CO2 emissions guide;

(iii) displaying posters in car showrooms;

(iv) the inclusion of fuel consumption and CO2 emissions data in advertisements, posters, brochures, etc.

(d) Implementation: Member States must notify the Commission of the competent body or bodies responsible for the implementation and functioning of the consumer information scheme. The Directive was to be implemented by 18 January 2001.

In the UK, the Directive was implemented by the Passenger Car (Fuel Consumption and CO2 Emissions Information) Regulations 2001.[481]

All Member States have notified implementing measures.

6. Council Directive 92/75 on the indication by labelling and standard product information of the consumption of energy and other resources by household appliances[482]

(a) Objective: The Directive aims to harmonise national measures relating to the publication of information on the consumption of energy and of other essential resources by household appliances, thereby allowing consumers to choose appliances on the basis of their energy efficiency

(b) Scope of application: The Directive applies to the following types of household appliances, even where these are sold for non-household uses: refrigerators, freezers and their combinations; washing machines, dryers and their combinations; dishwashers; ovens; water heaters and hot-water storage appliances; lighting sources; air-conditioning appliances.

(c) Labelling: Information relating to the consumption of electric energy, other forms of energy and other essential resources and supplementary information shall be brought to consumers' attention by means of a fiche and a label related to household appliances offered for sale, hire, hire-purchase or displayed to end-users. Details relating to the label and the fiche are to be further defined by directives.

The supplier must establish technical documentation sufficient to enable the accuracy of the information contained in the label and the fiche to be assessed, which must include the details set out in Article 2(3) .

All suppliers placing on the market the household appliances covered by this Directive and by implementing directives must supply a free label, to be attached to the appliance by the dealer in the appropriate position and in the appropriate language version; and a product fiche, contained in all the

481 SI 2001/3523.
482 [1992] OJ L297/16.

brochures relating to the product or, where these are not provided, in all other literature provided with the appliance.

Suppliers are responsible for the accuracy of the information contained in the labels. Where appliances are offered for sale, hire or hire-purchase by catalogue or by other means whereby the potential customer is unable to see the appliance displayed, the essential information contained in the label or fiche must be provided to the potential customer before purchase.

(d) Further measures: The Commission shall adopt, with the assistance of a Committee, directives for the implementation of the present Directive following the procedure described in Article 10.

(e) Implementation: The Directive was implemented in the UK by the Energy Information (Refrigerators and Freezers) Regulations 1994[483] and by the Energy Information (Dishwashers) Regulations 1999.[484]

All Member States except Germany and Luxembourg have notified implementing measures.

7. Parliament and Council Regulation (EC) 1980/2000[485] on a revised Community eco-label award scheme

(a) Objective: The Regulation repeals and replaces Council Regulation (EEC) 880/92[486] which had introduced the Community eco-label award scheme. The purpose of this scheme is to promote products which have a reduced environmental impact and to provide consumers with the relevant information and guidance on such products.

(b) Scope of application: The Regulation does not apply to foodstuffs, drinks, pharmaceutical products, medical devices, dangerous substances or preparations, or products manufactured by processes likely to significantly harm human beings and/or the environment.

(c) Eco-label: The eco-label may be awarded to products available in the EU which contribute significantly to improvements in relation to key environmental aspects and accordingly which comply with the essential environmental requirements referred to in Article 3 and the eco-label criteria referred to in Article 4.

The environmental requirements are defined with reference to the assessment matrix given in Annex I to the Regulation and must meet the methodological requirements set out in Annex II. The eco-label criteria are set out by product group. Eco-label criteria must be established by product group based on the product's prospects of market penetration; the technical and economic feasibility of the necessary adaptations; and the potential for environmental improvement.

483 SI 1994/3076.
484 SI 1999/1676.
485 [2000] OJ L237/1.
486 [1992] OJ L99/1.

The criteria are set and reviewed by the European Union Eco-Labelling Board (EUEB) , which is also responsible for the assessment and verification requirements relating to them.

(d) Applying for the award of a European eco-label: All manufacturers, importers, service providers, traders or retailers can apply for the award of an eco-label to the competent body designated by the Member State in which the product has been manufactured, first marketed or imported from a non-Member country. The competent body then assesses whether the product conforms to the criteria of the eco-label and decides whether or not to award the label.

Applications for the award of an eco-label are subject to payment of a fee. The use of the label is also subject to the payment of an annual fee by the user.

Products which have been awarded the eco-label are entitled to bear the 'daisy' logo described in Annex III to the Regulation.

(e) Follow-up work: By September 2005, the Commission must carry out an assessment of the application of the Regulation as applied and propose, if appropriate, amendments.

8. Labelling of medicinal products: Parliament and Council Directive 2001/83[487] on the Community code relating to medicinal products for human use

(a) Objective: The objective of the Directive is much broader than that of regulating the labelling of medicinal products, in that the Directive lays down the legal framework for the placing on the market, manufacture, import, classification, distribution, advertising and surveillance of medicinal products. For the purposes of this section, only the provisions concerning labelling and the package leaflet (Articles 54 to 69) are relevant.

(b) Scope of application: The Directive applies to industrially produced medicinal products for human use intended to be placed on the market in Member States. It does not apply to any medicinal product prepared in a pharmacy in accordance with a medical prescription for an individual patient; any medicinal product prepared in a pharmacy in accordance with the prescriptions of a pharmacopoeia and is intended to be supplied directly to the patients served by the pharmacy in question; medicinal products intended for research and development trials; intermediate products intended for further processing by an authorised manufacturer; any radionuclides in the form of sealed sources; whole blood, plasma or blood cells of human origin.

(c) Labelling: According to Article 54, the outer packaging of a medicinal product (or if there is not one, the immediate packaging) must contain the following particulars:

487 [2001] OJ L311/67.

(i) the name of the medicinal product followed by the common name where the product contains only one active substance and if its name is an invented name;

(ii) a statement of the active substances;

(iii) the pharmaceutical form and the contents by weight, by volume or by number of doses of the product;

(iv) a list of certain excipients known to have a recognised action or effect;

(v) the method and, if necessary, the route of administration;

(vi) a special warning that the medicinal product must be stored out of reach of children;

(vii) a special warning, if this is necessary for the medicinal product;

(viii) the expiry date in clear terms (month/year);

(ix) special storage precautions, if any;

(x) special precautions for disposal, if appropriate;

(xi) the name and address of the holder of the authorisation for placing the medicinal product on the market;

(xii) the number of the authorisation for placing the medicinal product on the market;

(xiii) the manufacturer's batch number;

(xiv) in the case of self-medication, instructions on the use of the medicinal products.

Further provisions are made in Article 55 concerning the particulars that must also appear on immediate packaging.

The particulars shall be easily legible, clearly comprehensible and indelible.

(d) Package leaflet: According to Article 59(1), the package leaflet included with the product must be drawn up in accordance with the summary of the product characteristics and shall include:

(i) information relevant for the identification of the medicinal product (eg, the name of the product followed by the common name if the product contains only one active substance);

(ii) the therapeutic indications;

(iii) a list of the information which is necessary before taking the medicinal product;

(iv) the necessary and usual instructions for proper use;

(v) a description of the undesirable effects which can occur under normal use of the medicinal product and, if necessary, the action to be taken in such a case; the patient should be expressly invited to communicate any undesirable effect which is not mentioned in the leaflet to his doctor or to his pharmacist;

(vi) a reference to the expiry date indicated on the label;

(vii) the date on which the package leaflet was last revised.

The inclusion in the packaging of all medicinal products of a package leaflet shall be obligatory unless all the above information is directly conveyed on the outer packaging or on the immediate packaging.

The package leaflet must be written in clear and understandable terms for the users and be clearly legible in the official language or languages of the Member State where the medicinal product is placed on the market. This does not prevent the package leaflet being printed in several languages, provided that the same information is given in all the languages used

(e) Presentation of particulars: According to Article 62, the outer packaging and the package leaflet may include symbols or pictogrammes designed to clarify certain information mentioned in Articles 54 and 59(1) and other information compatible with the summary of the product characteristics which is useful for health education, to the exclusion of any element of a promotional nature.

The particulars for labelling listed in Articles 54, 59 and 62 shall appear in the official language or languages of the Member State where the product is placed on the market. This does not prevent these particulars from being indicated in several languages, provided that the same particulars appear in all the languages used.

The competent authorities may exempt labels and package leaflets for specific medicinal products from the obligation that certain particulars shall appear, and that the leaflet must be in the official language or languages of the Member State where the product is placed on the market, when the product is not intended to be delivered to the patient for self-administration.

(f) Warnings and other information: As necessary, the Commission shall adopt, in the form of a directive, guidelines concerning in particular:

(i) the formulation of certain special warnings for certain categories of medicinal products,

(ii) the particular information needs relating to self-medication;

(iii) the legibility of particulars on the labelling and package leaflet;

(iv) methods for the identification and authentication of medicinal products;

(v) the list of excipients which must feature on the labelling of medicinal products and the way these excipients must be indicated.

(g) Homeopathic medicinal products: According to Article 68, the provisions above described also apply to homeopathic medicinals. Clear reference to their homeopathic nature shall also be made in the label. In addition, the package insert of these products must, where appropriate, contain the particulars listed in Article 69.

(h) Implementation: The time limits for transposition of this rather complex piece of legislation are set out in Annex II, Part B of the Directive.

D. LANGUAGE

1. Introduction

The issue of the language in which information must be conveyed to the consumer has in general received scarce attention at Community level, even after the 1993 Communication of the Commission to the Council and the Parliament on language use in the information of consumers in the Community.[488]

The language issue is tackled, often inconsistently, by several provisions on product labelling and has been the object of several judgements. The brief analysis carried out in this chapter reveals the need for a more coherent approach to language use.

2. Community legislation

The approach taken by Community measures to the language issue is not uniform. In some cases, the measure itself explicitly specifies the use of certain languages, such as Article 5 of Directive 2001/37 on the manufacture, presentation and sale of tobacco products[489] according to which certain information printed on the cigarette packet must be in the official language or languages of the Member State where the product is placed on the market. In other cases, the wording requires Member States to lay down rules. This is the case with foodstuffs labelling and nutrition labelling, which must be provided in a language 'easily understood' by the buyer. In some cases, the question of language is not mentioned at all (eg, misleading advertising, consumer credit), or it is left up to Member States to impose language requirements (eg, toy safety, cosmetic products).

Accordingly, there does not seem to have been a systematic approach in Community legislation as regards language use. This absence of consistency is only partially justified by the variety of domains covered (foodstuffs, cosmetic products, etc) and of the objectives envisaged by the different Community measures.

In addition, reference to a 'language easily understood' by the consumer has given rise to several interpretative doubts, from time to time clarified by a judgment of the ECJ.

488 COM(1993)456 final.
489 [2001] OJ L194/26.

3. The case law

Several references have been made to the ECJ concerning the interpretation of the requirement imposed by Directive 79/112 and now by Directive 2000/13 that labels of foodstuff contain information expressed in a language easily understood by the consumer.

In Case C-369/89 *Piageme v Peeters*,[490] for example, the Court ruled that a national law imposing a stricter obligation than the use of a language easily understood, that is to say the exclusive use of the language of a linguistic region and, on the other hand, failing to acknowledge the possibility of ensuring that the purchaser is informed by other measures, goes beyond the requirements of the Directive: the obligation exclusively to use the language of the linguistic region constitutes a measure having equivalent effect to a quantitative restriction on imports, prohibited by Article 28 (ex 30) of the EC Treaty.

The Court then further ruled in Case C-85/94 *Piageme v Peeters*[491] that the expression 'language easily understood by the consumer' is designed to ensure that the consumer is provided with information rather than to impose the use of a specific language and is therefore not equivalent to 'the official language of the Member State' or 'the language of the region', which are too restrictive.

Finally, in Case C-385/96 *Goerres*,[492] the Court ruled that Article 14 of Directive 79/112 does not preclude national legislation which, as regards language requirements, prescribes the use of a specific language for the labelling of foodstuffs but which also permits, as an alternative, the use of another language easily understood by purchasers.

Case C-366/98 *Criminal proceedings against Geffroy*[493] gives a last interpretation to the formula 'language easily understood by the consumer' by precluding national law from requiring the use of a specific language for the labelling of foodstuffs, without allowing for the possibility of using another language easily understood by purchasers or of ensuring that the purchaser is informed by other means.

The above judgments seek to clarify what a 'language easily understood by the consumer' is not; a judgment that clarifies what a 'language easily understood by the consumer' is, on the other hand, still being awaited.

4. Communication from the Commission to the Council and the Parliament concerning language use in the information of consumers in the Community[494]

In this Communication, the Commission surveyed the existing national and Community legislation relating to language requirements in the field of

490 [1991] ECR I-2971.
491 [1995] ECR I-2955.
492 [1998] ECR I-4431.
493 [2001] ECR I-222.
494 COM(1993)456 final.

consumer information in the areas of labelling, instructions for use, assembly instructions, precautions regarding employment or use, and any warning intended for the final user of the product or service.

At domestic level, the approaches adopted by the Member States are varied, since language problems are not identical in all Member States. However, more than half of the Member States have considered it necessary to inform the consumer in his own language. At European level, there does not seem to have been a systematic approach in Community legislation as regards language use and different measures make different provisions to address the issue of the language in which information is conveyed to the consumer. In addition, in cases where Community legislation gives Member States the option of stipulating language requirements in favour of consumers, this option is generally not very well taken up.

Yet, information which is difficult to understand or read may have serious repercussions for the health or safety of the consumer; for example, in the case of persons with allergies or diabetes or restricted to a particular diet, failure to understand the labelling may have serious health consequences.

The Commission therefore called for simplification of the Community provisions relating to language requirements and also put forward a number of ideas for strengthening consumer information. In particular, the Commission suggested that, in designing new measures, account should be taken of the competence of the Member States in defining national rules in this domain; the rules of the EC Treaty and the ECJ case law; and the legitimate right of consumers to receive the most exhaustive possible information on the products and services offered to them.

In the context of this new approach, the Commission proposed the following five themes for discussion:

(a) encourage multilingual information;

(b) preserve the freedom of Member States to require use of the language of the country of consumption;

(c) improve the consistency of the Community legal instruments with regard to the use of languages in the domain of consumption;

(d) improve information of the Commission, the Member States and the operators on the applicable language rules;

(e) assign responsibility to the economic operators (producers, distributors).

In practice, the Commission's Communication has not been followed by any initiative and has somehow remained a dead letter.

12

ADVERTISING AND UNFAIR COMMERCIAL PRACTICES

1. Introduction

Domestic rules on advertising have been on several occasions under the scrutiny of the ECJ as restrictions on the free movement of goods and/or services. In particular, it is not clear whether rules restricting or prohibiting advertising can be considered as MEQR within the meaning of Article 28 of the EC Treaty. In its most recent judgement, *KO v Gourmet International Products AB (GIP)* ,[495] the ECJ held that a prohibition of all advertising directed at consumers (such as of advertisements in the press, on the radio and on television, the direct mailing of unsolicited material or the placing of posters on the public highway) of alcoholic beverages, the consumption of which is linked to traditional social practices and to local habits and customs, is liable to impede access to the market by products from other Member States more than it impedes access by domestic products, with which consumers are instantly more familiar. Such a restriction, however, can be justified on grounds of protection of public health. [496]

The need to establish a European framework for advertising appears therefore rather clear, although it is understandable that Community intervention may not aim to interfere with certain types of advertising, or the advertising of certain products, which for social and cultural reasons are more satisfactorily dealt with at domestic level.

The general framework provided by Community law is limited to misleading and comparative advertising; there are, however, several sector-specific measures which deal with the advertisement of products such as tobacco[497] or medicinal products or certain foodstuffs. Another general framework for advertising is provided by a directive which harmonises the conditions upon which TV advertising may be carried out throughout the EU.

From a consumer point of view, the benefit of Community legislation on advertising is two-fold: first, harmonisation made at a relatively high level would assist consumers in countries with lower domestic levels of protection; second, adequate enforcement could prevent cross-border malpractices.

In this respect, the 2003 proposal for a Directive on unfair business-to-consumer commercial practices should be able to make cross-border trade simpler for consumers (and traders) by establishing a single, common, general prohibition of unfair commercial practices distorting

495 Case C-405/98 [2001] All ER (EC) 308.
496 See also Case C-362/88 GB-INNO [1990] ECR-I 667; Case C-292/92 Hünermund and others v Landesapothekerkammer Baden-Württemburg; Case C-412/93 Leclerc- Siplec [1995] ECR I-179.
497 See Chapter 9 on tobacco products.

consumers' economic behaviour. This single set of common rules will replace the existing multiple volumes of national rules and court rulings on commercial practices. This will give consumers the same protection against sharp business practices and rogue traders whether they buy from the shop around the corner or from a website in another Member State.

2. Council Directive (EEC) 84/450 concerning misleading and comparative advertising[498]

(a) Objective: The purpose of this Directive is to protect consumers, as well as persons carrying on a trade or business or practising a craft or profession, and the public in general against misleading advertising and the unfair consequences thereof. Since it was amended in 1997, it also aims to regulate comparative advertising. The reason for the amendment was that comparative advertising may be an important part of marketing strategy of a business and may be, upon certain conditions, beneficial to consumers. Legal regulation of comparative advertising in Europe differed dramatically from country to country (in countries such as Germany, Italy, Belgium, Luxembourg it was forbidden; in the Scandinavian countries strictly regulated; in others, such as the UK, controlled rather leniently) and it was therefore necessary to provide a common regulatory platform to allow such advertising throughout Europe.

(b) Scope of application: The Directive refers to 'advertising', meaning 'the making of a representation in any form in connection with a trade, business, craft or profession to promote the supply of goods or services including immovable property, rights and obligations' (Article 2(1)).

(c) Misleading advertising: Under Article 2, advertising is misleading when it 'in any way, including its presentation, deceives or is likely to deceive the person to whom it is addressed and which by reason of its deceptive nature, is likely to affect their economic behaviour or injures or is likely to injure a competitor'.[499]

Article 3 provides that, in judging whether an advertisement is misleading, account needs to be taken of:

498 [1984] OJ L250/17.

499 In the Nissan case (Case C-373/90 Complaint against X [1991] ECR I-131) the ECJ held that the Directive does not preclude vehicles from being advertised as new, less expensive and guaranteed by the manufacturer when the vehicles concerned are registered solely for the purpose of importation, have never been on the road, and are sold in a Member State at a price lower than that charged by dealers established in that Member State because they are equipped with fewer accessories. The ECJ's decision was probably also motivated by the desire to facilitate commercial opportunities of parallel importers; it also states, however, that a claim is misleading only if a 'significant number of consumers' may be misled, thus suggesting to national courts the adoption of a rather low level of consumer protection that would not save from harm the more vulnerable groups.

(i) the characteristics of the goods and services involved, such as availability, nature, method and date of manufacture, fitness for purpose, etc;

(ii) the price or the manner in which the price is calculated and the conditions upon which goods or services are supplied; and

(iii) the nature, attributes and rights of the advertiser, such as, for example, his identity and assets, his qualifications and ownership of the property rights.

3. Comparative advertising

Directive 97/55[500] introduced Article 3a that allows comparative advertising, ie, advertising which explicitly or by implication identifies a competitor or goods or services offered by a competitor.[501]

Comparative advertising is permitted under the following conditions:

(i) it is not misleading;

(ii) it compares goods or services meeting the same needs or intended for the same purpose;

(iii) it objectively compares one or more material feature which may include price;

(iv) it does not lead to confusion in the market place;

(v) it does not discredit or denigrate the trademarks, trade names, services, activities or circumstances of the competitor;

(vi) it does not take unfair advantage of the reputation of a trade mark;

(vii) it does not present goods or services as imitations of those bearing a protected trade mark.

Insofar as comparative advertising refers to any specific offer, it shall indicate in a clear way the date on which the offer ends, if it is subject to availability, and, if the offer has not yet begun, the date when it will commence.

(a) Member States' obligations: According to Article 4 , Member States are to ensure that adequate and effective means exist for the control of misleading and comparative advertising in the interests of consumers. Such means include legal provisions under which persons or organisations regarded by national law as having a legitimate interest in prohibiting misleading advertising may take legal action against such advertising, or bring such advertising before an administrative authority competent to decide on

500 [1999] OJ L151/40.

501 In Case C-112/99 Toshiba Europe GmbH v Katun Germany GmbH the ECJ held that the indication in the catalogue of a supplier of spare parts and consumable items suitable for the products of an equipment manufacturer, of product numbers (OEM numbers) by which the equipment manufacturer designates the spare parts and consumable items which he himself sells may constitute comparative advertising which objectively compares one or more material, relevant, verifiable and representative features of goods.

complaints, or initiate appropriate legal proceedings. Member States must confer on the courts powers enabling them to take appropriate action, including ordering the cessation of misleading or unpermitted comparative advertising or preventing the publication of it, even without proof of actual loss or damage or of intentional negligence on the part of the advertiser.

These measures may be the subject of an accelerated procedure with provisional or final effect.

The Member States may authorise their courts or administrative bodies to demand publication of the decision to withdraw the misleading advertising.

Where the above powers are exercised exclusively by an administrative authority, there must be provision for legal means of redress against any improper or unreasonable exercise of the administrative authority's powers.

In addition, under Article 6, Member States shall give the courts or administrative bodies powers enabling them, in civil or administrative proceedings, to:

(i) demand, if necessary, that the advertiser provide proof of the material accuracy of the facts contained in the advertising;

(ii) consider facts to be inaccurate if the proof demanded is lacking or insufficient.

(b) Composition of administrative authorities: Provision is made as to what administrative authorities would be suitable for the carrying out of the duties imposed by the Directive. The Directive does not exclude voluntary control of misleading advertising by self- regulatory bodies.

(c) Minimum harmonisation formula: Article 7 of the Directive enables Member States to obtain or adopt provisions with a view to ensuring more extensive protection of consumers, of persons carrying on a trade, business, craft or profession and of the general public. This does not apply to comparative advertising as far as the comparison is concerned.

The Directive does not oblige Member States who have bans regarding certain goods and services to permit comparative advertising regarding those goods and services and specifically allows bodies or organisations responsible under the law of the Member States to regulate the exercise of professional activities.

(d) Implementation: In the UK, the Directive was implemented by the Control of Misleading Advertisement Regulations 1988.[502]

All Member States have notified implementing measures.

502 SI 1988/915; see also SI 2000/914.

4. Television advertising: Council Directive (EEC) 89/552 of 3 October 1989 on the coordination of certain provisions laid down by law, regulation or administrative action in Member States concerning the pursuit of television broadcasting activities[503]

(a) Objective: The Directive (commonly called 'the Television without Frontiers' Directive) has a much broader scope than regulating advertising, in that it seeks to abolish all restrictions on the freedom to provide broadcasting services whilst at the same time coordinating the national laws. The Directive therefore lays down minimum rules needed to guarantee the freedom of transmission in broadcasting whilst enacting that all broadcasts emanating from and intended for reception within the EU and in particular those intended for reception in a Member State should respect the law of the originating Member State applicable to broadcasting intended for reception by the public in that Member State. The Directive also intends to deal with the promotion of markets for television productions, particularly those emanating from Europe and from independent producers. For the purposes of this work, only the provisions concerning TV advertising are taken into account.

As far as television advertising is concerned, the Directive lays down minimum rules and standards to protect consumers,[504] and aims to prohibit television advertising of medicinal products and medicinal treatment available only on prescription and to introduce strict criteria relating to the advertising of alcoholic products. It was also felt necessary to introduce rules to protect children in connection with both the content of programmes and the content of television advertising.

(b) Scope of application: The Directive regulates 'television advertising', ie, any form of announcement, broadcast whether in return for payment or for similar consideration or broadcast for self-promotional purposes by a public or private undertaking in connection with a trade, business, craft or profession in order to promote the supply of goods or services, including immovable property, rights and obligations, in return for payment. The Directive was

503 [1989] OJ L298/23.

504 In Case C-34–36/95 KO v De Agostini and TV Shop [1997] ECR I-3843 the ECJ ruled that this Directive does not exclude the application of rules other than those specifically concerning the broadcasting and distribution of programmes (eg, national rules on consumer protection). National rules will apply provided they do not represent a secondary control of broadcasting which stands in addition to the control carried out by the host Member State. However, the fact that the Directive provides a set of rules to govern TV advertising directed at minors precludes the operation of additional rules in this. In addition, the Court restated the principle that the protection of consumers is an overriding requirement in the public interest, which may under certain circumstances justify obstacles to the free movement of goods or restrictions on the freedom to provide services, and the extension of this principle to the area of advertising and television broadcasts.

amended in 1997[505] so as to include teleshopping within its scope of application.

The Directive also deals with 'sponsorship', ie, 'any contribution made by a public or private undertaking not engaged in television broadcasting activities or in the production of audio visual works, to the financing of television programmes with a view to promoting its name, its trademark, its image, its activities or its products'.

(c) Television advertising and sponsorship: general rules: Advertising and teleshopping must be readily recognisable as such and kept quite separate from other parts of programmes. Isolated advertising spots must be the exception, advertising and teleshopping must not use subliminal techniques and surreptitious advertising[506] must be prohibited (Article 10).

Article 11 provides that advertisements and teleshopping spots must be inserted between programmes in such a way that the integrity and value of the programme, taking into account natural breaks in and the duration and nature of the programme, and the rights of the rights holders are not prejudiced. In programmes consisting of autonomous parts, or in sports programmes and similarly structured events and performances comprising intervals, advertisements and teleshopping spots can only be inserted between parts or in intervals. In feature films and television films an interruption is only allowed once for each complete period of 45 minutes although a further interruption is allowed if the duration is at least 20 minutes longer than two or more complete periods of 45 minutes.[507]

There must be a period of least 20 minutes between each successive advertising break. Advertisements and teleshopping cannot be inserted in any broadcast of religious service. News, current affairs programmes, documentaries and childrens' programmes whose programme duration is less

505 Parliament and Council Directive (EC) 97/36 amending Council Directive (EEC) 89/552 on the coordination of certain provisions laid down by law, regulation or administrative action in Member States concerning the pursuit of television broadcasting activities ([1997] OJ L202/60).

506 'Surreptitious advertising' is defined in Art 1 as the representation in words or pictures of goods, services, the name, the trademark or activities of a producer of goods or provider of services in programmes when such representations are intended by the broadcasters to serve as advertising and might mislead the public as to its nature. The definition makes clear that the representation is considered to be intentional if it is done in return for payment or other similar consideration.

507 In Case C-6/98 Satellitenfernsehen GmbH, Kabel 1, K 1 Fernsehen GmbH [1999] ECR I-7599 the ECJ ruled that this latter restriction must be interpreted in the strictest possible sense. It is common ground that the gross principle (under which the duration of advertisements is included in the period of time taken into consideration for determining the number of advertising interruptions allowed) allows a greater number of interruptions for advertising than the net principle (under which only the duration of the works themselves is included). In the Directive, the interpretation to be taken is the one prescribing the gross principle, which means that, in order to calculate the 45-minute period for the purpose of determining the number of advertising slots authorised in the broadcasting of audiovisual works, such as feature films and films made for television, the duration of the advertisements must be included in that period.

than 30 minutes may not be interrupted. If the duration is of 30 minutes or more, the period of least 20 minutes must elapse.

(d) Advertising content: Article 12 provides that television advertising and teleshopping shall not:

(i) prejudice respect for human dignity;

(ii) include any discrimination on the grounds of race, sex or nationality;

(iii) be offensive to religious or political beliefs;

(iv) encourage behaviour prejudicial to health or safety;

(v) encourage behaviour prejudicial to the protection of the environment.

Article 13 bans tobacco advertising and tobacco teleshopping. Article 14 bans the advertising of medicinal products and medical treatment available only on prescription in the Member State within whose jurisdiction the broadcaster falls.

(e) Advertising of alcohol: Advertising and teleshopping relating to alcohol must comply with certain criteria. First, it is forbidden to aim these advertisements at children or show children consuming these drinks. The consumption of alcohol must not be linked to any enhanced physical performance or to drinking. Secondly, the consumption of alcohol must not be shown to contribute towards social or sexual success. Thirdly, alcohol must not be shown as having therapeutic qualities or that of a stimulant, sedative or means of resolving personal conflicts. Fourthly, advertising must not encourage immoderate consumption of alcohol or present abstinence or moderation in a negative light. Finally, it must not place emphasis on high alcoholic content as being a positive quality for drinkers.

(f) Advertisements and children: Television advertising and teleshopping must not cause moral or physical detriment to children and must comply with the following criteria:

(i) it must not directly put pressure on children to buy a product or service by exploiting their inexperience or credulity;

(ii) it must not directly encourage children to persuade their parents to purchase the goods or service being advertised;

(iii) it must not exploit the special trust minors place in their parents, teachers or other persons;

(iv) advertisements must not show minors in dangerous situations.

(g) Sponsored television programmes: Sponsored television programmes are allowed but must meet some strict requirements:

(i) the content and scheduling of the programmes may not be influenced by the sponsor;

(ii) they must be clearly identified as being sponsored;

(iii) they must not encourage the purchase or rental of products in particular by the making of promotional references to the product or services;

(iv) sponsorship cannot be provided by tobacco companies or the manufacturers of medicinal or medical treatment available only by prescription in Member States;

(v) news and current affairs programmes may not be sponsored.[508]

(h) Amount of advertising: Article 18 provides that the amount of advertising and teleshopping shall not exceed 15% of the daily transmission time. This percentage may be increased to 20% to include forms of advertisements such as direct offers to the public for sale provided the amount of spot advertising does not exceed 15%.[509]

The amount of advertising and teleshopping within a given one-hour period shall not exceed 20%.

Forms of advertisement such as direct offers to the public for sale shall not exceed one hour per day. These restrictions on advertising time may be made stricter by Member States' own rules.

(i) Implementation: The Directive was implemented in the UK by the Broadcasting Act 1990.

All Member States have notified implementing measures.

5. Advertising of medicinal products: Council and Parliament Directive 2001/83 relating to medicinal products for human use Directive (EC) 2001/83 on the Community code relating to medicinal products for human use[510]

(a) Objective: The objective of the Directive is much broader than that of regulating the advertising of medicinal products, in that the Directive lays

508 In Joined Cases C-320, 328, 329, 337, 338, 339/94 RTI (Reti Televise Italiane SpA) and Others v Ministero delle Poste e Telecomunicazioni [1996] ECR 1-6471, [1997] 1 CMLR 346, ECJ, the ECJ declared that the Directive, and in particular Art 17(1)(b) thereof, must be interpreted as permitting the insertion of the sponsor's name or logo at times other than at the beginning and/or the end of the programme.

509 See Joined Cases C-320, 328, 329, 337, 338,339/94 RTI (Reti Televise Italiane SpA) and Others v Ministero delle Poste e Telecomunicazioni [1996J ECR 1-6471, [1997] 1 CMLR 346, ECJ, in which the ECJ ruled that the second sentence of Art 18(1) of the Directive in no way obliges Member States to increase the daily transmission time allowed for advertising. Likewise, they are at liberty, should they choose to make use of the option introduced by the provision, to do so only in favour of certain more time-consuming forms of advertising. Indeed, inasmuch as Art 19 of the Directive provides that 'Member States may lay down stricter rules than those in Article 18 for programming time and the procedures for television broadcasting for television broadcasters under their jurisdiction', it must be interpreted as authorising Member States to lay down stricter rules for the definition of the types of publicity which may benefit from the additional transmission time provided for in the second sentence of Art 18(1), provided, however, that those rules are compatible with the EC Treaty.

510 [2001] OJ L311/67.

down the legal framework for the placing on the market, manufacture, import, classification, distribution, advertising and surveillance of medicinal products.

For the purposes of this chapter, only the provisions concerning advertising (Title VIII of the Directive) will be examined. The provisions of Directive 2001/83 concerning labelling and package leaflet are discussed in Part C of Chapter 11.

(b) Scope of application: According to Article 86, the provisions of the Directive on advertising apply to 'any form of door-to-door information, canvassing activity or inducement designed to promote the prescription, supply, sale or consumption of medicinal products', including in particular:

(i) the advertising of medicinal products to the general public;

(ii) the advertising of medicinal products to persons qualified to prescribe or supply them;

(iii) visits by medical sales representatives to persons qualified to prescribe medicinal products;

(iv) the supply of samples;

(v) the provision of inducements to prescribe or supply medicinal products by the gift, offer or promise of any benefit or bonus, whether in money or in kind, except when their intrinsic value is minimal;

(vi) sponsorship of promotional meetings and scientific congresses attended by persons qualified to prescribe or supply medicinal products.

The rules on advertising laid down in Title VIII do not cover:

(i) the labelling and the accompanying package leaflets, which are subject to the provisions of Title V (see Chapter 11, Part C);

(ii) correspondence, possibly accompanied by material of a non-promotional nature, needed to answer a specific question about a particular medicinal product;

(iii) factual, informative announcements and reference material relating, for example, to pack changes, adverse-reaction warnings as part of general drug precautions, trade catalogues and price lists, provided they include no product claims;

(iv) statements relating to human health or diseases, provided there is no reference, even indirect, to medicinal products.

The rules on advertising laid down in Title VIII (except Article 87(1)) also apply to homeopathic products.

(c) General rules: According to Article 87 , Member States are to prohibit any advertising of a medicinal product in respect of which a marketing authorisation has not been granted in accordance with Community law. All parts of the advertising of a medicinal product must comply with the particulars listed in the summary of product characteristics.

The advertising of a medicinal product:

(i) shall encourage the rational use of the medicinal product, by presenting it objectively and without exaggerating its properties;

(ii) shall not be misleading

(d) Medicinal products that cannot be advertised: Subject to certain exceptions, Member States shall prohibit the advertising to the general public of medicinal products which:

(i) are available on medical prescription only;

(ii) contain psychotropic or narcotic substances;

(iii) have certain therapeutic indications listed at Article 88(2) .

Medicinal products which, by virtue of their composition and purpose, are intended and designed for use without the intervention of a medical practitioner and, if necessary, with the advice of the pharmacist, may be advertised to the general public.

Member States shall prohibit the mentioning in advertising to the general public of therapeutic indications such as tuberculosis, sexually transmitted diseases, other serious infectious diseases, cancer and other tumoral diseases, chronic insomnia, diabetes and other metabolic illnesses.

Member States are entitled to ban, on their territory, advertising to the general public of medicinal products the cost of which may be reimbursed.

Member States shall prohibit the direct distribution of medicinal products to the public by the industry for promotional purposes; they may, however, authorise such distribution in special cases for other purposes.

(e) Advertising content: According to Article 89 , all advertising to the general public of a medicinal product shall:

(i) be set out in such a way that it is clear that the message is an advertisement and that the product is clearly identified as a medicinal product;

(ii) include the following minimum information:

– the name of the medicinal product, and in most cases the common name if the medicinal product contains only one active substance;

– the information necessary for correct use of the medicinal product;

– an express, legible invitation to read carefully the instructions on the package leaflet or on the outer packaging, as the case may be.

The advertising of a medicinal product to the general public shall not contain any material which:

(i) gives the impression that a medical consultation or surgical operation is unnecessary;

(ii) suggests that the effects of taking the medicine are guaranteed, are unaccompanied by adverse reactions or are better than, or equivalent to, those of another treatment or medicinal product;

(iii) suggests that the health of the subject can be enhanced by taking the medicine or affected by not taking the medicine, subject to certain exceptions;

(iv) is directed exclusively or principally at children;

(v) refers to a recommendation by scientists, health professionals or any way famous persons, who could encourage the consumption of medicinal products;

(vi) suggests that the medicinal product is a foodstuff, cosmetic or other consumer product;

(vii) suggests that the safety or efficacy of the medicinal product is due to the fact that it is natural;

(viii) could, by a description or detailed representation of a case history, lead to erroneous self-diagnosis;

(ix) refers, in improper, alarming or misleading terms, to claims of recovery or uses, in improper, alarming or misleading terms, pictorial representations of changes in the human body caused by disease or injury, or of the action of a medicinal product on the human body;

(x) mentions that the medicinal product has been granted a marketing authorisation.

(f) Other relevant provisions: Articles 91 to 96 lay down several detailed rules addressed to sales representatives and to those who are qualified to prescribe or supply medicinal products.

In brief, those provisions are aimed at ensuring that:

(i) any advertising or documentation of a medicinal product addressed to persons qualified to prescribe or supply such products includes certain essential information on the product (Articles 91 and 92);

(ii) medical sales representatives receive adequate training and are competent to provide precise and complete scientific information on the products which they promote. They should also ensure the transmission of certain relevant information concerning such products to the relevant authority in their Member State (Article 93);

(iii) where medicinal products are promoted to persons who are qualified to prescribe or supply them, the latter do not receive or solicit any inducements such as gifts or pecuniary advantages. Hospitality, for example at sales promotions, should always be reasonable in level and secondary to the main purpose of the meeting and must not be extended to those other than health professionals (Articles 94 and 95);

(iv) free samples are provided only subject to certain conditions (Article 96).

(g) Compliance: Member States must ensure that there are adequate and effective methods to monitor the advertising of medicinal products. Such methods, which may be based on a system of prior vetting, shall in any event include legal provisions under which persons or organisations regarded under national law as having a legitimate interest in prohibiting any advertisement inconsistent with the Directive may take legal action against such advertisement, or bring such advertisement before an administrative authority competent either to decide on complaints or to initiate appropriate legal proceedings.

The powers that shall be conferred upon courts or administrative authorities in the Member States and the specific remedies against advertising of medicinal products inconsistent with the Directive are laid down in Article 97.

(h) Implementation: The time limits for transposition of this rather complex piece of legislation are set out in Annex II, Part B of the Directive.

6. Proposal for a Parliament and Council Directive concerning business to consumer commercial practices in the internal market and amending Directives (EEC) 84/450, (EC) 97/7 and (EC) 98/27[511]

(a) Objective: The proposed Directive lays down rules aimed at laying down an EU-wide standard of protection against unfair commercial practices. The objective, as set out in Article 1, is to deliver a high degree of consumer protection and to facilitate the functioning of the internal market.

(b) Scope of application: The proposed Directive would apply to commercial practices, ie, to all acts, omissions, courses of conduct or representations, commercial communications including advertising and marketing by a trader, directly connected with the promotion, sale or supply of a product to consumers.

(c) Unfair practices: The Directive defines the conditions which determine whether a commercial practice is unfair: these are, in general, that the practice must be contrary to the requirements of professional diligence; and that the practice materially distorts or is likely to materially distort consumers' behaviour.

The benchmark consumer to be considered in assessing the impact of a practice is the 'average' European consumer who is 'reasonably well informed and reasonably observant and circumspect', as defined in the ECJ case law. However, where a specific group of consumers is targeted (for example, children or adolescents), the characteristics of the average member of that group must be taken into account in assessing the impact of the practice.

Practices that are misleading or aggressive are regarded as unfair.

(d) Internal market: The Directive contains an internal market clause which provides that traders have to comply only with the requirements of the

511 COM(2003)356 final.

country of origin and prevents other Member States from imposing additional requirements. This is to ensure that traders have the legal certainty they need to deal with cross-border consumers without imposing undue burden on them.

(e) Misleading and aggressive practices: A commercial practice is misleading either through action or omission. The Directive does not attempt to define a comprehensive list of information to be positively disclosed in all circumstances, but imposes on businesses the duty not to omit 'material' information which the average consumer needs to make an informed decision.

So, for example, the Directive regards as 'material' information on the main characteristics of the product to be bought the price inclusive of taxes and, where appropriate, delivery charges and the existence of a 'right of withdrawal' where one exists. Where this information is not apparent from the context, the trader will need to disclose it.

The Directive incorporates the current provisions of the Misleading Advertising Directive and applies them to other commercial practices, including those after sale.

A commercial practice can be aggressive in three possible ways, namely harassment, coercion and undue influence. Criteria are set out to be applied in differentiating between aggressive practices on the one hand and legitimate marketing on the other.

The proposed Directive lists in an Annex some specific types of unfair commercial practice that are banned in all circumstances. So, for example, using the expression 'liquidation sale' or equivalent when the trader is not about to cease trading or falsely arguing that the personal security of the consumer or his family is at risk if the consumer does not purchase the product are misleading claims; on the other hand, making persistent and unwanted solicitations by telephone, fax, e-mail or other remote media or advertising to children in a way which implies that their acceptance by their peers is dependent on them having a particular product are aggressive practices.

(f) Follow-up: The proposal, adopted by the Commission on 18 June 2003, is at the time of writing undergoing first reading in the European Parliament.

13
CONSUMER CONTRACTS

A. INTRODUCTION

Community action in the area of contract law has so far refrained from thorough harmonisation but has been limited to adopting directives for the protection of consumers in specific cases, for example, against high pressure marketing methods and against unfair terms, or in consumer credit or consumer sales contracts.

The relationship between these directives, commonly adopted on the legal basis of Article 95 (previously 100a) of the EC Treaty,[512] and the internal market is not very clear. If harmonisation of technical regulations can find a solid basis in the internal market programme and in the *Cassis de Dijon* jurisprudence, harmonisation of provisions of private law appears to be less evidently necessary for completing the internal market, while at the same time having quite drastic consequences for the national legal systems of private law.

While the first measures of consumer contract law were aimed at ensuring transparency of the market and consumer choice by imposing information duties on the trader and prescribing cooling-off periods in favour of the consumer, control of the substance of the transaction has progressively gained relevance and has resulted in the enactment of two directives, one on unfair contract terms and one on consumer sales, which have a landmark importance in the development of EC consumer law. Consumer information, however, remains an important target as demonstrated by the more recent enactment of the Directive on distance marketing of financial services.

The Commission issued in 2001 a Communication to the Council and Parliament on European Contract Law[513] aimed at triggering a debate on the desirability and viability of further harmonisation of European contract law. The 2001 Communication was followed by a second Communication proposing an action plan for more coherent contract law.[514]

While the scope of the debate is wider than merely that of consumer contracts, the improvement of the current Community *acquis* (ie, mainly made up of consumer law measures) is one of the most immediate targets of the action plans. This includes:

(a) remedying identified inconsistencies in EC contract law (eg, different modalities concerning the right of withdrawal in the Directives on

512 Or, for the earlier ones, Art 94 (ex 100).

513 COM(2001)398 final.

514 Communication from the Commission to the European Parliament and the Council: A more coherent contract law: An action plan, COM(2003)68 final.

doorstep selling, timeshare, distance selling and distance selling of financial services);

(b) reviewing the quality of drafting;

(c) simplifying and clarifying existing legislation;

(d) adapting existing legislation to economic, commercial and other developments which were not foreseen at the time of adoption;

(e) filling gaps in EC legislation which have led to problems in its application.

This chapter also discusses the issue of cross-border enforcement of consumers' rights: there is no point facilitating cross-border shopping by providing harmonised remedies throughout Europe if such remedies cannot be adequately pursued across the borders not only by consumers but also by associations that have a legitimate interest in the protection of consumers' rights.

B. MARKET TRANSPARENCY

1. Introduction

The Directives here examined[515] have as a common feature the fact that they require that the consumer is provided with certain information before he makes a choice.

This is a popular regulatory technique in EC consumer law and, with regard to contract law, it is often combined with the conferral, after the conclusion of the transaction, of a cooling-off period, ie, a lapse of time during which the consumer is entitled to exercise the right to withdraw from the contract. The conferral of a cooling-off period aims to ensure that the consumer can think over the transaction with peace of mind, with full knowledge of the bargain that he has concluded.

Techniques that ensure mere market transparency and consumer information are welcome to the extent that they promote an efficient market by supporting consumer choice; on the other hand, however, these techniques may be unsatisfactory in that they fail to address the substantive fairness of transactions, while it is well know that, because of his weaker bargaining position, the consumer is usually incapable of striking a fair deal with the economically more powerful seller or supplier.

515 Directive 94/47 on timeshare property, which also adopts this regulatory technique, is discussed in Chapter 15.

516 [1985] OJ L372/31.

2. Council Directive (EEC) 85/577 of 20 December 1985 to protect the consumer in respect of contracts negotiated away from business premises[516]

(a) Objective: This Directive, commonly known as the 'Doorstep Selling Directive', was adopted under Article 94 (ex 100) of the EC Treaty and stems from the preliminary programme for consumer protection and information policy which had provided that appropriate measures should be taken to protect consumers against unfair commercial practices in respect of doorstep selling.

The Directive takes into account the 'surprise element' of doorstep sales, ie, the fact that the consumer, often unprepared and facing an unexpected opportunity to make a transaction, is unable to cope with the high pressure selling methods of the trader.

(b) Scope of application: According to Article 1(1) , the Directive applies to contracts under which a trader supplies goods or services to a consumer and which are concluded during a visit organised by the trader away from his own business premises or during a visit by a trader to the consumer's home or to that of another consumer or to the consumer's place of work, and where the visit does not take place at the express request of the consumer. The Directive also applies (Article 1(2)) to a situation where the consumer having requested a visit for one purpose is then sold goods or services which he did not know were part of the trader's commercial or professional activities.

The Directive also applies to contracts in respect of which an offer was made by a consumer under the conditions similar to those described above although the consumer was not bound by that offer before its acceptance by the trader (Article 1(3)). Similarly, it applies to offers made contractually by the consumer under similar conditions where the consumer is bound by his offer (Article 1(4)).

The Directive applies to contracts between a trader and a consumer. The notion of 'consumer' as a 'natural person who, in transactions covered by this Directive, is acting for purposes which can be regarded as outside his trade or profession' is one which is commonly found in EC measures of consumer protection. It was, however, this specific provision that gave rise to two important cases concerning the exact definition of consumer: *Criminal proceedings against Di Pinto*[517] and *Bayerische Hypotheken- und Wechselbank AG v Edgard Dietzinger*[518] both discussed in Chapter 2.

'Trader' means a natural or legal person who, for the transaction in question, acts in his commercial or professional capacity, and anyone acting in the name or on behalf of that trader.

516 [1985] OJ L372/31.
517 Case C-361/89 [1991] ECR I-1189.
518 Case C-45/96 [1998] ECR I-1199.

Under Article 3, Member States may decide that the Directive shall apply only to contracts for which the payment to be made by the consumer exceeds a specified amount. This amount, however, may not exceed 60.

The Directive specifically does not apply to:

(i) contracts for the construction, sale and rental of immovable property.[519] However, contracts for the supply of goods and for their incorporation on to immovable property or contracts for the repair of immovable property do fall within the Directive;

(ii) contracts for the supply of foodstuffs, beverages or other goods intended for current consumption of a household and supplied by a regular roundsman;

(iii) contracts for the supply of goods or services provided that the contract is concluded on the basis of a trader's catalogue which the consumer has read in the absence of the representative;

(iv) the continuity of contract between the trader and the consumer;

(v) the catalogue and the contract clearly inform the consumer of his right to return goods to the supplier within a period of not less than seven days of receipt or otherwise to cancel the contract within that period without obligation;

(vi) contracts for securities.

Further, Member States may refrain from applying this Directive to contracts for the supply of goods or services having a direct connection with the goods or services concerning which the consumer requested the visit of the trader.

(c) Written notice: According to Article 4, traders are required to give consumers written notice of their right of cancellation together with the name and address of the person against whom that right may be exercised. The notice must be dated and give particulars enabling the contract to be identified. It must be given to the consumer either in connection with the

519 In Case C-423/97 Travel Vac SL v Manuel José Antelm Sanchis [1999] ECR-I 2195 the ECJ defined the exact scope of this exclusion in relation to timeshare property. The ECJ held that, while it is true that timeshare contracts are covered by Directive 94/47 on the protection of purchasers in respect of certain aspects of contracts relating to the purchase of the right to use immoveable properties on a timeshare basis, this does not preclude a contract having a timeshare element from being covered by Directive 85/577 if the conditions for the application of that Directive are otherwise fulfilled. Since a contract of that nature does not only concern the right to use timeshare property, but also concerns the provision of separate services of a value higher than that of the right to use the property, it is not covered by Directive 85/577, Art 3(2)(c), under which that Directive does not apply to contracts for the construction, sale and rental of immoveable property or contracts concerning other rights relating to immoveable property. Directive 85/577 can therefore apply to a contract relating to the acquisition of a right to use immoveable property on a timeshare basis and to the provision of services whose value is higher than that of the right to use the immoveable property.

cases identified in Article 1(1) at the time of conclusion of the contract or in the case of Article 1(2) not later than the time of the conclusion of the contract or in the case of Article 1(3) and Article 1(4) when the offer is made by the consumer. Member States shall ensure that the national legislation lays down appropriate consumer protection measures in cases where the information has not been supplied.

(d) Cancellation: Article 5 gives the consumer the right to cancel the contract by sending notice within a period of not less than seven days including the date of despatch. The effect of giving the notice releases the consumer from any obligations under the contract.

Under Article 6, the consumer may not waive the rights conferred on him by the Directive.

(e) Effect of cancellation of contract: If the consumer cancels the contract the legal effects of this shall be governed by the national laws of the Member States, particularly regarding the question of reimbursement of payment and the return of goods (Article 7).

(f) Minimum harmonisation formula: Article 8 allows Member States to adopt or maintain legislation more favourable to consumers.

In *Buet v Ministère Public*[520] the ECJ ruled that a French prohibition on canvassing in connection with the sale of educational material was not contrary to Article 28 (ex 30), first, because it was justified by the greater risk of ill-considered purchases in the area in question, and, secondly, because stricter rules on canvassing were allowed under Article 8 of Directive 85/577.

(g) Implementation: The Directive was implemented in the UK by the Consumer Protection (Cancellation of Contracts Concluded away from Business Premises) Regulations 1987 .[521]

All Member States have notified implementing measures. A delay in the Italian implementation has given rise to the well-known case of *Faccini Dori v Recreb*,[522] were a consumer sought to derive from the unimplemented Directive a right of cancellation as against traders with whom she had concluded a contract and to enforce such a right in a national court. In denying such possibility, the ECJ restated once again the principle that unimplemented directives can only have vertical direct effect.

3. Council Directive 87/102 on the approximation of the laws, regulations and administrative provisions of the Member States concerning consumer credit[523]

(a) Objective: The Directive seeks to approximate national measures in the field of consumer credit on grounds that differences between Member States' laws governing the supply of consumer credit distort competition between

520 Case 382/87 [1989] ECR 1235.
521 SI 1987/2117.
522 Case C-91/92 [1994] ECR I-3325.
523 [1987] OJ L42/48.

grantors of credit and impede consumers from obtaining credit in other Member States.

From the consumer's point of view, the Directive seeks to improve the transparency in the provision of credit by making sure that the consumer receives adequate information on the conditions and cost of credit.

(b) Scope of application: The Directive applies to all credit agreements entered into by consumers and creditors. These are broadly defined by Article 1(2)(c) so as to include deferred payments, loans or other similar financial accommodations.[524]

A creditor is any natural or legal person, or a group of such persons, who grants credit in the course of his trade, business or profession. There is therefore no requirement that the creditor pursues as his main activity that of lending as long as this is, even occasionally, part of his business.

Under Article 2, the Directive does not cover:

(i) credit agreements for the purpose of acquiring or retaining property rights in land or a building;[525]

(ii) credit agreements for the purpose of renovating or improving a building;

(iii) hiring agreements which do not provide for the title passing to the hirer;

(iv) credit free of interest or any other charge;

(v) interest-free credit agreements where the consumer repays the credit in a single payment;

(vi) credit in the form of advances on a current account granted by a credit institution or financial institution, subject to Article 6[526] and with the exception of credit card accounts;

524 In Case C-208/98 Berliner Kindl Brauerei AG v Andreas Siepert [2000] ECR-I 1741 the ECJ held that, on a proper construction of Directive 87/102 for the approximation of the laws, regulations and administrative provisions of the Member States concerning consumer credit, it does not cover a contract of guarantee for repayment of credit where neither the guarantor nor the borrower was acting in the course of his trade or profession.

525 Home loans are dealt with in Commission Recommendation of 1 March 2001 on pre-contractual information to be given to consumers by lenders offering home loans. The Recommendation lays down guidelines on harmonised information to be made available to consumers concerning home loans, so as to make it easier for them to compare loan products available from different lenders, including lenders from another Member State. The guidelines were incorporated in a Voluntary Code of Conduct agreed between the mortgage-lending industry and consumer groups. The Commission is responsible for monitoring implementation of the Code and will publish the list of mortgage lenders committed to respecting the Code.

526 Article 6 requires that, where there is an agreement between a consumer and a financial or credit institution for the granting of credit in the form of an advance on a current account (other than a credit card account), the following information must be provided in writing: the credit limit; the annual rate of interest and the charge applicable; the procedure for terminating the agreement. The consumer shall then be informed of any change of any charge.

(vii) credit agreements involving amounts less than 200 or more than 20,000, subject to Article 6 ;

(viii) credit agreements whereby the consumer undertakes to repay the credit either within three months or by a maximum of four payments within a 12-month period, subject to Article 6.

Member States may also exclude from the scope of the Directive certain types of credit which are granted at rates of charge below those prevailing in the market and which are not offered to the public generally.

(c) Advertising and marketing: Article 3 is central to the policy of information disclosure of the Directive. It requires that a statement of the annual percentage rate (APR) is provided whenever an advertisement or offer displayed at business premises indicates the rate of interest or any other figures relating to the cost of credit.

In fact, credit advertising is often much more strictly regulated in the Member States.

(d) Information: Unlike the Directive on doorstep sales and distance contracts, this Directive does not provide for any cancellation rights but simply requires that the credit agreement is made in writing and that the consumer receives a copy thereof. The written agreement must include certain information listed in Article 4(2) (eg, the APR and the conditions under which it may be amended) and other essential terms listed by way of illustration in what is now Annex I to the Directive.

(e) APR: The APR is 'the total cost of the credit to the consumer, expressed as an annual percentage of the amount of the credit granted and calculated in accordance with Article 1a'.

The APR is an important means of enabling consumers to compare interests since it provides a clear indication of the cost of credit. The amending Directive (EEC) 90/88[527] sets out a single mathematical formula for calculating the annual percentage rate of charge throughout the EU and for determining credit cost items to be used in the calculation. The amending Directive (EC) 98/7 Directive (EC) 98/7 amending Directive 87/102/EEC for the approximation of the laws, regulations and administrative provisions of the Member States concerning consumer credit ([1998] OJ L101/17)[528] further deals with the method of calculation of the annual percentage rate of credit charge.

(f) Repossession: The Directive sought to avoid the threat of repossession for consumers purchasing goods on credit, but due to its minimal character Article 7 leaves it to the Member States to lay down the conditions under which goods may be repossessed, with the only *caveat* that repossession should not entail unjust enrichment.

(g) Early repayment: Under Article 8 the consumer is entitled to discharge his obligations under the credit agreement before the time fixed by the

527 [1990] OJ L61/14.
528 [1998] OJ L101/17.

agreement and should then be entitled to an equitable reduction in the total charge for credit. The rules to calculate this reduction are to be laid down by the Member States.

(h) Liability of a third party creditor: In relation to assignment, Article 9 provides that where the creditor's rights are assigned to a third person, the consumer's rights remain unaffected and action to enforce any claim may be taken against that third person.

Article 10 aimed to make sure that a negotiable instrument could not be presented or transferred to a third party without being subject to any of the defences originally available under the original credit sale. In practice, however, it only requires Member States to ensure:

(i) that consumers using bills of exchange are suitably protected, when such practices are allowed;

(ii) that the existence of a credit agreement does not affect the rights of the consumer vis-à-vis the supplier of goods or services purchased by means of such an agreement in cases where the goods or services are not supplied or are not in conformity with the contract.

Article regulates the lender's liability. Provided that:

(i) the consumer has entered into a credit agreement with a person other than the supplier of the goods or services purchased;

(ii) the grantor of the credit and the supplier of the goods or services have a pre-existing agreement whereunder credit is made available exclusively by the former;

(iii) the consumer obtains his or her credit pursuant to that pre-existing agreement;

(iv) the goods or services covered by the credit agreement are not supplied or are not in conformity with the contract;

(v) the consumer has sought redress against the supplier but has failed to obtain satisfaction;

(vi) the individual transaction is for an amount of more than 200;

the consumer may seek redress against the grantor of credit. The rationale behind this is that the creditor works in cooperation with the supplier and should therefore not be able to escape when things go wrong. Also, creditors are able to exert a positive control over the behaviour of suppliers they work with.

(i) Enforcement: The Member States must provide one of the following means to ensure that the Directive is given effect:

(i) ensure that persons offering credit obtain official authorisation to do so;

(ii) ensure that the persons in question are subject to inspection by an official body;

(iii) promote the establishment of appropriate bodies for providing information and advice to consumers in respect of credit agreements and for receiving associated complaints.

All Member States have fortunately adopted one or both of the first two options, which appear to be much more effective than, and perhaps not even comparable to, the third one.

(j) Member States' obligations: The Member States must ensure that the rules set out in the Directive are complied with in credit agreements and are not circumvented as a result of the way in which agreements are formulated.

(k) Minimum harmonisation formula: Article 15 allows Member States to maintain or adopt more stringent measures for the protection of consumers. This provision, in combination with the fact that the Directive harmonises very few aspects of the provision of credit, has resulted in persisting divergence in the terms and conditions upon which credit services are provided in the Member States.

(l) Implementation: The Directive and its amendments were implemented in the UK by amending the existing Consumer Credit Act 1974. The Act goes is several respects much further than the Directive in the protection of consumers.

All Member States have notified implementing measures.[529]

(m) Follow-up: Article 17 of the Directive required the Commission to submit to the Council no later than January 1995 a report on the operation of the Directive. In its Report,[530] the Commission noted that most Member States had adopted stricter provisions than those envisaged by the Directive. This Report was followed by a second one where the Commission provided an overview of the comments made by the Member States, the financial services industry and consumer organisations on issues such as the extension of the scope of Directive 87/102 , the creation of bodies authorised to receive consumer complaints, cooling-off periods, usury, and over-indebteness.

More effective steps have been taken in recent years. On the ground of the outcome of a discussion entertained over several years with Member States and stakeholders, the Commission adopted in 2002 a Proposal for a Directive on harmonisation of the laws, regulations and administrative provisions of the Member States for credit for consumers.[531]

Unlike the present Directive, which lays down only the minimum basis of regulation leaving a large scope for Member States to go further, the new

529 In Case C-192/94 El Corte Inglés SA v Cristina Blázquez Rivero [1996] ECR-I 1281 the ECJ restated that, in the absence of measures implementing Directive 87/102 for the approximation of the laws, regulations and administrative provisions of the Member States concerning consumer credit within the period prescribed by that Directive, a consumer may not, even in view of Art 129a of the EC Treaty, base a right of action on the Directive itself against a lender who is a private person.

530 COM(1995)117 final.

531 COM(2002) 443 final.

Directive explicitly prevents Member States from adding to the new rules unless specifically stated.

The new Directive would cover all consumer credit no matter the form (loan, hire-purchase, overdraft facilities, rolling credit, financial lease, etc), amount (no floor, no ceiling) and any surety (a guarantor or a mortgage) or insurance; home loans would remain outside the scope but mortgage-backed consumer credit ('equity release') would still be covered.

The new Directive aims to harmonise the way that the cost of credit to the consumer is calculated. While the APR would express the total cost from the perspective of the consumer, the Directive introduces two new terms, the 'Sums Levied by the Creditor' (SLC) and the 'Total Lending Rate' (TLR): the former covers what the consumer pays to the lender while the latter expresses this in a percentage. They will provide a comparison of lender's offers on a national and cross-border basis.

The Directive imposes on the borrower a duty to disclose all relevant information when asked by the lender, but the latter must advise his client on the most appropriate product in his product range and conscientiously assess the borrower's ability to repay before granting new credit ('responsible lending'). This means that the lender must identify the most favourable or least expensive product in his product range for a consumer.

The new Directive also makes provisions to enhance circulation of quality solvency data across borders, to protect personal guarantors and to confer a 14 day right of cancellation on the consumer.

All Member States except Portugal, Italy, Ireland, Austria, Belgium and Greece have notified implementing measures.

4. Council and Parliament Directive (EC) 97/7 on the protection of consumers in respect of distance contracts[532]

(a) Objective: This Directive starts from the assumption that cross-border distance selling is increasingly popular among consumers as one of the main results of the completion of the internal market. The Directive also takes into account that the introduction of new technologies increases the ways in which consumers can obtain information about offers anywhere in the EU and place orders. The fact that various Member States had different laws to protect consumers in respect of distance selling could have a detrimental effect on the accomplishment of the internal market.

The purpose of the Directive is therefore to set down minimum levels of protection for consumers in connection with distance selling. It was also intended to protect the purchasers of goods and services from demands for payment of unsolicited goods and from high pressure selling methods, but also

532 [1997] OJ L144/19, as amended by Parliament and Council Directive (EC) 2002/65 concerning the distance marketing of consumer financial services and amending Council Directive (EEC) 90/619 and Directives (EC) 97/7 and (EC) 98/27.

to provide additional protection to transactions in which very often the quality of the goods bought cannot be checked by the consumer until the goods are already bought or in which the supplier may easily hide his identity.

The authors of the Directive appreciated that, in addition to setting down minimum binding rules itself, these would need to be supplemented by voluntary arrangements amongst the appropriate retailers concerned, in line with Commission Recommendation (EEC) 92/295 on the codes of practice for the protection of consumers in respect of contracts negotiated at a distance.[533]

(b) Scope of application: The Directive applies to distance contracts between traders and consumers. A 'consumer' is, as usual, any natural person who, in contracts covered by the Directive, is acting for purposes which are outside his trade, business or profession; a 'supplier' is any natural or legal person who, in contracts covered by the Directive, is acting in his commercial or professional capacity.

A distance contract is defined as meaning 'any contract concerning goods or services concluded between a supplier and a consumer under an organised distance sales or service provision scheme run by the supplier, who, for the purposes of the contract, makes exclusive use of one or more means of distance communication up to and including the moment at which the contract is concluded'.

'Means of distance communication' is said to mean 'any means which, without the simultaneous physical presence of the supplier and the consumer, may be used for the conclusion of the contract between those parties'. At Annex I to the Directive is a list of the sorts of procedure which might be indicative of such an arrangement. These include:

(i) printed matter sent through the post;

(ii) standard letters sent through the post;

(iii) press advertising with order form;

(iv) catalogues;

(v) telephone calls;

(vi) radio;

(vii) video-phone;

(viii) videotext;

(ix) electronic mail;

(x) fax machine; and

(xi) teleshopping.

The Directive does not apply to contracts relating to financial services (regulated by a specific directive), neither does it relate to contracts concluded by means of automatic vending machines or automated commercial premises

533 [1992] OJ L156/21.

or concluded with telecommunication operators through the use of public payphones or concluded for the construction and sale of immovable property or relating to other immovable property rights except for rental or any contracts concluded as an auction.

Further, provisions of the Directive relating to the need to give prior information to the consumer, providing written confirmation of that information, giving the consumer a right of withdrawal, and imposing upon the supplier a duty within 30 days of the contract to execute the order do not apply to either the contract for the supply of foodstuffs, beverages or other goods intended for everyday consumption which are supplied to the consumer's home or to his workplace by regular roundsmen. This would presumably include situations such as the daily delivery of milk in the United Kingdom.

Similarly, these provisions do not apply to contracts for the provision of accommodation, transport, catering or leisure services where the supplier undertakes to provide these services on a specific date or within a specific period. In the case of outdoor leisure activities, the supplier may also exceptionally reserve the right not to be bound by the provisions of the Directive whereby, if the supplier fails to perform his side of the contract, the consumer is able to obtain the refund of the monies he has paid.

(c) Prior information: Under Article 4, in good time prior to the conclusion of the contract, the consumer has to be provided with the following information:

(i) the name of the supplier, and, if payment is required in advance, his address;

(ii) the main characteristics of the goods or services;

(iii) the price of the goods, including all taxes;

(iv) delivery costs, if applicable;

(v) arrangements for payment, delivery or performance;

(vi) the existence of the right of withdrawal;

(vii) if communication is required by a specific format, eg, telephone, the cost of using it if it is greater than the basic rate usually charged;

(viii) the period for which the offer or price remains valid;

(ix) minimum duration of the contract if the contract provides for provision of services permanently or recurrently.

All of the above information must be provided in a clear and comprehensible way and having regard to the principles of good faith and the principles governing the protection of those such as children who are unable to enter into a contractual arrangement.

Finally, in the case of telephone sales, the identity of the supplier concerned and the commercial purpose of the call must be made clear at the beginning of any conversation with the consumer.

(d) Written confirmation of information: The consumer must receive written confirmation of the information referred to in (iii) above in good time during the contract and at the latest at the time of delivery. In any event, the following must be provided:

(i) written information on the condition for exercising the right of withdrawal;

(ii) the geographical address of the place of business of the supplier to which complaints may be addressed;

(iii) information on after-sales and guarantees which exist; and

(iv) the conditions for cancelling the contract where it is of unspecified duration or exceeds one year.

The right to written confirmation of the information does not apply to services which are performed through the use of distance communication where they are supplied only once and they are invoiced by the operator at that time. Nevertheless, the consumer must still be able to obtain the address of the place of business of the supplier to which he may address complaints.

(e) Withdrawal: The consumer shall have a period of seven working days in which to withdraw from the contract without penalty and without reason. The only charge which may be made is any direct cost of returning the goods to the supplier.

The period for exercise of this right shall begin, in the case of goods, from the day of receipt by the consumer provided that the supplier has given the written information which is required. In the case of services, this period begins from the date of completion of the contract or the date when the written information is given if this is after the date of completion of the contract, provided that the period must not exceed three months if the supplier has totally failed to provide the written information required.

If a supplier has failed to fulfil the obligations under Article 5 to provide the written information, the period is three months either from the date of the receipt of the goods or the date of conclusion of the contract. If information is supplied within the three-month period, then the seven working days for withdrawal starts to run from that moment. Upon the consumer exercising his right of withdrawal, the supplier must make the reimbursement to him within 30 days.

A consumer will not have the right of withdrawal (unless agreed in the contract) in the following cases:

(i) if performance of the contract has begun with the consumer's agreement before the end of seven working days;

(ii) for the supply of goods and services, the price of which is dependent on the fluctuations in the financial market;

(iii) for the supply of goods made to the consumer's own specifications or clearly personalised or which by reason of their nature cannot be returned or may deteriorate or expire;

(iv) for the supply of audio or video recordings or computer software which were unsealed by the consumer;

(v) for the supply of newspapers, periodicals and magazines;

(vi) for gaming and lottery services.

Member States are required to ensure that if the price of goods is covered by a credit agreement, the credit agreement itself can also be cancelled without penalty if the right of withdrawal is exercised.

(f) Performance: Unless the parties agree otherwise, the supplier must execute the order within 30 days from the date the consumer forwarded the order to the supplier. Where the supplier fails to perform the contract on the basis that the goods or services are unavailable, the consumer must be informed of the situation and must be able to obtain a refund within 30 days. However, Member States may lay down in their legislation that the supplier may provide the consumer with goods or services of equivalent quality and price provided that this possibility was provided for in the contract.

(g) Payment by credit or debit card: Member States must also put in place legislation which allows the consumer to request cancellation of a payment where fraudulent use has been made of his payment card in connection with distance contracts and to be re-credited with the sums paid.

(h) Inertia selling: National legislation must prohibit the supply of goods or services to a consumer when these are not ordered by the consumer beforehand, where such supply involves a demand for payment, and must exempt the consumer from having to pay for any such unsolicited supply.

(i) Restrictions on the use of certain means of distance communication: A supplier may not use an automatic calling machine or a fax machine to attempt sales to a consumer without the consumer's prior consent.

Member States may allow other forms of distance communication only where there is no clear objection from the consumer.

(j) Binding nature: A consumer is not entitled to waive the rights given to him by the Directive by virtue of any national law and the consumer must not be deprived of his protection by the supplier choosing the law of a non-Member country as the law applicable to the contract if the latter has close connection with the territory of one or more Member States.

(k) Minimum harmonisation: Article 14 makes it clear that Member States may introduce or maintain more stringent provisions compatible with the EC Treaty to ensure a higher level of consumer protection. Such provisions may include a ban on the marketing of certain goods or services, particularly medicinal products by means of distance contracts.

(l) Enforcement: Member States must include provisions in their legislation where either public bodies, consumer organisations or professional organisations have the power before the courts to ensure the national provisions for the implementation of the Directive are applied. National legislation may stipulate that the burden of proof concerning the existence of prior information, written confirmation, compliance with time limits or consumer consent is placed on the supplier and Member States are required to ensure that suppliers cease practices which do not comply with the terms of the Directive.

(m) Implementation: In Great Britain, the Directive was implemented by the Consumer Protection (Distance Selling) Regulations 2000.[534]

All Member States have notified implementing measures.

5. Parliament and Council Directive 2002/65 concerning the distance marketing of consumer financial services[535]

(a) Objective: The 1997 Directive on distance selling was adopted for all services other than financial services, which because of their complexity were thought to require specific rules. This Directive therefore seeks to harmonise the conditions for the provision of consumer financial services such as cards, investment funds, pension plans, etc, sold to the consumer by phone, fax or internet.

(b) Scope of application: The Directive applies to contracts concerning financial services (ie, any service of a banking, credit, insurance, personal pension, investment or payment nature) concluded between a supplier and a consumer under an organised distance sales or service-provision scheme run by the supplier, who, for the purpose of that contract, makes exclusive use of one or more means of distance communication up to and including the time at which the contract is concluded.

'Means of distance communication' refers to any means which, without the simultaneous physical presence of the supplier and the consumer, may be used for the distance marketing of a service between those parties.

In the case of contracts for financial services comprising an initial service agreement followed by successive operations or a series of separate operations of the same nature performed over time, the provisions of this Directive shall apply only to the initial agreement. In case there is no initial service agreement but the successive operations or the separate operations of the same nature performed over time are performed between the same contractual parties, Articles 3 (information prior to the conclusion of the contract) and 4

534 SI 2000/2334

535 [2002] OJ L271/16. The Directive amends Council Directives (EEC) 90/619, (EC) 97/7 and (EC) 98/27.

(additional information) apply only when the first operation is performed. Where, however, no operation of the same nature is performed for more than one year, the next operation will be deemed to be the first in a new series of operations and, accordingly, Articles 3 and 4 shall apply.

(c) Prior information: Sellers of financial services and products are obliged to provide consumers with a comprehensive package of information in good time before a contract is concluded. This includes details, listed in Article 3, concerning the supplier, the financial service, the distance contract, and means of redress.

This information, the commercial purpose of which must be made clear, shall be provided in a clear and comprehensible manner in any way appropriate to the means of distance communication used, with due regard, in particular, to the principles of good faith in commercial transactions, and the principles governing the protection of those who are unable, pursuant to the legislation of the Member States, to give their consent, such as minors.

Special provisions are made in Article 3(3) concerning voice telephony communications.

Information on contractual obligations, to be communicated to the consumer during the pre-contractual phase, shall be in conformity with the contractual obligations which would result from the law presumed to be applicable to the distance contract if the latter were concluded.

(d) Additional information requirements: Information on the technical quality and nature of the financial service must be also provided in accordance with the rules of the 'vertical' directives on credit, insurance and investment services or with relevant national rules for services not currently subject to EC legislation. National provisions must be communicated to the Commission.

(e) Communication of the contractual terms and conditions and of the prior information: The supplier must communicate to the consumer all the contractual terms and conditions and the information referred to above on paper or on another durable medium available and accessible to the consumer in good time before the consumer is bound by any distance contract or offer; however, if the contract has been concluded at the consumer's request using a means of distance communication which does not allow such communication, the supplier shall fulfil this obligation immediately after the conclusion of the contract.

At any time during the contractual relationship, the consumer is entitled, at his request, to receive the contractual terms and conditions on paper. In addition, the consumer is entitled to change the means of distance communication used, unless this is incompatible with the contract concluded or the nature of the financial service provided.

(f) Burden of proof: Member States may stipulate that the burden of proof in respect of the supplier's obligations to inform the consumer and the consumer's consent to conclusion of the contract and, where appropriate, its performance, can be placed on the supplier.

Any contractual term or condition providing that the burden of proof in respect of the supplier of all or part of the obligations incumbent on him pursuant to this Directive should lie with the consumer shall be an unfair term within the meaning of Council Directive (EEC) 93/13.

(g) Withdrawal: The consumer has the right to withdraw within 14 days, extended in the case of life insurance and pension plans to 30 days, in the following circumstances:

(i) when the contract has been signed before the consumer has received prior notice of the terms and conditions (eg, the consumer takes out an insurance policy in order to obtain immediate cover);

(ii) when the consumer has received the contractual terms and conditions but has been unfairly induced to conclude the contract during the reflection period.

If another distance contract concerning services provided by the supplier or by a third party has been attached to a given distance contract for a financial service, the additional distance contract shall be cancelled, without any penalty, if the consumer exercises his right of withdrawal.

If the consumer exercises his right of withdrawal after having already agreed to partial performance of the service, he may be required to pay the supplier for the service rendered. If the service has been rendered in its entirety before the right of withdrawal is exercised, that right can no longer be exercised and the consumer will have to pay for the service. Consumers must be informed in advance of the price to be paid (or of the basis on which it will be calculated).

In order to avoid speculative manoeuvres, the right of withdrawal does not apply to financial services that may be subject to fluctuations in the financial market, such as sales of foreign currency and securities.

Member States may also exclude mortgage or property credit from this right of withdrawal from a contract.

(h) Payments by card: Member States shall ensure that in the event of fraudulent use of payment cards or other non-cash means of payment, consumers will be able to cancel transactions and be entitled to reimbursement of any sums charged.

(i) Unsolicited services and communications: Article 9 prohibits the supply of financial services without the consumer's specific and valid consent when this supply includes a request for immediate or deferred payment and exempts him from any obligation in the event of unsolicited supplies. Article 10 also prohibits the use of automated distance communication systems without human intervention or faxes without the consumer's prior consent.

As regards other means of distance communication, such as 'cold calling' and 'spamming', Article 10 leaves Member States free to choose between two options: under the first option ('opt-in'), cold calling and spamming are prohibited unless the consumer has expressly consented; under the second option ('opt-out'), this is prohibited only if the consumer has signalled his objection, eg, by entering his name on a register set up for this purpose.

(j) Binding nature: Consumers may not waive the rights conferred on them by this Directive.

Member States shall take the measures needed to ensure that the consumer does not lose the protection granted by this Directive by virtue of the choice of the law of a non-Member country as the law applicable to the contract if this contract has a close link with the territory of one or more Member States.

(k) Enforcement and redress: Member States must provide for appropriate sanctions in the event of the supplier's failure to comply with national provisions adopted pursuant to this Directive. In particular, they may provide that the consumer may cancel the contract at any time, free of charge and without penalty.

The sanctions must be effective, proportional and dissuasive.

Member States must also ensure that adequate and effective means exist to ensure compliance with this Directive in the interests of consumers, such as provisions whereby one or more of the following bodies, as determined by national law, may take action in accordance with national law before the courts or competent administrative bodies to ensure that the national provisions for the implementation of this Directive are applied:

(i) public bodies or their representatives;

(ii) consumer organisations having a legitimate interest in protecting consumers;

(iii) professional organisations having a legitimate interest in acting.

Member States must take the measures necessary to ensure that operators and suppliers of means of distance communication put an end to practices that have been declared to be contrary to this Directive, on the basis of a judicial decision, an administrative decision or a decision issued by a supervisory authority notified to them, where those operators or suppliers are in a position to do so.

Member States must promote the setting up or development of adequate and effective out-of-court complaints and redress procedures for the settlement of consumer disputes concerning financial services provided at distance.

(l) Out-of-court settlement: Member States must encourage the bodies responsible for out-of-court settlement of disputes to cooperate in the resolution of cross-border disputes concerning financial services provided at distance.

(m) Implementation: Member States must implement the Directive not later than 9 October 2004.

(n) Follow-up: Following the implementation of this Directive, the Commission shall submit to the Parliament and the Council a report on the problems facing both consumers and suppliers seeking to buy and sell financial services, and shall submit, where appropriate, proposals to amend and/or further harmonise the Community legislation concerning financial services.

C. SUBSTANTIVE CONTROL

1. Introduction

Techniques aimed at simply ensuring market transparency may attract the criticism that information is not sufficient to achieve effective protection of the consumer since they assume that the consumer is able to fully understand the information provided to him and to choose accordingly. The increasing complexity of the goods and products offered, in combination with the fact that the consumer is usually deprived of any bargaining power, leads to the argument that the law needs to some extent to intervene more directly towards regulating the fairness of bargains.

The Community has therefore adopted two Directives aimed at ensuring protection in two areas where consumers are particularly vulnerable and subject to exploitation: unfair terms and non-conformity of the goods bought.

2. Council Directive (EEC) 93/13 on unfair terms in consumer contracts[536]

(a) Objective: The laws of the Member States relating to the terms of contracts between sellers of goods and suppliers of services on the one hand and the consumer on the other present a great number of disparities. As a result, the markets for the sale of goods and services to consumers varies substantially from State to State, and this may result in distortions of competition amongst retailers and suppliers, especially when goods are sold and supplied in other Member States.

Also, the Directive recognises that consumers do not know the rules of law in other Member States which govern the contracts for the sale of goods or services and that this deters them from purchasing directly from a retailer in another Member State.

As a result, the Directive sets a common platform to remove unfair terms from contracts between retailers and consumers.

(b) Scope of application: The Directive applies to contracts between a consumer (defined according to the formula commonly found in the other

536 [1993] OJ L95/29.

'contract directives')[537] and a seller or supplier. It applies equally to oral and written contracts. Contracts relating to employment, contracts relating to succession rights, contracts relating to rights under family law and contracts relating to the incorporation and organisation of companies or partnership agreements are excluded from the Directive.

Terms which reflect mandatory statutory or regulatory provisions of the Member States and the principles or the provisions of international conventions to which the Member States or the Community are party which directly or indirectly determine the terms of consumer contracts are not covered on the assumption that they cannot be unfair.

Article 2(c) of the Directive makes it clear that the public nature of a seller or supplier does not exclude the application of the Directive, thus making contracts for the supply of public services subject to the fairness control. This is subject, however, to the exclusion from control of terms that reflect mandatory statutory or regulatory provisions. Since, very often, mandatory statutory or regulatory provisions are reproduced in contracts for the provision of public services, the extent to which the Directive applies to public services is narrower than it may *prima facie* appear.

In addition, a report compiled for the Commission by a French/English 'task force' on public services[538] has revealed a wide variety, throughout Europe, of frameworks establishing the nature of the public service providers and the classification of the relationship between the latter and the customers. The nature of the relationship between the providers of public services and their citizen recipients varies, sometimes without apparent justification, not only from State to State, but also from area to area. As a consequence, the application of the Directive to public services will vary remarkably from State to State.

(c) Individually negotiated terms: According to Article 3(1), the Directive only applies to terms which have not been individually negotiated. This limitation appears to be like firing two shots at the same target: if the philosophy of the Directive is primarily to offer protection to the party who has been deprived of his right to influence the contract, and therefore focus only on non-negotiated terms, then there would be no need to have the scope strictly limited to consumers; if, on the other hand, the rationale is to protect the *per definitionem* weaker consumer, then the lack of protection against individual terms seems illogical.

537 In Case C-541/99 Cape SNC v Idealservice [2001] ECR I-9049 the ECJ clarified (should there be any need) that an undertaking, even if concluding a contract to acquire merchandise or services solely for the benefit of its employees, cannot be considered as a consumer for the purposes of Directive 93/13.

538 Institut National de la Consommation and National Consumer Council, Application de la Directive 93/13 aux prestations de service publique: Rapport final, 1997, available only in French at www.europa.eu.int/comm/consumers/policy/developments/unfa_cont_term/uct02_fr.html.

A term shall always be regarded as not individually negotiated where it has been drafted in advance and the consumer has therefore not been able to influence the substance of the term, particularly in the context of a pre-formulated standard contract. The concept of 'not individually negotiated terms' is rather wide as it covers not only standard terms but all terms where there has been no preliminary negotiation.

According to Article 3(2), a term has not been individually negotiated when it has been drafted in advance and the consumer has therefore not been able to influence the substance of the term. The following paragraph of this Article, however, raises some confusion where it states that the fact that certain aspects of a term or one specific term have been individually negotiated shall not exclude the application of the Directive if an overall assessment of the contract indicates that it is nevertheless a pre-formulated standard contract. This provision would make sense if the scope of the Directive was defined by reference to standard contracts: in this case, there is a risk that, if several terms of a standard contract have been, in a particular case, individually negotiated, the contract would lose its character of being a 'standard contract' and would therefore be subject to no control; on the other hand, the scope of the Directive is defined not by reference to standard contracts, but to consumer contracts, whether they are standard or not. The only limitation is that the Directive will not apply to the 'individually negotiated terms'. The provision in Article 3(2) may give another impression, because it would allow *a contrario* that in some cases the Directive would not be applicable to some non-negotiated terms in consumer contracts. That was obviously not the intention of the legislator and therefore the Article must be interpreted taking into account the other provisions and the rationale of the Directive.

Article 3(2) also introduces an irrebutable presumption of non-negotiation in the cases where the term has been drafted in advance; the Directive then gives as a typical example the case of standard form contracts.

(d) The fairness test: According to Article 3(1), a term which has not been individually negotiated is unfair if, contrary to the requirement of good faith, it causes a significant imbalance in the parties' rights and obligations, to the detriment of the consumer.

The inclusion of the requirement of good faith among the fairness criteria must be seen in the light of two factors: first, the importance of such a principle within the framework of continental systems, in particular Germany; secondly, the fact that one Member State had already used good faith alone as a general criterion for the assessment of unfairness: the Portuguese law of 1985 on contract terms established, at Article 16, that 'general contractual terms which are contrary to good faith shall be prohibited'. As far as other legal traditions (such as the common law) are concerned, the requirements of good faith and of contractual balance represent foreign notions, the meaning and effect of which is difficult to estimate.

The preamble seeks to clarify the meaning of the fairness test by stating that 'the assessment ... of the unfair character of terms ... must be supplemented by a means of making an overall evaluation of the different interests involved'. This 'constitutes the requirement of good faith', in making which particular regard shall be had to the strength of the bargaining positions of the parties, to whether the consumer had an inducement to agree to the term and whether the goods or services were sold or supplied to the special order of the consumer; and to whether the seller or supplier dealt fairly and equitably with the other party whose legitimate interests he has to take into account.

This does not clarify important issues such as whether the requirements of good faith and significant imbalance are alternative, cumulative or ancillary one to the other, or whether good faith should be given a procedural or rather a substantive meaning.

(e) 'Core' exclusions: According to Article 4(2) of the Directive, the main subject matter of the contract and the relationship between the good or service purchased and the price paid are outside the scope of the Directive provided that these parts of the contract are spelled out in 'plain, intelligible language'.

The preamble to the Directive makes it clear that the exemption of the price/quality ratio from the control of unfairness is limited to the ratio itself and not to any other term related to the price. Terms determining how the price is to be calculated or how it can be changed are fully submitted to the control of the Directive. Also, the main subject matter of the contract and the price/quality ratio may be taken into account in assessing the fairness of other terms. In that way, indirect control of the price is admitted. So, for example, a clause fixing a price cannot be considered unfair just because the price fixed is too high; but it cannot be ruled out that a contract clause that gives rise to significant imbalance can in practice be deemed not to be unfair if the contract provides for a particularly advantageous price for the consumer.

The exact scope of the subject matter exclusion is slightly more difficult to determine than the price exclusion, since it requires in the first place defining the 'main subject matter of the contract'. This evokes the puzzle, known to several legal traditions, of the distinction between terms defining the contractual obligations and terms excluding or restricting liability for breach of obligations. Obviously, only a term that excludes or restricts liability can be subject to the control of the Directive.

(f) The 'transparency' requirement: Article 5 of the Directive, by requiring that terms are drafted 'in plain, intelligible language', introduces a transparency requirement. 'Plain and intelligible' are not tautological in that a term is in 'plain' language when it is not surprising, it cannot be misunderstood and it does not give rise to any doubts; 'intelligibility', on the other hand, encompasses both the style used and how a contract term is actually printed on paper.

The transparency principle is deeply rooted in Community law, both in secondary legislation and in the case law of the ECJ. The importance of informing and protecting the consumer has been stressed since the first two programmes for consumer protection and information policy of the Community. Almost every consumer directive includes information duties: information should be given in a sufficient, precise and clear way;[539] 'when a brochure is made available to the consumer it shall indicate in a legible, comprehensible and accurate manner both the price and the adequate information';[540] it should respect ethical principles, human dignity as well as political beliefs ;[541] it must be easily accessible and it is often demanded that it is confirmed in writing.[542]

The sanctions for infringement of the transparency requirement are not clearly stated. Article 5 only deals with the case where more than one meaning can be attributed to a certain term: 'where there is doubt about the meaning of a term, the interpretation most favourable to the consumer shall prevail'. It does not indicate, however, what the sanction is if a contract term not only is recognised not to be written in plain and intelligible language, but does not appear to have a meaning, or has only one (unclear) meaning.

(g) *Interpretatio contra proferentem*: The principle stated in the second part of Article 5 that an ambiguous term must be interpreted in favour of the consumer is known with small variations to several European legal systems as the *contra proferentem* rule. It does not apply to the preventive actions of a collective nature envisaged in Article 7.

(h) The Annex: Since the negotiations leading to the first proposal for the Directive, there was concern that the notion of unfairness expressed by the general clause would lack sufficient accuracy and precision to be applied in a uniform way in all Member States. An Annex containing an indicative and non-exhaustive 'grey' list of terms that *may* be considered unfair was therefore added to the Directive with the purpose of providing a more detailed and practical elaboration of the notion of unfair term. Judges (or any other national competent authority) can assess the fairness of a clause corresponding to a model clause in the Annex with full freedom (even thought it would be *a priori* considered with suspicion[543]) and in conjunction with the criteria laid down in Article 3. Accordingly, a contractual term corresponding to one of the models

539 Directive 90/314, Art 3.2 on package travel, package holidays and package tours; see also Directive 97/7, Art 4.2 on distance contracts, according to which 'information ... shall be provided in a clear and comprehensible manner'.

540 Directive 90/314, Art 3.2 on package travel, package holidays and package tours.

541 Annex, Commission Recommendation of 7 April 1992 on Codes of Practice for the protection of consumers in respect of contracts negotiated at a distance ([1992] OJ L156/21).

542 See, eg, Directive 87/102 on consumer credit, Art 6; Directive 85/577 on doorstep selling, Art 4; Directive 97/7 on distance contracts, Art 5; Directive 94/47 on timeshare property, Art 3.

543 The 'serious' character of the list is confirmed by note 2 of the Annex, which aims to soften, for financial services, some of the terms listed in note 1.

in the Annex is not automatically unfair, and a contractual term not included in the list is not automatically fair.

The terms listed in the Annex can be grouped as follows:

(i) terms giving a party the control on the terms of the contract or the performance of the contract (eg, point j of the Annex: terms which enable the seller or supplier to alter the terms of the contract unilaterally without a valid reason which is specified in the contract; see also points i, k, l, m, p);

(ii) terms determining the duration of the contract (eg, point g: terms enabling the seller or supplier to terminate a contract of indeterminate duration without reasonable notice; see also point h);

(iii) terms restraining a party to have the same rights as the other (eg, point c: terms making an agreement binding on the consumer whereas provision of services by the seller or supplier is subject to a condition whose realisation depends on his own will alone; see also points d, f, o);

(iv) exemption and limitations clauses (eg, point a: terms excluding or limiting the legal liability of a seller or supplier in the event of the death of a consumer or personal injury to the latter resulting from an act or omission of that seller or supplier; see also points b, e, n, q).

(i) Unenforceability of unfair terms: Member States shall lay down that unfair terms used in a contract concluded with a consumer by a seller or supplier shall, as provided for under their national law, not be binding on the consumer and that the contract shall continue to bind the parties upon those terms if it is capable of continuing in existence without the unfair terms.

In *Oceano Grupo Editorial SA v Rocio Murciano Quintero*[544] the ECJ held that the protection provided for consumers by Directive 93/13 entails the national court being able to determine of its own motion whether a term of a contract before it is unfair when making its preliminary assessment as to whether a claim should be allowed to proceed before the national courts.

In *Cofidis SA v Jean Louis Fredout*[545] the ECJ further stated that the Directive precludes a national provision which, in proceedings brought by a seller or supplier against a consumer on the basis of a contract concluded between them, prohibits the national court, on expiry of a limitation period, from finding, of its own motion or following a plea raised by the consumer, that a term of the contract is unfair.

(j) Binding nature: Member States shall take the necessary measures to ensure that the consumer does not lose the protection granted by this Directive by virtue of the choice of the law of a non-Member country as the law applicable to the contract if the latter has a close connection with the territory of the Member States.

544 Cases C-240–244/98 [2000] ECR I-4941
545 Case C-473/00 [2002] ECR I-10875.

(k) Preventive actions: Member States shall ensure that, in the interests of consumers and of competitors, adequate and effective means exist to prevent the continued use of unfair terms in contracts concluded with consumers by sellers or suppliers. Such means shall include provisions whereby persons or organisations, having a legitimate interest under national law in protecting consumers, may take action according to the national law concerned before the courts or before competent administrative bodies for a decision as to whether contractual terms drawn up for general use are unfair, so that they can apply appropriate and effective means to prevent the continued use of such terms.

With due regard for national laws, the above legal remedies may be directed separately or jointly against a number of sellers or suppliers from the same economic sector or their associations which use or recommend the use of the same general contractual terms or similar terms.

(l) Minimum harmonisation: Member States may adopt or retain the most stringent provisions compatible with the EC Treaty in the area covered by the Directive, to ensure a maximum degree of protection for the consumer.

(m) Implementation: The Directive was implemented in the UK by the Unfair Terms in Consumer Contracts Regulations 1999.[546]

The Law Commission is currently drafting a measure aimed at merging and replacing the previously existing Unfair Contract Terms Act 1977 (which remained in force after the enactment of the Regulations) and the 1999 Regulations.

All Member States have notified implementing measures.[547]

(n) CLAB: The Commission has created a database accessible via the Internet (CLAB)[548] which collects all the existing case law in the Member States concerning unfair terms and is continuously updated. The aims pursued by this project are two: first, the Commission wanted to create a tool for the systematic monitoring of practical enforcement of the Directive in the Member States, with a view also to preparing its report; secondly, it wanted to provide this information to the public with a view to promoting the harmonious and consistent enforcement of the Directive in the Member States.

546 SI 1999/2083. Originally, the Directive was implemented by the Unfair Terms in Consumer Contract Regulations 1994, SI 1994/3159. The 1994 Regulations did not allow locus standi in preventive actions to bodies other than the OFT. Following an action brought by the consumers' associations for the review of the Regulations, the Government enacted the 1999 Regulations. This makes some minor amendments to the 1994 text and allows locus standi to other 'qualifying bodies' listed in Part I of Schedule 1.

547 Infringement proceedings for incorrect implementation have been mounted against several Member States. Some of those were later abandoned and others concluded without a declaration of infringement. To date, Italy (Case C-372/99 [2002] ECR-I 819) and the Netherlands (Case C-144/99 [2001] ECR I-3541) have been condemned.

548 CLAB can be viewed at europa.eu.int/clab/index.htm.

(o) Follow-up: Under Article 9, the Commission was to present a report to the European Parliament and to the Council concerning the application of this Directive five years at the latest after its implementation.

The Report,[549] drawn from Member States' experience in implementing the Directive, suggests a number of improvements concerning the Directive's limitations, the notion of unfair term, the list in the Annex to the Directive, the failure to supervise pre-contractual terms and conditions, the principle of transparency and the right to information, penalties, existing national arrangements for eliminating unfair terms, the problems posed by certain economic sectors, and the future of the CLAB database.

3. Council and Parliament Directive 1999/44 on certain aspects of the sale of consumer goods and associated guarantees[550]

(a) Objective: This Directive has been one of the most contentious consumer protection issues which has been before the Member States for many years. In the course of the adoption of the Directive, many national delegates expressed their misgivings with regard to the scope of the Directive, the ranking of the rights vested in the consumer by the legal guarantee, the limitation period for these rights, the moment from when the different periods would begin to run as well as the question as to whether the guarantee period should be stayed or interrupted in the event of the repair or replacement of the goods in question. Eventually, however, the Directive was adopted, although reduced to the minimum in many respects.

The proposed Directive aims to harmonise Member States' legislation on consumers' rights when they buy goods which do not conform to the sales contract. The purpose is to ensure a common minimal level of protection throughout the EU. The Directive provides for two types of guarantees: a legal guarantee which includes all legal protection of the purchaser in respect of defects in the goods acquired, resulting directly from the law, as a collateral effect of the contract of sale; and a 'commercial guarantee' (simply called 'guarantee' in the Directive) which expresses the will of one person, the guarantor, who assumes personal liability for certain defects.

(b) Scope of application: The Directive applies to contracts between a seller and a consumer (defined according to the formula commonly found in the other 'contract directives') for the sale of 'consumer goods'. These are defined as any tangible movable item, with the exception of: goods sold by way of execution or otherwise by authority of law; water and gas where they are not put up for sale in a limited volume or set quantity; electricity.

Member States may exclude from this definition second-hand goods sold at public auction where consumers have the opportunity of attending the sale in person.

549 COM(2000)248.
550 [1999] OJ L171/12.

The Directive applies to contracts for the supply of consumer goods to be manufactured or produced.

(c) Conformity with the contract: According to Article 2, goods delivered to the consumer must be in conformity with the contract of sale. Goods are presumed to be in conformity if, at the moment of delivery:

(i) they comply with the description given;

(ii) they are fit for the purposes for which goods of the same type are normally used;

(iii) they are fit for any particular purpose for which the consumer requires them and which was made known to the seller at the time of conclusion of the contract, and accepted by the seller;

(iv) their quality and performance are satisfactory, given the nature of the goods and taking into account the public statements made about them by the seller, the producer or his representative.

There is no lack of conformity if, at the time of the conclusion of the contract, the consumer was aware or could not reasonably be unaware of the lack of conformity, or if this is due to the material supplied by the consumer.

If the goods are not in conformity with the public statements made by the producer or his representative, the seller will not be liable if:

(i) the seller shows that he did not know and could not reasonably know the statement in question;

(ii) the seller shows that at the time of sale he corrected the statement;

(iii) the seller shows that the decision to buy the goods could not have been influenced by the statement.

Any lack of conformity resulting from incorrect installation of the consumer goods is deemed to be equivalent to lack of conformity of the goods if installation forms part of the contract of sale of the goods and the goods were installed by the seller or under his responsibility. This applies equally if the product, intended to be installed by the consumer, is installed by the consumer and the incorrect installation is due to a shortcoming in the installation instructions.

(d) Obligations of the seller: Article 3(1) of the Directive makes the seller liable for any lack of conformity appearing within two years of delivery. Any lack of conformity becoming apparent within six months of delivery will be presumed to have existed at the time of delivery, unless proof to the contrary is furnished or unless this presumption is incompatible with the nature of the goods or the nature of the lack of conformity.

(e) Remedies: In the case of non-conformity of the goods sold, Article 3(2) entitles the consumer to the following rights:

(i) a right to free repair or replacement, within a reasonable period and without major inconvenience to the consumer;

(ii) if repair or replacement is impossible or disproportionate or if the seller has not remedied the shortcoming within a reasonable period or without major inconvenience to the consumer, a right to an appropriate reduction of the price or to have the contract rescinded.

The consumer is not entitled to have the contract rescinded if the lack of conformity is minor.

Member States may provide that, in order to benefit from his rights, the consumer must inform the seller of the lack of conformity within a period of two months from the date on which he detected such lack of conformity.

(f) Right of redress: Under Article 4, where the final seller is liable to the consumer because of a lack of conformity resulting from an act or omission by the producer, a previous seller in the same chain of contracts or any other intermediary, the final seller shall be entitled to pursue remedies against the person responsible, under the terms of national law.

(g) (Commercial) guarantees: By effect of Article 6, commercial guarantees (ie, any additional undertaking given by a seller or producer, over and above the legal rules governing the sale of consumer goods, to reimburse the price paid, to exchange, repair or handle a product in any way, in the case of non-conformity of the product with the contract) are legally binding on the retailer under the conditions laid down in the guarantee document and the associated advertising. That would mean that commercial guarantees must put the consumer in a better position than that resulting from internal national consumer sales law.

The guarantee shall state in plain intelligible language its content and particulars and make clear that the consumer's rights under national law are not affected by the guarantee.

At the consumer's request, the guarantee shall be made available in writing or on another durable medium available and accessible to him. Within its own territory, the Member State in which the consumer goods are marketed may provide that the guarantee be drafted in one or more official languages of the Community.

Non-conformity of the guarantee with the provisions of the Directive does not affect its validity and the consumer may still require that the guarantee be honoured.

(h) Binding nature: Any contractual terms or agreements concluded with the seller which directly or indirectly waive or restrict the rights resulting from the proposed Directive are not binding on the consumer.

Member States shall take the necessary measures to ensure that the consumer does not lose the protection granted by this Directive by virtue of the choice of the law of a non-Member country as the law applicable to the contract if the latter has a close connection with the territory of the Member States.

(i) Minimum harmonisation: The rights resulting from this Directive shall be exercised without prejudice to other rights which may be conferred by national law to consumers.

Member States may adopt more stringent provisions, compatible with the EC Treaty, to ensure a higher level of consumer protection.

Those provisions are particularly important since domestic legislation in several Member States, including the UK, offers consumers a higher level of protection.

(j) Implementation: The Directive was implemented in the UK by the Sale and Supply of Goods to Consumers Regulations 2002,[551] which came into force on 31 March 2003.

All Member States except Belgium, France and Luxembourg have notified implementing measures.

(k) Follow-up: In 2006 at the latest, the Commission shall present to the European Parliament and the Council a report on the application of the Directive.

D. CROSS-BORDER PROTECTION OF CONSUMERS' INTERESTS

1 Introduction

Chapter 2 deals with recent Community initiatives to facilitate the resolution of consumer disputes, in particular where they entail a cross-border element, such as the 1998 Commission Communication on the out-of-court settlement of consumer disputes,[552] the 1998 Commission Recommendation on the principles applicable to the bodies responsible for out-of-court settlement of consumer disputes[553] and the 2000 Council Resolution on a Community-wide network of national bodies for the extra-judicial settlement of consumer disputes. [554]

Particular attention should now be devoted to a measure that aims to reinforce the use of collective actions of a preventive nature in cross-border cases.

Individual consumers often lack the motivation or means to bring cases to court or other alternative dispute resolution *fora*, especially in the case of cross-border claims. The possibility of consumers' associations and other bodies in charge of protecting consumers' interests being allowed to bring actions to prevent trade malpractices, even across border, makes not only litigation more affordable, but plays an important role in keeping under

551 SI 2002/3045.
552 COM(1998)198 final.
553 Recommendation (EC) 98/257 ([1998] OJ L115/31).
554 [2000] OJ C155/1.

control traders' behaviours and in enforcing consumer protection laws, no matter where the claimant and the defendant are based.

The reason why the Directive finds its place in this specific chapter is that it concerns the enforcement of provisions which are mainly contained in the 'consumer contract' directives (except the Misleading Advertising Directive).

2. Council and Parliament Directive 98/27 on injunctions for the protection of consumers' interests[555]

(a) Objective and scope of application: The aim of this Directive is to approximate the laws, regulations and administrative provisions of the Member States relating to actions for injunctions. Actions for injunctions are designed to put an end to any behaviour which adversely affects consumers and, in the specific case of this Directive, violates the collective interests of consumers enshrined in the Directives listed in the Annex, namely:

(i) Directive (EEC) 89/450 concerning misleading advertising;

(ii) Directive (EEC) 85/577 to protect consumers in contracts negotiated away from business premises;

(iii) Directive (EEC) 87/102 (as amended) concerning consumer credit;

(iv) Directive (EEC) 89/552 (as amended) concerning the pursuit of television broadcasting activities;

(v) Directive (EEC) 90/314 on package travel, package holidays and package tours;

(vi) Directive (EEC) 92/28 on the advertising of medicinal products (now repealed and replaced by Directive 2001/83);

(vii) Directive (EEC) 93/13 on unfair terms in consumer contracts;

(viii) Directive (EEC) 94/47 on certain aspects relating to the purchase of timeshare property;

(ix) Directive (EEC) 97/97 on the protection of consumers in relation to distance contracts.

Three amendments to Directive 1998/27 have allowed the inclusion in the Annex of the following other Directives:

(i) Directive (EC) 1999/44 on certain aspects of the sale of consumer goods and associated guarantees;

(ii) Directive (EC) 2000/31 on certain legal aspects of information society services, in particular electronic commerce, in the Internal Market ('the Directive on electronic commerce');

(iii) Directive (EC) 2002/65 concerning the distance marketing of consumer financial services.

555 [1998] OJ L166/51.

(b) Actions for injunctions: Member States must designate the court or the authority competent to rule on any proceedings instituted by entities qualified to bring actions seeking:

(i) to bring to an end or prohibit, possibly in the framework of an emergency procedure, any infringement, ie, any act contrary to the directives listed above;

(ii) the adoption of the measures needed, such as publication of the decision, to eliminate the effects of the infringement;

(iii) an order against the infringer for payment of a penalty in the event of failure to comply with the decision within the time limit specified.

The Directive shall not affect the operation of rules of private international law.

Member States may make provision to allow more extensive rights to bring actions at national level.

Provisions for actions of collective nature already exist in the Directives on misleading advertising, the advertising of medicinal products, unfair terms and distance contracts. The peculiarity of this Directive is that it seeks to reinforce the cross-border dimension of such actions by introducing specific provisions on intra-Community infringements.

(c) Intra-Community infringements: Member States must take the necessary measures to ensure that, in the event of infringement originating in that Member State, any qualified entity in another Member State in respect of which the interests it protects are adversely affected by the infringement may institute proceedings before the court or competent administrative authorities. Inclusion in the list mentioned in paragraph 2 of Article 4 constitutes proof of the qualified entity's legal capacity to institute proceedings.

The importance of this provision is in the fact that it sets a common platform for determining the *locus standi* of consumers' associations and other entities for the protection of consumers' interests. The difference in Member States' rules on *locus standi* of such bodies will no longer deter or prevent them from bringing actions against traders in other Member States.

(d) Prior consultation: Member States may maintain or adopt provisions pursuant to which a party may not bring an action for an injunction unless it has first tried to obtain the cessation of the infringement by consulting the offending party, possibly in cooperation with a qualified entity. If the infringement is not terminated within two weeks following receipt of the request for consultation, an action for an injunction may be brought.

(e) Qualified entities: The Directive does not, of course, list the entities which, in each member State, are entitled to bring actions for an injunction. Nevertheless, it lays down common criteria that such entities must fulfil in order to be granted such a possibility: those must be bodies or organisations which have a legitimate interest in ensuring that the collective interests of consumers are protected, and notably:

(i) independent public bodies, specifically responsible for protecting consumer interests in the Member States in which such bodies exist; and/or

(ii) bodies whose mission is to protect these interests in compliance with criteria laid down in national law.

For the purposes of cross-border actions and at the request of a qualified entity, a Member State must communicate to the Commission that such an entity is qualified to bring an action.

The Commission must also draw up a list of the qualified entities, which is published in the Official Journal of the European Communities and updated every six months.

(f) Implementation: In the UK, the Directive was implemented by the Consumer Protection Stop Now Orders (EC Directive) Regulations 2001.[556]

(g) Follow-up work: Every three years, the Commission must submit a report on the application of the Directive to the European Parliament and Council. The first report must be presented by 2003 at the latest and examine in particular the scope of the Directive and the effectiveness of the provisions concerning prior consultation.

556 SI 2001/1422.

14
ELECTRONIC COMMERCE

1. Introduction

Electronic commerce can bring significant benefits to consumers in many respects. It can provide greater choice, promote competition among suppliers, and allow businesses to develop new relationships with their customers to the advantage of both.

It also brings, however, new challenges and risks for consumer protection, especially in the case of cross-border transactions. In addition to the usual consumers' concerns about getting the right information on what they want to buy, cross-border shopping presents the additional risk of a major difficulty in seeking redress against traders established in another country.

In this respect, the Commission has sought to address consumers' lack of confidence in cross-border shopping by encouraging quality alternative dispute resolutions[557] and, with specific regard to e-commerce, it launched in 2002 an e-confidence initiative aimed at bringing to fruition an agreement between consumer and business representatives on good business practice for selling to consumers online.

The agreement establishes a common European standard for good business practice in dealing with consumers online. The standards agreed cover issues such as commercial communications and fair marketing practices, pre-contractual information, confirming and acknowledging orders, payment and security, data protection, handling complaints and alternative dispute resolution mechanisms. They are coupled with an effective monitoring and approval system including neutral third party assessment of trustmark schemes to ensure that commitments to these standards are met in practice.

The agreement reached should provide the basis for a Commission Recommendation to be adopted in the near future.

For the moment, though, the only measures which are directly relevant to consumer protection in the area of electronic commerce are contained in Directive 2000/31, here analysed for the parts which are relevant to this section.

557 See Commission Recommendation (EC) 2001/310 on the principles for out-of-court bodies involved in the consensual resolution of consumer disputes ([2001] OJ L109/56); Commission Communication on 'widening consumer access to alternative dispute resolution', 4 April 2001, COM(2001)161; Commission Recommendation (EC) 98/257 on the principles applicable to the bodies responsible for out-of-court settlement of consumer disputes ([1998] OJ L115/31).

2. Parliament and Council Directive 2000/31 on certain legal aspects of information society services, in particular electronic commerce, in the internal market[558]

(a) Objective: The objective of this Directive, commonly known as the 'E-commerce' Directive, is to lay down a common legal framework for the provision of information society services, ie, any service normally provided for remuneration, at a distance, by electronic means and at the individual request of a recipient of services. In particular, it aims to approximate certain national provisions on the establishment of service providers,[559] commercial communications, electronic contracts, the liability of intermediaries, codes of conduct, out-of-court dispute settlements, court actions and cooperation between Member States.

Although its priority is to facilitate the provision of information society services across borders, some of its provisions are directly beneficial to the consumer and are therefore examined in this chapter.

(b) Scope of application: This Directive does not establish any additional rules on private international law and does not affect the operation of other relevant Community directives, such as the directives on unfair terms in consumer contracts or on distance sales. This Directive shall not apply to:

(i) the field of taxation;

(ii) questions relating to information society services covered by Directives (EC) 95/46 and (EC) 97/66;

(iii) questions relating to agreements or practices governed by cartel law;

(iv) certain activities relating to the exercise of public authority, the representation and defence of clients or gambling activities such as lotteries and betting transactions.

(c) Information on the provider and on prices: The service provider must render easily, directly and permanently accessible to the recipients of the service and competent authorities at least the following information:

(i) the name of the service provider;

(ii) the geographic address at which the service provider is established;

(iii) the details of the service provider, including his electronic mail address, that allow him to be contacted rapidly and effectively;

(iv) the trade register in which the service provider is entered and his registration number, in case he is registered in a trade register;

558 Directive (EC) 2000/31 on certain legal aspects of information society services, in particular electronic commerce, in the Internal Market (Directive on electronic commerce) ([2000] OJ L178/1).

559 On this point, see the Commission Communication on the application to financial services of the E-commerce Directive, COM(2003)259, Art 3(4), discussed in section 3 of this work.

(v) if the activity is subject to an authorisation, the particulars of the relevant supervisory authority;

(vi) as concerns the regulated professions:

– any professional body or similar institution with which the service provider is registered,

– the professional title and the Member State where it has been granted,

– a reference to the applicable professional rules in the Member State of establishment and the means to access them;

(vii) where the service provider undertakes an activity that is subject to VAT, the identification number.

Where information society services refer to prices, these must be indicated clearly and unambiguously and, in particular, must indicate whether they are inclusive of tax and delivery costs.

(d) Commercial communications: Commercial communications which are part of, or constitute, an information society service must comply at least with the following conditions:

(i) the commercial communication, including unsolicited commercial communications, must be clearly identifiable as such;

(ii) the natural or legal person on whose behalf the commercial communication is made shall be clearly identifiable;

(iii) promotional offers, such as discounts, premiums and gifts must be clearly identifiable as such, and the conditions which are to be met to qualify for them shall be easily accessible and be presented clearly and unambiguously;

(iv) promotional competitions or games, where permitted in the Member State where the service provider is established, shall be clearly identifiable as such, and the conditions for participation shall be easily accessible and be presented clearly and unambiguously.

Service providers undertaking unsolicited commercial communications by electronic mail must consult regularly and respect the opt-out registers in which natural persons not wishing to receive such commercial communications can register themselves.

(e) Contracts: Member States must ensure that contracts can be concluded electronically. The Directive prescribes that the legal requirements applicable to the contractual process must not prevent the effective use and validity of electronic contracts but this excludes:

(i) contracts that create or transfer rights in real estate, except for rental rights;

(ii) contracts requiring by law the involvement of courts, public authorities or professions exercising public authority;

(iii) contracts of suretyship granted and on collateral securities furnished by persons acting for purposes outside their trade, business or profession;

(iv) contracts governed by family law or by the law of succession.

For the purposes of concluding a contract electronically, certain information must be provided, namely:

(i) the different technical steps to follow to conclude the contract;

(ii) whether or not the concluded contract will be filed by the service provider and whether it will be accessible;

(iii) the technical means for identifying and correcting input errors prior to the placing of the order;

(iv) the languages offered for the conclusion of the contract.

Member States shall ensure that, except if otherwise in business to business contracts, the service provider indicates any relevant codes of conduct to which he subscribes and information on how those codes can be consulted electronically.

Contract terms and general conditions provided to the recipient must be made available in a way that allows him to store and reproduce them.

The above provisions on information do not apply to contracts concluded exclusively by exchange of electronic mail or by equivalent individual communications.

Member States must make sure that, for orders placed electronically, the recipient receives from the service provider an electronic acknowledgement of receipt of the recipient's acceptance and confirms receipt of this acknowledgement.

(f) Codes of conduct: Member States and the Commission shall encourage the drawing up of codes of conduct at Community level, by trade, professional and consumer associations or organisations to contribute to the proper implementation of the Directive. These codes must be transmitted to the Commission and must be accessible in the EU languages by electronic means. Consumers' associations must be involved in drafting and implementing such codes of conduct.

(g) Out-of-court dispute settlement: Member States must ensure that, in the event of disagreement between an information society service provider and the recipient of the service, their legislation does not hamper the use of out-of-court schemes, available under national law, for dispute settlement, including appropriate electronic means.

Member States must also encourage bodies responsible for the out-of-court settlement of, in particular, consumer disputes to operate in a way which provides adequate procedural guarantees for the parties concerned. These bodies are also responsible for transmitting any relevant information on their decision to the Commission.

(h) Court actions: Court actions must be available under national law against the providers of information society services and Member States must allow the rapid adoption of measures, including interim measures, designed to terminate any alleged infringement and to prevent any further impairment of the interests involved.

(i) Cooperation: Member States must ensure that they put in place appropriate means of supervision and investigation for the implementation of this Directive and must cooperate with each other and with the Commission to ensure its effective application.

3. Communication from the Commission to the Council, the Parliament and the ECB – application to financial services of Article 3(4) to (6) of the Electronic Commerce Directive, COM(2003)259

The E-commerce Directive established, at Article 3, the principle of 'home state control' which enables a service provider to supply online services throughout the EU, as long as he complies with the rules and regulations laid down in the Member State where he is established. Member States may not, for reasons falling within the coordinated field, restrict the freedom to provide information society services from another Member State.

In the course of the adoption of the Directive, a number of states had expressed some concern that the full application of the 'home state control' clause might be detrimental in certain areas.

The principle of Article 3 is therefore subject to certain derogations which allow Member States to impose their own additional rules to all online services marketed within their territory in relation, for example, to the parties' freedom to choose the law applicable to their contract, the contractual obligations set out in contracts with consumers, etc. In addition, Article 3(4) to (6) allows Member States to take measures such as sanctions or injunctions that may restrict the provision of online services from other Member States on a number of grounds set out in Article 3(4) that include, *inter alia,* the protection of consumers, including investors.

The Commission's Communication seeks to reiterate and clarify, also by analysing the ECJ case law, the extent and scope of such restrictions in relation to the provision of financial services and to emphasise that such restrictions have to be proportionate to their objectives and can only be imposed:

(a) after the Member State where the service provider is established has been asked to take adequate measures and has failed to do so;

(b) if the intention to impose restrictions has been notified in advance to the Commission and to the Member State where the service provider is established.

The Commission additionally stated that the derogations imposed cannot have a general nature, ie, cover a whole category of financial services, but must be imposed on a case-by-case basis.

15

HOLIDAYS AND TRAVEL

1. Introduction

Community legislation in the area of holidays has been rather extensive. Two directives, Council Directive (EEC) 93/151[560] which relates to package travel, package holidays and package tours and Council Directive (EC) 94/47[561] which protects consumers in respect of timeshare properties, are discussed below. In addition, there are provisions in connection with air carriage, which are partly designed to assist consumers, which will be dealt with in this chapter.

2. Council Directive (EEC) 90/314 of 13 June 1990 on package travel, package holidays and package tours

(a) Objective: The aim of this Directive is to provide protection to consumers for what are normally called 'package holidays', ie, where the tour operator organises transport and accommodation. The Directive appreciates that package holidays are an important part of tourism and that tourism plays an increasingly important role in the economies of all Member States. The Commission saw this incentive as particularly effective in deterring consumers from buying packages outside their own Member States. Also, consumers would have the benefit of protection introduced by the Directive.

(b) Scope of application: The Directive applies to 'package' travel, holidays and tours. The definition of 'package' is a complicated one that has a number of components: first, it must be a pre-arranged combination of not fewer than two of three components. These components are:

(i) transport;

(ii) accommodation; and

(iii) other tourist services not ancillary to transport or accommodation and accounting for a significant proportion of the package.

Secondly, the holiday must be sold or offered for sale at an inclusive price and, thirdly, the service must cover a period of more than 24 hours or include overnight accommodation.

The mere fact that various components of the package are billed separately does not absolve the organiser or retailer from his obligations under the Directive. The Directive left in doubt to what extent the protection covers packages which are put together by a travel agent on behalf of a particular customer but the issue has been clarified in *Club-Tour, Viagens e Turismo SA v Alberto Carlos Lobo Gonçalves Garrido, and Club Med Viagens Ld*[562] where the ECJ held that that holidays organised at the request and in accordance with

560 [1993] OJ L121/20.
561 [1994] OJ L280/83.
562 Case C-400/00 [2002] ECR-I 4051.

the specifications of a consumer or a defined group of consumers can still be considered as 'package' holidays within the meaning of the Directive.

The second issue is to what extent accommodation is part of the package. There are, for example, certain flight-only offers which include accommodation. The accommodation is nominal and no-one uses it because it is part of a government-approved arrangement.

Thirdly, the issue of how one deals with accommodation which is provided as part of the transport is also unclear. Does a cruise on a cruise liner constitute both transport and accommodation? The answer may well be yes if the sole purpose of the holiday is a cruise. What then of the purchasing of tickets to travel to a specific country by boat? Is this both transport and accommodation? In most cases, it is sensible to believe that the Directive and the appropriate national legislation implementing it will apply.

The Directive makes provisions concerning both the organiser and the retailer. The 'organiser' is someone who regularly organises packages and sells or offers them for sale, whether directly or through a retailer. Whether an organisation which for charitable or educational purposes organises packages on a regular basis will be an organiser is open to doubt.

The retailer, on the other hand, is the person who sells or offers for sale the package put together by an organiser, eg, a travel agent whose prime job is to sell holidays from brochures.

The Directive applies in favour of 'consumers' but, contrary to the usual definition, this means 'the person who takes or agrees to take the package ("the principal contractor"), or any person on whose behalf the principal contractor agrees to purchase the package ("the other beneficiaries") or any person to whom the principal contractor or any of the other beneficiaries transfers the package ("the transferee")'. A customer taking a package trip for business reasons would therefore be covered by the Directive.

(c) Information: Article 3 of the Directive provides that any descriptive matter about the package must not contain misleading information. Brochures must contain in a legible, comprehensible and accurate manner the price and adequate information on:

(i) the destination, means, characteristics, and transport to be used;

(ii) the type of accommodation;

(iii) the meal plan;

(iv) the itinerary;

(v) general information on passport and visa requirements;

(vi) monetary amounts or the percentage of price to be paid on account and the timetable for the payment of the balance;

(vii) whether a minimum number of persons is required for the package.

The particulars contained in the brochure are to be binding on the organiser or the retailer unless the changes are communicated to the consumer before the conclusion of the contract or the changes are made later following an agreement between the parties.

Article 4 also imposes a duty on the organiser and the retailer to provide to the consumer in writing before the contract is concluded general information on passport and visa requirements, the times and places of intermediate stops and transport connections, details of the place to be occupied by the traveller (eg, cabin or berth on ship) and the name and address and telephone number of the organiser's and/or retailer's representative or of local agencies on whose assistance a consumer in difficulty could call.

In the case of journeys or stays abroad by minors, information must be provided enabling contact to be made with the child or the person responsible for his safety.

Information on the optional conclusion of insurance policies to cover the cost of cancellation by the consumer or the cost of assistance, including repatriation in the event of accident or illness, must also be given.

The contract must also contain certain compulsory information indicated in the Annex to the Directive and its terms must be set out in writing or any other comprehensible and accessible form.

(d) The right to transfer the booking: If the consumer cannot proceed with the package, he must be allowed to transfer his booking to a third party provided he and the transferee remain jointly and severally liable to pay the balance of the contract price and provided that he has given the organiser or retailer reasonable notice.

(e) Alteration in terms or price: If the organiser finds before departure that he has to alter significantly any of the terms such as price, he must notify the consumer as quickly as possible. The consumer may either withdraw from the contract without penalty or accept a rider to the contract specifying the alterations made and their impact on the price. The consumer must inform the organiser or the retailer as to which he wants to do as soon as possible.

The organiser or retailer may not change the prices laid down in the contract unless the contract reserves the right to do so and states precisely how the price is to be calculated. Any variations are only allowed in respect of transportation costs, dues, taxes or fees or exchange rate changes. In any event, during the 20 days prior to the departure, the price stated in the contract shall not be increased.

(f) Consumers' rights: If the consumer withdraws from the contract because of a significant alteration in the package holiday, or if the organiser cancels the package before the agreed date, the consumer is entitled:

(i) to a substitute package of equivalent or higher value; or

(ii) to be repaid as soon as possible all sums paid by him under the contract.

Where appropriate, the consumer is entitled to be compensated for non-performance of the contract.

It is for Member States to decide whether the consumer should be compensated by the organiser or the retailer or both.

(g) Substandard holiday: Where a significant proportion of the services contracted for is not provided or the organiser perceives he will be unable to secure their provision, the organiser shall make suitable arrangements at no extra cost to the consumer for the continuation of the package and where appropriate to compensate the consumer for the difference between the services offered and those supplied. If it is impossible to make these arrangements or the consumer will not accept them, the organiser shall provide the consumer with an equivalent transport back to the place of departure or to another return point which the consumer has agreed and, if appropriate, shall compensate the consumer.

(h) Liability: Article 5 provides that Member States shall take the necessary steps to ensure that the organiser and/or retailer to the contract is liable to the consumer for the proper performance of the obligations arising from the contract irrespective of whether the obligations are to be performed by that organiser and/or retailer or by other suppliers. With regard to damage resulting from breach of contract by the retailer or organiser, Member States must ensure that the organiser and/or retailer is liable unless failure to perform is attributable through no fault of theirs nor of any other supplier of services but because the failures are attributable to the consumer or to a third party who is not providing the service, or by reason of force majeure.

In *Leitner v TUI*[563] the ECJ held that that Article 5 of the Directive is to be interpreted as conferring, in principle, on consumers a right to compensation for non-material damage resulting from the non-performance or improper performance of the services constituting a package holiday.

Member States may limit compensation in accordance with international conventions governing such services and may also allow compensation to be limited other than for personal injury, but the limitation must not be unreasonable. It is impermissible to exclude liability under the Directive. However, the consumer's rights are subject to his obligation to communicate any breach of contract to the organiser or retailer in writing at the earliest opportunity. This obligation should be stated clearly in the contract.

(i) Security: It is an important element of the protection given by Article 7 of the Directive that the organiser and/or retailer to the contract shall provide sufficient evidence of security for the refund of the money paid by the consumer and for the repatriation of the consumer in the event of insolvency.

In *Dillenkofer*[564] the ECJ held that if a Member State allows the package travel organiser and/or retailer party to a contract to require payment of a

563 Case C-168/00 [2002] ECR-I 2631.

564 Cases C-178, 179, 188, 189, 190/94 Dillenkofer v Germany [1996] ECR I-4845.

deposit of up to 10% towards the travel price, the protective purpose pursued by Article 7 of Council Directive (EEC) 90/314 is not satisfied unless a refund of that deposit is also guaranteed in the event of the insolvency of the package travel organiser and/or retailer party to the contract.

In *Verein für Konsumenteninformation v Österreichische Kreditversicherungs AG*[565] the ECJ held that Article 7 also covers, as security for the refund of money paid over, a situation in which the purchaser of a package holiday who has paid the travel organiser for the costs of his accommodation before travelling on his holiday is compelled, following the travel organiser's insolvency, to pay the hotelier for his accommodation again in order to be able to leave the hotel and return home.

(j) Minimum harmonisation: Under Article 8, Member States may adopt or return more stringent provisions in the field to protect the consumer.

(k) Implementation: In the United Kingdom, the Directive was implemented by the Package Travel, Package Holiday and Package Tours Regulations 1992.[566]

All Member States have notified implementing measures.

3. Council and Parliament Directive (EC) 94/47 on the protection of purchasers in respect of certain aspects of contracts relating to the purchase of the right to use immovable properties on a timeshare basis[567]

(a) Objective: This Directive came about as the result of a number of major scandals involving the sale of timeshare in Member States. Besides, there were disparities between national legislation which created barriers to the proper operation of the internal market and distortion of competition. The aim of the Directive was therefore to establish a minimum basis of common rules which would make it possible to ensure that the internal market operates successfully and would protect consumers.

(b) Scope of application: The Directive covers only those aspects of timeshare properties which relate to information on the contract and the arrangements for the communication of that information and the procedures and arrangements for the cancellation and withdrawal from such contracts. Member States remain competent for other matters including determination of the legal nature of the rights which are the subject of contracts covered by the Directive.

The Directive applies to any contract or group of contracts concluded for at least three years under which, directly or indirectly on payment of a certain global price, a real property right or any other right relating to the use of one or more immovable properties for a specified or specifiable period of the year,

565 Case C-364/96 [1998] ECR-I 2949. See also Case C-410/96 Criminal proceedings against André Ambry [1998] ECR-I 7875.
566 SI 1992/3228.
567 [1994] OJ L280/83.

which may not be less than one week, is established or is the subject of a transfer or undertaking to transfer. It applies to a contract between the 'vendor' (ie, any natural or legal person who, acting in transactions covered by this Directive and in his professional capacity, establishes, transfers or undertakes to transfer the right which is the subject of the contract) and the 'purchaser' (ie, any natural person who acts in transactions covered by the Directive for purposes which may be regarded as being outwith his professional capacity).

(c) Information: Article 3 provides that Member States shall make provision in their legislation for measures to ensure the vendor is required to provide any person requesting information on immovable property or properties with a document which, in addition to the general description of the property, shall provide brief and accurate information on the points referred to in the Annex to the Directive. These items include:

(i) the identity of the parties and the information on the vendor's legal status and the identity and domicile of the owner;

(ii) the exact nature of the right which is the subject of the contract;

(iii) an accurate description of the property;

(iv) if the property is under construction, the state of it, the reasonable estimate of time for completion, the building permit and the names and addresses of the competent authority and the state of completion of the services rendering the property operational;

(v) a guarantee regarding completion of the property;

(vi) what services the purchaser will have access to;

(vii) what common facilities are to be provided and the principles based on which maintenance and repairs to the property will be arranged.

In addition, information must be given as to the price to be paid to exercise the contractual rights, an amount to be paid for the use of the common facilities and the basis of the calculation of the charges relating to the occupation of the property, including administrative overheads and mandatory statutory charges.

Finally, and perhaps most importantly, the purchaser must be given information on his right to cancel. In addition, Member States' legislation must ensure that all this information forms an integral part of the contract. The vendor cannot make any changes without the party's agreement unless the change results from circumstances outside its control. In any event, changes must be communicated to the purchaser before the contract is concluded. Any advertising relating to the timeshare must make it clear that this document with the information in it is available.

(d) The contract document: Article 4 provides that the contract must be in writing and must include not only the items referred to above, but the remainder of the information referred to in the Annex.

Secondly, the contract must be drawn up in one of the languages from the Member States in which the purchaser is resident, or the language of one of the Member States of which he is a national. If the Member State where the property is situated insists the contract is drawn up in its own language, then the vendor must provide the purchaser with a certified translation.

(e) Purchasers' rights: Member States' legislation must, pursuant to Article 5, allow the purchaser to withdraw without giving any reason within 10 calendar days of both parties signing the contract or, if the contract does not include the required information, a right to cancel within three months thereof. If the information is provided during the three months, the 10 days' withdrawal period then starts.

If at the end of the three-month period provided for the purchaser has not exercised the right to cancel, and the contract still does not include the required information, the purchaser has a further 10 days to terminate.

To exercise the right, the purchaser must notify the named person in the contract. For these purposes the deadline is observed if notice is despatched before the deadline expires. In the event of the purchaser withdrawing, he may be required to defray only those expenses which are incurred as the result of the conclusion of the withdrawal from the contract. These expenses should be expressly mentioned in the contract. Where the purchaser withdraws because of the failure of the vendor to provide the required information, he cannot be required to make any defrayal.

(f) Payment: Member States must ensure that their legislation prohibits any payments by the purchaser before the end of the period during which he may exercise the right of cancellation.

(g) Credit agreements: Member States must provide pursuant to Article 7 that, in the event of a lawful withdrawal by the purchaser, any credit agreement can similarly be cancelled without penalty.

(h) Binding nature: It is unlawful to make any provision to contract out of the obligations under the Directive.

Member States must take measures to ensure that, whatever the applicable law is, the purchaser is not deprived of his protection if the immovable property is situated within the territory of a Member State.

(i) Minimum harmonisation: The Directive allows Member States to adopt more favourable provisions for the protection of purchasers in the field in question.

(j) Implementation: In the UK, the Directive was implemented by the Timeshare Regulations 1997.[568]

568 SI 1997/1081.

4. Council Regulation (EEC) 295/91 of 4 February 1991 establishing common rules for a denied-boarding compensation scheme in scheduled air transport[569]

(a) Objective: The purpose of this Regulation is to ensure that, in the event of overbooking of scheduled air flights, air carriers should be obliged to pay compensation and to provide additional services to passengers who are denied boarding. The same standard should apply throughout the Community.

(b) Scope of application: The Regulation applies to passengers who are denied access to an overbooked scheduled flight for which they have a valid ticket and a confirmed reservation departing from an airport located in the territory of a Member State to which the EC Treaty applies, irrespective of the State where the air carrier is established, the nationality of the passenger and the point of destination.

Passengers must have a valid ticket, have a confirmed reservation on that flight, and have presented themselves for check-in within the required time limit and as stipulated.

'Confirmed reservation' means that a ticket sold by the air carrier or authorised travel agent contains the number, date and time of the flight and notification correctly showing the ticket has been registered by the air carrier.

An overbooked flight is one where the number of passengers holding a confirmed reservation and presenting themselves for check-in within the required time limit and as stipulated exceeds the number of available seats on that flight.

'Scheduled flight' means a flight possessing the following characteristics:

(i) seats are available for purchase by members of the public;

(ii) it is established to serve traffic between two points, according to a published timetable or according to a systematic series.

(c) Rules: Air carriers are obliged to lay down the rules which they will follow for boarding in the event of an over-booked flight. They shall notify these rules to the Member State concerned and to the Commission and they should also be available to the public. The rules must include the possibility of a call for volunteers prepared not to board.

In any event, the air carrier should take into consideration the interests of passengers who must be given boarding priority for legitimate reasons, such as handicapped persons and unaccompanied children.

(d) Passengers' rights: In the event of boarding being denied, the passenger shall have the choice either between reimbursement, re-routing at the earliest opportunity or re-routing at a later date, at the passenger's convenience. Irrespective of that choice, the carrier shall pay minimum compensation of 150 for flights up to 3,500km and 300 for flights of more than 3,500km. Provision exists for reductions in connection with re-routing.

569 [1991] OJ L36/5.

The amounts of compensation need not exceed the price of the ticket. Compensation should be paid in cash or, with agreement with the passenger, in travel vouchers.

(e) Package holidays: In the event of the boarding being denied on a package holiday flight, the air carrier is obliged to compensate a tour operator pursuant to Council Directive (EEC) 90/314.[570] The tour operator must pass on sums to the passenger.

(f) Other rights for the passenger: Apart from minimum compensation, the air carrier shall offer free of charge:

(i) the expense of a telephone call;

(ii) meals and refreshments which are reasonable in relation to the waiting time;

(iii) hotel accommodation where an additional stay of one or more nights is necessary.

If as part of an alternative route home, it is necessary for a passenger to travel to another airport within the same city, the air carrier shall pay that cost.

(g) Follow-up work: A Commission proposal[571] for a new Regulation is currently undergoing reading in the Council. The proposal has four main objectives:

(i) to extend its scope to non-scheduled flights;

(ii) to introduce rules whereby air carriers must ensure that, before denying boarding, they use the full capacity available on the aircraft, even if passengers are placed in a class higher than that for which a ticket has been purchased;

(iii) to make information compulsory by ensuring that a leaflet informing the passengers of their rights if denied boarding is available at the check-in counter;

(iv) to adapt to economic developments the level of compensation.

5. Council Regulation 2027/97 on air carrier liability in the event of accidents[572]

(a) Objective: This Regulation lays down the obligations of Community air carriers in relation to liability in the event of death or wounding of a passenger or any other bodily injury suffered by a passenger, if the accident which caused the damage so sustained took place on board an aircraft or in the course of any of the operations of embarking or disembarking.

It also clarifies some insurance requirements for Community air carriers and sets out some requirements on information to be provided by air carriers established outside the EU which operate to, from or within the EU.

570 [1990] OJ L158/59.
571 COM(1998)41 final.
572 [1997] OJ L285/1.

(b) Scope of application: The Regulation applies mainly to Community air carriers, ie, those with a valid operating licence granted by a Member State.

(c) Community air carrier's liability: The liability of a Community air carrier for damages sustained in the event of death, wounding or any other bodily injury by a passenger in the event of an accident shall not be subject to any financial limit, be it defined by law, convention or contract. This does not mean, however, that a Community air carrier is the sole party liable to pay damages or that the Community air carrier is not entitled to seek contribution or indemnity from any other party in accordance with applicable law.

Community air carriers are obliged to take out insurance.

For any damages up to the sum of the equivalent in Euros of 10,000 SDR (special drawing rights established by the International Monetary Fund), the carriers' liability is strict, ie, it cannot exclude or limit its liability by proving that all the necessary measures to avoid the damage had been taken or that it was impossible to take such measures. The carrier can only be discharged of its liability by proving that the damage was caused by the negligence of the injured or deceased passenger.

The Community air carrier shall without delay, and in any event not later than 15 days after the identity of the natural person entitled to compensation has been established, make to the victims or to those entitled such advance payments as may be required to meet immediate economic needs on a basis proportional to the hardship suffered. An advance payment shall not be less than the equivalent in Euros of 15,000 SDR per passenger in the event of death. The payment of an advance does not constitute recognition of liability but it is not returnable except in the cases prescribed in Article 3(3) or in circumstances where it is subsequently proved that the person who received the advance payment caused, or contributed to, the damage by negligence or was not the person entitled to compensation.

(d) Information: Information on the above liability must be included in the Community air carrier's conditions of carriage and, on request, be available to passengers at the Community air carrier's agencies, travel agencies and check-in counters and at points of sale. The ticket document or an equivalent shall contain a summary of the requirements in plain and intelligible language.

Air carriers established outside the EU operating to, from or within the EU and not applying the above provisions must expressly and clearly inform the passengers thereof.

(e) Follow-up work: A proposal for an amendment to Regulation 2027/97[573] is currently pending. This proposal is designed to incorporate the provisions of the Montreal Convention into the Regulation so as to bring it into line with the new international rules on air carriers' liability.

573 COM(2000)340 final.

16
FINANCIAL SERVICES

A. INTRODUCTION

Community measures in the area of financial services are targeted, with few exceptions, at financial institutions rather than at consumers. Their purpose is to facilitate the cross-border provision of financial services with a view to ensuring the smooth functioning of the common market.

They contribute, however, to consumer protection in several respects. First, they broaden consumer choice by promoting the offer of a wider range of products or services; secondly, they establish rules on authorisation, monitoring and supervision of financial institutions, which makes them more stable and trustworthy; thirdly, they require financial institutions to provide their clients with appropriate information, strengthen their legal position if something goes wrong, and provide systems of redress.

The latter objective, more directly relevant to consumer protection, is the object of the analysis carried out in this chapter. It must be noted, however, that this chapter only deals with measures which benefit a wider range of customers than 'consumers' (eg, 'policyholders') or which are indirectly aimed at consumer protection. Measures more directly concerned with consumer protection, such as the distance marketing of financial services or consumer credit, are dealt with elsewhere.

B. CREDIT TRANSFERS AND PAYMENT SYSTEMS

1 Introduction

The measures here examined are not limited in their scope to 'consumer' transactions, but apply to all credit transfers or payments. Since they aim to facilitate payments, especially those with an inter-State dimension, also for the benefit of consumers, they are nevertheless relevant to this work.

2. Council and Parliament Directive (EC) 97/5 on cross-border credit transfers[574]

(a) Objective: This Directive was made in recognition of the fact that the volume of cross-border payments was growing steadily as a result of the completion of the internal market and in the run-up to economic and monetary union. It was recognised that it was essential for individuals as well as businesses to have a reliable and cheap method of credit transfer and that those rules should be both transparent and clear.

574 [1997] OJ L43/25.

As a result, the Directive is designed to lay down the minimum requirements needed to ensure an adequate level of customer information both before and after execution of a cross-border credit transfer. This should include indication of complaints and redress procedures. The Directive deals with performance issues and its intention is to ensure that the maximum time taken to execute a cross-border credit transfer is reduced.

(b) Scope of application: The Directive, is not, strictly speaking, only a 'consumer' Directive since it applies to all cross-border credit transfers executed by credit institutions in currencies of the Member States and the ECU (Euro) up to the equivalent of 50,000 ECU (Euros) by named persons.

The definition of 'credit institution' is borrowed from Council Directive (EEC) 77/780[575] as 'an undertaking whose business is to receive deposits or other repayable funds from the public and to grant credits for its own account'. Such institutions will include their branches. Other institutions are those which carry out cross-border credit transfers. A cross-border credit transfer is 'a transaction carried out on the initiative of an originator via an institution or its branch in one Member State, with a view to making available an amount of money to a beneficiary at an institution or its branch in another Member State, the originator or beneficiary being one and the same person'.

(c) Transparency: Article 3 lays down information on conditions for cross-border transfers which must be made available to prospective customers in writing. These include the time needed for the transfer, the method of calculation of fees, the value date, details of any complaint procedures and an indication of the reference exchange rates which will be used.

Following the cross-border transfer, Article 4 provides that institutions must tell their customers the following:

(i) a reference enabling the customer to identify the transfer;

(ii) the original amount of the cross-border transfer;

(iii) the amount of charges;

(iv) the value date.

(d) Obligations on institutions: Article 5 provides that an institution must at a customer's request, for a cross-border credit transfer with stated specifications, give an undertaking concerning the time needed for execution of the transfer and the commission fees and charges payable, apart from those relating to the exchange rate used. The institution must execute the transfer in question within the time limit agreed. If those limits are not complied with or if in the absence of the time limit at the end of the fifth banking business day the funds have still not been credited to the beneficiary's institution, the institution shall pay compensation. This compensation will be the payment of interest.

575 [1977] OJ L322/30 (no longer in force).

The beneficiary's institution undertakes that it will make the transfer available to the beneficiary within the time limit agreed with him. Again, there are compensation provisions. No compensation is payable in either case if the error is that of the customer.

(e) Obligation to execute cross-border transfers: Article 7 provides that all the institutions involved in the transfer are obliged to execute the credit transfer for the full amount unless other instructions have been given.

(f) Refunds: Article 8 provides that if after acceptance of the instructions relevant amounts are not credited to the beneficiary, the originator's institution shall credit the beneficiary up to 12,500 plus the cross-border transfer, plus interest and plus charges. The amount should be payable to the customer within 14 banking business days following the date of his request.

(g) *Force majeure*: Institutions are released from their obligations in the event of *force majeure.*

(h) Settlement of disputes: Member States must have effective complaints and redress procedures for the settlement of disputes between the institution and the customers.

(i) Implementation: In Great Britain, the Directive was implemented by the Cross-Border Credit Transfers Regulations 1999.[576]

All Member States except Austria, Belgium, Greece, Ireland, Italy and Portugal have notified implementing measures.

3. Commission Recommendation (EEC) 88/590 of 17 November 1988 concerning payment systems and in particular the relationship between the cardholder and the card issuer[577]

(a) Objective: This recommendation follows the various consumer protection programmes of the Commission and is intended to accelerate consumer protection in the field of payment systems and certain other services available to consumers.

The Recommendation prescribes that the issuers of payment devices and system providers conduct their activities in accordance with the provisions contained in the Annex to the Recommendation.

Also, Member States should ensure that data relating to holders may be transmitted but that the data should be kept to the requisite minimum and be kept confidential by all persons to whose knowledge they are brought in the course of the operations.

(b) Scope of application: The Annex to the Recommendation applies to the following operations:

(i) the electronic payment involving the use of a card, in particular at the point of sale;

(ii) the withdrawing of bank notes from cash dispensing machines;

576 SI 1999/231.
577 [1988] OJ L317/55.

(iii) the non-electronic payment by card for which a signature is required and a voucher produced but not including guarantee payment cards;

(iv) electronic payment effected by a member of the public without the use of the card, such as through home banking.

There is no subjective limit to the application of the Recommendation, although the preamble refers to 'consumers'.

(c) The contract: Each issuer is to draw up full and fair terms of contract in writing to govern the issuing and use of the payment devices. Those terms shall be expressed in understandable words and in a form which is easy to read.

The contract shall specify:

(i) the basis of calculation and amount of charges, including interest;

(ii) whether crediting or debiting of operations will be instantaneous and, if not, over what period of time this will be done;

The terms of the contract will not be capable of being altered except by agreement but the issuer may propose an amendment and, if the contracting holder, having received notice thereof, continues to make use of the payment device, the contract will be deemed to be varied.

(d) Obligations on the cardholder: The cardholder will be obliged to take reasonable steps to keep the payment device safe and to notify the issuer after becoming aware of its loss or theft.

The cardholder must not record on the payment device his personal identification number nor record those things on anything he usually keeps or carries with the payment device. Neither may he countermand an order which he has given by means of his payment device.

(e) The issuer's obligations: The contract shall provide that the issuer shall not disclose the cardholder's personal identification number or any other confidential data. No payment device may be despatched to a member of the public except in response to an application.

(f) Disputes: In any dispute concerning an operation relating to liability for an unauthorised electronic fund transfer, the burden of proof is upon the issuer to show that the operation was accurately recorded and accurately entered into accounts and was not affected by technical breakdown.

(g) Details of transaction: The cardholder, if he requests it, may be supplied with a copy of the record of his operations simultaneously or shortly after he has completed them. The till receipt is sufficient evidence for these purposes.

(h) Loss of the card: The issuer is liable for the non-execution or defective execution of the cardholder's operation and where it has not been authorised by the cardholder.

Liability, however, is limited. In the case of non-execution or defective execution to the amount of the operation, or in the case of an unauthorised operation, the amount of liability shall extend to the sum required to restore the contracting holder to the position he was in before that operation took place. Any other consequences will be governed by the individual laws of Member States.

Provided the holder of the card notifies the issuer or a central agency of the loss of his card, he will not be liable thereafter for its wrongful use, but the provision does not apply if he has acted with extreme negligence or has himself been fraudulent. The cardholder bears the loss sustained up to the time of notification but only up to the equivalent of 150 for each event, again unless he acted negligently or fraudulently. The issuer is then obliged to take all action open to stop any further use of the payment device.

(i) Follow-up work: Although still in force, the Recommendation has in several respects been superseded by Recommendation 97/489 concerning transactions by electronic payment instruments and in particular the relationship between issuer and holder.

4. Recommendation 97/489 concerning transactions by electronic payment instruments and in particular the relationship between issuer and holder[578]

(a) Objective: The Recommendation is a follow-up to Commission Recommendation 87/598[579] laying down general principles relating to the contract between issuers (banks) and traders or consumers and is aimed at promoting security, convenience and efficiency to the advantage of consumers, traders and issuers.

(b) Scope of application: The Recommendation covers transactions effected by electronic payment instruments. These include instruments allowing for (remote) access to a customer's account, such as transfers of funds effected by means of electronic payment instruments and not ordered or executed by financial institutions, and cash withdrawals by the means of an electronic payment instrument and reloadable electronic money instruments at devices such as cash dispensing machines and automated teller machines and at the premises of the issuer or an institution who is under contract to accept the payment instrument.

The Recommendation does not apply to payments by cheques and to the guarantee function of certain cards in relation to payments by cheques.

(c) Transparency and conditions for transaction: Upon signature of the contract or in any event in good time prior to delivering an electronic payment instrument, the issuer must communicate to the holder the contractual terms and conditions (including an indication of the law applicable to the contract) governing the issue and use of that electronic payment instrument. The terms must be set out in writing, in easily understandable words and at least in the

578 [1997] OJ L208/52.
579 [1987] OJ L365/72.

official language or languages of the Member State in which the electronic payment instrument is offered.

The terms must include at least:

(i) a description of the electronic payment instrument, and the way in which it can be used, including the financial limits applied, if any;

(ii) a description of the holder's and issuer's respective obligations and liabilities;

(iii) where applicable, the normal period within which the holder's account will be debited or credited;

(iv) the types of any charges payable by the holder;

(v) the period of time during which a given transaction can be contested by the holder and an indication of the redress and complaints procedures available to the holder.

Additional information, such as an indication of the fees and charges levied for foreign currency transactions and an indication of the exchange rate used, must be given if the electronic payment instrument can be used abroad.

For each transaction, the issuer shall supply the holder with verifiable information enabling him to identify the transaction and details of the amounts and fees involved in it.

(d) Holder's obligations and liabilities: The holder must:

(i) use the electronic payment instrument in accordance with the terms governing the issuing and use of a payment instrument and take all reasonable steps to keep safe the electronic payment instrument;

(ii) notify the issuer without delay in case of the loss or theft of the electronic payment instrument, or the recording on his account of any unauthorised transaction, or any error or other irregularity in the account;

(iii) not record his personal identification number or other code in any easily recognisable form;

(iv) not countermand an order which he has given by means of his electronic payment instrument, except if the amount was not determined when the order was given.

The holder is liable, up to the time of notification, to bear the loss sustained in consequence of the loss or theft of the electronic payment instrument up to a limit, which may not exceed 150, except where he acted with extreme negligence or fraudulently, in which case such a limit does not apply. After the notification, he will not be liable for the losses.

The holder, however, is in no case liable if the payment instrument has been used without physical presentation or electronic identification (of the instrument itself).

(e) Obligations and liabilities of the issuer: The issuer may alter the terms of the contract by giving sufficient notice individually to the holder. After no less than one month, the holder is deemed to have accepted the terms if he has not withdrawn.

Changes to the interest rate, however, come into effect upon the date specified in the publication of such a change.

The issuer must:

(i) not disclose the holder's personal identification number or other code, except to the holder;

(ii) not dispatch an unsolicited electronic payment instrument, except where it is a replacement for an electronic payment instrument already held by the holder;

(iii) keep for a sufficient period of time internal records to enable the transactions to be traced and errors to be rectified;

(iv) ensure that appropriate means are available to enable the holder to notify loss of theft of a card.

(v) prove, in any dispute with the holder concerning a transaction, that the transaction was accurately recorded and entered into accounts and was not affected by technical breakdown or other deficiency.

The issuer should be liable for the non-execution or defective execution of the holder's transactions and for transactions not authorised by the holder, as well as for any error or irregularity attributable to the issuer in the maintaining of the holder's account.

The amount of the liability consists of the amount of the unexecuted or defectively executed transaction and, if any, interest thereon and/or of the sum required to restore the holder to the position he was in before the unauthorised transaction took place.

Any further financial consequences are regulated by the law applicable to the contract between the holder and the issuer.

The issuer is liable to the holder of an electronic money instrument for the lost amount of value stored on the instrument and for the defective execution of the holder's transactions, where the loss or defective execution is attributable to a malfunction of the instrument, of the device/terminal or any other equipment authorised for use, provided that the malfunction was not deliberately caused by the holder.

(f) Settlement of disputes: Member States are invited to ensure that there are adequate and effective means for the settlement of disputes between a holder and an issuer.

C. THE INSURANCE INDUSTRY

1. Introduction

The insurance industry in the EU has been the subject of a series of directives categorised either as 'life assurance directives' or 'non-life assurance directives'. The purpose of those directives as they now exist (as amended) is to liberalise the market in insurance in the EU so that an insurance company will be monitored solely by the competent authority of its home Member State.

Of all these measures, this chapter analyses only those directives and those provisions that have some relevance for the purpose of consumer protection.

2. Council Directive (EEC) 92/49[580] of 18 June 1992 on the coordination of the laws, regulations and administrative provisions relating to direct insurance other than life assurance and amending Council Directive (EEC) 73/239[581] and Council Directive 88/357[582]

(a) Objective: The prime purpose of this Directive is to regulate the provision of non-life assurance throughout the EU. Council Directive (EEC) 88/357 had urged the national market into an integrated market. This Directive lays down rules governing the introduction of a single authorisation system whereby any insurance undertaking whose head office is in one of the Member States of the EU can establish branches in other Member States and carry on business by way of provision of cross-border services under the supervision of the Member State in which its head office is situated.

The Directive also imposes on competent authorities of home Member States the duty of monitoring the financial health of the insurance undertakings in their control.

From the point of view of the consumer, the Directive is indirectly beneficial to him as it aims to give access to the widest possible range of insurance products within the EU so that he can choose what is best suited to his needs.

The Directive also intends to ensure that individual consumers as policyholders should be informed by the insurance company of the law which will apply to the contract and of the arrangements for handling policyholders' complaints concerning contracts. These are the provisions which are examined here.

(b) Scope: For the purposes of this work, suffice here to clarify that the Directive applies only to the types of insurance and undertakings referred to in Article 1 of Directive (EEC) 73/239[583] and for the benefits of 'policyholders' in general rather than simply consumers.

580 [1992] OJ L228/1 (as amended).
581 [1973] OJ L228/3 (as amended).
582 [1988] OJ L172/1 (as amended).
583 [1973] OJ L228/3.

(c) Relevant provisions: The following provisions are relevant for the purposes of consumer protection:

(i) Article 31 lays down a duty on the insurer to inform the policyholder, before the conclusion of the contract, of the law applicable to the contract where the parties do not have a free choice, or the fact that the parties are free to choose the law applicable and, in the latter case, the law the insurer proposes to choose; and the arrangements for handling the policyholder's complaints concerning contracts including, where appropriate, the existence of a complaints body, without prejudice to the policyholder's right to take legal proceedings. This obligation applies only where the policyholder is a natural person. The rules for implementing this Article shall be determined in accordance with the law of the Member State in which the risk is situated.

(ii) Article 42 provides for equal treatment of all creditors in the event of an insurance undertaking being wound up.

(iii) Article 43 provides that, where insurance is offered under the right of establishment or the freedom to provide services, the policyholder shall, before any commitment is entered into, be informed of the Member State in which the head office or, where appropriate, the branch with which the contract is to be concluded is situated. Any documents issued to the policyholder must convey this information. The contract or any other document granting cover, together with the insurance proposal where it is binding upon the policyholder, must state the address of the head office, or, where appropriate, of the branch of the insurance undertaking which grants the cover.

3. Parliament and Council Directive (EC) 2002/83 concerning life assurance[584]

(a) Objective: The purpose of this recast version is to simplify, clarify and repeal all the previously existing life assurance directives.

In relation to the consumer, the Directive is drafted upon the basis that, in a single assurance market, he has a wider and more varied choice of contracts, and that, to profit from this and from the increased competition, he must be provided with all the information that is necessary to enable him to choose the contract best suited to his needs. This is recognised as being exceptionally important, given that the duration of a contract of assurance can be very long. It is appreciated that, for the consumer to receive clear and accurate information on essential characteristics of the products as well as to whom he has to complain, national legislation needs to be coordinated.

584 [2002] OJ L345/1.

(b) Scope of application: The Directive applies to life assurance activities as defined in Article 2 of the Directive. It applies for the benefit of all policyholders.

(c) Relevant provisions

(i) Article 32 provides that the law applicable to contracts relating to the activities referred to in this Directive shall be, unless parties have expressed a different choice, the law of the Member State of the commitment. If the policy holder is a natural person and has his habitual residence in a Member State other than that of which he is a national, the parties may choose the law of the Member State of which he is a national.

(ii) Article 33 provides that Member States shall not prevent a policyholder from concluding a contract with an authorised assurance undertaking as long as it does not conflict with the legal provisions protecting the general good in the Member State of commitment.

(iii) Article 35. This provides for a cancellation period in favour of the policyholder of between 14 and 30 days from the time he was informed that the contract had been concluded. The giving of notice of cancellation by the policy holder shall have the effect of releasing him from any future obligation arising from the contract. The other legal effects and the conditions of cancellation shall be determined by the law applicable to the contract, notably as regards the arrangements for informing the policyholder that the contract has been concluded. The Member States need not provide for a cancellation period to contracts of six months' duration or less, nor where, because of the status of the policyholder or the circumstances in which the contract is concluded, the policyholder does not need this special protection. Member States shall specify in their rules where cancellation is not envisaged.

(iv) Article 36 states that before the assurance contract is concluded at least the information set out in Annex III(A) shall be provided. After the conclusion of the contract, the policyholder must be kept informed of any change concerning the information listed in Annex III(B). This information concerns the assurance undertaking or the commitment, any change in the name of the undertaking, its legal form or address.

585 [2002] OJ L181/65.
586 [1973] OJ L228/3.
587 [1988] OJ L172/1.

4. Parliament and Council Directive 2000/26[585] on the approximation of the laws of the Member States relating to insurance against civil liability in respect of the use of motor vehicles and amending Council Directives (EEC) 73/239[586] and (EEC) 88/357[587]

(a) Objective: The issue of compensation for victims of traffic accidents in the European Union has been one of the Commission's concerns since the adoption in 1972[588] of the first motor insurance directive which made third party insurance compulsory throughout the European Communities. That protection was then extended by further directives that concern accidents occurring in the victim's state of residence. None of the directives took account of the victims who whilst in another Member State suffered loss or injury by a vehicle registered in a Member State other than that where the victim resides.

Directive 2000/26 therefore aims to improve the present remedies available to persons who are injured in a road accident during a temporary stay in a Member State other than that of their residence. This is because it is recognised that settlement of damages is more complicated abroad than domestically because it is difficult for the claimant to collect evidence.

(b) Scope of application: The scope of the Directive is to cover claims for damages arising out of any accident occurring in a Member State other than the Member State of residence of the injured party which is caused by the use of vehicles insured and normally based in a Member State.

(c) Direct right of action: Article 3 gives a direct right of action to apply for compensation to the insurer providing civil liability motor cover for the person responsible for the accident, in addition to the right to sue the person responsible for the accident. It is hoped that this direct right of action will strengthen the victim's position, especially in situations where it is unclear as to who is the person liable or whether that person is still in the jurisdiction. It is also hoped that it will make it easier to reach out-of-court settlement.

(d) Claims representative: Article 4 sets out a duty for every insurance company of EU origin operating throughout the EU to appoint a claims representative in every Member State other than that in which they have received their official authorisation. The claims representative shall be responsible for handling and settling claims arising from an accident in the cases referred to in the Article. The claims representative shall be resident or established in the Member State where he is appointed and may work for one or more insurance undertaking.

Its task is, in relation to the claims, to collect all information necessary in connection with the settlement of the claims and to take the measures necessary to negotiate a settlement of claims. The requirement of appointing a

585 [2002] OJ L181/65.
586 [1973] OJ L228/3.
587 [1988] OJ L172/1.
588 Council Directive (EEC) 72/166 ([1972] OJ L103/1).

claims representative shall not preclude the right of the injured party or his insurance undertaking to institute proceedings directly against the person who caused the accident or his insurance undertaking.

Within three months of the date when the injured party presented his claim for compensation, the insurance undertaking of the person who caused the accident must make a reasoned offer of compensation or provide a reasoned reply to the points made in the claim in cases where liability is denied. Where the offer is not made within the three-month time limit, interest shall be payable on the amount of compensation.

(e) Information centres: Each Member State is obliged to establish or approve a body responsible for keeping the information listed in Article 5, such as the register of motor vehicles registered in the territory of that State, the insurance undertaking providing civil liability coverage for such vehicles and the claims representative notified by the appropriate undertaking. The purpose is that a victim of an accident may apply, for a period of seven years after the accident, to the information centre for details of the insurance of the vehicle, the number of the policy and the name of the insured's representative.

(f) Compensation bodies: Article 6 provides that Member States shall establish a compensation body which will be responsible for providing compensation where damage to property or personal injury is caused to a victim residing in a Member State by a vehicle registered and insured in a Member State other than the state of residence of the victim, and the accident giving rise to such damage occurs in a Member State other than the State of residence of the victim.

Injured parties may present a claim to the compensation body in their Member State of residence:

> (a) if, within three months of the date when the injured party presented his claim for compensation to the insurance undertaking of the vehicle which caused the accident, the insurance undertaking or its claims representative has not provided a reasoned reply; or
>
> (b) if the insurance undertaking has failed to appoint a claims representative in the State of residence of the injured party in accordance with Article 4(1) n this case, injured parties may not present a claim to the compensation body if they have presented a claim for compensation directly to the insurance undertaking of the vehicle which caused the accident and if they have received a reasoned reply within three months of presenting the claim.

Injured parties may not, however, present a claim to the compensation body if they have taken legal action directly against the insurance undertaking.

The compensation body shall take action within two months of the date when the injured party presented a claim for compensation

(g) Cases where the insurer cannot be identified: Article 7 states that, if the insurer cannot be identified, the vehicle is treated as uninsured and compensation for damage to property or personal injury shall be provided by the compensation body in the Member State where the victim resides in accordance with the provisions of Council Directive (EEC) 84/5.[589]

(h) Penalties: Article 12 states that Member States shall fix penalties for breaches of the national rules laid down under the Directive and take the steps necessary to secure their application. The penalties shall be effective, proportional and dissuasive.

589 [1984] OJ L8/17.

Index

Abstraction of drinking water 134
Abuse of dominant position 5
Acceptable daily intake (ADI) 82
Access to information
air carrier liability 284
Commission's projects 55–56
consumer credit 243
cosmetics 143, 147–150
dangerous substances 160
distance selling 249
distributors' obligations 68
electronic commerce 270–271
fourth three-year action plan (1999–2001) 34
importance 3
language *see* Language
medicinal products 218–219
motor insurance 296
package travel 276–277
preliminary programme (1975) 23–24
producers' obligations 68
product safety 69–71
rapid exchange system 54–55, 193, 194–197
second three-year action plan (1993–1995) 30–31
third three-year action plan (1996–1998) 31–33
timeshare 280
tobacco products 189
toys 184
see also Labelling
Access to justice
Commission projects 57
cross-border disputes *see* Cross-border disputes
preliminary programme (1975) 23
second three-year action plan (1993–1995) 31
Accidents
rapid exchange of information system 55, 193, 198
Accumulators 155
Acquis communautaire 58
Additives ***see*** **Food additives**
Advertising
Community intervention 223
consumer credit 243
cross-border disputes 223–224
free movement of goods and services 223
general framework 223
harmonisation 223
medicinal products 229, 230–234
tobacco products 190–192
see also Labelling; Misleading advertising; Price indication; Television advertising
Advice
preliminary programme (1975) 23, 24
first three-year action plan (1990–1992) 29
fourth three-year action plan (1999–2001) 34
AEC (Association of European Consumers) 42
Aerosol dispensers 155
After-sales service
second programme (1981) 25
Aggressive practices 235
Agricultural product safety
advertising 76
beef 209
crisis management 81
emergency measures 81
European Food Safety Authority 74, 75, 78–80
food 76
food trade 77
inspections 74–75
integrated approach 73
labelling 76
official control system 74
operators' responsibilities 77–78
precautionary principle 77
presentation 76
product liability 62
public confidence 73
rapid alert system 75, 79, 80–81
risk analysis 76–77
risk management 74
safety requirement 76
traceability 77
transparency 77

see also Hormones in meat; Organic food; Traditional products

Air carrier liability
- Community air carrier's liability 284
- follow-up work 284
- information 284
- objective 283
- scope of application 284

Air fares
- third three-year action plan (1996–1998) 32

Air transport compensation
- follow-up work 283
- objective 282
- package holidays 283
- passengers' rights 282–283
- rules 282
- scope of application 282

Air-conditioning appliances
- energy efficiency 215–216

Alcohol
- labelling 204, 210, 211
- television advertising 229

Allergies
- ingredients present in foodstuffs 203–204

Alternative dispute resolution *see* **Out-of-court settlement**

Ammonium polysuiphide 176

ANEC (European Association for the Coordination of Consumer Representation in Standardisation) 42, 45–46

Animal feed *see* **Agricultural product safety**

Animal testing
- ban 146
- legislative framework 146
- public concern 143–144

Antiques
- materials in contact with foodstuffs 83

Appliances *see* **Household appliances**

Applicable law *see* **Jurisdiction**

APR (annual percentage rate) 243

Aquatic pollutants 177–178

Arbitration *see* **Out-of-court settlement**

Aromatized wines 210–211

Arsenic compounds 177

Arsenic 179

Asbestos 176–177

Aspactame 97

Assistance *see* **Advice; Representation**

Association of European Consumers *see* **AEC**

Assorted chocolates 114

Average consumer 15

Azo-dye 179

Based table-top sweetener 97

Bathing water
- adaptation to technical progress 139–140
- Community measures 133
- conformity 138–139
- deemed conformity 139
- derogations 139
- implementation 140
- legal framework 133–134
- need for standards 133
- objective 138
- quality standards 138
- sampling 139
- scope of application 138

Batteries 155

Beef
- labelling 209

Benzene 176

Benzidine 178

Beta-agonists *see* **Hormones in meat**

BEUC (Bureau Européen des Unions de Consommateurs) 42

Blue asbestos *see* **Crocidolite**

Blue colourant (azo-dye) 179

Bovine spongiform encephalopathy *see* **BSE**

Brandy 210

Broadcasting *see* **Television advertising**

Bromacetic acid 176

BSE (bovine spongiform encephalopathy) 62

Bureau Européen des Unions de Consommateurs *see* **BEUC**

Cadmium 85–87, 178

Caffeine
- labelling 116, 208–209

Candy sugars 110

Carcinogens 174–175

Cars
- CO_2 emissions 214–215

fuel economy 214–215
CE marking 181, 182–183, 184
Cellulose film
in contact with foodstuffs 83, 87, 89–91
Ceramics
in contact with foodstuffs 83, 85–87
Cheese coatings 101
Cheese rinds 83
Chemicals *see* Dangerous preparations; Dangerous substances
Chestnut puree *see* Sweetened chestnut puree
Chicory extracts
further measures 116
implementation 116–117
labelling 116
Member States' obligations 116
objective 115–116
scope of application 116
Children
television advertising 229
Chocolate products
ECJ case law 115
further measures 115
general requirements 113–114
implementation 115
labelling114
Member States' obligations 115
objective 113
scope of application 113
Cider spirits 210
Cigarettes *see* Tobacco products
CLAB 261
Classification
dangerous preparations 165–171
dangerous substances 156–165
Climate
CO2 emissions 214–215
CO2 emissions
passenger cars 214–215
Cocoa
ECJ case law 115
further measures 115
general requirements 113–114
implementation 115
labelling 114
Member States' obligations 115
objective 113
scope of application 113
Codes of conduct
electronic commerce 272
COFACE (Confédération des organisations familiales de la Communauté européenne) 42
Coffee
further measures 116
implementation 116–117
labelling 116
Member States' obligations 116
objective 115–116
scope of application 116
Collective actions
cross-border disputes 20, 265–266
see also Injunctions
Colours
authorised substances 101
general principles 101
implementation 102
maximum levels 101
monitoring systems 102
objective 100
permitted uses 101
scope of application 100–101
Commission Programme of Community action in the field of public health (2003–2008) 194
Committee on Environment, Public Health and Consumer Protection 44
Committee on Legal Affairs and the Internal Market 44
Common agricultural policy, consumer interests
second programme (1981) 25
third three-year action plan (1996–1998) 32
Treaty of Rome (1957) 5
Community eco-label award scheme *see* Eco-label award scheme
Community institutions
legislative competence 2, 7
Community Tobacco Fund 187
Comparative advertising *see* Misleading and comparative advertising
Comparative testing
first three-year action plan (1990–1992) 29
Competition policy, consumer interests
Treaty of Rome (1957) 5

Confédération des organisations familiales de la Communauté européenne *see* COFACE
Confederation of European Cooperatives *see* EUROCOOP
Conformity assessment criteria
product safety 67–68
Consensual settlement procedures *see* Out-of-court settlement
Consultation
Community policies 28
Consumer Policy Strategy 2002–2006 36
EC decision-making process 41, 46
labelling requirements 3
preliminary programme (1975) 24
safety standards 3
second three-year action plan (1993–1995) 31
Consumer 36–40
Consumer Committee 2, 33, 43–44
Consumer Consultative Council 31
Consumer contracts
Community approach 237–238
cooling-off period 238
cross-border disputes 238
harmonisation 237
market transparency 238, 255
see also Consumer credit; Distance marketing of financial services; Distance selling; Doorstep selling; Electronic commerce; Injunctions; Timeshare; Unfair terms in consumer contracts
Consumer Councils 45
Consumer credit
advertising 243
APR 243
early repayment 243–244
enforcement 244–245
follow-up work 245–246
implementation 245
information 243
liability of third party creditors 244
marketing 243
Member States' obligations 245
minimum harmonisation formula 245
objective 241–242
repossession 243
scope of application 242–243
see also Cross-border credit transfers
Consumer Policy Strategy 2002–2006 35–36
Consumer protection 36
Consumer protection law
scope 37–40
Consumer-supplier dialogue 57–58
Consumer Voice 56
Consumption of energy *see* Energy efficiency
***Contra proferentem* rule 259**
Contracts *see* Consumer contracts
Cooling-off period 238, 241
Cooperation
between national authorities 54
Cosmetics
adaptation to technical problems 150–151
analysis 152–154
authorised substances 145–146
follow-up work 151–152
general obligations 145
implementation 151
information 143, 147–150
labelling requirements 147–150
legal framework 143
lists of ingredients 146–147
objective 144
safety 143
scope of application 143, 144–145
testing on animals *see* Animal testing
unauthorised substances 145–146
Council of Ministers meetings 45
Couverture 114
Credit *see* Consumer credit
Credit cards
distance marketing of financial services 253
distance selling 250
see also Payment systems
Credit market
third three-year action plan (1996–1998) 32
Creosote 179
Crocidolite 176–177
Cross-border credit transfers
force majeure 287
implementation 287
institutions' obligations 286–287
objective 285–286

refunds 287
scope of application 286
settlement of disputes 287
transparency 286
Cross-border disputes
access to justice 13, 16
advertising 223–224
collective actions 20, 265–266
consumer contracts 238
cooperation mechanisms 12
electronic commerce 269
enforcement 20–21
injunctions 20
jurisdiction 17
legal aid schemes 19–20
out-of-court settlement 13, 17–19, 57
second three-year action plan (1993–1995) 31
unfair commercial practices 223–224
Cross-border sales
consumer information centres 30–31
consumer information centres 56
first three-year action plan (1990–1992) 29
Cryogenic fluids 105
Damage 64
Dangerous liquid products 175
Dangerous preparations
adaptation to technical progress 170–171
assessment of environmental hazards 167–168
assessment of health hazards 167
classification 166–167
confidentiality 170
distance selling 170
implementation 171
labelling 169–170, 171
marketing restrictions 172–179
Member States' obligations 168
objective 165–166
packaging 168–169
restrictions 170
safety data sheet 170, 171–172
scope of application 166
see also Dangerous substances
Dangerous products
rapid exchange of information system 55
see also Dangerous preparations; Dangerous substances; Food imitation; Product liability; Product safety
Dangerous substances
adaptation to technical progress 163–164
circulation of information 160
classification 157–158
competent authority 158–159
confidentiality 160
criteria 157–158
derogations 162–163
exemptions from notification 160
general obligations 158
implementation 164
inventory of substances 160–161, 165
labelling 161–162
legislative framework 155–156
marketing restrictions 172–179
notification 158–159
objective 156
packaging 161
restrictions 163
scope of application 156–157
see also Dangerous preparations
Databases 57
Debit cards
distance marketing of financial services 253
distance selling 250
third three-year action plan (1996–1998) 32
see also Payment systems
Decision-making process
participation in *see* Consultation
Defective products *see* Product liability
Dehydrated preserved milk
authorised substances 112
further measures 113
implementation 113
labelling 112–113
Member States' obligations 113
objective 112
scope of application 112
Designations of origin *see* Traditional products
Development risks 16
Dietetic foodstuffs

composition 123–124
implementation 124
labelling 123
legislative framework 122–123
new foodstuffs 124
purpose 122
scope of application 123
see also Food supplements; Sweeteners
Dimethoxybenzidine 176
Directorate-General *see* Health and Consumer Protection Directorate-General
Dishwashers
energy efficiency 215–216
Disputes
cross-border *see* Cross-border disputes
Distance marketing of financial services
additional information requirements 252
binding nature 254
burden of proof 252–253
communication of prior information 252
communication of terms and conditions 252
enforcement 254
follow-up work 255
implementation 254
objective 251
out-of-court settlement 254
payments by card 253
prior information 252
redress 254
scope of application 251–252
unsolicited services and communications 253–254
withdrawal 253
Distance selling
binding nature 250
communication restrictions 250
dangerous preparations 170
enforcement 251
first three-year action plan (1990–1992) 29
implementation 251
inertia selling 250
minimum harmonisation 250–251
objective 246–247
payment by credit card or debit card 250
performance 250
prior information 248–249
scope of application 247–248
third three-year action plan (1996–1998) 32
withdrawal 249–250
written confirmation of information 249
see also Distance marketing of financial services
Distributors
product safety obligations 68–69
Domestic measures of consumer protection
relationship with EC law 40–41
Doorstep selling
cancellation 241
effect of cancellation of contract 241
implementation 241
minimum harmonisation formula 241
objective 239
scope of application 239–240
written notice 240–241
Drinking water
adaptation to technical progress 136–137
Community measures 133
derogations 135
emergency situations 136
implementation 137
labelling 136
legal framework 133–134
Member States' obligations 135
monitoring 136
need for standards 133
objective 134
quality standards 135
scope of application 134
Dryers
energy efficiency 215–216
EC consumer policy
future challenges 59–60
international dimension 59
EC decision-making process
consumer participation 41
EC external trade policy 58–59

EC law
breaches of 46
Eco-label award scheme
applications for 217
criteria 216–217
follow-up work 217
objective 216
scope of application 216
third three-year action plan (1996–1998) 33
Economic and Social Committee (ESC) 45
Economic interests
preliminary programme (1975) 22–23
second programme (1981) 25
1985 programme 27–28
fourth three-year action plan (1999–2001) 34
Education
Commission projects 56–57
preliminary programme (1975) 24
third three-year action plan (1996–1998) 31–32
EEJ-net *see* European extra-judicial network
EFSA *see* European Food Safety Authority
EFTA *see* European Free Trade Association
EHLASS (European Home and Leisure Accident Surveillance System) 55, 193, 198
EINECS (European Inventory of Existing Commercial Chemical Substances) 159
Elastomers
in contact with foodstuffs 87
Electronic commerce
benefits 269
codes of conduct 272
commercial communications 271
contracts 271–272
cooperation 273
court actions 273
cross-border disputes 269
home state control 273
information of provider and prices 270–271
objective 270
out-of-court settlement 272
scope of application 270
standards 269
Electronic payment instruments
conditions for transaction 289–290
holder's obligations and liabilities 290
issuer's obligations and liabilities 291
objective 289
scope of application 289
settlement of disputes 291
transparency 289–290
Energy efficiency
household appliances 215–216
passenger cars 214–215
Energy market
third three-year action plan (1996–1998) 32
Energy-reduced 96
Enforcement, consumer protection law
1985 programme 27
Consumer Policy Strategy 2002–2006 35–36
cross-border disputes 17, 20–21
Enlargement of the EU
third three-year action plan (1996–1998) 33
ENSP (European Network for Smoking Prevention) 187
Environment Agency 140
Environment Committee 44
Environmental hazards 167–168
Environmental pollutants 177–178
Environmental protection
CO2 emissions 214–215
see also Eco-label award scheme; Sustainable consumption
ENYPAT (European Network for Young People and Tobacco) 187
Enzymes 98
ESC *see* Economic and Social Committee
Ethyl alcohol
aromatized wines 211
spirit drinks 210
EUPHIN (European Union Public Health Information Network) 193–194, 198

Euro 24, 35, 54
EUROCOOP (Confederation of European Cooperatives) 42
Euroguichets 30–31, 34, 56
European Association for the Coordination of Consumer Representation in Standardisation *see* ANEC
European Commission
access-to-justice projects 57
consultation 46
consumer information projects 55–56
consumer-supplier dialogue, stimulation of 57–58
education programmes 56–57
framework proposal for financing EU activities 58
Green Paper on Consumer Access to Justice (1993) 57
Green Paper on Consumer Protection (2001) 54
Green Paper on Food Law (1997) 73
investigation of complaints 46
rapid exchange of information 194–196
research projects 57
training projects 57
White Paper on Food Safety (1999) 73–74
European Consumer Centres (ECC-Network) 56
European Consumers' Association *see* BEUC
European Council
co-decision procedure 8
qualified majority voting 8
European Court of Justice
preliminary references 46
European extra-judicial network (EEJ-net) 13, 18–19, 57
European Food Safety Authority (EFSA) 74, 75, 78–80
European Free Trade Association (EFTA) 58–59
European Home and Leisure Accident Surveillance System *see* EHLASS
European Inventory of Existing Commercial Chemical Substances *see* EINECS
European Network for Smoking Prevention *see* ENSP
European Network for Young People and Tobacco *see* ENYPAT
European Parliament
consumer committees 44–45
opinions 44
right to petition 46
European Product Safety Network 69–70
European Union Eco-Labelling Board (EUEB) 217
European Union Public Health Information Network *see* EUPHIN
Feed *see* **Agricultural product safety**
Fibres *see* **Textile names**
Final consumer 37
Financial services
Community measures 285
second three-year action plan (1993–1995) 31
third three-year action plan (1996–1998) 32
see also Cross-border credit transfers; Distance marketing of financial services; Electronic payment instruments; Insurance; Payment systems
Fire retardant products 175
First three-year action plan (1990–1992) 28–29
Flavourings
follow-up work 103–104
general principles 103
implementation 103
marketing 103
objective 102
scope of application 102–103
Food additives
amendments 95
authorised additives 92–93
colours 100–102
flavourings 92, 102–104
follow-up work 96

framework 91
harmonisation of national laws 91
implementation 95–96
labelling 94–95
limits 91
Member States' obligations 95
other than colours and sweeteners 98–100
public health measures 93–94
purity criteria 91
scientific and technological developments 94
scope of application 92
sweeteners 96–98
use 91

Food imitation
adjustments 208
implementation 208
Member States' obligations 208
objective 207
scope of application 207–208

Food labelling
third three-year action plan (1996–1998) 33

Food safety
advertising 76
crisis management 81
emergency measures 81
European Food Safety Authority 74, 75, 78–80
food 76
food trade 77
inspections 74–75
integrated approach 73
labelling
materials in contact with foodstuffs *see* Materials in contact with foodstuffs
official control system 74
operators' responsibilities 77–78
precautionary principle 77
presentation 76
public confidence 73
rapid alert system 55, 75, 79, 80–81, 196
risk analysis 76–77
risk management 74
safety requirement 76
traceability 77
transparency 77
see also Quick-frozen foodstuffs

Food supplements
further measures 126
implementation 126
labelling 126
manufacture 125
maximum amounts 125
Member States' obligations 126
objective 124
purpose 122
scope of application 124–125
see also Dietetic foodstuffs

Food trade 77

Footwear components
follow-up work 213
implementation 213
labelling 212–213
objective 212
scope of application 212

Fourth three-year action plan (1999–2001) 34

Framework directive 54

Framework proposal for financing EU activities 58

Free movement of goods and services
advertising restrictions 223
harmonisation measures 1
mutual recognition 7, 15

Freedom to trade
materials in contact with foodstuffs 85

Freezers
energy efficiency 215–216

Frozen foodstuffs ***see*** **Quick-frozen foodstuffs**

Fruit
materials in contact with foodstuffs 83

Fruit jams
further measures 110
implementation 110
ingredients 109
labelling 109
Member States' obligations 109
objective 109
scope of application 109

Fruit juices
authorised ingredients 107
authorised substances 107
authorised treatments 107
further measures 108
implementation 108
labelling 108

Member States' obligations 108
objective 107
scope of application 107
Fruit spirits 210
Fuel economy
passenger cars 214–215
Game
product liability 62
Genetically modified organisms (GMOs)
authorisation 121–122
deliberate release 121–122
further legislative initiatives 122
labelling 120
legislative framework 118–119
traceability 121
WTO dispute 122
Gentian spirit 210
Geographical indications *see* Traditional products
Globalisation of markets 34
Grain spirit 210
Grape marc 210
Green Paper on Consumer Access to Justice (1993) 57
Green Paper on Consumer Protection (2001) 54
Green Paper on Food Law (1997) 73
Greenhouse gases
passenger car emissions 214–215
Guarantees
binding nature 264
commercial guarantees 264
conformity with the contract 263
follow-up work 265
implementation 265
minimum harmonisation 265
objective 262
remedies 263–264
right of redress 264
scope of application 262–263
second programme (1981) 25
seller's obligations 263
Harmonisation
advertising 223
consumer contracts 237
cross-border disputes 16–17
minimum harmonisation 13–15
product liability 61
Health and Consumer Protection Directorate-General 34, 42–43, 47, 52, 56
Health and safety interests
preliminary programme (1975) 1, 22
products *see* Product liability; Product safety
standards 45, 68
Treaty of Rome (1957) 5
Hexachloroethane 179
High level of consumer protection
Consumer Policy Strategy 2002–2006 35
Hoaxes, substances used in 176
Holidays
legislation 275
see also Air carrier liability; Air transport compensation; Package travel; Timeshare
Home country shopping 15
Home-banking
second three-year action plan (1993–1995) 31
Homeopathic products 219–220
advertising 231
Honey
further measures 111–112
implementation 112
labelling 111
Member States' obligations 111
objective 111
scope of application 111
Hormones in meat
ban 117
WTO dispute 117–118
significance 104
Hot-water storage appliances
energy efficiency 215–216
Household appliances
energy efficiency 215–216
Hydromineral establishments 140
Ice cream 105
Ices 105
Icing sugars 110
Imitation food *see* Food imitation
Improvement of living and working conditions 6

Indication of prices *see* **Price indication**
Information *see* **Access to information**
Information society services *see* **Electronic commerce**
Information technology
third three-year action plan (1996–1998) 32
Ingredients *see* **Labelling**
Injunctions
actions for 267
follow-up work 268
implementation 268
intra-Community infringements 267
objective 266
prior consultation 267
qualified entities 267–268
scope of application 266
under Directive 98/27 20
Injuries
rapid exchange of information system 55, 193, 198
Injury Prevention Programme (IPP) 193
Injury Surveillance System (ISS) 193–194
Inspections
food safety 74–75
Instant coffee *see* **Coffee**
Insurance
consumer protection provisions 293
legislation 292
objective 292
scope of application 292
see also Life assurance; Motor insurance
Internal market policy
access to justice 11
Community consumer policy 28–29, 32
connection between consumer policy and 1, 11–16
cross-border disputes 21
potential 54
unfair commercial practices 234–235
see also Harmonisation measures
Internet
cross-border disputes 16
Ion-exchange resins
in contact with foodstuffs 87
Jams *see* **Fruit jams**
Jellies
further measures 110
implementation 110
ingredients 109
labelling 109
Member States' obligations 109
objective 109
scope of application 109
Jelly confectionery
food additive E 425 konjac 96
Jokes, substances used in 176
Juices *see* **Fruit juices**
Juniper-flavoured spirit drinks 210
Jurisdiction
cross-border disputes 17
Konjac 96
Labelling
alcoholic strength204, 211
aromatized wines 211
asbestos 176–177
beef 209
caffeine 208–209
chicory extracts 116
chocolate products 114
cocoa 114
coffee 116
compulsory indications 200–202
cosmetics 147–150
dangerous preparations 165–172
dangerous substances 156–165
dehydrated preserved milk 112–113
derogations 203
dietetic foods 123
drinking water 136
first three-year action plan (1990–1992) 29
food additives 94–95
food safety 76
food supplements 126
footwear components 212–213
fruit jams 109
fruit juices 108
further measures 203
genetically modified organisms (GMOs) 120
honey 111
household appliances 215–216
implementation 204
importance 199

ingredients present in foodstuffs 203–204
jellies 109
language *see* Language
legislative framework 199
marmalades 109
materials in contact with foodstuffs 84–85
medicinal products 217–219
Member States' obligations 203
national provisions 203
natural mineral waters 141–142
non-food products 211–212
novel foods 120
nutrition *see* Nutrition labelling
objective 200
organic food 127–128
presentation of particulars 202–203
quick-frozen foodstuffs 106–107
quinine 208–209
scope of applications 200
spirit drinks 210
sugars 110
sweetened chestnut puree 109
sweeteners 97
textile names 214
third three-year action plan (1996–1998) 33
tobacco products 188–189
see also Access to information

Language
case law 221
Commission's approach 221–222
legislation 220

Lead 85–87, 133, 178

Legal aid
for cross-border disputes 19–20

Legal basis for consumer protection
Paris summit (1972) 6
preliminary programme (1975) 6–7
Single European Act 1986 2, 7–8
Treaty of Amsterdam (1997) 10
Treaty of Rome (1957) 5–6
Treaty on European Union (1992) 2, 8–10

Legislative competence
Community institutions 2, 7

Liability
products *see* Product liability
service providers 29, 32
without fault *see* Strict liability

Life assurance
consumer protection provisions 294
objective 293
scope of application 294

Lighting sources
energy efficiency 215–216

Limitation period
product liability 64

Living and working conditions 6

Low calories diets *see* Sweeteners

Manufacturers, consumers and
second programme (1981) 25

Market surveillance 196–197

Market transparency
consumer contracts 238, 255

Marmalades
further measures 110
implementation 110
ingredients 109
labelling 109
Member States' obligations109
objective 109
scope of application 109

Materials in contact with foodstuffs
amendments 85
authorisation of substances 84
basic principle 83
cellulose film 83, 89–91
ceramics 83, 85–87
freedom to trade 85
implementation 85
labelling requirements 84–85
migration limits 82
plastics 83, 87–89
scope of application 83

Meat 209
see also Hormones in meat

Mediation *see* Out-of-court settlement

Medicinal products
advertising 229, 230–234
homeopathic medicinal products 219–220
implementation 220
labelling 217–219
objective 217
package leaflet 218–219
presentation of particulars 219
scope of application 217
television advertising 229
warnings 219

Medicinal waters 134, 140
Mercury compounds 177
Migrating products 67
Migration limits 82
plastics 87–88
Milk chocolate *see* Chocolate products
Minced beef
labelling 209
Mineral waters *see* Natural mineral waters
Minerals *see* Food supplements
Minimum harmonisation 13–15
consumer credit 245
distance selling 250–251
doorstep selling 241
guarantees 265
misleading and comparative advertising 226
package travel 279
price indication 205
timeshare 281
unfair terms in consumer contracts 261
Misleading and comparative advertising
comparative advertising 225
composition of administrative authorities 226
first three-year action plan (1990–1992) 29
implementation 226
Member States' obligations 225–226
minimum harmonisation formula 226
misleading advertising 224–225
objective 224
scope of application 224
see also Television advertising
Misleading practices 235
Mortgage credit offers
second three-year action plan (1993–1995) 31
Motor insurance
cases where insurer cannot be identified 296–297
claims representative 295–296
compensation bodies 296
direct right of action 295
information centres 296
objective 295
penalties 297
scope of application 295
Mutagens 174–175
Mutual recognition 7, 15
National consumer protection agencies *see* Advice; Representation
National Rivers Authority 140
Natural mineral waters
implementation 142
labelling 141–142
marketing 141
objective 140
scope of application 140–141
treatment 141
Natural rubber
in contact with foodstuffs 87
New approach doctrine 3, 26–27
Nicotine *see* Tobacco products
No added sugar 96
Non-conformity of goods *see* Guarantees
Non-food products
labelling 211–212
price indication 212
product safety 67
rapid exchange of information system 55
see also Cars; Footwear components; Household appliances; Medicinal products; Textile names
Novel foods
follow-up work 121
further measures 120–121
general principles 120
labelling 120
legislative framework 118–119
objective 119
placing on the market 120
scope of application 119
Nutrients *see* Food supplements
Nutrition labelling
content of labelling 206
form of the information 206
further measures 207
general rules 206
implementation 207
non pre-packaged foodstuffs 206 – 207
objective 205–206
presentation of the information 206

proposal for more restrictive rules 207
scope of application 206
Objective liability *see* Strict liability
Oestradiol 17 118
Organic food
advertising 127–128
labelling 127–128
legislative framework 127
objective 127
scope of application 127
success 127
Organostannic compounds 177, 179
Origin of food *see* Traceability; Traditional products
Out-of-court settlement 13, 17–19, 57
distance marketing of financial services 254
electronic commerce 272
Ovens
energy efficiency 215–216
Overall migration limit (OML) 82
Package travel
air transport compensation 283
alteration in terms or price 277
consumers' rights 277–278
implementation 279
information 276–277
liability 278
minimum harmonisation 279
objective 275
right to transfer booking 277
scope of application 275–276
security 278–279
substandard holidays 278
Packaging
dangerous preparations 165–171
dangerous substances 156–165
Paper
in contact with foodstuffs 87
Paperboard
in contact with foodstuffs 87
Paprika 100
Paraffin waxes
in contact with foodstuffs 87
Paris summit (1972) 6
Parma ham 130
Participation *see* Consultation
Partly dehydrated preserved milk *see* Dehydrated preserved milk
Passenger cars
CO_2 emissions 214–215
fuel economy 214–215
Payment systems
cardholder's obligations 288
contract 288
details of transaction 288
disputes 288
follow-up work 289
issuer's obligations 288
loss of card 288–289
objective 287
scope of application 287–288
see also Electronic payment instruments
PBBs 175
PCBs 175
PCTs 175
Pentachlorophenol 178
Pharmaceutical products *see* Medicinal products
Plant health products 92
Plastics
in contact with foodstuffs 83, 87–89
Polyols 97
Polyvinyl chloride (PVC) 178
Precautionary principle
food safety 77
Preliminary programme (1975) 1, 6–7, 21–25
Preliminary references 46
Prepared meat products
materials in contact with foodstuffs 83
Presentation *see* Labelling
Preserved milk *see* Dehydrated preserved milk
Price indication
advertising 205
implementation 205
Member States' obligations 205
Member States' powers 205
minimum harmonisation 205
non-food products 212
objective 204
scope of application 204
second programme (1981) 25
selling price 204–205
unit price 204–205

Processing aids 92
Producers 63, 68–69
Product liability
agricultural products 62
damage 64
defective products 63
domestic provisions 64–65
exceptions 63–64
exclusion of liability 63
follow-up work 65
implementation 65
joint and several liability 63
limitation period 64
new approach doctrine 61
producer 63
proving damage 62
strict liability 62–63
technical harmonisation 61
see also Agricultural product safety; Product safety
Product safety
assessing safety 67
conformity assessment criteria 67–68
distributor 69
distributors' obligations 68
domestic provisions 66
emergency situations 70–71
enforcement 69
European Product Safety Network 69–70
follow-up work 71
general safety obligation 66–67
implementation 71
information exchange 70
powers 69
producer 68–69
producers' obligations 68
product 67
recall of dangerous products 69
safety standards 68
see also Agricultural product safety; Product liability
Products appearing to be other than they are *see* Food imitation
Professional secrecy 71
Professionals
product safety 67
PROSAFE 197
Protected Designations of Origin (PDIs) 129
Protected Geographical Indications (PGIs) 129
Public utility services
third three-year action plan (1996–1998) 32
PVC *see* Polyvinyl chloride
Quality of goods and services
second programme (1981) 25
Quick-frozen foodstuffs
authorised substances 105–106
general principles 105
implementation 107
labelling 106–107
Member States' obligations 106
objective 104
packaging 106
sampling procedures 107
scope of application 104–105
temperature maintenance 106
Quinine
labelling 208–209
Radio advertising
tobacco products 191
Raisin spirit 210
RAPEX (rapid exchange of information on the dangers linked to the use of consumer products) 54–55, 69–71, 80–81, 193, 194–197
Rapid alert system
food safety 75, 79, 80–81
Recall of dangerous products 69
Recommended daily allowance (RDA) 206
Redress *see* Access to justice
Refrigerators
energy efficiency 215–216
Regenerated cellulose film
in contact with foodstuffs 87, 89–91
Representation
collective actions 20, 265–266
Consumer Committee 2
diversity of organisations 41–42
EC structures 42–46
first three-year action plan (1990–1992) 29
preliminary programme (1975) 24
second programme (1981) 26
third three-year action plan (1996–1998) 33
see also Legal aid

Reproduction, substances toxic to 174–175
Research
  Commission's projects 57
Retailers, consumers and
  second programme (1981) 25
Rights
  preliminary programme (1975) 6–7, 21–22
  recognition 6–7
Risk analysis
  food safety 76–77
Rubber
  in contact with foodstuffs 87
Rum 210
Safety of services 51
Safety standards
  1985 programme 27
  consultation 3
  fourth three-year action plan (1999–2001) 34
  toys 182–183
Saffron 100
Sausage casings 101
Scientific Committee on Cosmetic Products and Non-Food Products intended for Consumers 152–153
Scientific Committee on Food (SCF) 82, 84, 88
Scientific Committee on Veterinary measures relating to Public Health (SCVPH)118
Second programme (1981) 25–26
Second three-year action plan (1993–1995) 30–31
Second-hand products 67
Services
  equipment 67
  safety 51
Shoes *see* **Footwear components**
Silicones
  in contact with foodstuffs 87
Sneezing powders 176
Soluble coffee *see* **Coffee**
Specific migration limit (SML) 82
Spices 100
Spirit drinks 210
Sponsorship
  television advertising 228–230
  tobacco products 190–191
Standards
  new approach doctrine 26–27
Standing Committee on Foodstuffs 85, 95
Starches 98
State of the art defence 63–64
Strict liability 62–63
Substances toxic to reproduction 174–175
Sugars
  further measures 110
  implementation 110–111
  labelling 110
  Member States' obligations 110
  objective 110
  scope of application 110
  see also Chocolate products; Fruit jams; Fruit juices; Honey; Jellies; Marmalades; Sweetened chestnut puree; Sweeteners
Sums Levied by the Creditor (SLC) 246
Supplements *see* **Food supplements**
Suppliers
  dialogue between consumers and 57–58
Surface coatings
  in contact with foodstuffs 87
Sustainable consumption
  third three-year action plan (1996–1998) 33
Sutherland, Peter 30
Sweetened chestnut puree
  further measures 110
  implementation 110
  ingredients 109
  labelling 109
  Member States' obligations 109
  objective 109
  scope of application 109
Sweeteners
  authorised substances 97
  descriptions 97
  implementation 98
  labelling 97
  monitoring systems 97–98
  procedure 97
  scope of application 96
  see also Dietetic foods
Synthetic rubber

in contact with foodstuffs 87
Television advertising
advertising content 229
alcohol 229
amount of advertising 230
children 229
general rules 228–229
implementation 230
objective 227
scope of application 227–228
sponsorship 228–230
Testing on animals *see* Animal testing
Textile names
adaptation to technical progress 214
description 214
form of name 214
implementation 214
labelling 214
objective 213
scope of application 213–214
Third party creditors 244
Third three-year action plan (1996–1998) 31–33
Three-year action plans
first plan (1990–1992) 28–29
second plan (1993–1995) 30–31
third plan (1996–1998) 31–33
fourth plan (1999–2001) 34
Timeshare
binding nature 281
contract document 281
credit agreements 281
implementation 281
information 280
minimum harmonisation 281
objective 279
payment 281
purchasers' rights 281
scope of application 279–280
Tobacco products
adaptation to technical progress 189
advertising 190–192
Community measures 187
content of cigarettes 188
follow-up work 189–190
implementation 189
labelling 188–189
legislative framework 187
Member States' obligations 189
objective 188
oral use 189
product information 189
scope of application 188
sponsorship 190–191
television advertising 229
Tolerable daily intake (TDI) 82
Total Lending Rate (TLR) 246
Toy safety
approved bodies 183
checks 184
communication of information 184
Community measures 181
conformity assessment 182–183
examinations 183–184
harmonised safety standards 182
implementation 185
legislative framework 181
mandatory safety requirements 182
marks 183–184
new approach doctrine 181
objective 181–182
scope of application 182
Traceability
beef 209
food safety 77
Traditional products
certificates of special character 130–131
legal protection 128–129
objective 129
products that qualify 129–130
registration 130
scope of application 129
Traditional Speciality Guaranteed (TSG) 130–131
Training
Commission's projects 57
Transparency
cross-border credit transfers 286
electronic payment instruments 289–290
food safety 77
unfair terms in consumer contracts 258–259
Travel *see* Air carrier liability; Air transport compensation; Package travel
Tris-phosphate 175
Tris-phosphinozide 175
Turmeric 100
Ultimate consumer 37
Underprivileged consumers

second programme (1981) 25
Unfair commercial practices 5, 51
cross-border disputes 223–224
definition of unfair practices 234
follow-up work 235
internal market clause 234–235
misleading and aggressive practices 235
objective 234
scope of application 234
see also Misleading and comparative advertising
Unfair terms in consumer contracts
Annex of terms 259–260
binding nature 260
CLAB 261
contra proferentem rule 259
exclusions 258
fairness test 257–258
first three-year action plan (1990–1992) 29
follow-up work 262
implementation 261
individually negotiated terms 256–257
minimum harmonisation 261
objective 255
preventative actions 261
scope of application 255–256
second programme (1981) 25
transparency requirement 258–259
unenforceability of unfair terms 260
Unvarnished regenerated cellulose film
in contact with foodstuffs 87, 89–91
Varnished regenerated cellulose film
in contact with foodstuffs 87, 89–91
Vitamins *see* Food supplements
Voluntary agreements 25
Warnings *see* Access to information: rapid exchange system
Washing machines
energy efficiency 215–216
Water
additives 98
materials in contact with 83
see also Bathing water; Drinking water
Water heaters
energy efficiency 215–216
Weinbrand 210
Whisky 210
White chocolate *see* Chocolate products
White Paper on food safety (1999) 73–74
Wholly dehydrated preserved milk *see* Dehydrated preserved milk
Wine spirit 210
Wood preservation 178
World Health Organisation Framework Convention on Tobacco Control 190
WTO dispute 117–118, 122